HOME AND SCHOOL
READING AND STUDY GUIDES

THE NEW BOOK OF KNOWLEDGE

PART I.   READING GUIDE   PAGES 1–91

PART II. STUDY GUIDE   PAGES 1–93

HOME AND SCHOOL
READING GUIDE

THE NEW BOOK OF KNOWLEDGE

HOME AND SCHOOL READING GUIDE

THE NEW BOOK OF KNOWLEDGE

GROLIER
INCORPORATED
DANBURY, CONN

THE HOME AND SCHOOL READING GUIDE

HOME AND SCHOOL STUDY GUIDE

INTRODUCTION

The HOME AND SCHOOL READING GUIDE is a selected list of books for children at all reading levels. It is a source for books that will supplement the information contained in THE NEW BOOK OF KNOWLEDGE. It will also suggest books that answer the needs and interests of children. Every effort was made to include in this GUIDE recently published titles that reflect the trends, developments, and activities of today's rapidly changing world.

The READING GUIDE was not designed as a buying list for libraries. Its function is to direct young readers to titles that are fairly recent and readily available. Ideally, these suggestions will prompt the child to go to the school or public library, where many additional books will be available.

This GUIDE was organized as a separate unit to facilitate its frequent revision and to allow for a more extensive listing than is possible within the volumes of an encyclopedia. A separate reading guide also gives its user the opportunity to refer to all the related aspects of a subject without having to consult individual listings scattered through many volumes.

The attention of readers is called to book listings included in two articles in THE NEW BOOK OF KNOWLEDGE: "Children's Book Awards" (Vol. C, pp. 228–231) and "Children's Literature" (Vol. C, pp. 232–248).

THE NEW BOOK OF KNOWLEDGE Children's Literature Adviser, Nancy Larrick, helped establish the guidelines for the development of the READING GUIDE. The READING GUIDE was prepared by

John T. Gillespie
Professor
Palmer Graduate Library School
C. W. Post Center
of Long Island University

Christine B. Gilbert
Former Associate Professor
Palmer Graduate Library School
C. W. Post Center
of Long Island University

Professors Gillespie and Gilbert are co-editors of *Best Books for Children,* published by the R. R. Bowker Co.

Topics in the READING GUIDE are arranged in alphabetical order as they appear in THE NEW BOOK OF KNOWLEDGE. Books are graded according to reading level: P, Primary—from kindergarten through 4th grade; I, Intermediate—5th through 8th grade; A, Advanced—9th grade and up.

The following elementary and junior high school book lists are among the sources used in the preparation of the READING GUIDE:

Appraisal: Science Books for Young People. Published three times a year by the Children's Science Book Review Committee, sponsored by the Science and Mathematics Program of Boston University School of Education and the New England Roundtable of Children's Librarians.

Best Books for Children, by John T. Gillespie and Christine B. Gilbert. Bowker, 1985 (3rd ed.).

Children's Catalog. 14th ed. H. W. Wilson, 1981.

The Elementary School Library Collection. 15th ed. Bro-Dart Foundation, 1986.

Notable Children's Books, 1971–75. American Library Association, 1981.

Adventuring with Books: A Booklist for Pre-K–Grade 6. National Council of Teachers of English, 1981.

Children's Books. Library of Congress. Published annually.

Children's Books. New York Public Library. Published annually.

Outstanding Science Trade Books for Children. March issues of *Science and Children.*

Notable Children's Trade Books in the Field of Social Studies. Usually April issues of *Social Education.*

Booklist. American Library Association. Published twice a month September through June and monthly in July and August.

Bulletin of the Center for Children's Books. University of Chicago. Published monthly except for combined July–August issue.

The Horn Book Magazine. Horn Book, Inc. Published bimonthly.

School Library Journal. Bowker. Published monthly September through May.

Key to Abbreviations Used in the Home and School Reading Guide

(P)	primary (through 4th grade)	comp.	compiler; compiled
(I)	intermediate (5th through 8th grade)	ed.	editor; edition; edited
(A)	advanced (9th grade and up)	illus.	illustrator; illustrated
ad.	adapter; adapted	trans.	translator

ABACUS. See COMPUTERS.

ABORIGINES, AUSTRALIAN. See AUSTRALIA.

ABRAHAM. See BIBLE AND BIBLE STORIES.

ACID RAIN. See POLLUTION.

ADAMS, JOHN

Dwyer, Frank. *John Adams*. Chelsea House, 1989. *(I)*
Santrey, Laurence. *John Adams: Brave Patriot*. (Easy Biography Series) Troll, 1986. *(P; I)*
Stefoff, Rebecca. *John Adams: 2nd President of the United States*. Garrett Educational Corp., 1988. *(A)*

ADAMS, JOHN QUINCY

Kent, Zachary. *John Quincy Adams: Sixth President of the United States*. Childrens, 1987. *(I)*

ADAMS, SAMUEL

Fritz, Jean. *Why Don't You Get a Horse, Sam Adams?* Putnam, 1974. *(I)*

ADDAMS, JANE

Keller, Gail F. *Jane Addams*. Har-Row, 1971. *(P; I)*
Kittredge, Mary. *Jane Addams*. Chelsea House, 1988. *(I; A)*
Meigs, Cornelia Lynde. *Jane Addams: Pioneer for Social Justice*. Little, 1970. *(I)*

ADEN. See MIDDLE EAST.

ADOLESCENCE

Greenberg, Harvey R., M.D. *Hanging In: What You Should Know About Psychotherapy*. Scholastic, 1982. *(A)*
LeShan, Eda. *You and Your Feelings*. Macmillan, 1975; *What Makes Me Feel This Way? Growing Up with Human Emotions*, 1972. *(I)*
See also MENTAL HEALTH.

ADOPTION

Cohen, Shari. *Coping with Being Adopted*. Rosen, 1988. *(A)*
DuPrau, Jeanne. *Adoption: The Facts, Feelings and Issues of a Double Heritage*. Messner, 1990. *(I; A)*
Hyde, Margaret O. *Foster Care and Adoption*. Watts, 1982. *(I; A)*
Krementz, Jill. *How It Feels to Be Adopted*. Knopf, 1982. *(I)*
Nickman, Steven L. *The Adoption Experience*. Messner, 1985. *(A)*
Powledge, Fred. *So You're Adopted*. Scribner, 1982. *(I)*
Rosenberg, Maxine B. *Being Adopted*. Lothrop, 1984. *(P; I)*

Scott, Elaine. *Adoption*. Watts, 1980. *(I; A)*
Sobol, Harriet Langsam. *We Don't Look Like Our Mom and Dad*. Coward, 1984. *(P; I)*
Stewart, Gail B. *Adoption*. Macmillan/Crestwood, 1989. *(P; I)*

ADVERTISING

Greenberg, Jan. *Advertising Careers*. Holt, 1987. *(A)*
Larranaga, Bob. *Looking Forward to a Career: Advertising*. Dillon, 1977 (2nd ed.). *(I; A)*
Wiener, Solomon, and others. *Marketing and Advertising Careers*. Watts, 1977. *(I)*

AENEID

Church, Alfred J. *The Aeneid for Boys and Girls*. Macmillan, 1962. *(I)*

AERODYNAMICS. See AVIATION.

AFGHANISTAN

Afghanistan . . . in Pictures. Lerner, 1989. *(I; A)*
Clifford, Mary Louise. *The Land and People of Afghanistan*. Lippincott, 1989. (rev. ed.) *(I; A)*
Howarth, Michael. *Afghanistan*. Chelsea House, 1988. *(P)*

AFRICA

Morocco . . . in Pictures. Lerner, 1989. *(I; A)*
Tanzania . . . in Pictures. Lerner, 1988. *(I)*
Tunisia . . . in Pictures. Lerner, 1989. *(I)*
Anderson, Lydia. *Nigeria, Cameroon, and the Central African Republic*. Watts, 1981. *(I; A)*
Barker, Carol. *Kayode and His Village in Nigeria*. Merrimack, n.d. *(P; I)*
Baynham, Simon. *Africa; From 1945*. Watts, 1987. *(I; A)*
Bernheim, Marc, and Bernheim, Evelyne. *The Drums Speak: The Story of Kofi, a Boy of West Africa*. HarBraceJ, 1972. *(P)*
Blumberg, Rhoda. *Southern Africa: South Africa, Namibia, Swaziland, Lesotho, and Botswana*. Watts, 1981. *(I; A)*
Boyd, Herb. *The Former Portuguese Colonies: Angola, Mozambique, Guinea-Bissau, Cape Verde, São Tomé, and Príncipe*. Watts, 1981. *(I; A)*
Chiasson, John. *African Journey*. Macmillan/Bradbury, 1987. *(I; A)*
Conway, Jessica. *Swaziland*. Chelsea House, 1989. *(P; I)*
Ellis, Veronica Freeman. *Afro-Bets First Book About Africa: An Introduction for Young Readers*. Just Us Books, 1990. *(P)*
Fichter, George S. *The Bulge of Africa: Senegal, Guinea, Ivory Coast, Togo, Benin, and Equatorial Guinea*. Watts, 1981. *(I; A)*
Foster, F. Blanche. *East Central Africa: Kenya, Uganda, Tanzania, Rwanda, and Burundi*. Watts, 1981. *(I; A)*

Gilfond, Henry. *Gambia, Ghana, Liberia, and Sierra Leone*. Watts, 1981. *(I; A)*

Godbeer, Deardre. *Somalia*. Chelsea House, 1988. *(P; I)*

Gould, D. E. *Namibia*. Chelsea House, 1988. *(P; I)*

Hathaway, Jim. *Cameroon . . . in Pictures*. Lerner, 1989. *(I)*

Hintz, Martin. (Enchantment of the World Series). Childrens, 1985. *(P;I)*

Holmes, Timothy. *Zambia*. Chelsea House, 1988. *(P; I)*

Hornburger. *African Countries and Cultures: A Concise Illustrated Dictionary*. McKay, 1981. *(I; A)*

Jacobs, Francine. *Fire Snake: The Railroad That Changed East Africa*. Morrow, 1980. *(I)*

Lawson, Don. *Morocco, Algeria, Tunisia, and Libya*. Watts, 1978. *(I; A); South Africa*. Watts, 1986. *(I)*

McCulla, Patricia E. *Tanzania*. Chelsea House, 1988. *(I)*

Milsome, John. *Sierra Leone*. Chelsea House, 1988. *(P; I)*

Musgrove, Margaret. *Ashanti to Zulu: African Traditions*. Dial Bks Young, 1980. *(P; I)*

Newman, Gerald. *Zaire, Gabon, and the Congo*. Watts, 1981. *(I; A)*

Pomeray, J. K. *Rwanda*. Chelsea House, 1988. *(I)*

Taylor, L. B., Jr. *South East Africa: Zimbabwe, Zambia, Malawi, Madagascar, Mauritius, and Réunion*. Watts, 1981. *(I; A)*

Tonsing-Carter, Betty. *Lesotho*. Chelsea House, 1988. *(P; I)*

Wolbers, Marian F. *Burundi*. Chelsea House, 1989. *(I)*

Woods, Harold, and Woods, Geraldine. *The Horn of Africa: Ethiopia, Sudan, Somalia, and Djibouti*. Watts, 1981. *(I; A)*

AFRICAN ART

Kerina, Jane. *African Crafts*. Lion, 1970. *(P; I)*

Price, Christine. *Dancing Masks of Africa*. Scribner, 1975. *(P; I)*

AFRICAN LITERATURE

Aardema, Verna. *Bringing the Rain to Kapiti Plain*. Dial Bks Young, 1981; *Why Mosquitoes Buzz in People's Ears*, 1978. *(P)*

Feelings, Muriel. *Jambo Means Hello: Swahili Alphabet Book*. Dial Bks Young, 1981. *(P)*

McDermott, Gerald. *The Magic Tree: A Tale from the Congo*. Penguin, 1973. *(P)*

Parrinder, Geoffrey. *African Mythology*. Harper, 1986 (rev. ed.). *(A)*

AGING

Ancona, George. *Growing Older*. Dutton, 1978. *(P; I)*

Dychtwald, Ken, and Flower, Joe. *Age Wave: The Challenges and Opportunities of an Aging America*. Tarcher, 1989. *(A)*

Gelfand, Marilyn. *My Great-Grandpa Joe*. Four Winds, 1986. *(P)*

Landau, Elaine. *Growing Old in America*. Messner, 1985. *(I)*

LeShan, Eda. *Grandparents: A Special Kind of Love*. Macmillan, 1984. *(I)*

Silverstein, Alvin, and others. *Aging*. Watts, 1979. *(I; A)*

Worth, Richard. *You'll be Old Someday, Too*. Watts, 1986. *(A)*

AGRICULTURE

Bowman, Keith. *Agriculture*. Silver Burdett, 1987. *(I)*

Horwitz, Elinor L. *On the Land: The Evolution of American Agriculture*. Atheneum, 1980. *(I; A)*

Murphy, Wendy. *The Futureworld of Agriculture*. (An Epcot Center Book). Watts, 1985. *(I; A)*

White, William, C., and Collins, Donald N. *Opportunities in Agriculture Careers*. VGM Career Books, 1987. *(A)*

AIDS

Eagles, Douglas A. *The Menace of AIDS: A Shadow on Our Land*. Watts, 1988. *(I)*

Hausherr, Rosmarie. *Children and the AIDS Virus: A Book for Children, Parents, and Teachers*. *(P)*

Hawkes, Nigel. *AIDS*. Watts, 1987. *(I)*

Hyde, Margaret O., and Forsyth, Elizabeth H. *AIDS: What Does It Mean to You?* Walker, 1990. (rev. ed.) *(I; A)*

Kuklin, Susan. *Fighting Back: What Some People Are Doing About AIDS*. Putnam, 1989. *(A)*

Kurland, Morton L. *Coping with AIDS: Facts and Fears*. Rosen, 1988. *(A)*

Landau, Elaine. *We Have AIDS*. Watts, 1990. *(I; A)*

Madaras, Lynda. *Lynda Madaras Talks to Teens About AIDS: An Essential Guide for Parents, Teachers, and Young People*. Harper, 1988. *(A)*

Nourse, Alan E. *AIDS*. Watts, 1989. *(I; A)*

Turck, Mary. *AIDS*. Crestwood House, 1988. *(I; A)*

Wilson, Jonnie. *AIDS*. Lucent Books, 1989. *(I; A)*

AIRPLANE MODELS

Berliner, Don. *Flying-Model Airplanes*. Lerner, 1982; *Scale-Model Airplanes*, 1982. *(P; I)*

Curry, Barbara A. *Model Aircraft*. Watts, 1979. *(I)*

Herda, O. J. *Model Historical Aircraft*. Watts, 1982. *(I; A)*

Linsley, Leslie, and Aron, Jon. *Air Crafts: Playthings to Make and Fly*. Lodestar, 1982. *(P; I)*

Monfort, Platt. *Styro-Flyers: How to Build Super Model Airplanes from Hamburger Boxes and Other Fast-Food Containers*. Random, 1981. *(I)*

Radlauer, Ed. *Model Fighter Planes*. Childrens, 1983. *(P; I)*

AIR POLLUTION. See POLLUTION.

ALABAMA

McNair, Sylvia. *Alabama*. Childrens, 1989. *(P; I)*
Thompson, Kathleen. *Alabama*. Raintree, 1988. *(P; I)*

ALASKA

Cheney, Cora. *Alaska: Indians, Eskimos, Russians, and the Rest*. Dodd, 1980. *(I)*
Coombs, Charles. *Pipeline Across Alaska*. Morrow, 1978. *(I)*
Lewin, Ted. *World Within a World—Pribilofs*. Dodd, 1980. *(I)*
Redding, Robert H. *Alaska Pipeline*. Childrens, 1980. *(I)*
Stefansson, Evelyn, and Yahn, Linda. *Here Is Alaska*, Scribner, 1983 (4th ed.). *(I; A)*
Thompson, Kathleen. *Alaska*. Raintree, 1988. *(P; I)*

ALBANIA

Lear, Aaron E. *Albania*. Chelsea House, 1987. *(A)*

ALBERTA. See CANADA.

ALCOHOLISM

Claypool, Jane. *Alcohol and You*. Watts, 1988. (rev. ed.) *(I; A)*
Graeber, Laurel. *Are You Dying for a Drink?: Teenagers and Alcohol Abuse*. Messner, 1985. *(A)*
O'Neill, Catherine. *Focus on Alcohol*. 21st Century Books, 1990. *(I)*
Rosenberg, Maxine B. *Not My Family: Sharing the Truth About Alcoholism*. Bradbury, 1988. *(I)*
Seixas, Judith S. *Living with a Parent Who Drinks Too Much*. Greenwillow, 1979. *(I)*

ALCOTT, LOUISA MAY

Burke, Kathleen. *Louisa May Alcott*. Chelsea House, 1987. *(I; A)*
Greene, Carol. *Louisa May Alcott: Author, Nurse, Suffragette*. Childrens, 1984. *(I)*
Meigs, Cornelia. *Invincible Louisa*. Little, 1968. *(A)*
Santrey, Laurence. *Louisa May Alcott: Young Writer*. (Easy Biography Series) Troll, 1986. *(P;I)*

ALEXANDER THE GREAT

Krensky, Stephen. *Conqueror and Hero: The Search for Alexander*. Little, 1981. *(I)*

ALGAE

Kavaler, Lucy. *Green Magic: Algae Rediscovered*. Har-Row, 1983. *(I; A)*

ALGEBRA

Stallings, Pat. *Puzzling Your Way into Algebra*. Activity Resources, 1978 (new ed.). *(I; A)*

ALGERIA. See AFRICA.

ALLEN, ETHAN

Holbrook, Stewart. *America's Ethan Allan*. HM, n.d. *(I)*
Peck, Robert Newton. *Rabbits and Redcoats*. Regional Ctr Educ, 1976. *(I)*

ALPHABET

Fisher, Leonard Everett. *Alphabet Art: Thirteen ABCs from Around the World*. Scholastic, 1978. *(P)*
Kaye, Cathryn Berger. *Word works: Why the Alphabet is a Kid's Best Friend*. Little, Brown, 1985. *(I)*

ALPHABET BOOKS

Anno, Mitsumasa. *Anno's Alphabet: An Adventure in Imagination*. Har-Row, 1975. *(P)*
Balian, Lorna. *Humbug Potion: An A-B-Cipher*. Abington, 1984. *(P)*
Baskin, Leonard, and others. *Hosie's Alphabet*. Viking, 1972. *(P)*
Berger, Terry. *Ben's ABC Day*. Lothrop, 1982. *(P)*
Boynton, Sandra. *A Is for Angry*. Workman, 1983. *(P)*
Brown, Marcia. *All Butterflies: An ABC*. Scribner, 1974. *(P)*
Brunhoff, Laurent de. *Barbar's ABC*. Random, 1983. *(P)*
Crowther, Robert. *The Most Amazing Hide-and-Seek Alphabet Book*. Viking, 1978. *(P)*
Duvoisin, Roger. *A for the Ark*. Lothrop, 1952. *(P)*
Emberley, Edward R. *Ed Emberley's A B C*. Little, 1978. *(P)*
Gag, Wanda. *The ABC Bunny*. Putnam, 1978. *(P)*
Greenaway, Kate. *A Apple Pie*. Warne, 1987 (rev. ed.). *(P)*
Isadora, Rachel. *City Seen from A to Z*. Greenwillow, 1983. *(P)*
Jewell, Nancy. *ABC Cat*. Har-Row, 1983. *(P)*
Kitchen, Bert, illus. *Animal Alphabet*. Dial Bks Young, 1984. *(P)*
Lear, Edward. *An Edward Lear Alphabet*. Lothrop, 1983. *(P)*
Oxenbury, Helen. *Helen Oxenbury's ABC of Things*. Delacorte, 1983. *(P)*
Rey, H. A. *Curious George Learns the Alphabet*. HM, 1963. *(P)*
Scarry, Richard. *Richard Scarry's Find Your ABC's*. Random, 1973. *(P)*
Seuss, Dr. *Dr. Seuss' ABC*. Beginner, 1963. *(P)*
Wildsmith, Brian. *Brian Wildsmith's ABC*. Watts, 1963. *(P)*

ALUMINUM. See METALS AND METALLURGY.

AMAZON RIVER

Cheney, Glenn Alan. *The Amazon.* Watts, 1984. *(I; A)*

McConnell, Rosemary. *The Amazon.* Silver, 1978. *(I; A)*

AMERICAN COLONIES

Behrens, June, and Brower, Pauline. *Colonial Farm.* Childrens, 1976. *(P; I)*

Blackburn, Joyce. *James Edward Oglethorpe.* Dodd, 1983. *(I; A)*

DeLage, Ida. *Pilgrim Children Come to Plymouth.* Garrard, 1981. *(P; I)*

Fradin, Dennis B. *The Virginia Colony.* Childrens, 1987. *(I)*

Fritz, Jean. *The Double Life of Pocahontas.* Putnam, 1983; *Who's That Stepping on Plymouth Rock?* 1975. *(P; I)*

Knight, James E. *Sailing to America: Colonists at Sea; Salem Days: Life in a Colonial Seaport; The Village: Life in Colonial Times.* Troll, 1982. *(I; A)*

Reische, Diana. *Founding the American Colonies.* Watts, 1989. *(P; I)*

Sewall, Marcia. *The Pilgrims of Plimoth.* Atheneum, 1986. *(P)*

Siegal, Beatrice. *A New Look at the Pilgrims: Why They Came to America.* Walker, 1977. *(P; I)*

Tunis, Edwin. *Colonial Living.* Har-Row, 1976. *(I)*

AMERICAN LITERATURE. See UNITED STATES (ART, LITERATURE, AND MUSIC).

AMUSEMENT AND THEME PARKS. See PARKS AND PLAYGROUNDS.

ANCIENT CIVILIZATIONS

Board, Tessa. *Ancient Greece.* Watts, 1984 (rev. ed.). *(P; I)*

Bowra, C. M. *Classical Greece.* Time-Life, 1965. *(A)*

Cohen, Daniel. *Ancient Egypt.* Doubleday, 1990. *(P; I)*

Coolidge, Olivia E. *The Golden Days of Greece.* Har-Row, 1968; *The Trojan War.* HM, 1952. *(I; A)*

Corbishley, Mike. *The Roman World.* Watts, 1987. *(I; A)*

Garber, Janet, ed. *The Concise Encyclopedia of Ancient Civilizations.* Watts, 1978. *(I; A)*

Gibson, Michael, and Box, Sue. *Discovering Ancient Mysteries.* EMC, 1982. *(I; A)*

Goor, Ron, and Goor, Nancy. *Pompeii.* Harper/Crowell, 1987. *(I)*

Harris, Geraldine. *Ancient Egypt.* Facts on File, 1990. *(I)*

Katan, Norma J., and Mints, Barbara. *Hieroglyphs: The Writing of Ancient Egypt.* Atheneum, 1981. *(P; I)*

Macaulay, David. *Pyramid.* HM, 1975. *(I; A)*

Millard, Anne. *Ancient Civilizations.* Watts, 1983. *(P; I); Ancient Egypt,* 1979. *(I; A)*

Pace, Mildred Mastin. *Pyramids: Tombs for Eternity.* McGraw, 1981; *Wrapped for Eternity: The Story of the Egyptian Mummies,* 1974. *(I; A)*

Payne, Elizabeth. *The Pharaohs of Ancient Egypt.* Random, 1981. *(P; I)*

Perl, Lila. *Mummies, Tombs and Treasure: Secrets of Ancient Egypt.* Clarion, 1987. *(P)*

Purdy, Susan, and Sandak, Cass R. *Ancient Egypt; Ancient Greece* (Civilization Project Books). Watts, 1982. *(P; I)*

Robinson, Charles A., Jr. *First Book of Ancient Egypt; First Book of Ancient Greece.* Watts, 1984 (rev. by Lorna Greenberg). *(I; A)*

Stolz, Mary. *Zekmet, the Stone Carver: A Tale of Ancient Egypt.* Harcourt Brace Jovanovich, 1988. *(P; I)*

See also ARCHEOLOGY; ROME (ANCIENT).

ANDERSEN, HANS CHRISTIAN

Andersen, Hans Christian. *Hans Andersen's Fairy Tales.* Penguin, 1981; *Hans Christian Andersen's Favorite Fairy Tales.* Western, 1974; *Michael Hague's Favorite Hans Christian Andersen Fairy Tales.* HR&W, 1981. *(I)*

ANDES. See SOUTH AMERICA

ANGOLA. See AFRICA

ANIMALS

Arnosky, Jim. *Secrets of a Wildlife Watcher.* Lothrop, 1983. *(I; A)*

Attenborough, David. *Discovering Life on Earth.* Little, 1982. *(P; I; A)*

Bruemmer, Fred. *Arctic Animals.* North Word, 1987. *(A)*

Freedman, Russell. *Animal Superstars: Biggest, Strongest, Fastest, Smartest.* P-H, 1981. *(I; A)*

Hopf, Alice. *Animal and Plant Life Spans.* Holiday, 1978. *(I; A); Hyenas.* Dodd, 1983. *(P; I)*

Humphreys, Dena. *Animals Every Child Should Know.* Putnam, 1982. *(P)*

Johnston, Ginny, and Cutchins, Judy. *Windows on Wildlife.* Morrow, 1990. *(P; I)*

Kohl, Judith, and Kohl, Herbert. *The View from the Oak: The Private Worlds of Other Creatures.* Scribner, 1977. *(A)*

Komori, Atsushi. *Animal Mothers.* Putnam, 1983. *(P)*

Lambert, David. *First Picture Book of Animals.* Watts, 1982. *(P); Animal Life,* 1982. *(P; I)*

National Geographic editors. *Secrets of Animal Survival.* Natl Geog, 1983. *(I; A)*

Pringle, Laurence. *Feral: Tame Animals Gone Wild.* Macmillan, 1983. *(I; A)*

Selsam, Millicent E., and Hunt, Joyce. *A First Look at Animals with Backbones.* Walker, 1978; *A First Look at Animals Without Backbones,* 1976. *(P)*

Simon, Seymour. *Little Giants.* Morrow, 1983. *(P)*

Yabuuchi, Masayuki. *Animals Sleeping.* Putnam, 1983. *(P)*

ANIMALS: COMMUNICATION AND SOCIAL ORGANIZATION

Black, Hallie. *Animal Cooperation: A Look at Sociobiology*. Morrow, 1981. *(I)*

Johnson, Rebecca L. *The Secret Language: Pheromones in the Animal World*. Lerner, 1989. *(I)*

Kohl, Judith, and Kohl, Herbert. *Pack, Band, and Colony: The World of Social Animals*. FS&G, 1983. *(I; A)*

McGrath, Susan. *How Animals Talk*. National Geographic Society, 1987. *(P; I)*

Patent, Dorothy Hinshaw. *Singing Birds and Flashing Fireflies*. Watts, 1989. *(P)*

Vevers, Gwen. *Animal Partners*. Merrimack, 1982. *(P)*

ANIMALS: INTELLIGENCE AND BEHAVIOR

Arnold, Caroline. *Animals That Migrate*. Carolrhoda, 1982. *(P)*

Dinneen, Betty. *The Family Howl*. Macmillan, 1981. *(P; I)*

Freedman, Russell. *Can Bears Predict Earthquakes? Unsolved Mysteries of Animal Behavior*. P-H, 1982. *(I; A); How Animals Defend Their Young*. Dutton, 1978. *(I)*

Hewett, Joan. *When You Fight the Tiger*. Little, 1984. *(I)*

McClung, Robert M. *Mysteries of Migration*. Gerrard, 1983. *(I; A)*

National Geographic Soc. *Animal Architects*. National Geog., 1987. *(P; I)*

National Geographic Soc. *How Animals Behave: A New Look at Wildlife*. National Geog., 1984. *(I; A)*

Patent, Dorothy Hinshaw. *How Smart Are Animals?* Harcourt, Brace, Jovanovich, 1990. *(I)*

Powzyk, Joyce. *Animal Camouflage: A Closer Look*. Bradbury, 1990. *(P; I)*

Sanders, John. *All About Animal Migration*. Troll, 1984. *(P; I)*

Sattler, Helen Roney. *Fish Facts and Bird Brains: Animal Intelligence*. Lodestar, 1984. *(I)*

Simon, Seymour. *Secret Clocks: The Time Senses of Living Things*. Viking, 1979. *(P; I)*

Vevers, Gwen. *Animal Disguises; Animals That Sleep in Winter*. Merrimack, 1982. *(P)*

Walter, Eugene J., Jr. *Why Animals Behave the Way They Do*. Scribner, 1981. *(I; A)*

ANIMALS: LOCOMOTION

Goor, Ron. *All Kinds of Feet*. Har-Row, 1984. *(P)*

Gustafson, Anita. *Some Feet Have Noses*. Lothrop, 1983. *(P; I)*

Kaufman, Joe. *Wings, Paws, Hoofs, and Flippers: A Book About Animals*. Western, 1981. *(P)*

Sibbald, Jean H. *Sea Creatures on the Move*. Dillon, 1990. *(P; I)*

Simon, Hilda. *The Racers: Speed in the Animal World*. Lothrop, 1980. *(I)*

ANTARCTICA

Asimov, Isaac. *How Did We Find Out About Antarctica?* Walker, 1979. *(I)*

Hargreaves, Pat. *The Antarctic*. Silver, n.d. *(I; A)*

Lye, Keith. *Take a Trip to Antarctica*. Watts, 1984. *(P; I)*

Reader's Digest Press. *Antarctica*. Random, 1985. *(A)*

ANTHROPOLOGY

Bell, Neill. *Only Human: Why We Are the Way We Are*. Little, 1983. *(P; I)*

Branigan, Keith. *Prehistory*. Watts, 1984. *(I; A)*

Fisher, Maxine P. *Recent Revolutions in Anthropology*. Watts, 1986. *(A)*

Jaspersohn, William. *How People First Lived*. Watts, 1985. *(P)*

Leakey, Richard E. *Human Origins*. Dutton, 1982. *(I; A)*

Leakey, Richard E., and Lewin, Roger. *People of the Lake*. Avon, 1983. *(I; A)*

Merriman, Nick. *Early Humans*. Knopf, 1989. *(P; I; A)*

Milbauer, Barbara. *Suppose You Were a Netsilik: Teenagers in Other Societies*. Messner, 1981. *(A)*

Millard, Anne. *Early People*. Watts, 1982. *(I; A)*

Nance, John. *Lobo of the Tasaday: A Stone Age Boy Meets the Modern World*. Pantheon, 1982. *(A)*

Sattler, Helen Roney. *Hominids: A Look Back at Our Ancestors*. Lothrop, 1988. *(I; A)*

ANTIGUA AND BARBUDA. See CARIBBEAN SEA AND ISLANDS.

ANTS

Cook, David. *Small World of Ants*. Watts, 1981. *(P)*

Fischer-Nagel, Heiderose and Fischer-Nagel, Andrea. *An Ant Colony*. Carolrhoda, 1989. *(P; I)*

Overbeck, Cynthia. *Ants*. Lerner, 1982. *(P)*

Patent, Dorothy. *Looking at Ants*. Holiday, 1989. *(P; I)*

Sabin, Francene. *Amazing World of Ants*. Troll, 1981. *(P)*

AQUARIUMS

Braemer, Helga, and Scheurmann, Ines. *Tropical Fish*. Barron, 1983. *(I; A)*

Broekel, Ray. *Aquariums and Terrariums*. Childrens, 1982; *Tropical Fish*, 1983. *(P)*

Carrington, Neville. *A Fishkeeper's Guide to Maintaining a Healthy Aquarium*. Arco, 1986. *(A)*

Paige, David. *Behind the Scenes at the Aquarium*. Whitman, 1977. *(P; I)*

Sarnoff, Jane, and Ruffins, Reynold. *A Great Aquarium Book: The Putting-It-Together Guide for Beginners*. Scribner, 1977. *(P; I)*

Simon, Seymour. *Tropical Saltwater Aquariums: How to Set Them Up and Keep Them Going*. Viking, 1976. *(P; I)*

Watts, Barrie. *Keeping Minibeasts Series*. Watts, 1989. *(P)*

AQUINO, CORAZON

Chua-Eoan, Howard. *Corazon Aquino.* Chelsea House, 1987. *(A)*

Haskins, James. *Corazon Aquino: Leader of the Philippines.* Enslow, 1988. *(A)*

Siegel, Beatrice. *Cory: Corazon Aquino and the Philippines.* Dutton/Lodestar, 1988. *(I)*

ARABS. See MIDDLE EAST.

ARCHAEOLOGY

Anderson, Joan. *From Map to Museum: Uncovering Mysteries of the Past.* Morrow, 1988. *(P)*

Braymer, Marjorie. *Atlantis: The Biography of a Legend.* Atheneum, 1983; *The Walls of Windy Troy: A Biography of Heinrich Schliemann.* HarBraceJ, 1966. *(I; A)*

Cooke, Jean, and Others. *Archaeology.* Watts, 1982 (rev. ed.). *(I; A)*

Ford, Barbara, and Switzer, David C. *The Underwater Dig: The Excavation of a Revolutionary War Privateer.* Morrow, 1982. *(P; I)*

Goor, Ron. *Pompeii: Exploring a Roman Ghost Town.* Crowell, 1986. *(P; I)*

Hackwell, W. John. *Digging to the Past: Excavations in Ancient Lands.* Scribner, 1986. *(I; A)*

Kunhardt, Edith. *Pompeii: Buried Alive!* Random House, 1987. *(I)*

Lyttle, Richard B. *Waves Across the Past: Adventures in Underwater Archeology.* Atheneum, 1981. *(I; A)*

Marston, Elsa. *Mysteries in American Archeology.* Walker, 1986. *(A)*

Morrison, Velma Ford. *Going on a Dig.* Dodd, 1981. *(I)*

Olesky, Walter. *Treasures of the Land: Archaeology Today in America.* Messner, 1981. *(I; A)*

Rollin, Sue. *The Illustrated Atlas of Archaeology.* Watts, 1982. *(P; I)*

Snyder, Thomas F. *Archeology Search Book.* McGraw, 1982. *(P; I; A)*

Stuart, Gene S. *Secrets from the Past.* Natl Geog, 1979. *(P; I)*

Tantillo, Joe. *Amazing Ancient Treasures.* Pantheon, 1983. *(P; I)*

Ventura, Piero, and Ceserani, Gian Paolo. *In Search of Ancient Crete.* Silver Burdett, 1985. *(I; A); In Search of Troy,* 1985. *(I; A); In Search of Tutankhamun,* 1985. *(I; A)*

Williams, Barbara. *Breakthrough: Women in Archaeology.* Walker, 1981. *(I; A)*

ARCHERY

Boy Scouts of America. *Archery.* BSA, 1978. *(I; A)*

Heath, E. G. *Better Archery.* Sportshelf, 1976. *(I; A)*

Thomas, Art. *Archery Is for Me.* Lerner, 1981. *(P; I)*

ARCHITECTURE

Fagg, C. D. *How They Built Long Ago.* Watts, 1981. *(I; A)*

Giblin, James Cross. *The Skyscraper Book.* Har-Row, 1981. *(I)*

MacGregor, Anne, and MacGregor, Scott. *Domes: A Project Book.* Lothrop, 1982; *Skyscrapers: A Project Book,* 1981. *(I)*

Weiss, Harvey. *Shelters: From Teepee to Igloo.* Crowell, 1988. *(I; A)*

ARCTIC

Dekkers, Midas. *Arctic Adventure.* Watts, 1987. *(A)*

Hargreaves, Pat. *The Arctic.* Silver, n.d. *(I; A)*

Hiscock, Bruce. *Tundra: the Arctic Land.* Atheneum, 1986. *(P;I)*

Pluckrose, Henry, ed. *Small World of Arctic Lands.* Watts, 1982. *(P)*

ARGENTINA

Huber, Alex. *We Live in Argentina.* Watts, 1984. *(I; A)*

Peterson, Marge, and Peterson, Rob. *Argentina: A Wild West Heritage.* Dilon, 1990. *(I)*

ARITHMETIC. See Mathematics.

ARIZONA

Carpenter, Allan. *Arizona.* Childrens, 1979. *(I)*

Fradin, Dennis. *Arizona: In Words and Pictures.* Childrens, 1980. *(P; I)*

Wagoner, Jay. *Arizona's Heritage.* Peregrine Smith, 1977. *(I; A)*

ARKANSAS

Carpenter, Allan. *Arkansas.* Childrens, 1978. *(I)*

Fradin, Dennis. *Arkansas: In Words and Pictures.* Childrens, 1980. *(P; I)*

Heinrichs, Ann. *Arkansas.* Childrens, 1989. *(P; I)*

ARMOR

Gregor, Hugh. *Armor.* Silver, 1979. *(I; A)*

Mango, Karin. *Armor: Yesterday and Today.* Messner, 1980. *(I; A)*

Watts, Edith. *A Young Person's Guide to European Arms and Armor in the Metropolitan Museum of Art.* Metro Mus Art, 1982. *(I)*

Wilkinson, Frederick. *Arms and Armor.* Watts, 1984. *(P; I)*

ARNOLD, BENEDICT

Alderman, Clifford L. *The Dark Eagle: The Story of Benedict Arnold.* Macmillan, 1976. *(I; A)*

Fritz, Jean. *Traitor: The Case of Benedict Arnold.* Putnam, 1981. *(I; A)*

ART AND ARTISTS

Batterberry, Ariane (Ruskin). *The Pantheon Story of Art for Young People*. Pantheon, 1975. *(I)*

Grigson, Geoffrey, and Grigson, Jane. *Shapes and Stories: A Book About Pictures*. Vanguard, n.d.; *Shapes, Animals, and Special Creatures*, 1983. *(I; A)*

Janson, H. W., and Janson, Anthony F. *History of Art For Young People*. Abrams, 1987. *(A)*

Lynton, Norbert. *A History of Art*. Watts, 1982. *(I; A)*

Simon, Hilda. *The Magic of Color*. Lothrop, 1981. *(P; I)*

Smith, Dian G. *Careers in the Visual Arts*. Messner, 1980. *(I; A)*

Testa, Fulvio. *If You Take a Paintbrush: A Book of Colors*. Dial Bks Young, 1983. *(P)*

Waterford, Giles. *Faces*. Atheneum, 1982. *(I)*

Woolf, Felicity. *Picture This: A First Introduction to Paintings*. Doubleday, 1990. *(I)*

ARTHUR, CHESTER ALAN

Stevens, Rita. *Chester A. Arthur: 21st President of the United States*. Garrett Educational Corp., 1989. *(I)*

ARTHUR, KING

Hastings, Selina. *Sir Gawain and the Green Knight*. Lothrop, 1981. *(P; I)*

Malory, Thomas. *King Arthur and His Knights of the Round Table*, ed. by Sidney Lanier and Howard Pyle. Putnam, n.d. *(P; I)*

Pyle, Howard. *The Story of King Arthur and His Knights*. Scribner, 1903. *(I; A)*

Riordan, James. *Tales of King Arthur*. Rand, 1982. *(I)*

Sutcliff, Rosemary. *The Light Beyond the Forest*. Dutton, 1980; *The Road to Camlann: The Death of King Arthur*, 1982. *The Sword and the Circle: King Arthur and Knights of the Round Table*, 1981. *(I; A)*

ASIA

Asian Cultural Center for UNESCO, ed. *Folk Tales from Asia for Children Everywhere: Bks. 1–6*. Weatherhill, 1975–1978. *(P; I)*

St. Tamara. *Asian Crafts*. Lion, 1972. *(P; I)*

See also individual countries.

ASTRONOMY

Apfel, Necia H. *Astronomy Projects for Young Scientists*. Arco, 1984. *(A)*

Asimov, Isaac. *Astronomy Today*. Gareth Stevens, 1990. *(P; I); How Did We Find Out About the Universe?* Walker, 1983; *How Was the Universe Born?* Gareth Stevens, 1989. *(P; I); To the Ends of the Universe*, 1976 (new ed.). *(I; A)*

Berger, Melvin. *Bright Stars, Red Giants, and White Dwarfs*. Putnam, 1983; *Star Gazing, Comet Tracking and Sky Mapping*. Putnam, 1985. *(I; A)*

Branley, Franklyn M. *The Sky Is Full of Stars*. Har-Row, 1983. *(P); Space Telescope*. Crowell, 1985. *(P; I); Sun Dogs and Shooting Stars; A Skywatcher's Calendar*. HM, 1980. *(I)*

Chaple, Glenn F. *Exploring with a Telescope*. Watts, 1988. *(I)*

Fisher, David E. *The Origin and Evolution of Our Own Particular Universe*. Atheneum, 1988. *(A)*

Fradin, Dennis B. *Astronomy*. Childrens, 1987. *(A)*

Freeman, Mae, and Freeman, Ira. *The Sun, the Moon, and the Stars*. Random, 1979 (rev. ed.). *(P; I)*

Gallant, Roy A. *Once Around the Galaxy*. Watts, 1983. *(I; A); The Macmillan Book of Astronomy*. Atheneum, 1986. *(P; I)*

Herbst, Judith. *Sky Above and Worlds Beyond*. Atheneum, 1983. *(I; A)*

Kelsey, Larry, and Hoff, Darrel. *Recent Revolutions in Astronomy*. Watts, 1987. *(I; A)*

Moeschl, Richard. *Exploring the Sky: 100 Projects for Beginning Astronomers*. Chicago Review Press, dist. by Independent Publishers Group, 1988. *(I; A)*

Moore, Patrick, ed. *International Encyclopedia of Astronomy*. Orion Books, 1987. *(A)*

Simon, Seymour. *Galaxies*. Morrow, 1988. *(P)*

Vbrova, Zuza. *Space and Astronomy*. Gloucester Press, dist. by Watts, 1990. *(I)*

Yount, Lisa. *The Telescope*. Walker, 1983. *(I; A)*

ATHENS. See GREECE.

ATLANTA. See GEORGIA.

ATLANTIC OCEAN. See OCEANS AND OCEANOGRAPHY.

ATMOSPHERE

Jefferies, Lawrence. *Air, Air, Air*. Troll, 1983. *(P; I)*

Lloyd, David. *Air*. Dial Bks Young, 1983. *(P)*

Smith, Henry, *Amazing Air*. Lothrop, 1983. *(P; I)*

ATOMS

Asimov, Isaac. *How Did We Find Out About Atoms*. Walker, 1976. *Inside the Atom*. Har-Row, 1974. *(I; A)*

Mebane, Robert C., and Rybolt, Thomas R. *Adventures with Atoms and Molecules, Book II; Chemistry Experiments for Young People*. Enslow, 1987. *(I; A)*

AUDUBON, JOHN JAMES

Brenner, Barbara. *On the Frontier with Mr. Audubon*. Putnam, 1977. *(I)*

AUSTRALIA

Arnold, Caroline. *Australia Today*. Watts, 1987. *(P; I)*

Australia. Gareth Stevens, 1988. *(P)*

Dolce, Laura. *Australia*. Chelsea House, 1990. *(I)*

Ellis, Ronnie. *We Live in Australia*. Watts, 1983. *(I; A)*

Kelly, Andrew. *Australia*. Bookwright Press, dist. by Watts, 1989. *(I)*

Parker, K. Langloh. *Australian Legendary Tales*. Merrimack, 1980. *(P; I)*

Rau, Margaret. *Red Earth, Blue Sky: The Australian Outback*. Har-Row, 1981. *(I; A)*

Schneck, S., ed. *Australian Animals*. Western, 1983. *(I; A)*

Stark, Al. *Australia: A Lucky Land*. Dillon Press, 1987. *(P; I)*

Truby, David. *Take a Trip to Australia*. Watts, 1981. *(P)*

AUSTRIA

Wohlrabe, Raymond, and Krusch, Werner. *The Land and People of Austria*. Lippincott, 1972. *(I; A)*

AUTOMATION. See TECHNOLOGY.

AUTOMOBILE MODELS. See MODELMAKING.

AUTOMOBILE RACING

Abodaher, David J. *The Fantastic Formula 1 Racing Cars*. Messner, 1979; *Great Moments in Sports Car Racing*, 1981. *(I)*

Denan, Jay. *The Glory Ride: Road Racing; Hot on Wheels: The Rally Scene*. Troll, 1980. *(I; A)*

Harmer, Paul. *Racing Cars*. Rourke, 1988. *(P)*

Higdon, Hal. *Johnny Rutherford: Indy Champ*. Putnam, 1980. *(I; A)*

Knudson, Richard L. *Land Speed Record Breakers*. Lerner, 1981. *Racing Yesterday's Cars*, 1984. *(I; A)*

Sheffer, H. R. *Race Cars*. Crestwood, 1982. *(I; A)*

Wilkinson, Sylvia. *Stock Cars*. Childrens, 1981. *(I; A)*

AUTOMOBILES

Bendick, Jeanne. *The First Book of Automobiles*. Watts, 1984 (rev. ed.). *(I)*

Cave, Joyce, and Cave, Ronald. *Cars*. Watts, 1982. *(P)*

Cole, Joanna. *Cars and How They Go*. Har-Row, 1983. *(P)*

Ford, Barbara. *The Automobile*. Walker, 1987. *(I)*

Gunning, Thomas G. *Dream Cars*. Dillon, 1990. *(P; I)*

Kanetzke, Howard W. *The Story of Cars*. Raintree, 1978. *(P)*

Lord, Harvey G. *Car Care for Kids and Former Kids*. Atheneum, 1983. *(I; A)*

Taylor, John. *How Cars Are Made*. Facts on File, 1987. *(I)*

Tessendorf, K. C. *Look Out! Here Comes the Stanley Steamer*. Atheneum, 1984. *(P; I)*

Young, Frank. *Automobile: From Prototype to Scrapyard*. Watts, 1982. *(I)*

AVIATION

Ardley, Neil. *Air and Flight*. Watts, 1984. *(I)*

Barton, Byron. *Airport*. Har-Row, 1982. *(P)*

Bendick, Jeanne. *Airplanes*. Watts, 1982 (rev. ed.). *(I)*

Berliner, Don. *Personal Airplanes*. Lerner, 1982. *(I; A)*

Boyne, Walter J. *The Smithsonian Book of Flight for Young People*. Macmillan/Aladdin, 1988. *(I; A)*

Cave, Joyce, and Cave, Ronald, *Aircraft*. Watts, 1982. *(P)*

Corbett, Scott. *What Makes a Plane Fly?* Little, 1967. *(I)*

Dahnsen, Alan. *Aircraft*. Watts, 1978. *(P)*

Dwiggins, Don. *Flying the Frontiers of Space*. Dodd, 1982. *(I; A)*

Freeman. Tony. *Aircraft That Work for Us*. Childrens, 1981. *(P; I)*

Hodgman, Ann, and Djabbaroff, Ruby. *Skystars: The History of Women in Aviation*. Atheneum, 1981. *(I; A)*

Maynard, Chris, and Paton, John. *The History of Aircraft*. Watts, 1982. *(I)*

Moulton, Robert R. *First to Fly*. Lerner, 1983. *(I; A)*

Provenson, Alice, and Provenson, Martin. *The Glorious Flight: Across the Channel with Louis Blériot*. Viking, 1983. *(P)*

Rosenblum, Richard. *The Golden Age of Aviation*. Atheneum, 1984. *(P; I)*

Sabin, Francene. *Amelia Earhart: Adventure in the Sky*. Troll, 1983. *(P; I)*

Schleier, Curt. *The Team Behind Your Airline Flight*. Westminster, 1981. *(I)*

Sloate, Susan. *Amelia Earhart: Challenging the Skies*. Fawcett, 1990. *(I)*

Zisfein, Melvin B. *Flight: A Panorama of Aviation*. Pantheon, 1981. *(I)*

BABY

Banish, Roslyn. *I Want to Tell You About My Baby*. Wingbow, 1982. *(P)*

Harris, Robbie H., and Levy, Elizabeth. *Before You Were Three: How You Began to Walk, Talk, Explore and Have Feelings*. Delacorte, 1981. *(A)*

Ormerod, Jan. *101 Things to Do with a Baby*. Lothrop, 1984. *(P)*

See also REPRODUCTION, HUMAN.

BACTERIA. See MICROBIOLOGY.

BADGERS. See OTTERS AND OTHER MUSTELIDS.

BADMINTON

Wright, Len. *Your Book of Badminton*. Transatlantic, 1972. *(I; A)*

BAHAMAS. See CARIBBEAN SEA AND ISLANDS.

BAHRAIN. See MIDDLE EAST.

BALLADS. See FOLK MUSIC.

BALLET. See DANCE.

BALLOONS AND BALLOONING

Briggs, Carole S. *Ballooning*. Lerner, 1986. *(P; I)*
Coombs, Charles. *Hot-Air Ballooning*. Morrow, 1981. *(I)*
Scarry, Huck. *Balloon Trip: A Sketchbook*. P-H, 1983. *(I)*

BALTIMORE. See MARYLAND.

BANDS AND BAND MUSIC. See MUSIC AND MUSICIANS.

BANGKOK (KRUNG THEP). See SOUTHEAST ASIA.

BANGLADESH. See PAKISTAN AND BANGLADESH.

BANKS AND BANKING

Cantwell, Lois. *Money and Banking*. Watts, 1984. *(I; A)*
Scott, Elaine. *The Banking Book*. Warne, 1981. *(I; A)*

BARBADOS. See CARIBBEAN SEA AND ISLANDS.

BAROMETER. See WEATHER.

BARTON, CLARA

Bains, Rae. *Clara Barton: Angel of the Battlefield*. Troll, 1982. *(P; I)*
Kraske, Robert. *Clara Barton*. Winston, 1980 (new ed.). *(P)*
Stevenson, Augusta. *Clara Barton: Founder of the American Red Cross*. Bobbs, 1983. *(P; I)*

BASEBALL

Aaseng, Nate. *Baseball: You Are the Manager*. Lerner, 1983. *(P; I)*
Arnow, Jan. *Louisville Slugger: The Making of a Baseball Bat*. Pantheon, 1984. *(P; I)*
Brewster, Benjamin. *The First Book of Baseball*. Watts, 1979 (rev. ed.). *(P; I)*
Clark, Steve. *The Complete Book of Baseball Cards*. Putnam, 1982. *(P; I; A)*
Cluck, Bob. *The Winning Edge: Baserunning; The Winning Edge: Catching; The Winning Edge: Hitting; The Winning Edge: Shortstop*. Pantheon, 1987. *(I; A)*
Dolan, Edward F. *Great Moments in the World Series*. Watts, 1982. *(I)*
Earle, Vana. *The All-Star Book of Baseball Fun*. Macmillan, 1982. *(P; I)*
Frommer, Harvey. *A Hundred and Fiftieth Anniversary Album of Baseball*. Watts, 1988. *(I; A); Baseball's Hall of Fame*. Watts, 1985. *(P; I)*
Jaspersohn, William. *The Ballpark: One Day Behind the Scenes at a Major League Game*. Little, Brown, 1980. *(I; A); Bat, Ball, Glove: The Making of Major League Baseball Gear*. Little, 1989. *(I; A)*
Kreutzer, Peter, and Kerley, Ted. *Little League's Official How-to-Play Baseball Book*. Doubleday, 1990. *(I)*
Ritter, Lawrence S. *The Story of Baseball*. Morrow, 1983. *(I)*

Sandak, Cass R. *Baseball and Softball*. Watts, 1982. *(P)*
Sullivan, George. *All About Baseball*. Putnam, 1989. *(P; I); The Art of Base-Stealing*. Dodd, 1982; *Better Baseball for Boys*, 1981 (rev. ed.). *(I); Baseball Backstage*. Holt, 1986. *(I)*
Thorn, John. *Baseball's 10 Greatest Games*. Scholastic, 1981. *(I)*
Walker, Henry. *Illustrated Baseball Dictionary for Young People*. P-H, 1978. *(P; I)*
Williams, Ted, and Underwood, John. *The Science of Hitting*. Simon & Schuster, 1986. *(I; A)*
See also LITTLE LEAGUE BASEBALL.

BASKETBALL

Aaseng, Nate. *Basketball: You Are the Coach; Basketball's Playmakers; Basketball's Sharpshooters*. Lerner, 1983. *(I; A)*
Anderson, Dave. *The Story of Basketball*. Morrow, 1988. *(I; A)*
Beard, Butch and others. *Butch Beard's Basic Basketball*. Michael Kesend, 1985. *(A)*
Clark, Steve. *Illustrated Basketball Dictionary for Young People*. Harvey. 1977. *(I)*
Finney, Shan. *Basketball*. Watts, 1982. *(P)*
Lerner, Mark. *Careers in Basketball*. Lerner, 1983. *(P; I)*
Liss, Howard. *Strange but True Basketball Stories*. Random, 1983. *(I; A)*
Radlauer, Ruth, and Radlauer, Ed. *Some Basics About Women's Basketball*. Childrens, 1982. *(P; I; A)*
Rosenthal, Bert. *Basketball*. Childrens, 1983. *(P)*
Sullivan, George. *Better Basketball for Boys*. Dodd, 1980; *Better Basketball for Girls*, 1978. *(I; A)*
Young, Faye, and Coffey, Wayne. *Winning Basketball for Girls*. Facts on File, 1984. *(I; A)*

BATS

Hopf, Alice L. *Bats*. Dodd, 1985. *(P; I)*
Johnson, Sylvia A. *Bats*. Lerner, 1985. *(P; I)*
Mulleneux, Jane. *Discovering Bats*. Bookwright, dist. by Watts, 1989. *(P)*
Pringle, Laurence. *Vampire Bats*. Morrow, 1982. *(I; A)*
Schlein, Miriam. *Billions of Bats*. Har-Row, 1982. *(I)*

BATTERIES. See ELECTRICITY.

BEARS

Banks, Martin. *The Polar Bear on the Ice*. Gareth Stevens, 1990. *(I)*
Calabro, Marian. *Operation Grizzly Bear*. Four Winds, 1989. *(I)*
Harrison, Virginia. *The World of Polar Bears*. Gareth Stevens, 1990. *(P)*
Patent, Dorothy H. *Bears of the World*. Holiday, 1980. *(I; A)*
Weaver, John L. *Grizzly Bears*. Dodd, 1982. *(P; I)*

BEATLES, THE

Evans, Mike. *The Art of the Beatles.* Morrow/Beechtree. 1985. *(A)*

Harry, Bill. *The Book of Beatle Lists.* Javelin Books, 1985. *(A)*

Hoffmann, Dezo. *The Beatles Conquer America.* Avon, 1985. *(A)*

BEAVERS

Lane, Margaret. *The Beaver.* Dial Bks Young, 1982. *(P)*

Nentl, Jerolyn. *Beaver.* Crestwood, 1983. *(P; I)*

Ryden, Hope. *The Beaver.* Putnam, 1987. *(I; A)*

BEES

Cook, David. *Small World of Bees and Wasps.* Watts, 1981. *(P)*

Fischer-Nagel, Heiderose, and Fischer-Nagel, Andreas. *Life of the Honeybee.* Carolrhoda, 1985. *(P)*

Hogan, Paula Z. *The Honeybee.* Raintree, 1979. *(P)*

Migutsch, Ali. *From Blossom to Honey.* Carolrhoda, 1981. *(P)*

BEETHOVEN, LUDWIG VAN

Blackwood, Alan. *Beethoven.* Watts, 1987. *(I)*

Jacobs, David. *Beethoven.* Har-Row, 1970. *(I; A)*

Johnson, Ann D. *The Value of Giving: The Story of Beethoven.* Value Comm, 1979. *(P; I)*

BELGIUM

Goldstein, Frances. *Children's Treasure Hunt Travel to Belgium and France.* Paper Tiger Pap, 1981. *(P; I)*

Hargrove, Jim. *Belgium.* Childrens, 1988. *(P; I)*

Lye, Keith. *Take A Trip to Belgium.* Watts, 1984. *(P; I)*

BELIZE. See CENTRAL AMERICA.

BELL, ALEXANDER GRAHAM

Quackenbush, Robert. *Ahoy! Ahoy! Are You There? A Story of Alexander Graham Bell.* P-H, 1981. *(P; I)*

Shippen, Katherine B. *Alexander Graham Bell Invents the Telephone.* Random, 1982. *(P; I)*

BELLS AND CARILLONS. See MUSICAL INSTRUMENTS.

BENIN. See AFRICA.

BEOWULF

Crossley-Holland, Kevin, tr. *Beowulf.* Oxford U Pr, 1984. *(I; A)*

Hieatt, Constance B., ed. *Beowolf and Other Old English Poems.* Bantam, 1982. *(A)*

Nye, Robert. *Beowulf.* Dell, 1982. *(I; A)*

BERLIN. See GERMANY.

BERLIOZ, HECTOR. See MUSIC AND MUSICIANS.

BHUTAN. See NEPAL, SIKKIM, AND BHUTAN.

BIBLE AND BIBLE STORIES

Holy Bible. *King James Version.* Holy Bible. *Rev. Standard Version (Catholic Edition).* Many publishers.

Asimov, Isaac. *Animals of the Bible.* Doubleday, 1978. *(I); The Story of Ruth.* 1972. *(I)*

Daniel, Rebecca. *Women of the Old Testament.* Good Apple, 1983. *(I; A)*

DePaola, Tomie. *Noah and the Ark.* Winston, 1983. *(P)*

Gibson, Katharine. *The Tall Book of Bible Stories.* Har-Row, 1980. *(P)*

Haley, Gail E. *Noah's Ark.* Atheneum, 1971!. *(P)*

Hutton, Warwick, ad. and illus. *Jonah and the Great Whale.* Atheneum, 1984. *(P)*

Leeton, Will C. *David and Goliath.* Dandelion, 1979. *(P; I)*

LeFevre, G. L. *Favorite Bible Stories.* Standard Pub, 1982. *(P; I)*

Maves, Paul B., and Maves, Mary C. *Exploring How the Bible Came to Be.* Abingdon, 1973; *Finding Your Way Through the Bible,* 1971. *(P; I)*

Petersham, Maud, and Petersham, Miska. *The Christ Child.* Macmillan, 1931; 1980 (paper). *(P)*

Reed, Gwendolyn E. *Adam and Eve.* Lothrop, 1968. *(P)*

Singer, Isaac Bashevis. *The Wicked City.* FS&G, 1972. *(I)*

Stoddard, Sandol. *Doubleday Illustrated Children's Bible.* Doubleday, 1983. *(P; I); Five Who Found the Kingdom: New Testament Stories,* 1981. *(I)*

Turner, Philip. *The Bible Story.* Merrimack, 1982. *(P; I)*

BICYCLING

Berto, Frank J. *Bicycling Magazine's Complete Guide to Upgrading Your Bike.* Rodale, 1988. *(A)*

Coombs, Charles. *BMX: A Guide to Bicycle Motocross.* Morrow, 1983. *(I)*

Eds. of *Bicycling. Bicycling's Complete Guide to Bicycle Maintenance and Repair.* Rodale, 1986. *(A)*

LeMond, Greg, and Gordis, Kent. *Greg LeMond's Complete Book of Bicycling.* Putnam, 1987. *(A)*

Murphy, Jim. *Two Hundred Years of Bicycles.* Lippincott, 1983. *(I)*

Olney, Ross. *Riding High: Bicycling for Young People.* Lothrop, 1981. *(I; A)*

Roth, Harold. *Bike Factory.* Pantheon, 1985. *(I)*

Scioscia, Mary. *Bicycle Rider.* Har-Row, 1983. *(P; I)*

Wilhelm, Glenda, and Wilhelm, Tim. *Bicycle Basics.* P-H, 1982. *(P; I)*

BIOLOGY

Evans, Ifor. *Biology.* Watts, 1984. *(I)*

Silver, Donald M. *Life on Earth: Biology Today.* Random, 1983. *(A)*

Tocci, Salvatore. *Biology Projects for Young Scientists.* Watts, 1987. *(A)*

BIOLUMINESCENCE

Jacobs, Francine. *Nature's Light: The Story of Biolumi-nescence.* Morrow, 1974. *(P; I)*

BIRDS

Barrie, Anmarie. *A Step-by-Step Book About Canaries; A Step-by-Step Book About Cockatiels.* TFH Publications, 1988. *(I; A)*

Blassingame, Wyatt. *Wonders of Egrets, Bitterns, and Herons.* Dodd, 1982. *(I; A)*

Board, Tessa. *Birds.* Watts, 1983. *(P; I)*

Burnie, David. *Bird.* Knopf, 1988. *(I)*

Burton, Maurice. *Birds.* Facts on File, July, 1985. *(I)*

Cole, Joanna. *A Bird's Body.* Morrow, 1982. *(P)*

Freedman, Russell. *How Birds Fly.* Holiday, 1977. *(I)*

Greenberg, Polly. *Birds of the World.* Putnam, 1983. *(P; I)*

Mansell, William C. *North American Birds of Prey.* Morrow, 1980. *(I; A)*

McCauley, Jane B. *Baby Birds and How They Grow.* Natl Geog, 1984. *(P)*

McGowen, Tom. *Album of Birds.* Rand, 1982. *(I; A)*

Milkins, Colin S. *Discovering Songbirds.* Bookwright Press, dist. by Watts, 1990. *(P; I)*

Sattler, Helen Roney. *The Book of Eagles.* Lothrop, 1989. *(I)*

Selsam, Millicent, and Hunt, Joyce. *A First Look at Birds.* Walker, 1973. *(P)*

Stone, Lynn M. *Birds of Prey.* Childrens, 1983. *(P)*

Wharton, Anthony. *Discovering Ducks, Geese, and Swans.* Watts, 1987. *(P)*

BIRDS (Extinct and Endangered Species)

Heilmen, Joan R. *Bluebird Rescue.* Lothrop, 1982. *(I; A)*

Hendrich, Paula. *Saving America's Birds.* Lothrop, 1983. *(I; A)*

McClung, Robert M. *America's Endangered Birds: Programs and People Working to Save Them.* Morrow, 1979. *(I; A)*

BLACK AMERICANS

Adams, Russell L. *Great Negroes Past and Present.* Afro-American Pub., 1984. *(I)*

Altman, Susan. *Extraordinary Black Americans: From Colonial to Contemporary Times.* Childrens, 1989. *(I)*

Andrews, Bert. *In the Shadow of the Great White Way: Images from the Black Theatre.* Thunder's Month Press, 1989. *(I; A)*

Bellegarde, Ida R. *Black Heroes and Heroines.* Bell Ent, 1979. *(I; A)*

Du Bois, W. E. *The Souls of Black Folk.* Dodd, 1979. *(I; A)*

Evitts, William J. *Captive Bodies, Free Spirits: The Story of Southern Slavery.* Messner, 1985. *(I)*

Fields, Julia. *The Green Lion of Zion Street.* McElderry, 1988. (Fiction) *(I)*

Flournoy, Valerie. *The Patchwork Quilt.* Dutton, 1985. (Fiction) *(P)*

Greenfield, Eloise. *Grandpa's Face.* Philomel, 1988. (Fiction) *(P)*

Hancock, Sibyl. *Famous Firsts of Black Americans.* Pelican, 1983. *(P; I)*

Hughes, Langston. *Not Without Laughter.* Macmillan, 1969. *(I; A)*

Jackson, Florence. *The Black Man in America.* Watts, 1975. *(A)*

Johnston, Johanna. *A Special Bravery.* Dodd, 1967. *(I)*

Katz, William L. *Black People Who Made the Old West.* Har-Row, 1977. *(I; A)*

Lester, Julius. *Long Journey Home: Stories from Black History.* Dial, 1972. *(I)*; *This Strange New Feeling.* Dial Bks Young, 1982. *(A)*

McKissack, Patricia. *Flossie and the Fox.* Dial, 1986. (Fiction) *(P)*; *Mirandy and Brother Wind.* Knopf, 1988. (Fiction) *(P)*; *Nettie Jo's Friends.* Knopf, 1989. (Fiction) *(P)*

Myers, Walter Dean. *The Mouse Rap.* Harper, 1990. (Fiction) *(I)*

Otfinoski, Steven. *Jesse Jackson: A Voice for Change.* Fawcett, 1990. *(I)*

Patterson, Lillie G. *Benjamin Banneker: Genius of Early America.* Abingdon, 1978. *(P; I)*

Richardson, Ben. *Great Black Americans.* Crowell, 1976. *(I)*

Rummel, Jack. *Malcolm X: Militant Black Leader.* Chelsea House, 1989. *(I; A)*

Spangler, Earl. *Blacks in America.* Lerner, 1980 (rev. ed.). *(I; A)*

Sterling, Dorothy, ed. *The Trouble They Seen: Black People Tell the Story of Reconstruction.* Doubleday, 1976. *(A)*

Taylor, Mildred. *The Gold Cadillac.* Dial, 1987. (Fiction) *(I)*

Thum, Marcella. *Exploring Black America: A History and Guide.* Atheneum, 1975. *(A)*

BLIND, EDUCATION OF THE

Brighton, Catherine. *My Hands, My World.* Macmillan, 1984. *(P)*

Curtis, Patricia. *Greff, The Story of a Guide Dog.* Dutton, 1982. *(P; I; A)*

Davidson, Margaret. *Louis Braille: The Boy Who Invented Books for the Blind.* Hastings, 1972. *(I)*

Jensen, Virginia, and Haller, Dorcas. *What's That?* Putnam, 1979. *(P)*

Marcus, Rebecca B. *Being Blind.* Hastings, 1981. *(I)*

Weiss, Malcolm E. *Blindness.* Watts, 1980. *(P; I)*

BLOOD

Showers, Paul. *A Drop of Blood*. Har-Row, 1967. *(P)*

Silverstein, Alvin, and Silverstein, Virginia. *Circulatory Systems: The Rivers Within*. P-H, 1969. *(P; I)*

Ward, Brian R. *The Heart and Blood*. Watts, 1982. *(I)*

BOATS AND BOATING

Gelman, Rita G., and Buxbaum, Susan K. *Boats That Float*. Watts, 1981. *(P)*

Gibbons, Gail. *Boat Book*. Holiday, 1983. *(P)*

Lippman, Peter. *Busy Boats*. Random, 1980. *(P)*

Rockwell, Anne. *Boats*. Dutton, 1982. *(I)*

See also SAILING.

BODY, HUMAN

Avraham, Regina. *The Circulatory System*. Chelsea House, 1989. *(I)*

Baldwin, Dorothy, and Lister, Claire. *How You Grow and Change*. Watts, 1984. *(P; I)*

Berger, Gilda. *The Human Body*. Doubleday, 1989. *(P); The Whole World of Hands*. HM, 1982. *(P; I)*

Berger, Melvin. *Why I Cough, Sneeze, Shiver, Hiccup, and Yawn*. Har-Row, 1983. *(P)*

Branley, Franklyn M. *Shivers and Goose Bumps: How We Keep Warm*. Crowell, 1984. *(I; A)*

Brunn, Ruth Dowling, M.D., and Brunn, Bertel, M.D. *The Human Body: Your Body and How It Works*. Random, 1982. *(I; A)*

Buxbaum, Susan Kovacs, and Gelman, Rita Golden. *Body Noises: Where They Come From, Why They Happen*. Knopf, 1983. *(P; I)*

Cole, Joanna. *Cuts, Breaks, Bruises, and Burns: How Your Body Heals*. Crowell, 1985. *(I); The Human Body: How We Evolved*. Morrow, 1987. *(P)*

Cosgrove, Margaret. *Your Muscles and Ways to Exercise Them*. Dodd, 1980. *(P; I)*

Facklam, Margery, and Facklam, Howard. *Spare Parts for People*. Harcourt, Brace, Jovanovich, 1987. *(I; A)*

Fekete, Irene, and Ward, Peter D. *Your Body. Facts on File*, 1984. *(I)*

Gamlin, Linda. *The Human Body*. Watts, 1988. *(I; A)*

Gilbert, Sara D. *Feeling Good: A Book About You and Your Body*. Scholastic, 1979. *(I; A)*

Goode, Ruth. *Hands Up!* Macmillan, 1983. *(I)*

Goor, Ron, and Goor, Nancy. *All Kinds of Feet*. Crowell, 1984. *(P)*

Kettelkamp, Larry. *A Partnership of Mind and Body: Biofeedback*. Morrow, 1976. *(A)*

Klein, Aaron E. *You and Your Body*. Doubleday, 1977. *(I)*

Miller, Jonathan. *The Human Body*. Viking, 1983 (a pop-up book). *(P; I; A)*

Parker, Steve. *Food and Digestion*. Watts, 1990. *(I)*

Pluckrose, Henry. *Feet*. Watts, 1988. *(P)*

Reader's Digest ABC's of the Human Body. Reader's Digest Press (dist. by Random), 1987. *(I; A)*

Settel, Joanne, and Baggett, Nancy. *Why Does My Nose Run?: (and Other Questions Kids Ask About Their Bodies)*. Atheneum, 1985. *(I; A)*

Showers, Paul. *You Can't Make a Move Without Your Muscles*. Har-Row, 1982. *(P)*

Silverstein, Alvin, and Silverstein, Virginia B. *The Digestive System: How Living Creatures Use Food*. P-H, 1970; *The Story of Your Mouth*. Coward, 1984. *(I; A); The Story of Your Foot*. Putnam, 1987. *(I; A)*

Thomson, Ruth. *Hands*. Watts, 1988. *(P)*

BODY, HUMAN (Body's Senses)

Baldwin, Dorothy, and Lister, Claire. *Your Senses*. Watts, 1984. *(I; A)*

Cobb, Vicki. *How to Really Fool Yourself: Illusions for All Your Senses*. Har-Row, 1981. *(I)*

DeBruin, Jerry. *Young Scientists Explore the Five Senses*. Good Apple, 1983. *(P; I)*

Hoover, Rosalie, and Murphy, Barbara. *Learning About Our Five Senses*. Good Apple, 1981. *(P)*

Martin, Paul D. *Messengers to the Brain: Our Fantastic Five Senses*. National Geog., 1984. *(I)*

Parker, Steve. *Touch, Taste, and Smell*. Watts, 1989. *(P; I)*

Silverstein, Alvin, and Silverstein, Virginia. *The Story of Your Hand*. Putnam, 1985. *(I)*

Sullivan, Tom. *Common Senses*. Childrens, 1982. *(P)*

Ward, Brian R. *Touch, Taste, and Smell*. Watts, 1982. *(I; A)*

BODYBUILDING. See HEALTH AND PHYSICAL FITNESS.

BOLIVIA

Visual Geography. *Bolivia . . . In Pictures*. Lerner, 1987. *(I; A)*

Morrison, Marion. *Bolivia*. Childrens, 1988. *(I)*

Warren, Leslie F. *The Land and People of Bolivia*. Har-Row, 1974. *(A)*

BOOKS

Ahlstrom, Mark. *Books*. Crestwood, 1983. *(P; I)*

Althea. *Making a Book*. Cambridge U Pr, 1983. *(I; A)*

Greenfeld, Howard. *Books: From Writer to Reader*. Crown, 1989 (rev. ed.). *(I)*

Kehoe, Michael. *The Puzzle of Books*. Carolrhoda, 1982. *(P)*

BOONE, DANIEL

Brandt, Keith. *Daniel Boone: Frontier Adventures*. Troll, 1983. *(P; I)*

Stevenson, Augusta. *Daniel Boone: Young Hunter and Tracker*. Bobbs, 1983. *(P; I)*

BORNEO. See SOUTHEAST ASIA.

BOSTON

Monke, Ingrid. *Boston*. Dillon, 1989. *(P; I)*

Vanderwarker, Peter. *Boston Then and Now: Sixty-Five Boston Sites Photographed in the Past and Present*. Dover, 1982. *(P; I)*

See also MASSACHUSETTS.

BOTANY. See PLANTS.

BOTSWANA. See AFRICA.

BOWLING

Holman, Marshall, and Nelson, Roy G. *Marshall Holman's Bowling Tips and Techniques*. Contemporary Books, 1985. *(A)*

Lerner, Mark. *Bowling Is for Me*. Lerner, 1981. *(P; I)*

BOXER REBELLION. See CHINA.

BOXING

Edwards, Audrey, and Wohl, Gary. *Muhammed Ali, the People's Champ*. Little, 1977. *(I)*

Riciutti, Edward R. *How to Box: Boxing for Beginners*. Har-Row, 1982. *(P; I)*

BOY SCOUTS

Blassingame, Wyatt. *Story of the Boy Scouts*. Garrard, 1968. *(I)*

Boy Scouts of America. *Bear Cub Scoutbook*. BSA, 1973. *(I)*; *Boy Scout Fieldbook*. Workman, 1967. *(A)*; *Scout Handbook*. BSA, 1972. *(I)*; *Wolf Cub Scoutbook*. 1986 (rev. ed.). *(I)*

BRAHMS, JOHANNES. See MUSIC AND MUSICIANS.

BRAIN

Baldwin, Dorothy, and Lister, Claire. *Your Brain and Nervous System*. Watts, 1984. *(I; A)*

Berger, Melvin. *Exploring the Mind and Brain*. Har-Row, 1983. *(I; A)*

Facklam, Margery, and Facklam, Howard. *The Brain: Magnificent Mind Machine*. HarBraceJ, 1982. *(A)*

Parker, Steve. *The Brain and Nervous System*. Watts, 1990. *(I)*

Silverstein, Alvin, and Silverstein, Virginia. *World of the Brain*. Morrow, 1986. *(P;I)*

BRAZIL

Bennett, Olivia. *A Family in Brazil*. Lerner, 1986. *(P; I)*

Carpenter, Mark L. *Brazil: An Awakening Giant*. Dillon Press, 1987. *(P; I)*

Cross, Wilbur, and Cross, Susanna. *Brazil*. Childrens, 1984. *(I; A)*

Haverstock, Nathan A. *Brazil in Pictures*. Lerner, 1987. *(I)*

Lye, Keith. *Take a Trip to Brazil*. Watts, 1983. *(P; I)*

Sherwood, Rhoda. *Brazil*. Gareth Stevens, 1988. *(P)*

BREAD AND BAKING

Lucas, Angela. *A Loaf of Bread*. Watts, 1983. *(I)*

Meyer, Carolyn. *The Bread Book: All About Bread and How to Make It*. HarBraceJ, 1976. *(I; A)*

Mitgutsch, Ali. *From Grain to Bread*. Carolrhoda, 1981. *(P; I)*

Ogren, Sylvia. *Shape It and Bake It: Quick and Simple Ideas for Children from Frozen Bread Dough*. Dillon, 1981. *(I)*

Sumption, Lois L., and Ashbrook, Marguerite L. *Breads from Many Lands*. Dover, 1982. *(I)*

Williams, Vera B. *It's a Gingerbread House: Bake It, Build It, Eat It!* Greenwillow, 1978. *(P)*

BRICKS AND MASONRY. See BUILDING CONSTRUCTION.

BRIDGES

Carlisle, Norman, and Carlisle, Madelyn. *Bridges*. Childrens, 1983. *(P)*

Mitgutsch, Ali. *From Cement to Bridge*. Carolrhoda, 1981. *(P)*

Pelta, Kathy. *Bridging the Golden Gate*. Lerner, 1987. *(P)*

St. George, Judith. *The Brooklyn Bridge: They Said It Couldn't Be Built*. Putnam, 1982. *(I; A)*

Sandak, Cass R. *Bridges*. Watts, 1983. *(P)*

Warren, Sandra, and Sjoerdsma, Tom. *The Great Bridge Lowering*. Good Apple, 1983. *(P; I)*

BRITISH COLUMBIA. See CANADA.

BRONTË SISTERS

Brontë, Charlotte. *Jane Eyre*, ad. by Diana Stewart. Raintree, 1983. *(I)*

Brontë, Emily. *Wuthering Heights*, ad. by Betty K. Wright. Raintree, 1983. *(I; A)*

Martin, Christopher. *The Brontës*. Rourke, 1989. *(I; A)*

Sarnoff, Jane. *That's Not Fair*. Scribner, 1980. *(P)*

BRUNEI. See SOUTHEAST ASIA.

BUCHANAN, JAMES

Brill, Marlene Targ. *James Buchanan*. Childrens, 1988. *(I)*

BUCK, PEARL

La Farge, Ann. *Pearl Buck*. Chelsea House, 1988. *(A)*

BUDDHA AND BUDDHISM. See RELIGIONS OF THE WORLD.

BUFFALO AND BISON

Freedman, Russell. *Buffalo Hunt*. Holiday, 1988. *(P; I)*
Patent, Dorothy Hinshaw. *Buffalo: The American Bison Today*. Clarion/Houghton, 1986. *(I)*
Scott, Jack. *Return of the Buffalo*. Putnam, 1976. *(I)*

BUFFALO BILL

D'Aulaire, Ingri, and D'Aulaire, Edgar Parin. *Buffalo Bill*. Doubleday, 1952. *(I)*

BUILDING CONSTRUCTION

Barton, Byron. *Building a House*. Greenwillow, 1981. *(P)*
Fagg, C. D. *How They Built Long Ago*. Watts, 1981. *(I)*
Horwitz, Elinor L. *How to Wreck a Building*. Pantheon, 1982. *(I)*
Robbins, Ken. *Building a House*. Four Winds, 1984. *(P; I)*
Stephen, R. J. *Cranes*. Watts, 1987. *(P); Earthmovers*, 1987. *(P)*
Younker, Richard. *On Site: The Construction of a High-Rise*. Har-Row, 1980. *(I)*

BULGARIA. See BALKANS.

BULLETIN BOARDS

Finton, Esther. *Bulletin Boards Are More Than Somethng to Look At*. Good Apple, 1979; *Bulletin Boards for Science and Health*, 1980; *Math Bulletin Boards*, 1981. *(P; I)*
Jenkins, Betty. *Bulletin Board Book No. 1*. Good Apple, 1977; *Bulletin Board Book No. 2*, 1979. *(P)*

BULLFIGHTING. See SPAIN.

BURBANK, LUTHER

Quakenbush, Robert. *Here a Plant, There a Plant, Everywhere a Plant, Plant! A Story of Luther Burbank*. P-H, 1982. *(P; I)*

BURMA. See SOUTHEAST ASIA.

BURR, AARON. See HAMILTON, ALEXANDER.

BURUNDI. See AFRICA.

BUSES AND BUS TRAVEL. See TRANSPORTATION.

BUSH, GEORGE

Schneiderman, Ron. *The Picture Life of George Bush*. Watts, 1989. *(I)*
Sufrin, Mark. *George Bush: The Story of the Forty-first President of the United States*. Dell, 1989. *(I)*

BUTTERFLIES AND MOTHS

Cook, David. *Small World of Butterflies and Moths*. Watts, 1981. *(P)*
Dallinger, Jane, and Overbeck, Cynthia. *Swallowtail Butterflies*. Lerner, 1983. *(P; I)*
Gibbons, Gail. *The Monarch Butterfly*. Holiday, 1989. *(P; I)*
Jourdan, Eveline. *Butterflies and Moths Around the World*. Lerner, 1981. *(I; A)*
Mitchell, Robert T., and Zim, Herbert S. *Butterflies and Moths: A Guide to the More Common American Species*. Western, 1964. *(I)*
Norsgaard, E. Jaediker. *How to Raise Butterflies*. Putnam/Dodd, 1988. *(P)*
Overbeck, Cynthia. *The Butterfly Book*. Lerner, 1978. *(I)*
Penn, Linda. *Young Scientists Explore Butterflies and Moths*. Good Apple, 1983. *(P)*
Reidel, Marlene. *From Egg to Butterfly*. Carolrhoda, 1981. *(P)*
Ryder, Joanne. *Where Butterflies Grow*. Dutton, 1989. *(P)*
Sabin, Louis. *Amazing World of Butterflies and Moths*. Troll, 1981. *(P; I)*
Tarrant, Graham. *Butterflies*. Putnam, 1983. *(P)*
Whalley, Paul. *Butterfly & Moth*. Knopf, 1988. *(P; I)*

BYRD, RICHARD EVELYN. See POLAR REGIONS.

CABOT, JOHN AND SEBASTIAN

Goodnough, David. *John Cabot and Son*. Troll, 1979 (new ed.). *(P; I)*

CACTUS

Busch, Phyllis S. *Cactus in the Desert*. Har-Row, 1979. *(I)*
Holmes, Anita. *Cactus: The All-American Plant*, Scholastic, 1982; *The 100-Year-Old Cactus*, 1983. *(P; I)*
Overbeck, Cynthia. *Cactus*. Lerner, 1982. *(I)*

CAESAR, GAIUS JULIUS

Peach, L. Dugarde. *Julius Caesar and Roman Britain*. Merry Thoughts, n.d. *(I)*
Matthews, Rupert. *Julius Caesar*. Bookwright, dist. by Watts, 1989. *(P; I)*
Shakespeare, William. *Julius Caesar;* ad. by Diana Stewart. Raintree, 1983. *(I; A)*
See also ROME (ANCIENT)

CALENDAR

Apfel, Necia H. *Calendars*. Watts, 1985. *(I; A)*
Bolton, Carole. *The Good-Bye Year*. Lodestar, 1982, *(I; A)*
Borland, Hal. *The Golden Circle: A Book of Months*. Har-Row, 1977. *(I)*
Brindze, Ruth. *The Story of Our Calendar*. Vanguard, 1968. *(I)*

Hughes, Paul. *The Days of the Week: Stories, Songs, Traditions, Festivals, and Surprising Facts About the Days of the Week from All Over the World.* Garrett Educational Corp., 1989. *(P; I)*; *The Months of the Year: Stories, Songs, Traditions, Festivals, and Surprising Facts About the Months of the Year from All Over the World.* Garrett Educational Corp., 1989. *(P; I)*

Perry, Susan. *How Did We Get Clocks and Calendars?* Creative Ed, 1981. *(P; I)*

Watkins, Peter, and Hughes, Erica. *Here's the Year.* Watts, 1982. *(I; A)*

CALIFORNIA

Cash, Judy. *Kidding Around Los Angeles: A Young Person's Guide to the City.* John Muir, 1989. *(I; A)*

Haddock, Patricia. *San Francisco.* Dillon, 1988. *(P)*

King, David, and others. *Windows on California.* HM, 1978. *(P)*

Oliver, Rice D. *Student Atlas of California.* Calif Weekly, 1982. *(I; A)*

Pack, Janet. *California.* Watts, 1987. *(I; A)*

Starr, Kevin. *California!* Peregrine Smith, 1980. *(I; A)*

Stein, R. Conrad. *California.* Childrens, 1988. *(P)*

CAMELS

Cloudsley-Thompson, John. *Camels.* Raintree, 1980. *(I; A)*

Waters, John F. *Camels: Ships of the Desert.* Har-Row, 1974. *(P)*

Wexo, John Bonnett. *Camels.* Creative Education, 1988. *(P)*

CAMEROON. See AFRICA.

CAMPING

Dolan, Edward. *Bicycle Camping and Touring.* Wanderer Bks, 1982. *(I; A)*

National Geographic Society. *Wilderness Challenge.* National Geog, 1980. *(I; A)*

Neimark, Paul. *Camping and Ecology.* Childrens, 1981. *(I)*

Riviere, Bill. *Camper's Bible.* Doubleday, 1984 (3rd rev. ed.). *(I; A)*

Roscoe, D. T. *Your Book of Camping.* Faber & Faber, 1980. *(A)*

Ryalls, Alan, and Marchant, Roger. *Better Camping.* Sportshelf, 1979. *(I; A)*

Zeleznak, Shirley. *Camping.* Crestwood, 1980. *(P; I; A)*

See also HIKING AND BACKPACKING.

CAMPING, ORGANIZED

Arnold, Eric H., and Loeb, Jeffrey, eds. *Lights Out!: Kids Talk About Summer Camp.* Little Brown, 1986. *(P;I)*

Marsoli, Lisa Ann. *Things to Know Before Going to Camp.* Silver Burdett, 1985. *(I)*

Schneider, Susan. *Please Send Junk Food: A Camp Survival Guide.* Pacer, 1985 *(P; I)*

CANADA

Berucson. *Opening the Canadian West.* Watts, 1980. *(I; A)*

Brickenden, Jack. *Canada.* Bookwright Press, dist. by Watts, 1989. *(I)*

Ferguson, Linda. *Canada.* Scribner, 1979. *(I; A)*

Holbrook, Sabra. *Canada's Kids.* Atheneum, 1983. *(I)*

Kurelek, William. *A Prairie Boy's Summer.* HM, 1975. *(I)*; *A Prairie Boy's Winter,* 1973. *(P)*

Lye, Keith. *Take a Trip to Canada.* Watts, 1983. *(P)*

Martin, Eva, ed. *Canadian Fairy Tales.* Douglas & McIntyre, 1984. *(P; I)*

Morton, Desmond. *New France and War.* Watts, 1984. *(I; A)*

Patterson, E. Palmer. *Inuit Peoples of Canada.* Watts, 1982. *(I; A)*

Shepherd, Jennifer. *Canada.* Children's, 1988. *(P; I)*

Skeoch, Alan. *The United Empire Loyalists and the American Revolution.* Watts, 1983. *(I; A)*

Thompson, Wayne C. *Canada 1985.* Stryker-Post Pubs., 1985. *(A)*

CANALS

Boyer, Edward. *River and Canal.* Holiday, 1986. *(I)*

Sandak, Cass R. *Canals.* Watts, 1983. *(P)*

Scarry, Huck. *Life on a Barge: A Sketchbook.* P-H, 1982. *(I)*

St. George, Judith. *Panama Canal: Gateway to the World.* Putnam, 1989. *(I; A)*

CANCER AND CANCER RESEARCH

Burns, Sheila L. *Cancer: Understanding and Fighting It.* Messner, 1982. *(I; A)*

Fine, Judylaine. *Afraid to Ask: A Book About Cancer.* Kids Can Pr., 1984. *(A)*

Gaes, Jason. *My Book for Kids with Cansur.* Melius & Peterson Publishing Corporation, 1988. *(P; I)*

Holleb, Arthur I., Ed. *The American Cancer Society Cancer Book.* Doubleday, 1986. *(A)*

Hyde, Margaret Oldroyd, and Hyde, Lawrence E. *Cancer in the Young: A Sense of Hope.* Westminster, 1985. *(A)*

Rodgers, Joann Ellison. *Cancer.* Chelsea House, 1990. *(I; A)*

Silverstein, Alvin and Virginia B. *Cancer: Can It Be Stopped?* Lippincott, 1987. *(A)*

Swenson, Judy Harris, and Kunz, Roxanne Brown. *Cancer: The Whispered Word.* Dillon Pr., 1986. *(P;I)*

Trull, Patti. *On with My Life.* Putnam, 1983. *(I; A)*

CANDLES

Yonck, Barbara. *Candle Crafts*. Lion, 1981. *(P; I)*

CANDY. See RECIPES; FOOD AROUND THE WORLD.

CANOEING

Boy Scouts of America. *Canoeing*. BSA, 1977. *(I; A)*
Koon, Celeste A. *Canoeing*. Harvey, 1981. *(I; A)*
Mohn, Peter B. *Whitewater Challenge*. Crestwood, 1975. *(I)*
Moran, Tom. *Canoeing Is for Me*. Lerner, 1983. *(P; I)*

CAPITALISM. See ECONOMICS.

CARD GAMES

Belton, John, and Cramblit, Joella. *Card Games*. Raintree, 1976. *(P; I)*; *Let's Play Cards*, 1975. *(P)*; *Solitaire Games*, 1975. *(P; I)*
Perry, Susan. *How to Play Rummy Card Games*. Creative Ed, 1980. *(P; I)*
Reisberg, Ken. *Card Games*. Watts, 1979. *(P; I)*; *Card Tricks*, 1980. *(P)*
Sackson, Sid. *Playing Cards Around the World*. P-H, 1981. *(I; A)*

CAREERS. See VOCATIONS AND CAREERS.

CARIBBEAN SEA AND ISLANDS

Bryan, Ashley, ed. *The Dancing Granny*. Atheneum, 1977. *(P)*
Carroll, Raymond. *The Caribbean: Issues in U.S. Relations*. Watts, 1984. *(I; A)*
Saunders, Dave. *Through the Year in the Caribbean*. David & Charles, 1981. *(I; A)*
Wolkstein, Diane, ed. *The Magic Orange Tree and Other Haitian Folktales*. Schocken, 1980. *(I)*

CARNIVALS. See FAIRS AND EXPOSITIONS.

CAROLS

Cope, Dawn, and Cope, Peter, eds. *Christmas Carols for Young Children*. Evergreen, 1981. *(P; I)*
Cusack, Margaret. *The Christmas Carol Sampler*. HarBraceJ, 1983. *(P; I; A)*
Langstaff, John M., comp. *The Season for Singing: American Christmas Songs and Carols*. Doubleday, 1974. *(P; I; A)*
Mohr, Joseph. *Silent Night*. Dutton, 1984. *(P; I; A)*
Tennyson, Noel, illus. *Christmas Carols: A Treasury of Holiday Favorites with Words and Pictures*. Random, 1983. *(I; A)*

CARROLL, LEWIS

Carroll, Lewis. *Alice's Adventures in Wonderland* (many editions and publishers); *Through the Looking Glass and What Alice Found There*, illus. by Barry Moser. U of Cal Pr, 1983. *(I; A)*

CARSON, KIT

McCall, Edith. *Hunters Blaze the Trails*. Childrens, 1980. *(P; I; A)*

CARTER, JAMES EARL, JR.

Richman, Daniel A. *James E. Carter*. Garrett Educational Corp., 1989. *(I)*

CARTIER, JACQUES

Averill, Esther. *Cartier Sails the St. Lawrence*. Har-Row, 1956. *(I)*
Syme, Ronald. *Cartier: Finder of the St. Lawrence*. Morrow, 1958. *(I)*

CARTOONS

Hoff, Syd. *How to Draw Cartoons*. Scholastic, 1975. *(P)*
Weiss, Harvey. *Cartoons and Cartooning*. Houghton, 1990. *(I; A)*

CARVER, GEORGE WASHINGTON

Holt, Rackham. *George Washington Carver: An American Biography*. Doubleday, 1963. *(I; A)*

CASTLES

Chisholm. *Castle Times*. EDC, 1983. *(I; A)*
Davison, Brian. *Explore a Castle*. David & Charles, 1983. *(I)*
Monks, John. *Castles*. Rourke, 1988. *(P)*
Smith, Beth. *Castles*. Watts, 1988. *(I; A)*
Vaughan, Jennifer. *Castles*. Watts, 1984. *(P)*

CASTRO, FIDEL. See CUBA.

CATHEDRALS

Gallagher, Maureen. *The Cathedral Book*. Paulist Pr., 1983. *(I; A)*
Macaulay, David. *Cathedral: The Story of Its Construction*. HM, 1973. *(A)*
Watson, Percy, *Building the Medieval Cathedrals*. Lerner, 1978. *(I; A)*

CATS

Barrett, N. S. *Big Cats*. Watts, 1988. *(P; I)*
Cajacob, Thomas. *Close to the Wild: Siberian Tigers in a Zoo*. Carolrhoda, 1985. *(P;I)*
Eaton, Randall L. *Cheetah: Nature's Fastest Racer*. Dodd, 1981. *(I; A)*
Hamer, Martyn. *Cats*. Watts, 1983. *(P)*
Levitin, Sonia. *All the Cats in the World*. HarBraceJ, 1982. *(P)*
McDearmon, Kay. *Cougar*. Dodd, 1977. *(P)*

Ryden, Hope, *Bobcat*. Putnam, 1983. *(I; A)*

Winston, Peggy D. *Wild Cats*. National Geog, 1981. *(P)*

CATS, DOMESTIC

Cole, Joanna. *A Cat's Body*. Morrow, 1982. *(I)*

Fischer-Nagel, Heiderose, and Fischer-Nagel, Andreas. *A Kitten Is Born*. Putnam, 1983. *(P)*

Hess, Lilo. *A Cat's Nine Lives*. Scribner, 1984; *Listen to Your Kitten Purr*, 1980. *(P; I)*

Selsam. Millicent E., and Hunt, Joyce. *A First Look at Cats*. Walker, 1981. *(P; I)*

Steneman, Shep. *Garfield: The Complete Cat Book*. Random, 1981. *(I; A)*

CATTLE. See RANCH LIFE.

CAVES AND CAVERNS

Dean, Anabel. *Going Underground: All About Caves and Caving*. Dillon, 1984. *(I)*

Gans, Roma. *Caves*. Har-Row, 1977. *(P)*

Kerbo, Ronal C. *Caves*. Childrens, 1981. *(P; I)*

CELLS

Fichter, George S. *Cells*. Watts, 1986. *(I; A)*

CELTS. See ENGLAND, HISTORY OF.

CENTIPEDES AND MILLIPEDES

Preston-Mafham, Ken. *Discovering Centipedes & Millipedes*. Bookwright Press, dist. by Watts, 1990. *(I)*

CENTRAL AFRICAN REPUBLIC. See AFRICA.

CENTRAL AMERICA

Adams, Faith. *El Salvador: Beauty Among the Ashes*. Dillon Pr., 1986. *(P;I)*

Cheney, Glenn Alan. *El Salvador: Country in Crisis*. Watts, 1990. *(A)*

Hanmer, Trudy J. *Nicaragua*. Watts, 1986. *(I)*

Haverstock, Nathan A. *El Salvador in Pictures*. Lerner, 1987. *(I); Nicaragua . . . In Pictures*, 1987. *(I; A)*

Markun, Maloney P. *Panama Canal*. Watts, 1979 (rev. ed.). *(P; I)*

Markun, Patricia M. *Central America and Panama*. Watts, 1983 (rev. ed.). *(P; I)*

Perl, Lila. *Guatemala: Central America's Living Past*. Morrow, 1982. *(I; A)*

Visual Geography. *Costa Rica in Pictures*. Lerner, 1987. *(I); Guatemala in Pictures*, 1987. *(I)*

CERAMICS

Gilbreath, Alice. *Slab, Coil and Pinch: A Beginner's Pottery Book*. Morrow, 1977. *(P; I)*

Price, Christine. *Arts of Clay*. Scribner, 1977. *(P; I)*

Weiss, Harvey. *Ceramics: from Clay to Kiln*. A-W, 1982. *(I; A)*

CHAD. See AFRICA.

CHAMBER MUSIC. See MUSIC AND MUSICIANS.

CHAMPLAIN, SAMUEL DE

Grant, Matthew G. *Champlain*. Creative Ed, 1974. *(I)*

CHAPLIN, CHARLIE. See MOTION PICTURE INDUSTRY.

CHARLEMAGNE

Winston, Richard. *Charlemagne*. Har-Row, 1968. *(I; A)*

CHAUCER, GEOFFREY

Chaucer, Geoffrey. *Canterbury Tales*. Hyman, 1988. *(P; I; A); The Canterbury Tales*. adapt. by Geraldine McCaughrean. Rand McNally, 1985. *(I; A)*

Cohen, Barbara. *Canterbury Tales*. Lothrop, 1988. *(P; I; A)*

CHEMISTRY

Chishom, J., and Lynnington, M. *Understanding Chemistry*. EDC, 1983. *(I; A)*

Cobb, Vicki. *Chemically Active! Experiments You Can Do at Home*. Lippincott, 1985. *(A)*

Conway, Lorraine. *Chemistry Concepts*. Good Apple, 1983. *(I; A)*

Mebane, Robert C., and Rybolt, Thomas R. *Adventures with Atoms and Molecules, Book II: Chemistry Experiments for Young People*. Enslow, 1987. *(P; I)*

Walters, Derek. *Chemistry*. Watts, 1983. *(I; A)*

See also EXPERIMENTS AND OTHER SCIENCE ACTIVITIES.

CHESS

Caldwell. *Playing Chess*. EDC, 1980. *(P; I)*

Langfield, Paul. *A Picture Guide to Chess*. Har-Row, 1977. *(I)*

Marsh, Carole. *Go Queen Go! Chess for Kids*. Gallopade, 1983. *(P; I)*

Pandolfini, Bruce. *Let's Play Chess: A Step-by-Step Guide for Beginners*. Messner, 1980. *(I; A)*

Reinfeld, Fred. *Chess for Children*. Sterling, 1980 (rev. ed.). *(P; I; A)*

CHIANG KAI-SHEK. See CHINA.

CHICAGO. See ILLINOIS.

CHILD ABUSE

Benedict, Helen. *Safe, Strong and Streetwise*. Joy Street Books/Little Brown, Feb. 1987. *(A)*

Dolan, Edward F., Jr. *Child Abuse*. Watts, 1984. *(A)*

Hall, Lynn. *The Boy in the Off-White Hat*. Scribner, 1984. *(I; A)*

Haskins, James. *The Child Abuse Help Book*. A-W, 1981. *(A)*

Hyde, Margaret O. *Cry Softly! The Story of Child Abuse*. Westminster, 1986 (rev. ed.). *(I; A); Sexual Abuse: Let's Talk About It*. 1984. *(A)*

Irwin, Hadley. *Abby, My Love*. Atheneum, 1985. *(A)*

Landau, Elaine. *Child Abuse: An American Epidemic*. Messner, 1990 (rev. ed.). *(A)*

Morgan, Marcia. *My Feelings*. Equal Justice (Eugene, OR 97405), 1984. *(P; I)*

Newman, Susan. *Never Say Yes to a Stranger*. Putnam, 1985. *(I; A)*

Stanek, Muriel. *Don't Hurt Me, Mama*. Whitman, 1983. *(P)*

Terkel, Susan N., and Rench, Janice E. *Feeling Safe, Feeling Strong: How to Avoid Sexual Abuse and What to Do if it Happens to You*. Lerner, 1984. *(P; I; A)*

Wachter, Oralee. *No More Secrets for Me*. Little, 1983. *(P)*

CHILE

Haverstock, Nathan A. *Chile in Pictures*. Lerner, 1988. *(I; A)*

Huber, Alex. *We Live in Chile*. Watts/Bookwright Pr., 1986. *(P;I)*

CHINA

Bradley, John. *China: A New Revolution?* Gloucester Press, dist. by Watts, 1990. *(I; A)*

Buck, Pearl. *Chinese Story Teller*. Har-Row, 1971. *(P)*

Feinstein, Stephen C. *China . . . in Pictures*. Lerner, 1989. *(I)*

Fritz, Jean. *China's Long March: 6,000 Miles of Danger*. Putnam, 1988. *(I; A)*

Hacker, Jeffrey H. *The New China*. Watts, 1986. *(A)*

Keeler, Stephen. *Passport to China*. Watts, 1987. *(I; A)*

Lawson, Don. *The Long March: Red China Under Chairman Mao*. Har-Row, 1983. *(I; A)*

Loescher, Gil, and Loescher, Ann D. *China: Pushing Toward the Year Two Thousand*. HarBraceJ, 1981. *(I; A)*

Major, John S. *The Land and People of China*. Lippincott, 1989. *(I; A)*

Merton, Anna, and Kan, Shio-yun. *China: The Land and Its People*. Silver Burdett, 1987. *(P; I)*

Murphey, Rhoads, ed. *China*. Gateway Press, 1988. *(I; A)*

Newlon, Clarks. *China: The Rise to World Power*. Dodd, 1983. *(I; A)*

Perl, Lila. *Red Star and Green Dragon: Looking at New China*. Morrow, 1983. *(A)*

Poole, Frederick K. *Album of Modern China*. Watts, 1981. *(I; A)*

Roberson, John R. *China from Manchu to Mao*. Atheneum, 1980. *(I; A)*

Ross, Stewart. *China Since 1945*. Bookwright Press, dist. by Watts, 1989. *(I; A)*

Sadler, Catherine E. *Two Chinese Families*. Atheneum, 1981. *(P; I)*

Sherwood, Rhoda, with Sally Tolan. *China*. Gareth Stevens, 1988. *(P)*

Steele, Philip. *China*. Steck-Vaughn, 1989. *(I)*

Yee, Paul. *Tales from Gold Mountain*. Macmillan, 1989. *(I; A)*

Yep, Lawrence. *The Rainbow People*. Harper, 1989. *(I; A); The Serpent's Children*. Har-Row, 1984. *(I)*

Young, Ed. *Lon Po Po: A Red-Riding Hood Story from China*. Philomel, 1989. *(P)*

CHOCOLATE

Ammon, Richard. *The Kids' Book of Chocolate*. Atheneum, 1987. *(P; I)*

CHOPIN, FRÉDÉRIC. See MUSIC AND MUSICIANS.

CHORAL MUSIC. See MUSIC AND MUSICIANS.

CHRISTMAS CUSTOMS AROUND THE WORLD

Barth, Edna. *Holly, Reindeer, and Colored Lights: The Story of the Christmas Symbols*. HM, 1981. *(P; I)*

Daniel, Mark. *A Child's Christmas Treasury*. Dial, 1988. *(P)*

Hunt, Roderick. *The Oxford Christmas Book for Children*. Merrimack, 1983. *(P; I)*

Jupo, Frank. *Christmas Here, There, and Everywhere*. Dodd, 1977. *(P)*

Patent, Dorothy Hinshaw. *Christmas Trees*. Dodd, 1987. *(P)*

Purdy, Susan. *Christmas Cooking Around the World*. Watts, 1983. *(I; A)*

Sawyer, Ruth. *Joy to the World: Christmas Legends*. Little, 1966. *(P; I)*

Thomas, Dylan. *A Child's Christmas in Wales*. Holiday, 1985. *(P; I)*

Wilson, Robina B. *Merry Christmas! Children at Christmastime Around the World*. Putnam, 1983. *(P; I)*

CHURCHILL, SIR WINSTON

Driemen, J. E. *Winston Churchill: An Unbreakable Spirit*. Dillon, 1990. *(I)*

Finlayson, Iain. *Winston Churchill*. David & Charles, 1981. *(P; I)*

CIRCUS

Cross, Helen Reeder. *The Real Tom Thumb*. Scholastic, 1980. *(P; I)*

Fenton, Don, and Fenton, Barb. *Behind the Circus Scene*. Crestwood, 1980. *(P; I)*

Harmer, Mabel. *Circus*. Childrens, 1981. *(P)*

Machotka, Hana. *The Magic Ring: A Year with the Big Apple Circus*. Morrow, 1988. *(P; I; A)*

CITIES

Beekman, Daniel. *Forest, Village, Town, City.* Har-Row, 1982. *(P; I)*

Carey, Helen. *How to Use Your Community as a Resource.* Watts, 1983. *(I; A)*

Hanmer, Trudy. *The Growth of Cities.* Watts, 1985. *(A)*

Isadora, Rachael. *City Seen from A to Z.* Greenwillow, 1983. *(P)*

Macaulay, David. *Underground.* HM, 1976. *(P; I; A)*

Switzer, Ellen. *Our Urban Planet.* Atheneum, 1980. *(A)*

CITIZENSHIP

Abel, Sally. *How to Become a U.S. Citizen.* Nolo Pr, 1983. *(I; A)*

Burt, Olive W. *I Am an American.* Har-Row, 1968. *(I)*

CIVIL LIBERTIES AND CIVIL RIGHTS

Anders, Rebecca. *A Look at Prejudice and Understanding.* Lerner, 1976. *(P; I)*

Bach, Julie S., ed. *Civil Liberties.* Greenhaven Press, 1988. *(A)*

Bolton, Carole. *Never Jam Today.* Atheneum, 1971. *(I; A)*

Bradley, John. *Human Rights.* Gloucester Press (dist. by Watts), 1987. *(I)*

Cook, Fred J. *The Ku Klux Klan: America's Recurring Nightmare.* Messner, 1980. *(A)*

Englebardt, Leland S. *You Have a Right.* Lothrop, 1979. *(I; A)*

Lapping, Brian. *Apartheid: A History.* Braziller, 1987. *(A)*

McKissack, Patricia, and McKissack, Frederick. *The Civil Rights Movement in America From 1865 to the Present.* Childrens, 1987. *(I; A)*

Morrison, Dorothy Nafus. *Chief Sarah: Sarah Winnemucca's Fight for Indian Rights.* Atheneum, 1980. *(I)*

Pascoe, Elaine. *Racial Prejudice.* Watts, 1985. *(I; A)*

Price, Janet R., and others. *The Rights of Students; the Basic ACLU Guide to a Student's Rights.* Southern Illinois University, 1988. *(A)*

Selby, David. *Human Rights.* Cambridge, 1987. *(I; A)*

CIVIL WAR, UNITED STATES

Foster, Genevieve. *Year of Lincoln, 1861.* Scribner, 1970. *(I)*

Fritz, Jean. *Stonewall.* Putnam, 1979. *(I; A)*

Goldston, Robert. *The Coming of the Civil War.* Macmillan, 1972. *(I; A)*

Hunt, Irene. *Across Five Aprils.* Ace Bks, 1982. *(A)*

Levenson, Dorothy. *The First Book of the Civil War.* Watts, 1977 (rev. ed.). *(P; I)*

Meltzer, Milton, ed. *Voices from the Civil War: A Documentary History of the Great American Conflict.* Crowell, 1989. *(I; A)*

Steele, William O. *The Perilous Road.* HarBraceJ, 1965. *(P; I)*

Stein, R. Conrad. *The Story of the Monitor and the Merrimack.* Childrens, 1983. *(P; I)*

CLAY, HENRY

Kelly, Regina Z. *Henry Clay: Statesman and Patriot.* HM, 1960. *(I)*

CLAY MODELING

McTwigan, M., and Post, H. *Clay Play: Learning Games for Children.* P-H, 1973. *(P)*

CLEMENS, SAMUEL. See TWAIN, MARK.

CLEVELAND, GROVER

Collins, David R. *Grover Cleveland: 22nd and 24th President of the United States.* Garrett Educational Corp., 1988. *(A)*

Kent, Zachary. *Grover Cleveland: Twenty-second and Twenty-fourth President of the United States.* Childrens, 1988. *(P; I)*

See also PRESIDENCY OF THE UNITED STATES.

CLIMATE

Gallant, Roy A. *Earth's Changing Climate.* Scholastic, 1979. *(I; A)*

Newton, James R. *Rain Shadow.* Har-Row, 1983. *(P; I)*

Pringle, Laurence. *Frost Hollows and Other Microclimates.* Morrow, 1981. *(P; I)*

Updegraffe, Imelda, and Updegraffe, Robert. *Continents and Climates.* Penguin, 1983. *(I; A)*

See also WEATHER.

CLOTHING

Bowood, Richard. *The Story of Clothes and Costumes.* Merry Thoughts, n.d. *(P; I)*

Cooke, Jean. *Costumes and Clothes.* Watts, 1987. *(P)*

Dru, Ricki. *The First Blue Jeans.* Silver, 1978. *(I; A)*

Thompson, Stephanie. *Clothes and Ornaments.* Silver, 1978. *(I; A)*

Weil, Lisl. *New Clothes: What People Wore—From Cavemen to Astronauts.* Atheneum, 1988. *(I)*

Wilson, K. *Costumes and Uniforms.* Starlog, 1980. *(I; A)*

CLOUDS. See WEATHER; CLIMATE.

CLOWNS

Fife, Bruce, and others. *Creative Clowning.* Java Publishing, 1988. *(A)*

COAL AND COAL MINING

Asimov, Isaac. *How Did We Find Out About Coal?* Walker, 1980. *(I; A)*

Davis, Bertha, and Whitfield, Susan. *The Coal Question.* Watts, 1982. *(I; A)*

Kraft, Betsy. *Coal.* Watts, 1982 (rev. ed.). *(P; I)*

CODES AND CIPHERS

Albert, Burton. *Code Busters!* 1985. *(I); More Codes for Kids.* Whitman, 1979. *(P; I); Top Secret! Codes to Crack,* 1987. *(P; I)*

Baker, Eugene. *Secret Writing—Codes and Messages.* Childrens, 1980. *(P; I)*

Brandreth, Gyles. *Writing Secret Codes and Sending Hidden Messages.* Sterling, 1984. *(I)*

Fletcher, Helen J. *Secret Codes.* Watts, 1980. *(P)*

Garden, Nancy. *The Kid's Code and Cipher Book.* HR&W, 1981. *(I; A)*

Grant, E. A. *The Kids' Book of Secret Codes, Signals, and Ciphers.* Running Press, 1989. *(P; I)*

Janeczko, Paul B. *Loads of Codes and Secret Ciphers.* Macmillan, 1984. *(I)*

Mango, Karin N. *Codes, Ciphers and Other Secrets.* Watts, 1988. *(P; I)*

COINS AND COIN COLLECTING

Boy Scouts of America. *Coin Collecting.* BSA, 1975. *(I; A)*

Hobson, Burton H. *Coin Collecting as a Hobby.* Sterling, 1982 (rev. ed.). *(I; A)*

Reinfeld, Fred, and Hobson, Burton H. *How to Build a Coin Collection.* Sterling, 1977. *(P; I; A)*

Reisberg, Ken. *Coin Fun.* Watts, 1981. *(P)*

COLLAGE

Beaney, Jan. *Fun with Collage.* Sportshelf, 1980. *(P; I)*

COLOMBIA

Jacobsen, Peter O., and Kristensen, Preben S. *A Family in Colombia.* Watts-Bookwright Press, 1986. *(P)*

Visual Geography. *Colombia in Pictures.* Lerner, 1987. *(I; A)*

COLONIAL LIFE IN AMERICA. See AMERICAN COLONIES.

COLORADO

Kent, Deborah. *Colorado.* Childrens, 1989. *(P; I)*

Spies, Karen. *Denver.* Dillon, 1988. *(P)*

COLUMBUS, CHRISTOPHER

Ceserani, Gian Paolo. *Christopher Columbus.* Random, 1979. *(P)*

Columbus, Christopher. *The Log of Christopher Columbus' First Voyage to America in the Year 1492: As Copied out in Brief by Bartholomew Las Casas.* Linnet Books, 1989. *(P; I)*

D'Aulaire, Ingri, and D'Aulaire, Edgar P. *Columbus.* Doubleday, n.d. *(P)*

Foster, Genevieve. *Year of Columbus, 1492.* Scribner, 1969. *(P; I)*

Fritz, Jean. *Where Do You Think You're Going, Christopher Columbus?* Putnam, 1980. *(I)*

Levinson, Nancy Smiler. *Christopher Columbus.* Lodestar, 1990. *(I; A)*

Meltzer, Milton. *Columbus and the World Around Him.* Watts, 1990. *(I; A)*

Weil, Lisl. *I, Christopher Columbus.* Atheneum, 1983. *(A)*

COMETS, METEORS, AND METEORITES

Anderson, Norman D., and Brown, Walter R. *Halley's Comet.* Dodd, 1981. *(I)*

Asimov, Isaac. *Comets and Meteors.* Gareth Stevens, 1990. *(P; I); Asimov's Guide to Halley's Comet.* 1985. *(I; A); How Did We Find Out About Comets?* Walker, 1975. *(I)*

Berger, Melvin. *Comets, Meteors, and Asteroids.* Putnam, 1981. *(A)*

Branley, Franklyn M. *Comets.* Har-Row, 1984. *(P); Halley: Comet 1986.* Lodestar, 1983. *(I; A)*

Darling, David J. *Comets, Meteors, and Asteroids: Rocks in Space.* Dillon, 1984. *(P)*

Fichter, George S. *Comets and Meteors.* Watts, 1982. *(P; I)*

Hamer, Martyn. *Comets.* Watts, 1984. *(P; I)*

Krupp, Edwin C. *The Comet and You.* Macmillan, 1985. *(P)*

Simon, Seymour. *The Long Journey from Space.* Crown, 1982. *(P)*

Vogt, Gregory. *Halley's Comet: What We've Learned.* Watts, 1987. *(I)*

COMIC BOOKS

Rovin, Jeff. *The Encyclopedia of Superheroes.* Facts on File, 1985. *(A)*

COMMUNICATION

Aylesworth, Thomas G. *Understanding Body Talk.* Watts, 1979. *(I; A)*

Fisher, Trevor. *Communications.* David & Charles, 1985. *(I; A)*

Graham, Ian. *Communications.* Watts, 1989. *(P; I)*

Herda, D. J. *Communication Satellites.* Watts, 1988. *(I; A)*

Jespersen, James, and Fitz-Randolph, Jane. *Mercury's Web: The Story of Telecommunications.* Atheneum, 1981. *(I; A)*

Schefter, James L. *Telecommunications Careers.* Watts, 1988. *(A)*

Storrs, Graham. *The Telecommunications Revolution.* Watts/Bookwright Pr., 1985. *(I; A)*

Sullivan, George. *How Do We Communicate?* Watts, 1983. *(P)*

Wolverton, Ruth, and Wolverton, Mike. *The News Media*. Watts, 1981. *(I; A)*
See also SATELLITES; TELEPHONE.

COMMUNISM

Forman, James D. *Communism*. Watts, 1979 (2nd ed.). *(I; A)*

COMPUTERS

Asimov, Isaac. *How Did We Find Out About Computers?* Walter, 1984. *(I)*
Ault, Rosalie S. *BASIC Programming for Kids*. HM, 1983. *(I; A)*
Berger, Melvin. *Computer Talk*. Messner, 1984. *(I)*; *Computers in Your Life*. Crowell, 1984. *(I; A)*
Bly, Robert W. *A Dictionary of Computer Words*. Dell, 1983. *(I; A)*
Howard, Penny. *Looking at Computers; Looking at Computer Programming; Looking at LOGO*. Watt, 1984. *(P)*
Lampton, Christopher. *Advanced BASIC for Beginners; BASIC for Beginners; COBOL for Beginners; FORTRAN for Beginners; The Micro Dictionary; PASCAL for Beginners; PILOT for Beginners*. Watts, 1984. *(I; A)*; *Super-Conductors*. Enslow, 1989. *(I; A)*
Lipson, Shelley. *It's BASIC: The ABC's of Computer Programming*. HR&W, 1982. *(P; I)*
Norback, Judith. *The Complete Computer Career Guide*. TAB, 1987. *(A)*
Petty, Kate. *Computers*. Watts, 1984. *(P)*
Sullivan, George. *Computer Kids*. Dodd, 1984. *(I; A)*

CONFEDERATE STATES OF AMERICA. See CIVIL WAR.

CONGO. See AFRICA.

CONGO RIVER

Lauber, Patricia. *The Congo: River into Central Africa*. Garrard, 1964. *(I)*

CONNECTICUT

Carpenter, Allan. *Connecticut*. Childrens, 1979. *(P; I)*
Fradin, Dennis. *Connecticut: In Words and Pictures*. Childrens, 1980. *(P; I)*

CONSERVATION. See ENVIRONMENT.

CONSTELLATIONS. See STARS.

CONSUMER EDUCATION

Arnold, Caroline. *What Will We Buy?* Watts, 1983. *(P)*
Berger, Melvin. *Consumer Protection Labs*. Har-Row, 1975. *(A)*
Kelly, Brendan. *Consumer Math*. EDC, 1981. *(I)*

Riekes, Linda, and Ackerly, Salley M. *Young Consumers*. West Pub, 1980 (2nd ed.). *(I; A)*

COOKING

Betty Crocker's Cookbook for Boys and Girls. Western, 1984. *(P; I)*
Borghese, Anita. *The Down to Earth Cookbook*. Scribner, 1980 (rev. ed.). *(P; I)*
Cooper, Terry T., and Ratner, Marilyn. *Many Friends Cooking: An International Cookbook for Boys and Girls*. Putnam, 1980. *(P; I)*
Coronado, Rosa. *Cooking the Mexican Way*. Lerner, 1982. *(I; A)*
Delmar, Charles. *The Essential Cook: Everything You Really Need to Know About Foods and Cooking Except the Recipes*. Hill House Pub., dist. by Ingram, 1989. *(I; A)*
Goldstein, Helen H. *Kid's Cuisine*. News & Observer, 1983. *(P; I)*
Greene, Karen. *Once Upon a Recipe: Delicious, Healthy Foods for Kids of All Ages*. New Hope Press, 1988. *(P; I)*
John, Sue. *The Special Days Cookbook*. Putnam, 1982. *(P; I)*
Moore, Carolyn E., and others. *Young Chef's Nutrition Guide and Cookbook*. Barron's, 1990. *(I)*
Pfommer, Marian. *On the Range: Cooking Western Style*. Atheneum, 1981. *(P; I)*
Sanderson, Marie C., and Schroeder, Rosella J. *It's Not Really Magic: Microwave Cooking for Young People*. Dillon, 1981. *(I; A)*

COOLIDGE, CALVIN

Kent, Zachary. *Calvin Coolidge: Thirtieth President of the United States*. Childrens, 1988. *(P; I)*

COPLAND, AARON. See MUSIC AND MUSICIANS.

COPPER. See METALS AND METALLURGY.

CORALS

Bender, Lionel. *Life on a Coral Reef*. Gloucester Press, dist. by Watts, 1989. *(P; I)*
Berger, Gilda. *The Coral Reef: What Lives There*. Putnam, 1977. *(P; I)*
Jacobson, Morris K., and Franz, David R. *Wonders of Coral Reefs*. Dodd, 1979. *(I; A)*
Reese, Bob. *Coral Reef*. Childrens, 1983. *(P)*

CORN

Aliki. *Corn Is Maize: The Gift of the Indians*. Har-Row, 1976. *(P)*
Selsam, Millicent E. *Popcorn*. Morrow, 1976. *(P; I)*

CORTES, HERNANDO

Dorner, Jane. *Cortes and the Aztecs*. Longman, 1972. *(I; A)*

Marrin, Albert. *Aztecs and Spaniards: Cortes and the Conquest of Mexico*. Atheneum, 1986. *(A)*

Wilkes, John. *Hernan Cortes: Conquistador in Mexico*. Lerner, 1977. *(I; A)*

COSMIC RAYS. See NUCLEAR ENERGY.

COSTA RICA. See CENTRAL AMERICA.

COTTON

Miles, Lewis. *Cotton*. (Spotlight on Resources) Rourke Enterprises, 1987. *(P; I)*

Mitgutsch, Ali. *From Cotton to Pants*. Carolrhoda, 1981. *(P)*

Selsam, Millicent E. *Cotton*. Morrow, 1982. *(P; I)*
See also TEXTILES.

COUNTRY AND WESTERN MUSIC

Harris, Stacy, and Krishef, Robert K. *The Carter Family: Country Music's First Family*. Lerner, 1978. *(I; A)*

Krishef, Robert K. *The Grand Ole Opry*. Lerner, 1978; *Introducing Country Music,* 1979. *(I; A)*

Lomax, John. *Nashville: Music City USA*. Abrams, 1985. *(A)*

COURTS. See LAW AND LAW ENFORCEMENT; SUPREME COURT OF THE UNITED STATES.

COWBOYS

Dean, Frank. *Cowboy Fun*. Sterling, 1980. *(I)*

Freedman, Russell. *Cowboys of the Wild West*. Clarion/T&F, 1985. *(A)*

Gorsline, Marie, and Gorsline, Douglas. *Cowboys*. Random, 1980. *(P)*

Helberg, Kristin. *Cowboys*. Troubador, 1982. *(I; A)*

Malone, Margaret G. *Cowboys and Computers: Life on a Modern Ranch*. Messner, 1982. *(P; I)*

Patent, Dorothy Hinshaw. *The Sheep Book*. Dodd, 1985. *(I)*

Wellman, Paul I. *The Greatest Cattle Drive*. HM, 1964. *(A)*

CRABS

Bailey, Jill. *Discovering Crabs and Lobsters*. Watts, 1987. *(P)*

Johnson, Sylvia A. *Crabs*. Lerner, 1982. *(P; I; A)*

CRIME AND CRIMINOLOGY. See JUVENILE CRIME; LAW AND LAW ENFORCEMENT; POLICE.

CROCKETT, DAVY

McCall, Edith. *Hunters Blaze the Trails*. Childrens, 1980. *(P; I; A)*

Santrey, Laurence. *Davy Crockett: Young Pioneer*. Troll, 1983. *(P; I)*

Townsend, Tom. *Davy Crockett: An American Hero*. Eakin Press, 1987. *(I)*

CROCODILES AND ALLIGATORS

Bare, Colleen Stanley. *Never Kiss An Alligator!* Dutton/Cobblehill, 1989. *(P)*

Bender, Lionel. *Crocodiles and Alligators*. Gloucester Press, dist. by Watts, 1988. *(I)*

Gross, Ruth B. *Alligators and Other Crocodilians*. Scholastic, 1978. *(I)*

Harris, Susan. *Crocodiles and Alligators*. Watts, 1980. *(P)*

Scott, Jack Denton. *Alligators*. Putnam, 1984. *(P; I; A)*

CRUSADES

Williams, Ann. *The Crusades*. Longman, 1975. *(I; A)*

Williams, Jay. *Knights of the Crusades*. Har-Row, 1962. *(I; A)*

CRYSTALS

Gans, Roma. *Millions and Millions of Crystals*. Crowell, 1973. *(P)*

CUBA

Cannon, Terence. *Revolutionary Cuba*. Har-Row, 1981. *(A)*

Cowan, Rachel. *Growing Up Yanqui*. Viking, 1975. *(I; A)*

Dolan, Edward D., and Scariano, Margaret M. *Cuba and the United States*. Watts, 1987. *(A)*

Haverstock, Nathan. *Cuba . . . In Pictures*. Lerner, 1987. *(I; A)*

Lindon, Edmund. *Cuba*. Watts, 1980. *(P; I)*

Vazquez, Ana Maria, and Casas, Rosa E. *Cuba*. Children's, 1988. *(P; I)*

CURIE, MARIE AND PIERRE

Birch, Beverley. *Marie Curie: The Polish Scientist Who Discovered Radium and Its Life-Saving Properties*. Gareth Stevens, 1988. *(I)*

Brandt, Keith. *Marie Curie: Brave Scientist*. Troll, 1983. *(I)*

Conner, Edwina. *Marie Curie*. Watts, 1987. *(I)*

Keller, Mollie. *Marie Curie*. Watts, 1982. *(I; A)*

CZECHOSLOVAKIA

Hall, Elvajean. *The Land and People of Czechoslovakia*. Har-Row, 1972 (rev. ed.). *(I; A)*

Ish-Kishor, S. *A Boy of Old Prague*. Scholastic, 1980. *(P; I)*

DAIRYING AND DAIRY PRODUCTS

Dineen, Jacqueline. *Food from Dairy and Farming*. Enslow, 1988. *(P; I)*

Gibbons, Gail. *The Milk Makers*. Macmillan, 1985. *(P)*

Moon, Cliff. *Dairy Cows on the Farm; Pigs on the Farm; Poultry on the Farm; Sheep on the Farm*. Watts, 1983. *(P)*

Patterson, Geoffrey. *Dairy Farming*. Andre Deutsch, 1984. *(P)*

Scuro, Vincent. *Wonders of Dairy Cattle*. Dodd, 1986. *(P; I)*

DALLAS. See TEXAS.

DAMS

Sandak, Cass R. *Dams*. Watts. 1983. *(P)*

DANCE

Ancona, George. *Dancing Is*. Dutton, 1981. *(P)*

Brown, LouLou, ed. *Ballet Class*. Arco, 1985. *(I)*

Collard, Alexandra. *Two Young Dancers: Their World of Ballet*. Messner, 1984. *(I; A)*

Finney, Shan. *Dance*. Watts, 1983. *(I; A)*

Haney, Lynn. *I Am a Dancer*. Putnam, 1981. *(I; A)*

Isadora, Rachel. *Opening Night*. Greenwillow, 1984. *(P)*

Kuklin, Susan. *Reaching for Dreams: A Ballet From Rehearsal to Opening Night*. Lothrop, 1987. *(I; A)*

Nadell, Bonnie. *Break Dance*. Running Press, 1984. *(I; A)*

Rosenberg, Jane. *Dance Me a Story*. Norton, 1985. *(I; A)*

Royal Academy of Dancing. *Ballet Class*. Arco, 1985. *(P; I)*

Sinibaldi, Thomas. *Tap Dancing Step by Step*. Sterling, 1981. *(I; A)*

Sorine, D. *Imagine That! It's Modern Dance; At Every Turn: It's Ballet*. Knopf, 1981. *(P)*

Switzer, Ellen E. *Dancers!* Atheneum, 1982. *(I; A)*

DARWIN, CHARLES ROBERT

Karp, Walter. *Charles Darwin and the Origin of Species*. Har-Row, 1968. *(I; A)*

Skelton, Renee. *Charles Darwin and the Theory of Natural Selection*. Barron's, 1987. *(P; I)*

Ward, Peter. *The Adventures of Charles Darwin: A Story of the Beagle Voyage*. Cambridge U Pr, 1982. *(A)*

DAVIS, JEFFERSON. See CIVIL WAR, UNITED STATES.

DEAFNESS

Aseltine, Lorraine and others. *I'm Deaf and It's Okay*. Albert Whitman, 1986. *(P)*

Bourke, Linda, illus. *Handmade ABC: A Manual Alphabet*. A-W, 1981. *(P; I; A)*

Charlip, Remy, and others. *Handtalk: An ABC of Finger Spelling and Sign Language*. Scholastic, 1974. *(P; I)*

Curtis, Patricia. *Cindy: A Hearing Ear Dog*. Dutton, 1981. *(P; I)*

Hlibok, Bruce. *Silent Dancer*. Messner, 1981. *(I)*

LaMore, Gregory S. *Now I Understand: A Book About Hearing Impairment*. Gallaudet College Pr., 1986. *(P;I)*

Neimark, Anne E. *A Deaf Child Listened: Thomas Gallaudet, Pioneer in American Education*. Morrow, 1983. *(I; A)*

Walker, Lou Ann. *Amy: The Story of a Deaf Child*. Lodestar, 1985. *(P; I)*

Wolf, Bernard. *Anna's Silent World*. Har-Row, 1977. *(I)*

DEATH

Alexander, Sue. *Nadia the Willful*. Pantheon, 1983. *(P)*

Clardy, Andrea Fleck. *Dusty Was My Friend: Coming to Terms with Loss*. Human Sciences Pr., 1984. *(P; I)*

Donnelley, Elfie. *So Long, Grandpa;* tr. from the German by Anthea Bell. Crown, 1981. *(P; I)*

Hermes, Patricia. *Who Will Take Care of Me?* HarBraceJ, 1983. *(P; I)*

Krementz, Jill. *How It Feels When a Parent Dies*. Knopf, 1981. *(I)*

LeShan, Eda. *Learning to Say Good-by: When a Parent Dies*. Macmillan, 1976. *(P; I; A)*

Miles, Miska. *Annie and the Old One*. Little, 1971. *(P)*

Rofes, Eric E., ed. *The Kids' Book About Death and Dying: By and For Kids*. Little, 1985. *(I; A)*

Rohr, Janelle. *Death and Dying*. Greenhaven Press, 1987. *(A)*

DECLARATION OF INDEPENDENCE

Commager, Henry Steele. *The Great Declaration*. Bobbs, 1958. *(I; A)*

Dalgliesh, Alice. *The Fourth of July Story*. Scribner, 1956. *(P; I)*

Fradin, Dennis B. *The Declaration of Independence*. Childrens, 1988. *(P)*

Giblin, James C. *Fireworks, Picnics, and Flags: The Story of the Fourth of July*. HM, 1983. *(I)*

Munves, James. *Thomas Jefferson and the Declaration of Independence*. Scribner, 1978. *(I)*

See also REVOLUTIONARY WAR; UNITED STATES (HISTORY AND GOVERNMENT).

DÉCOUPAGE

Gilbreath, Alice Thompson. *Simple Decoupage: Having Fun with Cutouts*. Morrow, 1978. *(I)*

Linsley, Leslie. *Decoupage for Young Crafters*. Dutton, 1977. *(I)*

DEER

Ahlstrom, Mark. *The Whitetail*. Crestwood, 1983. *(P; I)*

Bailey, Jill. *Discovering Deer*. Watts, 1988. *(P)*

Brady, Lillian. *The Saga of a Whitetail Deer*. Bk Pools, 1981. *(I; A)*

McClung, Robert M. *White Tail*. Morrow, 1987. *(P; I)*

DE GAULLE, CHARLES. See FRANCE.

DELAWARE

Carpenter, Allan. *Delaware*. Childrens, 1979. *(I)*
Fradin, Dennis. *Delaware: In Words and Pictures*. Childrens, 1980. *(P; I)*

DELHI. See INDIA.

DEMOCRACY

Chute, Marchette. *The Green Tree of Democracy*. Dutton, 1971. *(I)*
Crout, George. *The Seven Lives of Johnny B. Free*. Denison, n.d. *(P; I)*

DENMARK

Andersen, Ulla. *We Live in Denmark*. Watts, 1984. *(P; I)*
Anderson, Madelyn Klein. *Greenland: Island at the Top of the World*. Dodd, 1983. *(I; A)*
Haugaard, Erik C. *Leif the Unlucky*. HM, 1982. *(I)*
Lepthien, Emilie U. *Greenland*. Childrens, 1989. *(I)*
Mussari, Mark. *The Danish Americans*. Chelsea House, 1988. *(I; A)*

DENTISTS AND DENTISTRY

Betancourt, Jeanne. *Smile: How to Cope with Braces*. Knopf, 1982. *(I; A)*
Boy Scouts of America. *Dentistry*. BSA, 1975. *(I; A)*
Krauss, Ronnie. *Mickey Visits the Dentist*. Putnam, 1980. *(P)*
Marsoli, Lisa Ann. *Things to Know Before Going to the Dentist*. Silver Burdett, 1985. *(I)*
Silverstein, Alvin, and Silverstein, Virginia B. *So You're Getting Braces: A Guide to Orthodontics*. Har-Row, 1978. *(I; A)*
Ward, Brian R. *Dental Care*. Watts, 1986. *(I; A)*
See also TEETH.

DENVER. See COLORADO.

DEPARTMENT STORES. See RETAIL STORES.

DESERTS

Baylor, Byrd. *Desert Voices*. Scribner's, 1981. *(P)*
Bramwell, Martyn. *Deserts*. Watts, 1988. *(I)*
Dixon, Dougal. *Deserts and Wastelands*. Watts, 1985. *(I)*
George, Jean Craighead. *One Day in the Desert*. Har-Row, 1983. *(P; I)*
Graham, Ada, and Graham, Frank. *The Changing Desert*. Scribner, 1981. *(I; A)*
Lye, Keith. *Deserts*. Silver Burdett, 1987. *(P)*
Posell, Elsa. *Deserts*. Childrens, 1982. *(P)*
Pringle, Laurence. *The Gentle Desert: Exploring an Ecosystem*. Macmillan, 1977. *(P; I)*
Sanders, John. *All About Deserts*. Troll, 1984. *(P; I)*

Watson, Jane W. *Deserts of the World; Future Threat or Promise?* Putnam, 1981. *(A)*
Wiewandt, Thomas. *The Hidden Life of the Desert*. Crown, 1990. *(I)*

DESIGN AND COLOR

Branley, Franklyn M. *Color: From Rainbows to Lasers*. Har-Row, 1978. *(A)*
Hoban, Tana. *Is It Red? Is It Yellow? Is It Blue? An Adventure in Color*. Greenwillow, 1978. *(P)*
O'Neill, Mary. *Hailstones and Halibut Bones*. Doubleday, 1961. *(P; I; A)*

DE SOTO, HERNANDO. See EXPLORATION AND DISCOVERY.

DETROIT. See MICHIGAN.

DIAMONDS

Campbell, Archie. *Diamonds in the Dirt*. Childrens, 1978. *(P; I)*
Rickard, Graham. *Spotlight on Diamonds*. Rourke, 1988. *(P; I)*

DICKENS, CHARLES

Dickens, Charles. *The Magic Fishbone*. Retold by Hans J. Schmidt. Coach Hse, 1961. *(P; I)*

DICKINSON, EMILY

Barth, Edna. *I'm Nobody! Who Are You? The Story of Emily Dickinson*. HM, 1971. *(I)*
Dickinson, Emily. *Poems for Youth*. Little, 1934. *(I; A)*
Longsworth, Polly. *Emily Dickinson: Her Letter to the World*. Har-Row, 1965. *(I; A)*

DICTIONARIES

Karske, Robert. *The Story of the Dictionary*. HarBraceJ, 1975. *(I; A)*

DIESEL ENGINES. See ENGINES.

DINOSAURS

Aliki. *Digging Up Dinosaurs*. Har-Row, 1981. *(P); My Visit to the Dinosaurs*. 1969. *(P)*
Bates, Robin and Simon, Cheryl. *The Dinosaurs and the Dark Star*. Macmillan, 1985. *(I)*
Booth, Jerry. *The Big Beast Book: Dinosaurs and How They Got That Way*. Little, Brown, 1988. *(P; I)*
Branley, Franklyn M. *Dinosaurs, Asteroids, and Superstars: Why the Dinosaurs Disappeared*. Har-Row, 1982. *(I)*
Clark, Mary L. *Dinosaurs*. Childrens, 1981. *(P)*
Cobb, Vicki. *The Monsters Who Died*. Putnam, 1983. *(P; I)*
Cohen, Daniel. *Dinosaurs*. Doubleday, 1987. *(P; I)*

Dixon, Dougal. *Be a Dinosaur Detective*. Lerner, 1988. *(I)*

Eldredge, Niles, and others. *The Fossil Factory: A Kid's Guide to Digging Up Dinosaurs, Exploring Evolution, and Finding Fossils*. Addison-Wesley, 1990. *(I)*

Freedman, Russell. *Dinosaurs and Their Young*. Holiday, 1983. *(P)*

Horner, John R., and Gorman, James. *Maia: A Dinosaur Grows Up*. Courage Books, 1987. *(P)*

Jacobs, Francine. *Supersaurus*. Putnam, 1982. *(P)*

Kaufmann, John. *Little Dinosaurs and Early Birds*. Har-Row, 1977. *(P)*

Lambert, David. *Dinosaur World*. Watts, 1982. *(I)*

Lasky, Kathryn. *Dinosaur Dig*. Morrow, 1990. *(P; I)*

Lauber, Patricia. *Dinosaurs Walked Here: and Other Stories Fossils Tell*. Bradbury, 1987. *(P)*; *The News About Dinosaurs*. Bradbury, 1989. *(I)*

Mannetti, William. *Dinosaurs in Your Backyard*. Atheneum, 1982. *(P; I)*

Moseley, Keith. *Dinosaurs: A Lost World*. Putnam, 1984. *(P; I)*

Norman, David and Milner, Angela. *Dinosaur*. Knopf, 1989. *(I)*

Parker, Steve. *Dinosaurs and Their World*. Putnam/Grosset, 1988. *(P; I)*

Sattler, Helen Roney. *Dinosaurs of North America*. Lothrop, 1981. *(P; I; A)*; *The Illustrated Dinosaur Dictionary*, 1983. *(P; I)*; *Pterosaurs, the Flying Reptiles*. Lothrop, 1985. *(P;I)*

Simon, Seymour. *The Largest Dinosaurs*. Macmillan, Oct. 1986. *(P; I)*; *New Questions and Answers About Dinosaurs*. Morrow, 1990. *(P; I)*

DISABLED PEOPLE

Allen, Anne. *Sports for the Handicapped*. Walker, 1981. *(I; A)*

Boy Scouts of America. *Handicapped Awareness*. BSA, 1981. *(I; A)*

Brown, Tricia. *Someone Special: Just Like You*. HR&W, 1984. *(P)*

Cattoche, Robert J. *Computers For the Disabled*. Watts, 1987. *(I)*

Haskins, James, and Stifle, J. M. *The Quiet Revolution: The Struggle for the Rights of Disabled Americans*. Har-Row, 1979. *(I; A)*

Kamien, Janet. *What If You Couldn't . . . ? A Book About Special Needs*. Scribner, 1979. *(P; I; A)*

Mitchell, Joyce S. *See Me More Clearly: Career and Life Planning for Teens with Physical Disabilities*. Har-BraceJ, 1980. *(I; A)*

Rosenberg, Maxine B. *My Friend Leslie: The Story of a Handicapped Child*. Lothrop, 1983. *(P; I)*

Roy, Ron. *Move Over, Wheelchairs Coming Through!* Houghton/Clarion, 1985. *(I)*

Savitz, Harriet M. *Wheelchair Champions: A History of Wheelchair Sports*. Har-Row, 1978. *(P; I; A)*

Weiss, Malcolm. *Blindness*. Watts, 1980. *(I; A)*

See also BLIND, EDUCATION OF THE; DEAF, EDUCATION OF THE.

DISEASES

Anderson, Madelyn Klein. *Environmental Diseases*. Watts, 1987. *(A)*

Berger, Melvin. *Disease Detectives*. Har-Row, 1978. *(A)*

Brown, Fern G. *Hereditary Diseases*. Watts, 1987. *(A)*

Check, William A. *Alzheimer's Disease*. Chelsea House, 1989. *(A)*

Eagles, Douglas A. *Nutritional Diseases*. Watts, 1987. *(A)*

Edelson, Edward. *Allergies*. Chelsea House, 1989. *(I; A)*

Fekete, Irene, and Ward, Peter Dorrington. *Disease and Medicine*. World of Science Series, 1985. *(A)*

Frank, Julia. *Alzheimer's Disease: The Silent Epidemic*. Lerner, 1985. *(I; A)*

Hughes, Barbara. *Drug Related Diseases*. Watts, 1987. *(A)*

Jacobs, Francine. *Breakthrough—the True Story of Penicillin*. Dodd, 1985. *(I)*

Klein, Aaron E. *The Parasites We Humans Harbor*. Elsevier/Nelson, 1981. *(A)*

Landau, Elaine. *Alzheimer's Disease*. Watts, 1987; *Why Are They Starving Themselves? Understanding Anorexia Nervosa and Bulimia*. Messner, 1983. *(I; A)*

Metos, Thomas A. *Communicable Diseases*. Watts, 1987. *(A)*

Patent, Dorothy Hinshaw. *Germs!* Holiday, 1983. *(I)*

Riedman, Sarah R. *Allergies*. Watts, 1978. *(P; I)*; *Diabetes*, 1980. *(P; I; A)*

Silverstein, Alvin, and Silverstein, Virginia. *Itch, Sniffle, and Sneeze: All About Asthma, Hay Fever, and Other Allergies*. Scholastic, 1978. *(P)*

Silverstein, Alvin, Silverstein, Virginia, and Silverstein, Robert. *Overcoming Acne: The How and Why of Healthy Skin Care*. Morrow, 1990. *(I; A)*

Tiger, Steven. *Diabetes*. Messner, 1987. *(P; I)*

Zizmor, Jonathan. *The Doctor's Do-It-Yourself Guide to Clearer Skin*. Har-Row, 1980. *(I; A)*

DISNEY, WALT

Fisher, Maxine R. *Walt Disney*. Watts, 1988. *(I)*

Ford, Barbara. *Walt Disney*. Walker, 1989. *(I; A)*

DIVING. See SWIMMING AND DIVING.

DIVORCE

Bienenfeld, Florence. *My Mom and Dad Are Getting a Divorce*. EMC, 1980. *(P)*

Blume, Judy. *It Isn't the End of the World*. Bantam, 1977. *(P; I)*

Coleman, William L. *What Children Need to Know When Parents Get Divorced*. Bethany, 1983. *(P; I)*

Craven, Linda. *Stepfamilies: New Patterns of Harmony*. Messner, 1982. *(I; A)*

Krementz, Jill. *How It Feels When Parents Divorce.* Knopf, 1984. *(I)*

Lazo, Caroline Evensen. *Divorce.* Macmillan/Crestwood House, 1989. *(P; I)*

LeShan, Eda. *What's Going to Happen to Me? When Parents Separate or Divorce.* Scholastic, 1978. *(I)*

Ourth, John. *Help! for Children of Divorce at Home and School.* Good Apple, 1983. *(I; A)*

Sinberg, Janet. *Divorce Is a Grown Up Problem: A Book About Divorce for Young Children and Their Parents.* Avon, 1978. *(P)*

DOCTORS

Bluestone, Naomi. *So You Want to Be a Doctor: The Realities of Pursuing Medicine as a Career.* Lothrop, 1981. *(I; A)*

Forsey, Chris. *At the Doctor.* Watts, 1984. *(P)*

Oxenbury, Helen. *The Checkup.* Dutton, 1983. *(P)*

See also MEDICINE.

DOG FAMILY

Hansen, Rosanna. *Wolves and Coyotes.* Putnam, 1981. *(P; I; A)*

Lavine, Sigmund L. *Wonders of Coyotes.* Dodd Mead, 1984. *(A)*

Pringle, Laurence. *The Controversial Coyote.* HarBraceJ, 1977. *(I; A)*

See also FOXES; WOLVES.

DOGS

Benjamin, Carol Lea. *Dog Training for Kids.* Howell, 1988. *(I)*

Caras, Roger, and Graham, Pamela C. *Dogs: Records, Stars, Feats, and Facts.* HarBraceJ, 1979. *(P; I)*

Casey, Brigid, and Haugh, Wendy. *Sled Dogs.* Dodd, 1983. *(I)*

Cole, Joanna. *My Puppy Is Born.* Morrow, 1973. *(P); A Dog's Body,* 1987. *(P)*

Hart, Angela. *Dogs.* Watts, 1982. *(P)*

Rinard, Judith E. *Puppies.* National Geog, 1982. *(P)*

Schoder, Judith. *Canine Careers: Dogs at Work.* Messner, 1981. *(P; I)*

Silverstein, Alvin, and Silverstein, Virginia. *Dogs: All About Them.* Lothrop, 1986. *(I; A)*

DOLLS AND DOLLHOUSES

Glubok, Shirley. *Doll's Houses: Life in Miniature.* Har-Row, 1984. *(I; A)*

Horwitz, Joshua. *Doll Hospital.* Pantheon, 1983. *(I)*

Nicklaus, Carol. *Making Dolls.* Watts, 1981. *(P)*

Radlauer, Ruth. *Dolls.* Childrens, 1980. *(P; I)*

Roche, P. K. *Dollhouse Magic: How to Make and Find Simple Dollhouse Furniture.* Dial Bks Young, 1977. *(P; I)*

Schnurnberger, Lynn Edelman. *A World of Dolls That You Can Make.* Har-Row, 1982. *(P; I)*

DOLPHINS AND PORPOISES

Fox, Michael. *The Way of the Dolphin.* Acropolis, 1981. *(I; A)*

Hinshaw, Dorothy. *Dolphins and Porpoises.* Patent, 1987. *(I; A)*

Leatherwood, Stephen, and Reeves, Randall. *The Sea World Book of Dolphins.* HBJ, 1987. *(P; I)*

Patent, Dorothy Hinshaw. *Dolphins and Porpoises.* Holiday, 1988. *(I); Looking at Dolphins and Porpoises.* Holiday, 1989. *(P; I)*

Smith, Elizabeth Simpson. *A Dolphin Goes to School: The Story of Squirt, a Trained Dolphin.* Morrow, 1986. *(P)*

Torgersen, Don. *Killer Whales and Dolphin Play.* Childrens, 1982. *(P; I)*

Wise, Terence. *Whales and Dolphins.* Raintree, 1980. *(P; I)*

DOMINICA. See CARIBBEAN SEA AND ISLANDS.

DOMINICAN REPUBLIC

Creed, Alexander. *Dominican Republic.* Chelsea House, 1987. *(A)*

Haverstock, Nathan A. *Dominican Republic in Pictures.* Lerner, 1988. *(P; I)*

DOUGLASS, FREDERICK

Davis, Ossie. *Escape to Freedom: The Story of Young Frederick Douglass.* Viking, 1978. *(A)*

Douglass, Frederick. *Narrative of the Life of Frederick Douglass, an American Slave.* NAL, 1968. *(I; A)*

Miller, Douglas T. *Frederick Douglass and the Fight For Freedom.* Facts on File, 1988. *(A)*

DOYLE, SIR ARTHUR CONAN

Doyle, Arthur Conan. *The Adventures of Sherlock Holmes, Books One–Four.* Adapted by Catherine E. Sadler. Avon, 1981. *(P; I); Sherlock Holmes,* adapted by Diana Stewart. Raintree, 1983. *(P; I; A)*

DRAKE, SIR FRANCIS

Goodnough, Davis. *Francis Drake.* Troll, 1979 (new ed.). *(P; I)*

DRAMA. See THEATER.

DRAWING

Albert, Gretchen D. *Scribble Art: Kindergarten and Preschool.* GDA, 1980. *(P)*

Ames, Lee J. *Draw Fifty Airplanes, Aircraft, and Spacecraft.* Doubleday, 1977; *Draw Fifty Dogs,* 1981; *Draw Fifty Monsters, Creepy Creatures, Superheroes,* 1983; and other titles. *(P; I; A)*

Arnosky, Jim. *Drawing Life in Motion.* Lee & Shepard,

1984. *(I; A); Drawing from Nature.* Lothrop, 1982. *(P; I)*

Bolognese, Don. *Drawing Dinosaurs and Other Prehistoric Animals.* Watts, 1982; *Drawing Spaceships and Other Spacecraft,* 1982. *(P; I)*

Emberley, Ed. *Ed Emberley's Big Green Drawing Book,* Little, 1979; *Big Purple Drawing Book,* 1981; *Little Drawing Book of Birds,* 1973; and other titles. *(P; I; A)*

Ivenbaum, Elliott. *Drawing People.* Watts, 1980. *(P; I; A)*

Nicklaus, Carol. *Drawing Pets; Drawing Your Family and Friends.* Watts, 1980. *(P)*

Witty, Ken. *A Day in the Life of an Illustrator.* Troll, 1981. *(I; A)*

DREAMING. See SLEEP.

DRESSMAKING. See SEWING.

DREYFUS, ALFRED

Schechter, Betty. *The Dreyfus Affair: A National Scandal.* HM, 1965. *(I; A)*

DRUGS AND DRUG ABUSE

Berger, Gilda. *Addiction: Its Causes, Problems and Treatment.* Watts, 1982. *(I; A); Crack: The New Drug Epidemic!; Drug Abuse: The Impact on Society.* Watts, 1988. *(A); Drug Testing.* Watts, 1987. *(A)*

Browne, David. *Crack and Cocaine.* Watts, 1987. *(I; A)*

Childress, Alice. *A Hero Ain't Nothin' But a Sandwich.* Putnam, 1973. *(I; A)*

Cohen, Susan, and Cohen, Daniel. *What You Can Believe and Drugs.* Evans, dist. by Holt, 1988. *(A)*

Dolan, Edward F. *Drugs in Sports.* Watts, 1986. *(A)*

Friedman, David. *Focus on Drugs and the Brain.* 21st Century Books, 1990. *(P; I)*

Hyde, Margaret O. *Mind Drugs.* McGraw, 1981 (4th ed.). *(A)*

Hyde, Margaret, and Hyde, Bruce G. *Know About Drugs.* McGraw, n.d. *(P; I)*

Madison, Arnold. *Drugs and You.* Messner, 1990 (rev. ed.). *(I)*

Perry, Robert. *Focus on Nicotine and Caffeine.* 21st Century Books, 1990. *(P; I)*

Shulman, Jeffrey. *Focus on Cocaine and Crack.* 21st Century Books, 1990. *(P; I)*

Washton, Arnold M., and Boundy, Donna. *Cocaine and Crack: What You Need to Know.* Enslow, 1989. *(I; A)*

Woods, Geraldine, and Woods, Harold. *Cocaine.* Watts, 1985. *(A)*

Zeller, Paul Klevan. *Focus on Marijuana.* 21st Century Books, 1990. *(P; I)*

DRUM. See MUSICAL INSTRUMENTS.

DUCKS

Burton, Jane. *Dabble the Duckling.* Gareth Stevens, 1989. *(P)*

Wharton, Anthony. *Discovering Ducks, Geese, and Swans.* Watts, 1987. *(P)*

DUNBAR, PAUL LAURENCE

McKissack, Patricia. *Paul Laurence Dunbar: A Poet to Remember.* Childrens, 1984. *(I)*

DUST

McFall, Christie. *Wonders of Dust.* Dodd, 1980. *(I; A)*

EAGLES

McConoughey, Jane. *Bald Eagle.* Crestwood, 1983. *(P; I)*

Patent, Dorothy Hinshaw. *Where the Bald Eagles Gather.* HM, 1984. *(P; I)*

Ryden, Hope. *America's Bald Eagle.* Putnam, 1985. *(I; A)*

Sattler, Helen Roney. *The Book of Eagles.* Lothrop, 1989. *(P; I)*

Van Wormer, Joe. *Eagles.* Lodestar, 1985. *(P; I)*

Wildlife Education Staff. *Eagles.* Wildlife Educ, 1983. *(I; A)*

EAR

Showers, Paul. *Ears Are for Hearing.* Harper/Crowell, 1990. *(P)*

EARTH

Asimov, Isaac. *Earth: Our Home Base.* Gareth Stevens, 1989. *(P; I)*

Bain, Iain. *Mountains and Earth Movements.* Bookwright/Watts, 1984. *(I)*

Ballard, Robert D. *Exploring Our Living Planet.* Natl Geog, 1983. *(I; A)*

Bennett, David. *Earth.* Bantam, 1988. *(P)*

Berger, Melvin. *The New Earth Book: Our Changing Planet.* Har-Row, 1980. *(I; A)*

Brandreth, Gyles. *Amazing Facts About Our Earth.* Doubleday, 1981. *(I)*

Chisholm. *Our Earth: Let's Find Out About It.* EDC, 1982. *(P; I)*

George, Jean C. *The Talking Earth.* Har-Row, 1983. *(I; A)*

Lambert, David. *The Active Earth.* Lothrop, 1982. *(P; I); Planet Earth.* Watts, 1983. *(I; A)*

Lampton, Christopher. *Planet Earth.* Watts, 1982. *(I)*

Lauber, Patricia. *Seeing Earth From Space.* Orchard Books, dist. by Watts, 1990. *(I)*

Markle, Sandra. *Digging Deeper: Investigations into Rocks, Shocks, Quakes, and Other Earthly Matters.* Lothrop, 1987. *(I)*

O'Donnell, James J. *Earthly Matters: A Study of Our Planet.* Messner, 1982. *(A)*

Rutland, Jonathan. *Exploring the Violent Earth*. Watts, 1980. *(P; I)*

Scarry, Huck. *Our Earth*. Messner, 1984. *(I)*

Selden, Paul. *The Face of the Earth*. Childrens, 1982. *(P; I)*

Silver, Donald M. *Earth: The Ever-Changing Planet*. Random, 1989. *(I)*

Simon, Seymour. *Earth: Our Planet in Space*. Scholastic, 1984. *(P)*

See also GEOLOGY AND GEOPHYSICS.

EARTHQUAKES

Asimov, Isaac. *How Did We Find Out About Earthquakes?* Walker, 1978. *(I)*

Dudman, John. *The San Francisco Earthquake*. Bookwright, dist. by Watts, 1988. *(P; I)*

Fradin, Dennis Brindell. *Disaster! Earthquakes*. Childrens, 1982. *(P; I)*

Golden, Frederic. *The Trembling Earth: Probing and Predicting Earthquakes*. Scribner, 1983. *(I; A)*

Lambert, David. *Earthquakes*. Watts, 1982. *(P)*

Levine, Ellen. *If You Lived at the Time of the Great San Francisco Earthquake*. Scholastic, 1987. *(P)*

Nixon, Hershell H., and Nixon, Joan L. *Earthquakes: Nature in Motion*. Dodd, 1981. *(P; I)*

Paananen, Eloise. *Tremor! Earthquake Technology in the Space Age*. Messner, 1982. *(A)*

EASTER

Barth, Edna. *Lillies, Rabbits, and Painted Eggs: The Story of the Easter Symbols*. HM, 1970. *(P; I)*

Berger, Gilda. *Easter and Other Spring Holidays*. Watts, 1983. *(P; I; A)*

Fisher, Aileen. *Easter*. Har-Row, 1968. *(P)*

Lloyd, Rawson. *The Easter Story*. EDC, 1981. *(P; I)*

Milhous, Katherine. *The Egg Tree*. Scribner, n.d. *(P)*

Sandak, Cass R. *Easter*. Watts, 1980. *(P)*

ECLIPSES. See MOON; SUN.

ECOLOGY. See ENVIRONMENT.

ECONOMICS

Abels, Harriette S. *Future Business*. Crestwood, 1980. *(I; A)*

Adler, David A. *Prices Go Up, Prices Go Down: The Law of Supply and Demand*. Watts, 1984. *(P)*

Armstrong, Louise. *How to Turn Lemons into Money: A Child's Guide to Economics*. HarBraceJ, 1976; *How to Turn Up into Down into Up: A Child's Guide to Inflation, Depression, and Economic Recovery*, 1978. *(P; I)*

James, Elizabeth, and Barkin, Carol. *How to Grow a Hundred Dollars*. Lothrop, 1979. *(P; I)*

Killen, M. Barbara. *Economics and the Consumer*. Lerner, 1990. *(I; A)*

Marsh, Carole. *The Teddy Bear Company: Easy Economics for Kids; The Teddy Bear's Annual Report: Tomorrow's Books*. Gallopade, 1983. *(P; I)*

Schmitt, Lois. *Smart Spending: A Young Consumer's Guide*. Scribners, 1989. *(I; A)*

Shanaman, Fred, and Malnig, Anita. *The First Official Money Making Book for Kids*. Bantam, 1983. *(I)*

ECUADOR

Sterling Editors, ed. *Ecuador in Pictures*. Sterling, 1973. *(I)*

EDISON, THOMAS A.

Buranelli, Vincent. *Thomas Alva Edison*. Silver Burdett, 1989. *(I)*

Cousins, Margaret. *The Story of Thomas Alva Edison*. Random, 1981. *(I)*

Greene, Carol. *Thomas Alva Edison: Bringer of Light*. Childrens Pr., 1985. *(I)*

Guthridge, Sue. *Thomas A. Edison: Young Inventor*. Bobbs, 1983. *(P; I)*

Lampton, Christopher. *Thomas Alva Edison*. Watts, 1988. *(P; I)*

Mintz, Penny. *Thomas Edison: Inventing the Future*. Fawcett, 1990. *(I)*

Quackenbush, Robert. *What Has Wild Tom Done Now?* P-H, 1981. *(P)*

Sabin, Louis. *Thomas Alva Edison: Young Inventor*. Troll, 1983. *(P; I)*

EDUCATION

Fisher, Leonard Everett. *The Schools*. Holiday, 1983. *(I)*

Hand, Phyllis. *The Name of the Game Is . . . Learning*. Good Apple, 1983. *(P; I)*

Lenski, Lois. *Prairie School*. Dell, 1967. *(I)*

Loeper, John J. *Going to School in 1776*. Atheneum, 1984. *(I)*

EELS

Friedman, Judi. *The Eels' Strange Journey*. Har-Row, 1976. *(P)*

Waters, John F. *The Mysterious Eel*. Hastings, 1973. *(I)*

EGGS AND EMBRYOS

Burton, Robert. *Eggs: Nature's Perfect Package*. Facts on File, 1987. *(I; A)*

Johnson, Sylvia A. *Inside an Egg*. Lerner, 1982. *(I)*

May, Julian. *Million of Years of Eggs*. Creative Ed, 1970. *(P)*

McClung, Robert M. *The Amazing Egg*. Dutton, 1980. *(I)*

EGYPT

Egypt . . . in Pictures. Lerner, 1988. *(I)*

Cross, Wilbur. *Egypt*. Childrens, 1982. *(I; A)*

Kristensen, Preben, and Cameron, Fiona. *We Live in Egypt*. Watts/Brookwright Press, 1987. *(P)*
Lengyel, Emil. *Modern Egypt*. Watts, 1978 (rev. ed.). *(I)*
Lye, Keith. *Take a Trip to Egypt*. Watts, 1983. *(P)*
Sullivan, George. *Sadat: The Man Who Changed Mid-East History*. Walker, 1981. *(I; A)*
See also ANCIENT CIVILIZATIONS.

EGYPTIAN ART AND ARCHITECTURE. See EGYPT; ANCIENT CIVILIZATIONS.

EINSTEIN, ALBERT

Apfel, Necia H. *It's All Relative: Einstein's Theory of Relativity*. Lothrop, 1981. *(I; A)*
Dank, Milton. *Albert Einstein*. Watts, 1983. *(I; A)*
Hunter, Nigel. *Einstein*. Watts/Bookwright Press, 1987. *(P; I)*

EISENHOWER, DWIGHT D.

Ambrose, Stephen E. *Ike: Abilene to Berlin*. Har-Row, 1973. *(I; A)*
Cannon, Marian G. *Dwight David Eisenhower: War Hero and President*. Watts, 1990. *(I; A)*
Ellis, Rafaela. *Dwight D. Eisenhower: 34th President of the United States*. Garret Ed. Corp., 1989. *(I)*
Hargrove, Jim. *Dwight D. Eisenhower: Thirty-fourth President of the United States*. Children's, 1987. *(P; I)*
Lovelace, Delos W. *Ike Eisenhower: Statesman and Soldier of Peace*. Har-Row, 1969. *(I)*
See also PRESIDENCY OF THE UNITED STATES.

ELECTIONS

Modl, Thomas, ed. *America's Elections*. Greenhaven Press, 1988. *(A)*
Priestly, E. J. *Finding Out About Elections*. David & Charles, 1983. *(I; A)*

ELECTRICITY

Bailey, Mark W. *Electricity*. Raintree, 1978. *(P; I)*
Bains, Rae. *Discovering Electricity*. Troll, 1981. *(P)*
Berger, Melvin. *Switch On, Switch Off*. Crowell, 1989. *(P)*
Epstein, Sam, and Epstein, Beryl. *The First Book of Electricity*. Watts, 1976. *(I)*
Grossman, Peter Z. *In Came the Darkness: The Story of Blackouts*. Scholastic, 1981. *(I; A)*
Keating, Joni. *Watt's Happening?* Good Apple, 1981. *(P; I)*
Math, Irwin. *More Wires and Watts: Understanding and Using Electricity*. Scribner, 1988. *(I; A); Wires and Watts: Understanding and Using Electricity*. Scribner, 1981. (I; A)

ELECTRIC MOTORS. See TECHNOLOGY.

ELECTRONICS

Berger, J. Louis. *How Electronic Gadgets Work*. Stratford, 1982. *(I; A)*
Billings, Charlene W., *Microchip: Small Wonder*. Dodd, 1984. *(I)*
Laron, Carl. *Electronics Basics*. P-H, 1984. *(I; A)*
Renowden, Gareth. *Video,* Watts, 1983. *(I; A)*
Tatchess, J., and Cutter, N. *Practical Things to Do*. EDC, 1983. *(I; A)*

ELEMENTS

Asimov, Isaac. *Building Blocks of the Universe*. Abelard, 1974 (rev. ed.). *(I; A)*

ELEPHANTS

Aliki. *Wild and Wooly Mammoths*. Har-Row, 1983. *(P)*
Barrett, N. S. *Elephants*. Watts, 1988. *(P; I)*
Bright, Michael. *Elephants*. Gloucester Press, dist. by Watts, 1990. *(P; I)*
Hintz, Martin. *Tons of Fun: Training Elephants*. Messner, 1982. *(P; I)*
Holbrook, John. *A Closer Look at Elephants*. Watts, 1978. *(P; I)*
Petty, Kate. *Elephants*. Gloucester Press, dist. by Watts, 1990. *(P; I)*
Posell, Elsa. *Elephants*. Childrens, 1982. *(P)*
Schlein, Miriam. *Elephants*. Atheneum, 1990. *(I)*
Stewart, John. *Elephant School*. Pantheon, 1982. *(I; A)*
Torgersen, Dan. *Elephant Herds and Rhino Horns*. Childrens, 1982. *(I; A)*

ELIZABETH I

Turner, Dorothy. *Queen Elizabeth I*. Watts, 1987. *(I)*
Zamoyska, Betka. *Queen Elizabeth I*. McGraw, 1981. *(I; A)*

ELIZABETH II

Lacey, Robert. *Elizabeth II: The Work of the Queen*. Viking, 1977. *(I; A)*
Turner, Dorothy. *Queen Elizabeth II*. Watts/Bookwright Pr., 1985. *(I)*

EL SALVADOR. See CENTRAL AMERICA.

EMANCIPATION PROCLAMATION. See SLAVERY; LINCOLN, ABRAHAM; CIVIL WAR, UNITED STATES.

EMBROIDERY. See NEEDLECRAFT.

ENDANGERED SPECIES

Arnold, Caroline. *Saving the Peregrine Falcon*. Carolrhoda, 1985. *(I)*
Banks, Martin. *Endangered Wildlife*. Rourke, 1988. *(I)*
Bloyd, Sunni. *Endangered Species*. Lucent Books, 1989. *(I; A)*

Burton, John. *Close to Extinction*. Gloucester Press, dist. by Watts, 1988. *(I)*

Hendrich, Paula. *Saving America's Birds*. Lothrop, 1982. *(I; A)*

Lampton, Christopher. *Endangered Species*. Watts, 1988. *(A)*

Pringle, Laurence. *Saving Our Wildlife*. Enslow, 1990. *(I; A)*

Schlein, Miriam. *Project Panda Watch*. Atheneum, 1984. *(I; A)*

See also BIRDS (EXTINCT AND ENDANGERED SPECIES OF BIRDS).

ENERGY

Energy. Raintree, 1988. *(I)*

Adler, David. *Wonders of Energy*. Troll, 1983. *(P; I)*

Asimov, Isaac. *How Did We Find Out About Energy?* Avon, 1981. *(I)*

Berger, Melvin. *Energy*. Watts, 1983. *(P; I)*

Boyle, Desmond. *Energy*. Silver, 1982. *(I)*

Carey, Helen H. *Producing Energy*. Watts, 1984. *(I; A)*

Fogel, Barbara R. *Energy Choices for the Future*. Watts, 1985. *(A)*

Gardiner, Brian. *Energy Demands*. Gloucester Press, dist. by Watts, 1990. *(I)*

McKie, Robin. *Energy*. Watts, 1989. *(P; I)*

Millard, Reed, and Editors of Science Book Associates. *Energy: New Shapes/New Careers*. Messner, 1982. *(I; A)*

Rice, Dale. *Energy from Fossil Fuels*. Raintree, 1983. *(P; I)*

See also COAL AND COAL MINING; NUCLEAR ENERGY; PETROLEUM; SOLAR ENERGY.

ENGINEERING. See TECHNOLOGY.

ENGINES

Olney, Ross R. *The Internal Combustion Machine*. Har-Row, 1982. *(I; A)*

Weiss, Harvey. *Motors and Engines and How They Work*. Har-Row, 1969. *(I)*

ENGLAND

Fairclough, Christ. *Take a Trip to England*. Watts, 1982. *(P)*

Ferguson, Sheila. *Village and Town Life*. David & Charles, 1983. *(I; A)*

Greene, Carol. *England*. Children's, 1982. *(I; A)*

James, Ian. *Inside Great Britain*. Watts, 1988. *(P; I)*

Sproule, Anna. *Great Britain*. Bookwright, dist. by Watts, 1988. *(P); Living in London*. Silver Burdett, 1987. *(P)*

St. John, Jetty. *A Family in England*. Lerner, 1988. *(P)*

ENGLAND, HISTORY OF

Barber, Richard. *A Strong Land and a Sturdy: Life in Medieval England*. HM, 1976. *(I)*

Branley, Franklyn. *The Mystery of Stonehenge*. Har-Row, 1969. *(I)*

Brooks, Polly Schoyer. *Queen Eleanor: Independent Spirit of the Medieval World: A Biography of Eleanor of Aquitaine*. Lippincott, 1983. *(I; A)*

Clarke, Amanda. *Growing Up in Ancient Britain*. David & Charles, 1981; *Growing Up in Puritan Times*, 1980. *(I; A)*

Corbishley, Mike. *The Romans*. Warwick, 1984. *(I)*

Fyson, Nance L. *Growing Up in Edwardian Britain*. David & Charles, 1980. *(I; A)*

Goodall, John S. *The Story of an English Village*. Atheneum, 1979. *(I)*

Hamilton, Alan. *Queen Elizabeth II*. Hamish Hamilton, 1983. *(I)*

Jones, Madeline. *Growing Up in Regency England*. David & Charles, 1980; *Growing Up in Stuart Times*, 1979. *(I; A)*

Lane, Peter. *Elizabethan England*, David & Charles, 1981; *Norman England*, 1980. *(I; A)*

Wilkins, Frances. *Growing Up During the Norman Conquest*. David & Charles, 1980. *(I; A)*

ENVIRONMENT

Banks, Martin. *Conserving Rain Forests*. SteckVaughn, 1990. *(I)*

Bash, Barbara. *Desert Giant*. Little, 1989. *(P; I)*

Cherry, Lynne. *The Great Kapok Tree: A Tale of the Amazon Rain Forest*. Harcourt, Brace, Jovanovich, 1990. *(P; I)*

Cook, David. *Environment*. Crown, 1985. *(I)*

Gates, Richard. *Conservation*. Childrens, 1982. *(P)*

George, Jean Craighead. *One Day in the Tropical Rain Forest*. Crowell, 1990. *(P; I)*

Johnson, Rebecca. *The Greenhouse Effect: Life on a Warmer Planet*. Lerner, 1990. *(I)*

Kudlinski, Kathleen V. *Rachel Carson: Pioneer of Ecology*. Viking Kestrel, 1988. *(I)*

Landau, Elaine. *Tropical Rain Forests Around the World*. Watts, 1990. *(P)*

Mabey, Richard. *Oak and Company*. Greenwillow, 1983. *(P; I)*

Milne, Margery, and Milne, Lorus J. *Dreams of a Perfect Earth*. Atheneum, 1982. *(I; A)*

Nations, James D. *Tropical Rainforests: Endangered Environment*. Watts, *(I; A)*

Peacock, Howard. *The Big Thicket of Texas: America's Ecological Wonder*. Little, 1984. *(I; A)*

Pringle, Laurence. *Global Warming: Assessing the Greenhouse Threat*. Arcade, 1990. *(I); Lives At Stake: The Science and Politics of Environmental Health*. Macmillan, 1980. *(I); Natural Fire, Its Ecology in Forests*. Morrow, 1979. *(I); Restoring Our*

Earth. Enslow, 1987. *(P); What Shall We Do with the Land?* Har-Row, 1981. *(I)*

Rice, Paul, and Mayle, Peter. *As Dead As a Dodo.* Godine, 1981. *(I)*

Scott, Jack Denton. *Orphans from the Sea.* Putnam, 1982. *(I; A)*

Skurzynski, Gloria. *Safeguarding the Land: Women at Work in Parks, Forests, and Rangelands.* Har-Row, 1981. *(I)*

Stone, Lynn M. *Marshes and Swamps.* Childrens, 1983. *(P)*

Taylor, Paula. *The Kids' Whole Future Catalog: A Book About Your Future.* Random, 1982. *(I; A)*

Vandivert, Rita. *To the Rescue: Seven Heroes of Conservation.* Warne, 1982. *(I; A)*

Weinstock, Edward B. *The Wilderness War: The Struggle to Preserve Our Wildlands.* Messner, 1982. *(I; A)*

Wild, Russell, Ed. *The Earth Care Annual 1990.* National Wildlife Federation: Rodale Press, 1990. *(I; A)*

EQUATORIAL GUINEA. See AFRICA.

ERICSON, LEIF

Humble, Richard. *The Age of Leif Eriksson.* Watts, 1989. *(I)*

Jensen, Malcolm C. *Leif Erikson the Lucky.* Watts, 1979. *(A)*

ERIE CANAL. See CANALS.

ESKIMOS (INUIT)

Alexander, Bryan, and Alexander, Cherry. *An Eskimo Family.* Lerner, 1985. *(P)*

Ekoomiak, Normee. *Arctic Memories.* Holt, 1988. *(P; I)*

Hughes, Jill. *Eskimos.* Watts, 1984 (rev. ed.). *(P; I)*

Patterson, E. Palmer. *Inuit Peoples of Canada.* Watts, 1982. *(I; A)*

Pluckrose, ed. *Small World of Eskimos.* Watts, 1980. *(P)*

Purdy, Susan, and Sandak, Cass R. *Eskimos.* Watts, 1982. *(P; I)*

Rogers, Jean. *Goodbye, My Island.* Greenwillow, 1983. *(I)*

ETHICS

Dronenwetter, Michael. *Journalism Ethics.* Watts, 1988. *(A)*

Hyde, Margaret O., and Forsyth, Elizabeth H. *Medical Dilemmas.* Putnam, 1990. *(I; A)*

ETHIOPIA

Abebe, Daniel. *Ethiopia in Pictures.* Lerner, 1988. *(I)*

Fradin, Dennis Brindell. *Ethiopia.* Childrens, 1988. *(I)*

Kleeberg, Irene Cumming. *Ethiopia.* Watts, 1986. *(I; A)*

ETIQUETTE

Adamson, Elizabeth C. *Mind Your Manners.* Good Apple, 1981. *(P)*

Allison, Alida. *The Children's Manners Book.* Price Stern, 1981. *(P; I)*

Baker, Eugene H. *Your Manners Are Showing: A Handbook About Etiquette.* Childs World, 1980. *(P; I)*

Brown, Fern G. *Etiquette.* Watts, 1985. *(I)*

Brown, Marc, and Krensky, Stephen. *Perfect Pigs: An Introduction to Manners.* Atlantic, 1983. *(P)*

Howe, James. *The Muppet Guide to Magnificent Manners.* Muppet Pr/Random, 1984. *(P)*

Scarry, Richard. *Richard Scarry's Please and Thank You Book.* Random, 1978. *(P)*

Zeldis, Yona. *Coping with Social Situations: A Handbook of Correct Behavior.* Rosen, 1988. *(A)*

EUROPE

Cairns, Trevor. *Europe Around the World.* Lerner, 1982. *(I; A)*

Roberts, Elizabeth. *Europe 1992: The United States of Europe?* Gloucester Press, dist. by Watts, 1990. *(I; A)*

EVEREST, MOUNT. See MOUNTAINS AND MOUNTAIN CLIMBING.

EVOLUTION

Asimov, Isaac. *How Did We Find Out About the Beginning of Life?* Walker, 1982. *(I)*

Attenborough, David. *Life on Earth: A Natural History.* Little, 1981. *(I)*

British Museum of Natural History. *Origin of Species.* Cambridge U Pr, 1982. *(A)*

Gallant, Roy A. *Before the Sun Dies: The Story of Evolution.* Macmillan, 1989. *(A)*

Gamlin, Linda. *Origins of Life.* Watts, 1988. *(I; A)*

Matthews, Rupert. *How Life Began.* Bookwright Press, dist. by Watts, 1989. *(P; I)*

McLoughlin, John C. *The Tree of Animal Life: A Tale of Changing Forms and Fortunes.* Dodd, 1981. *(I)*

EXPERIMENTS AND OTHER SCIENCE ACTIVITIES

Apfel, Necia H. *Astronomy Projects for Young Scientists.* Arco, 1984. *(A)*

Challand, Helen J. *Science Projects and Activities.* Children's, 1985. *(I)*

Cobb, Vicki. *Chemically Active! Experiments You Can Do at Home.* Lippincott, 1985. *(A). Lots of Rot,* 1981. *(P); The Secret Life of Hardware: A Science Experiment Book.* 1982. *(I; A); The Secret Life of School Supplies.* 1981. *(I)*

Cobb, Vicki, and Darling, Kathy. *Bet You Can't! Science Impossibilities to Fool You.* Lothrop, 1980. *(I)*

Filson, Brent. *Famous Experiments and How to Repeat Them.* Messner, 1986. *(P; I)*

Gardner, Robert. *Kitchen Chemistry: Science Experiments to Do at Home.* Messner, 1982. *(I)*

Orii, Eiji and Masako. *Simple Science Experiments with Circles; Simple Science Experiments with Marbles; Simple Science Experiments with Ping-Pong Balls; Simple Science Experiments with Water.* Gareth Stevens, 1989. *(P)*

Scienceworks: An Ontario Science Centre Book of Experiments. Kids Can Pr., 1984. *(I)*

Smith, Norman F. *How Fast Do Your Oysters Grow?* Messner, 1982. *(I; A)*

Walpole, Brenda. *175 Science Experiments to Amuse and Amaze Your Friends.* Random, 1988. *(P; I)*

Webster, Vera. *Science Experiments.* Childrens, 1982. *(P)*

White, Laurence B. *Science Games and Puzzles.* A-W, 1979. *(P; I); Science Toys and Tricks,* 1980. *(P)*

Willow, Daine, and Curran, Emily. *Science Sensations.* Addison-Wesley, 1989. *(P; I)*

Zubrowski, Bernie. *Balloons: Building and Experimenting with Inflatable Toys.* Morrow, 1990. *(P; I); Messing Around with Baking Chemistry: A Children's Museum Activity Book.* Little, 1981. *(P; I)*

EXPLORATION AND DISCOVERY

Barden, Renardo. *The Discovery of America.* Greenhaven, 1990. *(I; A)*

Brosse, Jacques. *Great Voyages of Discovery.* Facts On File, 1985. *(A)*

Fradin, Dennis B. *Explorers.* Childrens, 1984. *(P)*

Grosseck, Joyce. *Great Explorers.* Fideler, 1981 (rev. ed.). *(I; A)*

Lomask, Milton. *Great Lives: Exploration.* Scribner, 1988. *(I; A)*

Poole, Frederick. *Early Exploration of North America.* Watts, 1989. *(P; I)*

Sandak, Cass R. *Explorers and Discovery.* Watts, 1983. *(I; A)*

See also FUR TRADE IN NORTH AMERICA; POLAR REGIONS; WESTWARD MOVEMENT; VIKINGS; and individual explorers.

EXPLOSIVES

Anderson, Norman D., and Brown, Walter R. *Fireworks! Pyrotechnics on Display.* Dodd, 1983. *(P; I)*

Gleasner, Diana C. *Dynamite.* Walker, 1982. *(I; A)*

EXTRASENSORY PERCEPTION

Akins, William R. *ESP: Your Psychic Powers and How to Test Them.* Watts, 1980. *(P; I; A)*

Aylesworth, Thomas. *Spoon Bending and Other Impossible Feats.* EMC, 1980. *(P; I; A)*

Cohen, Daniel. *How to Test Your ESP.* Dutton. 1982. *(A)*

EYE

Parker, Steve. *The Eye and Seeing.* Watts, 1989. *(P; I)*

Thomson, Ruth. *Eyes.* Watts, 1988. *(P)*

FABLES

Aesop. *Aesop's Fables;* illus. by Heidi Holder. Viking, 1981. *(I)*

Caldecott, Randolph. *The Caldecott Aesop—Twenty Fables.* Doubleday, 1978. *(I)*

Michie, James. *LaFontaine: Selected Fables.* Viking, 1979. *(P; I)*

Winter, Milo. *The Aesop for Children.* Rand, 1984. *(P; I)*

FAIRS AND EXPOSITIONS

Pierce, Jack. *The State Fair Book.* Carolrhoda, 1980. *(P)*

Marsh, Carole. *A Fun Book of World's Fairs.* Gallopade, 1982. *(P; I)*

FAIRY TALES. See FOLKLORE AND FAIRY TALES.

FAMILY

Abels, Harriette S. *Future Family.* Crestwood, 1980. *(I; A)*

Cannon, Ann. *My Home Has One Parent.* Broadman, 1983. *(I; A)*

Gilbert, Sara. *How to Live with a Single Parent.* Morrow, 1982. *(I)*

Jenness, Aylette. *Families: A Celebration of Diversity, Commitment, and Love.* Houghton, 1990. *(P; I)*

LeShan, Eda. *Grandparents: A Special Kind of Love.* Macmillan, 1984. *(P; I)*

Rossel, Seymour. *Family.* Watts, 1980. *(P; I; A)*

Worth, Richard, *The American Family.* Watts, 1984. *(I; A)*

FARMS AND FARMING

Ancona, George, and Anderson, Joan. *The American Family Farm.* Harcourt, Brace, Jovanovich, 1989. *(I)*

Bellville, Charyl Walsh. *Farming Today Yesterday's Way.* Carolrhoda, 1984. *(P)*

Bushey, Jerry. *Farming the Land: Modern Farmers and Their Machines.* Carolrhoda, 1987. *(P; I)*

Gibbons, Gail. *Farming.* Holiday, 1988. *(P)*

Gorman, Carol. *America's Farm Crisis.* Watts, 1987. *(A)*

Graff, Nancy Price. *The Strength of the Hills: A Portrait of a Family Farm.* Little, 1989. *(P; I: A)*

Jeffries, Tony, and Hindley, Judy. *Farm Animals.* Watts, 1982. *(P)*

Kushner, Jill Menkes. *The Farming Industry.* Watts, 1984. *(I; A)*

Marston, Hope I. *Machines on the Farm.* Dodd, 1982. *(P; I)*

Murphy, Jim. *Tractors: From Yesterday's Steam Wagons to Today's Turbocharged Giants.* Lippincott, 1984. *(P; I)*

Olney, Ross Robert. *Farm Giants.* Atheneum, 1982. *(P)*

Patent, Dorothy Hinshaw. *Farm Animals.* Holiday, 1984. *(P; I)*

Stephen, R. J. *Farm Machinery.* Watts, 1987. *(P)*

FARRAGUT, DAVID

Latham, Jean Lee. *Anchor's Aweigh: The Story of David Glasgow Farragut*. Har-Row, 1968. *(I)*

FASCISM. See HITLER, ADOLF; MUSSOLINI, BENITO.

FEET AND HANDS. See BODY, HUMAN.

FERDINAND AND ISABELLA. See SPAIN.

FERNS, MOSSES, AND LICHENS

Johnson, Sylvia A. *Mosses*. Lerner, 1983. *(P; I; A)*
Shuttleworth, Floyd S., and Zim, Herbert. *Non-Flowering Plants*. Western, 1967. *(I)*
Wexler, Jerome. *From Spore to Spore: Ferns and How They Grow*. Dodd, 1985. *(I)*

FEUDALISM. See MIDDLE AGES.

FIBERS. See TEXTILES.

FIELD HOCKEY

Preston-Mauks, Susan. *Field Hockey Is for Me*. Lerner, 1983. *(P; I)*
Sullivan, George. *Better Field Hockey for Girls*. Dodd, 1981. *(I; A)*

FILLMORE, MILLARD

Casey, Jane Clark. *Millard Fillmore: Thirteenth President of the United States*. Children's, 1988. *(P; I)*
See also PRESIDENCY OF THE UNITED STATES.

FINLAND

Hentz, Martin. *Finland*. Childrens, 1983. *(I; A)*
Lander, Patricia, and Charbonneau, Claudette. *The Land and People of Finland*. Lippincott, 1990. *(I; A)*

FIRE AND COMBUSTION

Fradin, Dennis B. *Disaster! Fires*. Childrens, 1982. *(I)*
Satchwell, John. *Fire*. Dial Bks Young, 1983. *(P)*

FIRE AND EARLY PEOPLE. See ANTHROPOLOGY.

FIRE FIGHTING AND PREVENTION

Broekel, Ray. *Fire Fighters*. Childrens, 1981. *(P)*
Bundt, Nancy. *The Fire Station Book*. Carolrhoda, 1981. *(P)*
Fichter, George. *Disastrous Fires*. Watts, 1981. *(I)*
Loeper, John. *By Hook and Ladder*. Atheneum, 1981. *(I)*
Madison, Arnold. *Arson!* Watts, 1978. *(I)*
Poynter, Margaret. *Wildland Fire Fighting*. Atheneum, 1982. *(I; A)*
Stephen, R. J. *Fire Engines*. Watts, 1987. *(P)*
Wolf, Bernard. *Firehouses*. Morrow, 1983. *(I)*

FIREWORKS. See EXPLOSIVES.

FIRST AID

Boy Scouts of America. *First Aid*. BSA, 1981. *(I; A)*
Freeman, Lory. *What Would You Do If? A Children's Guide to First Aid*. Parenting Pr, 1983. *(P)*
Gore, Harriet M., and Lindroth, D. *What to Do When There's No One But You*. P-H, 1974. *(I)*
Nourse, Alan. *Fractures, Dislocations and Sprains*. Watts, 1978. *(I)*

FIRST LADIES

Boller, Paul F. *Presidential Wives*. Oxford, 1988. *(I; A)*
Butwin, Miriam, and Chaffin, Lillie. *America's First Ladies*. (2 volumes). Lerner, n.d. *(I; A)*
Caroli, Betty Boyd. *First Ladies*. Oxford, 1987. *(A)*
Healy, Diana Dixon. *America's First Ladies*. Atheneum, 1988. *(I; A)*
See also PRESIDENCY OF THE UNITED STATES.

FISHES

Broekel, Ray. *Dangerous Fish*. Childrens, 1982. *(P)*
Castro, Jose I. *The Sharks of North American Waters*. Tex A&M Univ Pr., 1983. *(I; A)*
Freedman, Russell. *Killer Fish*. Holiday, 1982. *(P)*
Graham-Barber, Lynda. *Round Fish, Flatfish, and Other Animal Changes*. Crown, 1982. *(I)*
Harris, Jack C. *A Step-by-Step Book About Goldfish*. TFH Publications, 1988. *(I; A)*
Henrie, Fiona. *Fish*. Watts, 1981. *(P; I)*
Lane, Margaret. *The Fish: The Story of the Stickleback*. Dial Bks Young, 1982. *(P)*
Zim, Herbert S., and Shoemaker, Hurst H. *Fishes: A Guide to Fresh- and Salt-Water Species*. Western, n.d. *(I)*

FISHING

Arnosky, Jim. *Flies in the Water, Fish in the Air; A Personal Introduction to Fly Fishing*. Lothrop, 1986. *(I; A)*; *Freshwater Fish and Fishing*. Macmillan/Four Winds, 1982. *(P; I)*
Evanoff, Vlad. *A Complete Guide to Fishing*. Har-Row, 1981 (rev. ed.). *(I; A)*
Fabian, John. *Fishing for Beginners*. Atheneum, 1980. *(P; I)*
Randolph, John. *Fishing Basics*. P-H, 1981. *(P; I)*
Roberts, Charles P., and Roberts, George F. *Fishing for Fun: A Freshwater Guide*. Dillon, 1984. *(I)*

FISHING INDUSTRY

Ferrell, Nancy Warren. *The Fishing Industry*. Watts, 1984. *(I; A)*

Scarry, Huck. *Life on a Fishing Boat: A Sketchbook*. P-H, 1983. *(I; A)*

FLAGS

Crampton, William. *Flag*. Knopf, 1989. *(I)*
Crouthers, David D. *Flags of American History*. Hammond, 1973. *(I)*
Swanson, June. *I Pledge Allegiance*. Carolrhoda, 1990. *(P)*
White, David. *Flags*. Rourke, 1988. *(P)*

FLORENCE. See ITALY.

FLORIDA

Coil, Suzanne M. *Florida*. Watts, 1987. *(P; I)*
Fradin, Dennis. *Florida: In Words and Pictures*. Childrens, 1980. *(P; I)*
Stone, Lynn M. *Florida*. Childrens, 1988. *(P; I)*

FLOWERS AND SEEDS

Allen, Sarah, ed. *Wildflowers: Eastern Edition; Western Edition*. Little, 1981. *(I; A)*
Crowell, Robert L. *The Lore and Legend of Flowers*. Har-Row, 1982. *(I; A)*
Dowden, Anne Ophelia. *The Clover & the Bee: A Book of Pollination*. Harper/Crowell, 1990. *(I; A)*
Fichter, George S. *Wildflowers of North America*. Random, 1982. *(P; I)*
Kuchalla, Susan. *All About Seeds*. Troll, 1982. *(P)*
Lerner, Carol. *Plant Families*. Morrow, 1989. *(P; I)*
Overbeck, Cynthia. *How Seeds Travel*. Lerner, 1982; *Sunflowers*. 1981. *(I; A)*
Patent, Dorothy Hinshaw. *Flowers for Everyone*. Cobblehill: Dutton, 1990. *(I)*
Selsam, Millicent E., and Wexler, Jerome. *Eat the Fruit, Plant the Seed*. Morrow, 1980. *(P)*

FLYING SAUCERS

Branley, Franklyn M. *A Book of Flying Saucers for You*. Har-Row, 1973, *(I)*
Cohen, Daniel. *Creatures from UFO's*. Dodd, 1978. *(I)*
Gurney, Clare, and Gurney, Gene. *Unidentified Flying Objects*. Har-Row, 1970. *(A)*
Knight, David C. *Those Mysterious UFO's: The Story of Unidentified Flying Objects*. Enslow, 1975. *(I)*

FOG AND SMOG. See POLLUTION; WEATHER.

FOLK ART

Fowler, Virginia. *Folk Arts Around the World: And How to Make Them*. P-H, 1981. *(I; A)*
Horwitz, Elinor L. *Contemporary American Folk Artists*. Har-Row, 1975. *(I; A)*

FOLKLORE AND FAIRY TALES

Aardema, Verna. *Oh Kojo! How Could You?: An Ashanti Tale*. Dial, 1984. *(P)*
Briggs, Raymond. *The Fairy Tale Treasury*. Dell, 1980. *(P; I)*
Brown, Beth, comp. *Fairy Tales of Birds and Beasts*. Lion, 1982. *(P; I)*
Climo, Shirley. *The Egyptian Cinderella*. Crowell, 1989. *(P; I)*
Colwell, Eileen, ed. *The Magic Umbrella and Other Stories for Telling*. Merrimack, 1977. *(P; I)*
Corrin, Sara, ed. *The Faber Book of Modern Fairy Tales*. Faber, 1981. *(I)*
Crouch, Marcus. *The Whole World Storybook*. Oxford, 1983. *(I)*
Cummings, E. E. *Fairy Tales*. HarBraceJ, 1975. *(P)*
Goble, Paul. *Buffalo Woman*. Bradbury Press, 1984. *(P; I)*
Grifalconi, Ann. *The Village of Round and Square Houses*. Little, Brown, 1986. *(P)*
Hamilton, Virginia. *The People Could Fly: American Black Folktales*. Knopf, 1985. *(I; A)*
Haviland, Virginia, ed. *The Fairy Tale Treasury*. Putnam, 1980. *(P)*
Lanes, Selma, ed. *A Child's First Book of Nursery Tales*. Western, 1983. *(P)*
Lang, Andrew. *Blue Fairy Book*. Viking, 1978; *Green Fairy Book*, 1978 (and other Lang Fairy Books). *(I)*
Leach, Maria, ed. *Whistle in the Graveyard: Folktales to Chill Your Bones*. Penguin, 1982. *(P; I)*
Lester, Julius. *The Tales of Uncle Remus: The Adventure of Brer Rabbit*. Dial, 1987. *(I; A)*
MacDonald, George. *The Complete Fairy Tales of George MacDonald*. Schocken, 1979. *(P; I; A)*
Perrault, Charles. *Perrault's Complete Fairy Tales*, tr. by A. E. Johnson. Dodd, 1982. *(P; I)*
Pyle, Howard. *The Wonder Clock: Of Four and Twenty Marvelous Tales*. Dover, n.d. *(P)*
Rackham, Arthur, ed. *The Arthur Rackham Fairy Book*. Har-Row, 1950. *(I)*
Rohmer, Harriet. *The Invisible Hunters: A Legend from the Miskito Indians of Nicaragua*. Childrens, 1987. *(P; I)*; *Uncle Nacho's Hat*, Childrens, 1989. *(P; I)*
Sanfield, Steve. *The Adventures of High John the Conqueror*. Watts, 1989. *(I; A)*
San Souci, Robert. *The Talking Eggs*. Dial, 1989. *(P; I)*
Steptoe, John. *Mufaro's Beautiful Daughters: An African Tale*. Lothrop, 1987. *(P)*
Tudor, Tasha. *Tasha Tudor Book of Fairy Tales*. Platt, 1961. *(P)*
See also ANDERSEN, HANS CHRISTIAN; GRIMM, JACOB AND WILHELM.

FOLK MUSIC

Berger, Melvin. *The Story of Folk Music*. S. G. Phillips, 1976. *(I; A)*

Fox, Dan, ed. *Go In and Out the Window: An Illustrated Songbook for Young People.* Holt, 1987. *(P; I; A)*

Glazer, Tom. *Eye Winker, Tom Tinker, Chin Chopper.* Doubleday, 1978. *(P)*

Seeger, Ruth C. *American Folk Songs for Children.* Doubleday, 1980. *(P; I)*

Yolen, Jane, ed. *The Lullaby Songbook.* HarBraceJ, 1986. *(P; I)*

FOOD AROUND THE WORLD

Cooper, Terry, and Ratner, Marilyn. *Many Friends Cookbook: An International Cookbook for Boys and Girls.* Putnam, 1980. *(P; I)*

Hayward, Ruth Ann, and Warner, Margaret Brink. *What's Cooking: Favorite Recipes from Around the World.* Little, 1981. *(I; A)*

Pizer, Vernon. *Eat the Grapes Downward: An Uninhibited Romp Through the Surprising World of Food.* Dodd, 1983. *(I; A)*

Van der Linde, Polly, and Van der Linde, Tasha. *Around the World in Eighty Dishes.* Scroll, n.d. *(P; I)*

FOOD SHOPPING. See CONSUMER EDUCATION.

FOOD SUPPLY

Blumberg, Rhoda. *Famine.* Watts, 1978. *(A)*

Bonner, James. *The World's People and the World's Food Supply.* Carolina Biological, 1980. *(A)*

FOOTBALL

Aaseng, Nate. *Football: You Are the Coach.* Lerner, 1983. *(I; A)*

Anderson, Dave. *The Story of Football.* Morrow, 1985. *(I; A)*

Barrett, Norman. *Football.* Watts, 1989. *(P)*

Berger, Melvin. *The Photo Dictionary of Football.* Methuen, 1980. *(P; I)*

Broekel, Ray. *Football.* Children's, 1982. *(P)*

Fox, Larry. *Football Basics.* P-H, 1981. *(P; I)*

Madden, John. *The First Book of Football.* Crown, 1988. *(I; A)*

Namath, Joe. *Football for Young Players and Parents.* Simon & Schuster, 1986. (I)

Sandak, Cass R. *Football.* Watts, 1982. *(P)*

Sullivan, George. *All About Football.* Dodd, 1987. *(P)*

FORD, GERALD R. See PRESIDENCY OF THE UNITED STATES.

FORESTS AND FORESTRY

Bellamy, David. *The Forest.* Clarkson N. Potter; dist. by Crown, 1988. *(P)*

Dixon, Dougal. *Forests.* Watts, 1984. *(P; I)* (Atlas format)

List, Albert, and List, Ilka. *A Walk in the Forest: The Woodlands of North America.* Har-Row, 1977. *(I)*

Milne, Lorus J., and Milne, Margery. *The Mystery of the Bog Forest.* Dodd, 1984. *(I; A)*

Newton, James. *A Forest Is Reborn.* Har-Row, 1982. *(P)*

Sabin, Francene. *Wonders of the Forest.* Troll, 1981. *(P)*

FORTS AND FORTIFICATION

Peterson, Harold L. *Forts in America.* Scribner, 1964. *(I)*

Stiles, David. *The Kids' Fort Book.* Avon, 1982. *(P; I)*

FOSSILS

Aliki. *Fossils Tell of Long Ago.* Crowell, 1990 (rev. ed.). *(P)*

Arnold, Caroline. *Trapped in Tar: Fossils From The Ice Age.* Clarion Books, 1987. *(P)*

Curtis, Neil. *Fossils.* Watts, 1984. *(P; I)*

Eldredge, Niles. *The Fossil Factory.* Addison-Wesley, 1989. *(I)*

Gallant, Roy A. *Fossils.* Watts, 1985. *(P)*

Lasky, Kathryn. *Dinosaur Dig.* Morrow, 1990. *(I)*

Lauber, Patricia. *Dinosaurs Walked Here (And Other Stories Fossils Tell).* Bradbury Press, 1987. *(I; A)*

Pringle, Laurence P. *Dinosaurs and People: Fossils, Facts, and Fantasies.* HarBraceJ, 1978. *(I)*

Roberts, Allan. *Fossils.* Childrens. 1983. *(P)*

Rydell, Wendy. *Discovering Fossils.* Troll, 1984. *(P; I)*

FOSTER CARE. See ADOPTION AND FOSTER CARE.

FOUNDERS OF THE UNITED STATES

Benchley, Nathaniel. *Sam the Minuteman.* Har-Row, 1969. *(P)*

Bennett, Wayne, ed. *Founding Fathers.* Garrard, 1975. *(I; A)*

Bliven, Bruce, Jr. *The American Revolution, 1760–1783.* Random, 1981. *(I)*

Coolidge, Olivia E. *Tom Paine, Revolutionary.* Scribner, 1969. *(I)*

De Pauw, Linda G. *Founding Mothers: Women of America in the Revolutionary Era.* HM, 1975. *(I; A)*

FOXES

Ahlstrom, Mark. *The Foxes.* Crestwood, 1983. *(P; I)*

Burton, Jane. *Trill the Fox Cub.* Gareth Stevens, 1989. *(P)*

Lane, Margaret. *The Fox.* Dial Bks Young, 1982. *(P)*

McDearmon, Kay. *Foxes.* Dodd, 1981. *(P; I)*

FRACTIONS. See MATHEMATICS.

FRANCE

Balderdi, Susan. *France: The Crossroads of Europe.* Dillon, 1983. *(I; A)*

Blackwood, Alan, and Chosson, Brigitte. *France.* Bookwright, dist. by Watts, 1988. *(P)*

Harris, Jonathan. *The Land and People of France.* Lippincott, 1989. *(I; A)*

Jacobsen, Peter O., and Kristensen, Preben S. *A Family in France.* Watts, 1984. *(P; I)*

James, Ian. *France.* Watts, 1989. *(P; I)*

Morrice, Polly. *The French Americans.* Chelsea House, 1988. *(I; A)*

Moss, Peter, and Palmer, Thelma. *France.* Children's, 1986. *(P)*

Rutland, Jonathan. *Take a Trip to France.* Watts, 1981. *(P)*

Tomlins, James. *We Live in France.* Watts, 1983. *(I; A)*

FRANKLIN, BENJAMIN

Adler, David A. *A Picture Book of Benjamin Franklin.* Holiday, 1990. *(P)*

Aliki. *The Many Lives of Benjamin Franklin.* P-H, 1977. *(P)*

Cousins, Margaret. *Ben Franklin of Old Philadelphia.* Random, 1981. *(I; A)*

D'Aulaire, Ingri, and D'Aulaire, Edgar P. *Benjamin Franklin.* Doubleday, 1950. *(P)*

Franklin, Benjamin. *The Autobiography of Benjamin Franklin.* Airmont, n.d. *(A)*; *Poor Richard.* Peter Pauper, n.d. *(I; A)*

Fritz, Jean. *What's the Big Idea, Ben Franklin?* Putnam, 1982. *(I)*

Lampton, Christopher. *Thomas Alva Edison.* Watts, 1988. *(I)*

Looby, Chris. *Benjamin Franklin.* Chelsea House, 1990. *(I; A)*

Meltzer, Milton. *Benjamin Franklin: The New American.* Watts, 1988. *(I; A)*

Sandak, Cass R. *Benjamin Franklin.* Watts, 1986. *(P;I)*

Santrey, Laurence. *Young Ben Franklin.* Troll, 1982. *(P; I)*

Stevens, Byrna. *Ben Franklin's Glass Armonica.* Carolrhoda, 1983. *(P)*

FREEDOM OF RELIGION, SPEECH, AND PRESS. See Civil Liberties and Civil Rights.

FRENCH AND INDIAN WAR. See United States (History and Government).

FRENCH REVOLUTION

Cairns, Trevor. *Power for the People.* Cambridge U Pr, 1978. *(A)*

Dickens, Charles. *A Tale of Two Cities.* Putnam, 1982. *(I)*

Lacey, Robert. *The French Revolution.* Viking, 1977. *(I; A)*

Powers, Elizabeth. *The Journal of Madame Royale.* Walker, 1976. *(I; A)*

Pratt, Stephen. *The French Revolution.* Har-Row, 1971. *(I; A)*

FREUD, SIGMUND

Lager, Marilyn. *Sigmund Freud: Doctor of the Mind.* Enslow, 1986. *(A)*

FROGS, TOADS, AND OTHER AMPHIBIANS

Cole, Joanna. *A Frog's Body.* Morrow, 1980. *(P)*

Dallinger, Jane, and Johnson, Sylvia A. *Frogs and Toads.* Lerner, 1982. *(I; A)*

Lacey, Elizabeth A. *The Complete Frog: A Guide for the Very Young Naturalist.* Lothrop, 1989. *(I)*

Lane, Margaret. *The Frog.* Dial Bks Young, 1982. *(P)*

Lavies, Bianca. *Lily Pad Pond.* Dutton, 1989. *(P)*

Modiki, Masuda. *Tree Frogs.* Lerner, 1986. *(I)*

Tarrant, Graham. *Frogs.* Putnam, 1983. *(P)*

FROST, ROBERT

Bober, Natalie S. *A Restless Spirit: The Story of Robert Frost.* Atheneum, 1981. *(I; A)*

Frost, Robert. *The Road Not Taken: An Introduction to Robert Frost.* HR&W, 1951. *(A)*

FRUITGROWING

Ancona, George. *Bananas: From Manolo to Margie.* Clarion, 1982. *(P; I)*

Gemming, Elizabeth. *The Cranberry Book.* Putnam, 1983. *(I)*

Johnson, Sylvia A. *Apple Trees.* Lerner, 1983. *(P; I; A)*

Mitgutsch, Ali. *From Seed to Pear.* Carolrhoda, 1981. *(P)*

Potter, Marian. *A Chance Wild Apple.* Morrow, 1982. *(P; I)*

FUELS. See Energy.

FULTON, ROBERT

Philip, Cynthia. *Robert Fulton: A Biography.* Franklin Watts, 1985. *(A)*

Quackenbush, Robert. *Watt Got You Started, Mr. Fulton?* P-H, 1982. *(P; I)*

FUNGI

Johnson, Sylvia A. *Mushrooms.* Lerner, 1982. *(I; A)*

Selsam, Millicent E. *Mushrooms.* Morrow, 1986. *(I)*

FUR TRADE IN NORTH AMERICA

Siegel, Beatrice. *Fur Trappers and Traders; The Indians, the Pilgrims, and the Beaver.* Walker, 1981. *(P; I)*

GABON. See Africa.

GALILEO. See Astronomy.

GAMA, VASCO DA

Knight, David. *Vasco Da Gama*. Troll, 1979 (new ed.). *(P; I)*

GAMBIA, THE. See AFRICA.

GAMES

Bernarde, Anita. *Games from Many Lands*. Lion, 1971. *(P; I)*

Cline, Dallas, and Tornborg, Pat. *How to Play Almost Everything*. Putnam, 1982. *(P; I)*

D'Amato, Alex, and D'Amato, Janet. *Galaxy Games*. Doubleday, 1981. *(P; I)*

Ferretti, Fred. *The Great American Book of Sidewalk, Stoop, Dirt, Curb, and Alley Games*. Workman, 1975. *(P; I)*

Gould, Marilyn. *Playground Sports: A Book of Ball Games*. Lothrop, 1978. *(I)*

Hass, E. A. *Come Quick! I'm Sick*. Atheneum, 1982. *(P)*

McToots, Rudi. *Best-Ever Book of Indoor Games*. Arco, 1985. *(I; A)*

GANDHI, MOHANDAS KARAMCHAND

Cheney, Glenn A. *Mohandas Gandhi*. Watts, 1983. *(I; A)*

Rawding, F. W. *Gandhi*. Cambridge U Pr, 1980. *(I); Gandhi and the Struggle for India's Independence*. Lerner, 1982. *(I; A)*

GANGES RIVER. See INDIA.

GARDENS AND GARDENING

Brown, Marc. *Your First Garden Book*. Little, 1981. *(P)*

Murphy, Louise. *My Garden: A Journal for Gardening Around the Year*. Scribner, 1980. *(P; I)*

Vogel, Antje, illus. *The Big Book for Little Gardners*. Green Tiger, 1983. *(P)*

Waters, Marjorie. *The Victory Garden Kid's Book*. Houghton, 1988. *(P; I)*

GARFIELD, JAMES A.

Lillegard, Dee. *James A. Garfield*. Children's, 1988. *(P; I)*

See also PRESIDENCY OF THE UNITED STATES.

GARIBALDI, GIUSEPPE. See ITALY.

GASES

Griffin, Frank. *Industrial Gases*. Sportshelf, n.d. *(I; A)*

Pechey, Roger. *Gas*. (Spotlight on Resources) Rourke Enterprises, 1987. *(P; I)*

GASOLINE. See PETROLEUM.

GEESE

Hirschi, Ron. *City Geese*. Dodd, 1987. *(P; I)*

Wharton, Anthony. *Discovering Ducks, Geese, and Swans*. Watts, 1987. *(P)*

GEMSTONES. See ROCKS, MINERALS, AND ORES.

GENEALOGY

Barnes, Kathleen, and Pearce, Virginia. *You and Yours*. Desert Bk, 1980. *(P; I)*

Cooper, Kay. *Where Did You Get Those Eyes? A Guide to Discovering Your Family History*. Walker, 1988. *(I)*

Stryker-Rodda, Harriet. *How to Climb Your Family Tree: Genealogy for Beginners*. Har-Row, 1977. *(I; A)*

Wubben, Pamela G. *Genealogy for Children*. One Percent, 1981. *(P; I)*

GENETICS AND GENETIC ENGINEERING

Arnold, Caroline. *Genetics: From Mendel to Gene Splicing*. Watts, 1986. *(I; A)*

Asimov, Isaac. *How Did We Find Out About Our Genes?* Walker, 1983. *(I)*

Bornstein, Sandy, and Bornstein, Jerry. *New Frontiers in Genetics*. Simon & Schuster, 1984 *(A)*

Goldstein, Philip. *Genetics Is Easy: A Handbook of Information*. Lantern, n.d. *(A)*

Hyde, Margaret O., and Hyde, Lawrence E. *Cloning and the New Genetics*. Enslow, 1984. *(A)*

Silverstein, Alvin, and Silverstein, Virginia. *The Genetics Explosion*. Scholastic, 1980. *(A)*

Snyder, Gerald S. *Test Tube Life: Scientific Advance and Moral Dilemma*. Messner, 1982. *(I; A)*

Stwertka, Eve, and Stwertka, Albert. *Genetic Engineering*. Watts, 1982. *(I; A)*

GEOGRAPHY

Adler, Peggy. *Geography Puzzles*. Watts, 1979. *(P; I)*

Bell, Neill. *The Book of Where or How to Be Naturally Geographic*. Little, 1982. *(I; A)*

Grolier Incorporated. *Lands and Peoples* (6 volumes). Grolier, 1988. *(I)*

National Geographic Society. *Nature's World of Wonders*. Natl Geog, 1983. *(I; A)*

GEOLOGY AND GEOPHYSICS

Boy Scouts of America. *Geology*. BSA, 1981. *(I; A)*

Dixon, Dougal. *Geology*. Watts, 1983. *(I; A)*

Jacobs, Linda. *Letting Off Steam: The Story of Geothermal Energy*. Carolrhoda, 1989. *(I; A)*

Lambert, David, and the Diagram Group. *The Field Guide to Geology*. Facts on File, 1988. *(A)*

Markle, Sandra. *Digging Deeper: Investigations into Rocks, Shocks, Quakes, and Other Earthly Matters*. Lothrop, 1987. *(I)*

McNulty, Faith. *How to Dig a Hole to the Other Side of the World.* Har-Row, 1979. *(P)*

Rossbacher, Lisa A. *Recent Revolutions In Geology.* Watts, 1986. *(I; A)*

See also EARTH.

GEOMETRY AND GEOMETRIC FORMS

Diggins, Julia E. *String, Straightedge, and Shadow: The Story of Geometry.* Viking, 1965. *(I)*

Froman, Robert. *Angles Are Easy as Pie.* Har-Row, 1976. *(P)*

Hoban, Tana. *Circles, Triangles, and Squares.* Macmillan, 1974. *(P)*

Kelly, Brendan. *Geometrics.* EDC, 1980. *(I)*

Phillips, Jo. *Exploring Triangles: Paper-Folding Geometry.* Har-Row, 1975. *(P); Right Angles: Paper-Folding Geometry,* 1972. *(P)*

Srivastava, Jane J. *Spaces, Shapes, and Sizes.* Har-Row, 1980. *(P)*

GEORGIA

Blackburn, Joyce. *James Edward Oglethorpe.* Dodd, 1983. *(I; A)*

Fradin, Dennis. *Georgia: In Words and Pictures.* Childrens, 1981. *(P; I)*

Hepburn, Lawrence R. *The Georgia History Book.* U. of Georgia Inst. Govt., 1982. *(I; A)*

Kent, Zachary A. *Georgia.* Childrens, 1988. *(P; I)*

Pedersen, Anne. *Kidding Around Atlanta: A Young Person's Guide to the City.* John Muir Publications, 1989. *(I; A)*

Snow, Pegeen. *Atlanta.* Dillon Press, 1989. *(P; I)*

GERMANY

Einhorn, Barbara. *West Germany.* Bookwright, dist. by Watts, 1988. *(P)*

Fairclough, Chris. *Take a Trip to West Germany.* Watts, 1981. *(P)*

Goldston, Robert. *Sinister Touches: The Secret War Against Hitler.* Dial Bks Young, 1982. *(I; A)*

Hintz, Martin. *West Germany.* Childrens, 1983. *(I; A)*

James, Ian. *West Germany.* Watts, 1989. *(P; I)*

McKenna, David. *East Germany.* Chelsea House, 1988. *(P; I)*

Pfeiffer, Christine. *Germany: Two Nations, One Heritage.* Dillon Press, 1987. *(P; I)*

Sharman, Tim. *We Live in East Germany.* Watts/Bookwright Pr., 1986. *(P;I)*

Singer, Julia. *Impressions: A Trip to the German Democratic Republic.* Atheneum, 1979. *(A)*

Stadtler, Christa. *We Live in West Germany.* Watts, 1984. *(I; A)*

GERONIMO

Wilson, Charles M. *Geronimo.* Dillon, 1973. *(I; A)*

GERSHWIN, GEORGE. See MUSIC AND MUSICIANS.

GETTYSBURG ADDRESS. See LINCOLN, ABRAHAM.

GEYSERS AND HOT SPRINGS

Lauber, Patricia. *Tapping Earth's Heat.* Garrard, 1978. *(P; I)*

GHANA

Ghana . . . in Pictures. Lerner, 1988. *(P; I)*

Barnett, Jeanie M. *Ghana.* Chelsea House, 1988. *(I)*

GIOTTO DI BONDONE. See ART AND ARTISTS.

GIRAFFES

Arnold, Caroline. *Giraffe.* Morrow, 1987. *(P; I)*

Brown, Louise. *Giraffes.* Dodd, 1980. *(P; I)*

Bush, John. *This Is a Book About Giraffes.* Watts, 1983. *(P)*

Lavine, Sigmund A. *Wonders of Giraffes.* Dodd, Mead, 1986. *(I; A)*

Sattler, Helen Roney. *Giraffes, the Sentinels of the Savannahs.* Lothrop, 1990. *(I)*

Torgersen, Don. *Giraffe Hooves and Antelope Horns.* Childrens, 1982. *(P; I)*

GIRL SCOUTS

Girl Scouts of the United States of America. *Daisy Low of the Girl Scouts: The Story of Juliette Gordon Low, Founder of the Girl Scouts of America.* GS, 1975 (rev. ed.). *(I; A); Wide World of Girl Guiding and Girl Scouting.* 1980. *(P; I); Worlds to Explore for Brownie and Junior Girl Scouts.* 1977. *(P; I)*

World Association of Girl Guides and Girl Scouts. *The Story of the Four World Centres: For Girls and Leaders.* GS, 1982 (rev. ed.). *(P; I); Trefoil Round the World.* 1978. *(P; I; A)*

GLACIER NATIONAL PARK. See NATIONAL PARK SYSTEM.

GLACIERS. See ICEBERGS AND GLACIERS.

GLASS

Cackett, Susan. *Glass.* Gloucester, dist. by Watts, 1988. *(P; I)*

Corning Museum of Glass. *Masterpieces of Glass from the Corning Museum.* Dover, 1983. *(I; A)*

Giblin, James Cross. *Let There Be Light.* Harper/Crowell, 1988. *(A)*

Kolb, Kenneth E. and Doris K. *Glass: Its Many Facets.* Enslow, 1988. *(I; A)*

Mitgutsch, Ali. *From Sand to Glass.* Carolrhoda, 1981. *(P)*

Paterson, Alan J. *How Glass Is Made*. Facts on File, 1985. *(P;I)*

GLIDING AND SOARING

Penzler, Otto. *Hang Gliding*. Troll, 1976. *(I; A)*
Schmetz, Dorothy C. *Hang Gliding*. Crestwood, 1978. *(P)*

GOLD. See METALS AND METALLURGY.

GOLD, DISCOVERIES OF

Cooper, Michael. *Klondike Fever: The Famous Gold Rush of 1898*. Clarion, 1989. *(I; A)*
Gough, Barry. *Gold Rush!* Watts, 1983. *(I; A)* (Canada)
McCall, Edith. *Gold Rush Adventures*. Childrens, 1980. *(P; I; A)*
Poynter, Margaret. *Gold Rush! The Yukon Stampede of .1898*. Atheneum, 1979. *(A)*
Stein, R. Conrad. *The Story of the Gold at Sutter's Mill*. Childrens, 1981. *(P; I)*

GOLF

Golf Digest Editors. *Better Golf*. Sportshelf, n.d. *(I; A)*
Merrins, Eddie, and Mcteigue, Michael. *Golf for the Young*. Atheneum, 1983. *(I; A)*

GORBACHEV, MIKHAIL

Caulkins, Janet. *The Picture Life of Mikhail Gorbachev*. Watts, 1989 (rev. ed.). *(P)*
Oleksy, Walter. *Mikhail Gorbachev: A Leader for Soviet Change*. Childrens, 1989. *(P; I)*
Sullivan, George. *Mikhail Gorbachev*. Messner, 1988. *(I)*

GOTHIC ART AND ARCHITECTURE

Gallagher, Maureen. *The Cathedral Book*. Paulist Pr, 1983. *(P; I)*
Macaulay, David. *Castle*. HM, 1977. *(P; I; A)*; *Cathedral: The Story of Its Construction*. 1973. *(P; I)*
Watson, Percy. *Building the Medieval Cathedrals*. Lerner, 1978. *(I; A)*

GOYA, FRANCISCO. See ART AND ARTISTS.

GRAIN AND GRAIN PRODUCTS

Blackwood, Alan. *Grain*. (Spotlight on Resources) Rourke Enterprises, 1987. *(P; I)*
Johnson, Sylvia A. *Wheat*. Lerner, 1990. *(P; I)*
Mitgutsch, Ali. *From Grain to Bread*. Carolrhoda, 1981. *(P)*
Patent, Dorothy Hinshaw. *Wheat: The Golden Harvest*. Mead, 1987. *(P; I)*

GRANT, ULYSSES S.

Falkof, Lucille. *Ulysses S. Grant: 18th President of the United States*. Garrett, 1988. *(A)*

Kent, Zachary. *Ulysses S. Grant*. Childrens, 1989. *(P; I)*
See also PRESIDENCY OF THE UNITED STATES.

GRAPES AND BERRIES. See FRUITGROWING.

GRAPHS

Fry, Edward B. *Graphical Comprehension: How to Read and Make Graphs*. Jamestown Pubs, 1981. *(I; A)*
Stwertka, Eve, and Stwertka, Albert. *Make It Graphic!: Drawing Graphs for Science and Social Studies Projects*. Messner, 1985. *(A)*

GRASSES

Horton, Casey. *Grasslands*. Watts, 1985. *(I)*
Horton, Catherine. *A Closer Look at Grasslands*. Watts, 1979. *(P; I)*; *Grasslands and People*. Silver, n.d. *(I; A)*

GRAVITY AND GRAVITATION

Branley, Franklyn M. *Gravity Is a Mystery*. Har-Row, 1970; *Weight and Weightlessness*. 1972. *(P)*
Brewer, Mary. *What Floats?* Childs World, 1976. *(P)*
Smith, Howard E., Jr. *Balance It!* Scholastic, 1982. *(I; A)*

GREAT LAKES

Adamson, Wendy W. *Saving Lake Superior*. Dillon, 1974. *(I; A)*
Henderson, Kathy. *The Great Lakes*. Childrens, 1989. *(P)*

GREECE

Elliott, Drossoula V., and Elliott, Sloane. *We Live in Greece*. Watts, 1984. *(I; A)*
Lye, Keith. *Take a Trip to Greece*. Watts, 1983. *(P)*
Monos, Dimitris. *The Greek Americans*. Chelsea House, 1988. *(I; A)*
Stein, R. Conrad. *Greece*. Children's, 1988, *(P; I)*
Warren, Ruth. *Modern Greece*. Watts, 1979 (rev. ed.). *(I; A)*
See also ANCIENT CIVILIZATIONS.

GREEK MYTHOLOGY

Billout, Guy. *Thunderbolt and Rainbow: A Look at Greek Mythology*. P-H, 1981. *(P; I)*
Colum, Padraic. *Golden Fleece and the Heroes Who Lived Before Achilles*. Macmillan. 1983. *(I)*
Coolidge, Olivia. *Greek Myths*. HM, 1949. *(I; A)*
D'Aulaire, Ingri, and D'Aulaire, Edgar. *D'Aulaires' Book of Greek Myths*. Doubleday, 1962. *(I)*
Fisher, Leonard Everett. *The Olympians: Great Gods and Goddesses of Ancient Greece*. Holiday, 1984. *(P; I)*
Gates, Doris. *A Fair Wind for Troy*. Viking, 1976. *(I)*
Green, Roger L. *Tales of Greek Heroes*. Penguin, 1974. *(I)*
Homer. *The Voyage of Odysseus*. Troll, 1984. *(P; I)*

Low, Alice. *Greek Gods and Heroes*. Macmillan, 1985. *(P)*

Wise, William. *Monster Myths of Ancient Greece*. Putnam, 1981. *(I; A)*

GREENAWAY, KATE

Greenaway, Kate. *A—Apple Pie*. Warne, 1987 (rev. ed.); *The Language of Flowers*, 1977; *Mother Goose: Or, the Old Nursery Rhymes*, 1882. *(P; I)*

GREENLAND. See DENMARK.

GRENADA. See CARIBBEAN SEA AND ISLANDS.

GRIMM, JACOB AND WILHELM

Grimm Brothers. *The Best of Grimms' Fairy Tales*. Larousse, 1980. *(P)*

Manheim, Ralph, ed. *Grimms' Tales for Young and Old: The Complete Stories*. Doubleday, 1977. *(P; I; A)*

GUATEMALA. See CENTRAL AMERICA.

GUIANA. See SOUTH AMERICA.

GUINEA. See AFRICA.

GUINEA PIGS, HAMSTERS, AND GERBILS

Barrie, Anmarie. *A Step-by-Step Book About Guinea Pigs; A Step-by-Step Book About Hamsters*. TFH Publications, 1988. *(I; A)*

Burton, Jane. *Dazy the Guinea Pig*. Gareth Stevens, 1989. *(P)*

Henrie, Fiona. *Gerbils*. Watts, 1980; *Guinea Pigs*, 1981; *Hamsters*, 1981. *(P; I)*

Hess, Lilo. *Making Friends with Guinea Pigs*. Scribner, 1983. *(P; I)*

Rubins, Harriett. *Guinea Pigs: An Owner's Guide to Choosing, Raising, Breeding, and Showing*. Lothrop, 1982. *(I; A)*

Silverstein, Alvin, and Silverstein, Virginia B. *Gerbils*. Har-Row, 1976. *(I)*; *Hamsters: All About Them*. Lothrop, 1974. *(I)*

GUYANA

Guyana in Pictures. Lerner, 1988. *(P; I)*

Sterling Editors. *Guyana—In Pictures*. Sterling, 1975. *(I)*

GYMNASTICS

Barrett, Norman. *Gymnastics*. Watts, 1989. *(P)*

Berke, Art. *Gymnastics*. Watts, 1988. *(P; I)*

Dolan, Edward. *The Complete Beginners Guide to Gymnastics*. Doubleday, 1980. *(I)*

Gribble, McPhee. *Body Tricks: To Teach Yourself*. Penguin, 1982. *(I; A)*

Krementz, Jill. *A Very Young Gymnast*. Knopf, 1978. *(I)*

Murdock, Tony, and Nik, Stuart. *Gymnastics*. Watts, 1985. *(I)*

HAIR AND HAIRSTYLING

Blakely, Pat. *Why Do We Have Hair?* Creative Ed, 1982. *(P; I; A)*

Bozic, Patricia, and Lee, Pola. *Cutting Hair at Home*. NAL/Plume, 1986. *(A)*

Tether, Graham. *The Hair Book*. Random, 1979. *(P)*

HAITI

Hanmer, Trudy J. *Haiti*. Watts, 1988. *(I; A)*

HALE, NATHAN

Poole, Susan. *Nathan Hale*. Dandelion, 1979. *(P)*

HALLOWEEN

Barth, Edna. *Witches, Pumpkins, and Grinning Ghosts: The Story of the Halloween Symbols*. HM, 1972. *(I)*.

Corwin, Judith Hoffman. *Halloween Fun*. Messner, 1983. *(I)*

Dobrin, Arnold. *Make a Witch, Make a Goblin: A Book of Halloween Crafts*. Scholastic, 1977. *(P)*

Gibbons, Gail. *Halloween*. Holiday, 1984. *(P)*

Herda, D. J. *Halloween*. Watts, 1983. *(P; I)*

Hopkins, Lee Bennett, ed. *Hey-How for Halloween!* HarBraceJ, 1974. *(P)*

HAMILTON, ALEXANDER

Kurland, Gerald. *Alexander Hamilton: Architect of American Nationalism*. SamHar Pr, 1972. *(I; A)*

HAMLET. See SHAKESPEARE, WILLIAM.

HANCOCK, JOHN

Fritz, Jean. *Will You Sign Here, John Hancock?* Putnam, 1976. *(I)*

HANDWRITING

Gourdie, Tom. *Handwriting*. Merry Thoughts, n.d. *(P; I)*

Sassoon, Rosemary. *A Practical Guide to Children's Handwriting*. Thames Hudson, 1983. *(P; I)*

Steinberg, Margery A. *Handwriting*. Putnam, 1979. *(P; I)*

HANNIBAL

Hirsh, Marilyn. *Hannibal and His 37 Elephants*. Holiday, 1977. *(P)*

HANOI. See SOUTHEAST ASIA.

HANUKKAH

Adler, David A. *Hanukkah Game Book: Games, Riddles, Puzzles, and More.* Hebrew Pub, 1978. *(P; I); A Picture Book of Hanukkah.* Holiday, 1982. *(P)*

Aleichem, Sholem. *Hanukkah Money.* Greenwillow, 1978. *(P)*

Becker, Joyce. *Hanukkah Crafts.* Hebrew Pub, 1978. *(P; I)*

Behrens, June. *Hanukkah.* Childrens, 1983. *(P; I)*

Chaikin, Miriam. *Light Another Candle: The Story and Meaning of Hanukkah.* HM, 1981. *(P; I)*

Drucker, Malka. *Hanukkah: Eight Nights, Eight Lights.* Holiday, 1980. *(I; A)*

Hirsh, Marilyn. *The Hanukkah Story.* Hebrew Pub, 1977. *(P; I); I Love Hanukkah,* Holiday, 1984. *(P)*

Levoy, Myron. *The Hanukkah of Great-Uncle Otto.* Jewish Pubn, 1984. *(P)*

Singer, Isaac B. *The Power of Light: Eight Stories for Hanukkah.* FS&G, 1980. *(P; I; A)*

HARDING, WARREN G.

Wade, Linda R. *Warren G. Harding.* Childrens, 1989. *(P; I)*

HARP. See MUSICAL INSTRUMENTS.

HARRISON, BENJAMIN. See PRESIDENCY OF THE UNITED STATES.

HARRISON, WILLIAM HENRY

Fitz-Gerald, Christine Maloney. *William Henry Harrison.* Children's, 1988. *(P; I)*

Peckham, Howard H. *William Henry Harrison: Young Tippecanoe.* Bobbs, 1951. *(I)*

See also PRESIDENCY OF THE UNITED STATES.

HAWAII

Bauer, Helen. *Hawaii: The Aloha State.* Bess Pr, 1982 (new ed.). *(I)*

Dunford, Elizabeth P. *The Hawaiians of Old.* Bess Pr, 1980. *(P; I)*

Fradin, Dennis. *Hawaii: In Words and Pictures.* Childrens, 1980. *(P; I)*

Jacobsen, Peter O., and Kristensen, Preben S. *A Family In Hawaii.* Watts/Bookwright Press, 1987. *(P)*

Potter, Norris, and Kasdon, Lawrence. *The Hawaiian Monarchy.* Bess Pr, 1982. *(I)*

Rizzuto, Shirley O. *Hawaii's Pathfinders.* Bess Pr, 1983. *(I)*

Rublowsky, John. *Born in Fire: A Geological History of Hawaii.* Har-Row, 1981. *(I)*

Williams, Jay. *The Surprising Things Maui Did.* Scholastic, 1979. *(P)*

HAWTHORNE, NATHANIEL

Gaeddert, LouAnn. *A New England Love Story: Nathaniel Hawthorne and Sophia Peabody.* Dial Bks Young, 1980. *(I; A)*

Wood, James P. *Unpardonable Sin: A Life of Nathaniel Hawthorne.* Pantheon, 1970. *(I; A)*

See also UNITED STATES (ART, LITERATURE, AND MUSIC).

HAYDN, JOSEPH. See MUSIC AND MUSICIANS.

HAYES, RUTHERFORD B.

Kent, Zachary. *Rutherford B. Hayes.* Childrens, 1989. *(P; I).*

HAZARDOUS WASTES. See POLLUTION.

HEALTH AND PHYSICAL FITNESS

Bershad, Carol, and Bernick, Deborah. *Bodyworks: The Kids' Guide to Food and Physical Fitness.* Random, 1981. *(I; A)*

Carr, Rachel. *Be a Frog, a Bird, or a Tree: Creative Yoga Exercises for Children.* Doubleday, 1973. *(P; I); Wheel, Camel, Fish, and Plow: Yoga for You.* P-H, 1981. *(I; A)*

Feder, R. F., and Taylor, G. J. *Junior Body Building.* Sterling, 1982. *(I; A)*

Gagliostro, Vincenzia, Sr. *Am I OK—If I Feel the Way I Do?* Collins, 1980. *(I)*

Heron, Jackie. *Careers in Health and Fitness.* Rosen, 1988. *(A)*

Lindquist, Marie. *Body Makeovers.* Pinnacle, 1985. *(A)*

Lubowe, Irwin I., and Huss, Barbara. *A Teenage Guide to Healthy Skin and Hair.* Dutton, 1979 (rev. ed.). *(I; A)*

Lyttle, Richard B. *The New Physical Fitness: Something for Everyone.* Watts, 1981. *(I; A)*

Trier, Carola S. *Exercise: What It Is, What It Does.* Greenwillow, 1982. *(P)*

Ward, Brian. *Health and Hygiene.* Watts, 1988. *(I)*

HEALTH FOODS. See NUTRITION.

HEART

McGowan, Tom. *The Circulatory System: From Harvey to the Artificial Heart.* Watts, 1988. *(I)*

Silverstein, Alvin, and Silverstein, Virginia B. *Heartbeats: Your Body, Your Heart.* Har-Row, 1983. *(I); Heart Disease: America's #1 Killer.* Lippincott, 1985. *(A)*

Ward, Brian. *The Heart and Blood.* Watts, 1982. *(I)*

HEAT

Ardley, Neil. *Hot and Cold*. Watts, 1983. *(P)*
Ross, Dave. *How to Keep Warm in Winter*. Har-Row, 1980. *(I; A)*

HELICOPTERS

Berliner, Don. *Helicopters*. Lerner, 1983. *(I; A)*
Delear, Frank J. *Airplanes and Helicopters of the U.S. Navy*. Dodd, 1982; *Helicopters and Airplanes of the U.S. Army*. 1977. *(I; A)*
Petersen, David. *Helicopters*. Childrens, 1983. *(P)*
White, David. *Helicopters*. Rourke, 1988. *(P)*

HENRY, PATRICK

Fritz, Jean. *Where Was Patrick Henry on the 29th of May?* Putnam, 1975. *(P; I)*
Reische, Diana. *Patrick Henry*. Watts, 1987. *(P)*
Sabin, Louis. *Patrick Henry: Voice of the American Revolution*. Troll, 1982. *(P; I)*

HERALDRY. See MIDDLE AGES.

HERBS, SPICES, AND CONDIMENTS

Barker, Albert. *The Spice Adventure*. Messner, 1980. *(P; I)*
Gabriel, Ingrid. *Herb Identifier and Handbook*. Sterling, 1975. *(I; A)*

HEREDITY. See GENETICS AND GENETIC ENGINEERING.

HIBERNATION

Busch, Phyllis. *The Seven Sleepers: The Story of Hibernation*. Macmillan, 1985. *(I)*
Facklam, Margery. *Do Not Disturb: The Mysteries of Animal Hibernation and Sleep*. Sierra Club Books/Little, 1989. *(P; I)*
Ward, Andrew. *Baby Bear and the Long Sleep*. Little, 1980. *(P)*

HIKING AND BACKPACKING

Larson, Randy. *Backpacking*. Harvey, 1979; *Illustrated Backpacking and Hiking Dictionary for Young People*. P-H, 1981. *(P; I; A)*
Peterson, P. J. *Nobody Else Can Walk It for You*. Delacorte, 1982. *(I; A)*
Randolph, John. *Backpacking Basics*. P-H, 1982. *(P; I)*
Thomas, Art. *Backpacking Is for Me*. Lerner, 1980. *(P; I)*

HIMALAYAS. See ASIA; INDIA; MOUNTAINS AND MOUNTAIN CLIMBING.

HINDUISM. See RELIGIONS OF THE WORLD.

HIPPOPOTAMUSES

Arnold, Caroline. *Hippo*. Morrow, 1989. *(P; I)*

HISPANIC AMERICANS

Catalano, Julie. *The Mexican Americans*. Chelsea House, 1988. *(P; I)*
Larsen, Ronald J. *The Puerto Ricans in America*. Lerner, 1989. *(I)*
Maynes, J. O. Hispanic Heroes of the U.S.A. (English version, 4 bks.): Bk. 1, *Raul H. Castro, Tony Nunez, and Vikki Carr;* Bk. 2, *Henry Gonzalez, Trini Lopez, and Edward Roybal;* Bk. 3, *Carmen R. Maymi, Roberto Clemente, and Jose Feliciano;* Bk. 4, *Tony Perez, Lee Trevino, and Jim Plunkett*. EMC, 1975. *(P; I; A)*
Meltzer, Milton. *The Hispanic Americans*. Har-Row, 1982. *(I; A)*
Morey, Janet, and Dunn, Wendy. *Famous Mexican Americans*. Cobblehill, 1989. *(I)*
Pinchot, Jane. *The Mexicans in America*. Lerner, 1989. *(I)*
Raintree Hispanic Stories. (Written in both English and Spanish) *Simon Bolivar; Hernando De Soto; David Farragut; Miguel Hildago Y Costilla; Jose Marti; Luis Munoz Marin; Diego Rivera; Junipero Serra; Luis W. Alvarez; Juana Ines De La Cruz; Carlos Finlay; Bernardo De Galvez; Queen Isabella I; Benito Juarez; Vilma Martinez; Pedro Menendez De Aviles*. Raintree, 1989–90. *(P; I)*

HISTORY

Chisholm. *First Guide to History*. EDC, 1983. *(I; A)*
Foster, Genevieve. *Birthdays of Freedom: From Early Egypt to July 4, 1776*. Scribner, 1974. *(I)*
Van Loon, Hendrik W. *The Story of Mankind*. Liveright, 1972. *(A)*

HITLER, ADOLF

Devaney, John. *Hitler, Mad Dictator of World War II*. Putnam, 1978. *(I)*
Dolan, Edward F., Jr. *Adolph Hitler: A Portrait in Tyranny*. Dodd, 1981. *(I; A)*
Gray, Ronald. *Hitler and the Germans*. Lerner, 1983. *(I; A)*

HOBBIES AND CRAFTS

Bottomly, Jim. *Paper Projects for Creative Kids of All Ages*. Little, 1983. *(P; I; A)*
Fletcher, Helen. *Carton Crafts*. Lion, 1981. *(P; I)*
Greene, Peggy R. *Things to Make*. Random, 1981. *(P)*
Lewis, Shari. *The Do-It-Better Book; Things Kids Collect*. HR&W, 1981. *(P; I)*
Scarry, Richard. *Richard Scarry's Best Make-It Book Ever*. Random, 1977. *(P)*

Schulz, Charles M. *Charlie Brown's Super Book of Things to Do and Collect*. Random, 1975. *(P; I)*

Supraner, Robyn. *Fun-to-Make Nature Crafts*. Troll, 1981. *(P; I)*

Volpe, Nancee. *Good Apple and Seasonal Arts and Crafts*. Good Apple, 1982. *(P; I)*

HO CHI MINH CITY (SAIGON). See SOUTHEAST ASIA.

HOCKEY. See FIELD HOCKEY or ICE HOCKEY.

HOISTING AND LOADING MACHINERY. See TECHNOLOGY.

HOLIDAYS

Berger, Gilda. *Easter and Other Spring Holidays*. Watts, 1983. *(I)*

Burnett, Bernice. *Holidays*. Watts, n.d. *(I)*

Greene, Carol. *Holidays*. Children's, 1982. *(P)*

Grigoli, Valorie. *Patriotic Holidays and Celebrations*. Watts, 1985. *(P;I)*

Hautzig, Esther. *Make It Special: Cards, Decorations, and Party Favors for Holidays and Other Celebrations*. Macmillan, 1986. *(P)*

Livingston, Myra Cohn. *Celebrations*. Holiday House, 1985. *(I; A)*

Livingston, Myra Cohn, ed. *O Frabjous Day: Poetry for Holidays and Special Occasions*. Atheneum, 1977. *(I; A)*

Perl, Lila, and Ada, Alma F. *Pinatas and Paper Flowers (Pinatas y Flores de Papel): Holidays of the Americas in English and Spanish*. HM, 1983. *(P; I)*

Quackenbush, Robert, ed. *The Holiday Song Book*. Lothrop, 1977. *(I)*

Scott, Geoffrey. *Memorial Day*. Carolrhoda, 1983. *(P)*

Van Straalen, Alice. *The Book of Holidays Around The World*. Dutton, 1987. *(A)*

Zalben, Jane B. *Happy Passover, Rosie*. Holt, 1990. *(P)*

See also DECLARATION OF INDEPENDENCE (Fourth of July holiday) and names of other well-known holidays.

HOLLAND. See NETHERLANDS.

HOLOCAUST

Abells, Chana Byers. *The Childen We Remember*. Greenwillow, 1986. *(I)*

Bernbaum, Israel. *My Brother's Keeper*. Putnam, 1985. *(I:A)*

Chaikin, Miriam. *A Nightmare in History: The Holocaust*. Clarion Books, 1987. *(P; I)*

Finkelstein, Norman H. *Remember Not to Forget: A Memory of the Holocaust*. Watts, 1985. *(P)*

Friedman, Ina R. *The Other Victims: First Person Stories of Non-Jews Persecuted by the Nazis*. Houghton, 1990. *(I)*

Meltzer, Milton. *Never to Forget: The Jews of the Holocaust*. Har-Row, 1976. *(I; A)*

Orlev, Uri. *The Island on Bird Street*, tr. by Hillel Halkin. HM, 1984. *(I)*

Patterson, Charles. *Anti-Semitism: The Road to the Holocaust and Beyond*. Walker, 1982. *(I; A)*

Rogasky, Barbara. *Smoke and Ashes: The Story of the Holocaust*. Holiday, 1988 *(A)*

Rossel, Seymour. *The Holocaust: The Fire that Raged*. Watts, 1989. *(I; A)*

HOMER, WINSLOW

Goldstein, Ernest. *Winslow Homer: The Gulf Stream*. NAL, 1983. *(I; A)*

Hyman, Linda. *Winslow Homer: America's Old Master*. Doubleday, 1973. *(I; A)*

HOMES. See ARCHITECTURE; BUILDING CONSTRUCTION.

HOMING AND MIGRATION. See ANIMALS: INTELLIGENCE AND BEHAVIOR; BIRDS.

HONDURAS. See CENTRAL AMERICA.

HONG KONG

Fairclough, Chris. *We Live in Hong Kong*. Watts/Bookwright Pr., 1986. *(P;I)*

Lye, Keith. *Take a Trip to Hong Kong*. Watts, 1984. *(P; I)*

McKenna, Nancy Durrell. *A Family in Hong Kong*. Lerner, 1987. *(P)*

HOOVER, HERBERT

Clinton, Susan. *Herbert Hoover; Thirty-first President of the United States*. Children's, 1988. *(P; I)*

See also PRESIDENCY OF THE UNITED STATES.

HORSEBACK RIDING

Dumas, Philippe. *The Lippizaners: And the Spanish Riding School*. P-H, 1981. *(P; I)*

Haney, Lynn. *Show Rider*. Putnam, 1982. *(I; A)*

Krementz, Jill. *A Very Young Rider*. Knopf, 1977. *(I)*

Reimer, Dianne, and Lee, Carol. *Horsebackriding Basics*. P-H, 1980. *(I; A)*

Van Steenwyck, Elizabeth. *Illustrated Riding Dictionary for Young People*. Harvey, 1981. *(I; A)*

Wheatley, George. *The Young Rider's Companion*. Lerner, 1981. *(P; I)*

HORSES AND THEIR RELATIVES

Clay, Patrice A. *We Work with Horses*. Putnam, 1980. *(I)*

Cole, Joanna. *A Horse's Body*. Morrow, 1981. *(P)*

Freedman, Russell. *Getting Born*. Holiday, 1978. *(I)*

Lavine, Sigmund A., and Casey, Brigid. *Wonders of Draft*

Horses. Dodd, 1983; *Wonders of the World of Horses*. 1972. *(P; I)*

Lavine, Sigmund A. and Scuro, Vincent. *Wonders of Donkeys*. Dodd, 1979; *Wonders of Mules*. 1982. *(P; I)*

Patent, Dorothy. *Arabian Horses*. Holiday, 1982; *Horses and Their Wild Relatives*, 1981; *Horses of America*, 1981; *Picture Book of Ponies*, 1983. *(P; I); Thoroughbred Horses*, 1985. *(A)*

Philp, Candace T. *Rodeo Horses*. Crestwood, 1983. *(P; I)*

Popescu, Charlotte. *Horses at Work*. David & Charles, 1983. *(P)*

HOSPITALS

Elliott, Ingrid G. *Hospital Roadmap: A Book to Help Explain the Hospital Experience to Young Children*. Resources Children, 1982. *(P)*

Fisher, Leonard. *The Hospitals*. Holiday, 1980. *(I; A)*

Holmes, Burnham. *Early Morning Rounds: A Portrait of a Hospital*. Scholastic, 1981. *(I; A)*

Howe, James. *The Hospital Book*. Crown, 1981. *(P)*

Rogers, Fred. *Going to the Hospital*. Putnam, 1988. *(P)*

Wolfe, Bob, and Wolfe, Diane. *Emergency Room*. Carolrhoda, 1983. *(I)*

HOUSEPLANTS. SEE PLANTS.

HOUSTON, SAMUEL. See MEXICAN WAR; TEXAS.

HUDSON, HENRY

Harley, Ruth. *Henry Hudson*. Troll, 1979 (new ed.). *(P; I)*

HUGHES, LANGSTON

Hughes, Langston. *Don't You Turn Back: Poems Selected by Lee Bennett Hopkins*. Knopf, 1969. *(P; I)*

Larson, Norita D. *Langston Hughes, Poet of Harlem*. Creative Ed, 1981. *(I; A)*

Walker, Alice. *Langston Hughes, American Poet*. Har-Row, 1974. *(P; I)*

HUMOR

Bodecker, N. M. *Hurry, Hurry, Mary Dear! And Other Nonsense Poems*. Atheneum, 1976. *(I)*

Ciardi, John. *Fast and Slow: Poems for Advanced Children and Beginning Parents*. HM, 1978. *(P)*

Cole, Joanna, and Calmenson, Stephanie. *The Laugh Book*. Doubleday, 1987. *(I; A)*

Corbett, Scott. *Jokes to Tell Your Worst Enemy*. Dutton, 1984. *(P; I)*

Fleischman, Albert Sidney. *McBroom's Almanac*. Little, 1984. *(P; I)*

Lear, Edward. *Complete Nonsense Book*. Dodd, n. d. *(P; I)*

Leonard, Marcia, and Cricket Magazine Editors. *Crick-*

et's Jokes, Riddles, and Other Stuff. Random, 1977. *(P; I)*

Maestro, Giulio. *A Raft of Riddles*. Dutton, 1982. *(P; I); Riddle Romp*, HM, 1983. *(P)*

Schwartz, Alvin. *Flapdoodle: Pure Nonsense from American Folklore*. Har-Row, 1980. *(I; A); Unriddling: All Sorts of Riddles to Puzzle Your Guessery*, 1983. *(P; I)*

HUNGARY

Hintz, Martin. *Hungary*. Childrens, 1988. *(I)*

Siegal, Aranka. *Upon the Head of a Goat: A Childhood in Hungary*. FS&G, 1981. *(I; A)*

St. John, Jetty. *A Family in Hungary*. Lerner, 1988. *(P)*

HURRICANES AND TORNADOES

Alth, Max, and Alth, Charlotte. *Disastrous Hurricanes and Tornadoes*. Watts, 1981. *(P; I)*

Fradin, Dennis Brindel. *Disaster! Tornadoes; Disaster! Hurricanes*. Childrens, 1982. *(I)*

McNulty, Faith. *Hurricane*. Har-Row, 1983. *(P; I)*

Ruckman, Ivy. *Night of the Twisters*. Crowell, 1984. *(P)*

Simon, Seymour. *Storms*. Morrow, 1989. *(P)*

HYMNS AND SPIRITUALS

Bryan, Ashley. *I'm Going to Sing: Black American Spirituals*, Vol II. Atheneum, 1982; *Walk Together, Children*. 1974. *(P; I)*

Curry, W. Lawrence, ed. *Songs and Hymns for Primary Children*. Westminster, 1978. *(P)*

Griffin, Steve. *Children's Guitar Hymnal*. Impact Bks, 1978. *(P; I)*

Konkel, Wilbur. *Living Hymn Stories*. Bethany, 1982. *(P; I)*

Krull, Kathleen, collector and arranger. *Songs of Praise*. Har Brace J, 1988. *(P)*

HYPNOTISM

Kirby, Vivian. *Hypnotism: Hocus Pocus or Science?* Messner, 1985. *(I; A)*

ICE AGES

Cole, Joanna. *Saber-Toothed Tiger and Other Ice-Age Mammals*. Enslow, 1981. *(P; I)*

Fodor, R. V. *Frozen Earth: Explaining the Ice Ages*. Enslow, 1981. *(I; A)*

Maynard, Christopher. *Exploring the Great Ice Age*. Watts, 1979. *(P; I)*

ICEBERGS AND GLACIERS

Greenberg, Jan. *The Iceberg and Its Shadow*. Dell, 1982. *(I; A)*

Nixon, Hershell H., and Nixon, Joan L. *Glaciers: Nature's Frozen Rivers*. Dodd, 1980. *(P; I)*

Robin, Gordon De Q. *Glaciers and Ice Sheets*. Watts, 1984. *(I)*

Simon, Seymour. *Icebergs and Glaciers*. Morrow, 1987. *(P; I)*

Walker, Sally M. *Glaciers: Ice on the Move*. Carolrhoda, 1990. *(I)*

ICE CREAM

Jaspersohn, William. *Ice Cream*. Macmillan, 1988. *(P)*

ICE HOCKEY

Aaseng, Nathan. *Hockey's Fearless Goalies; Hockey's Super Scores*. Lerner, 1983. *(P; I)*

Coombs, Charles I. *Be a Winner in Ice Hockey*. Morrow, 1974. *(I; A)*

Kalb, Jonah. *The Easy Hockey Book*. HM, 1977. *(P; I)*

MacLean, Norman. *Hockey Basics*. P-H, 1983. *(P; I)*

Olney, Ross R. *Winners! Super-Champions of Ice Hockey*. HM, 1982. *(I; A)*

Paulsen, Gary. *Facing Off, Checking, and Goaltending— Perhaps*. Raintree, 1979. *(P; I)*

ICELAND

Berry, Erick. *The Land and People of Iceland*. Har-Row, 1972 (new rev. ed.). *(I)*

Lepthien, Emilie U. *Iceland (Enchantment of the World)*. Childrens, 1987. *(P; I)*

ICE-SKATING

Dickmeyer, Lowell A., and Rolens, Lin. *Ice Skating Is for Me*. Lerner, 1980. *(P; I)*

Fox, Mary V. *The Skating Heidens*. Enslow, 1981. *(I; A)*

Hamill, Dorothy, and Clairmont, Elva. *Dorothy Hamill on and off the Ice*. Knopf, 1983. *(P; I; A)*

Haney, Lynn. *Skaters: Profile of a Pair*. Putnam, 1983. *(I; A)*

Kalb, Jonah, and Kalb, Laura. *The Easy Ice Skating Book*. HM, 1981. *(P; I)*

Krementz, Jill. *A Very Young Skater*. Knopf, 1979. *(P; I)*

MacLean, Norman. *Ice Skating Basics*. Prentice-Hall, 1984. *(P; I)*

IDAHO

Carpenter, Allan. *Idaho*. Childrens, 1979. *(I)*

Fradin, Dennis. *Idaho: In Words and Pictures*. Childrens, 1980. *(P; I)*

ILIAD

Picard, Barbara L., ed. *The Iliad of Homer*. Oxford U Pr, 1980. *(I)*

ILLINOIS

Carpenter, Allan. *Illinois*. Children's, 1979. *(I)*

Carter, Alden R. *Illinois*. Watts, 1987. *(P; I)*

Fradin, Dennis. *Illinois: In Words and Pictures*. Children's, 1976. *(P; I)*

Pfeiffer, Christine. *Chicago*. Dillon, 1989. *(P; I)*

IMMIGRATION

Anderson, Lydia. *Immigration*. Watts, 1981. *(I; A)*

Ashabranner, Brent. *The New Americans: Changing Patterns in U.S. Immigration*. Dodd, 1983. *(I; A)*

Blumenthal, Shirley. *Coming to America: Immigrants from Eastern Europe*. Delacorte, 1981. *(I; A)*

Bouvier, Leon F. *Immigration: Diversity in the U.S*. Walker, 1988. *(A)*

Caroli, Betty Boyd. *Immigrants Who Returned Home*. Chelsea House, 1990. *(A)*

Day, Carol Olsen, and Day, Edmund. *The New Immigrants*. Watts, 1985. *(A)*

Dixon, Edward H., and Galan, Mark A. *The Immigration and Naturalization Service*. Chelsea House, 1990. *(I; A)*

Freedman, Russell. *Immigrant Kids*. Dutton, 1980. *(P; I)*

Garver, Susan, and McGuire, Paula. *Coming to North America: From Mexico, Cuba, and Puerto Rico*. Delacorte, 1981. *(I; A)*

Kennedy, John F. *A Nation of Immigrants*. Har-Row, 1964 (rev. ed.). *(A)*

Kurelek, William. *They Sought a New World: The Story of European Immigration to North America*. Tundra, 1985. *(I; A)*

Meltzer, Milton. *The Chinese Americans*. Crowell, 1980. *(I; A)*

Perrin, Linda. *Coming to America: Immigrants from the Far East*. Delacorte, 1980. *(A)*

Reimers, David M. *The Immigrant Experience*. Chelsea House, 1989. *(I; A)*

Rips, Gladys N. *Coming to America: Immigrants from Southern Europe*. Dell, 1981. *(A)*

Robbins, Albert. *Coming to America: Immigrants from Northern Europe*. Dell, 1982. *(A)*

INCOME TAX. See TAXATION.

INDIA

India . . . in Pictures. Lerner, 1989. *(I)*

Galbraith, Catherine A., and Mehta, Rama. *India Now and Through Time*. HM, 1980. *(I; A)*

Jacobsen, Peter O., and Kristensen, Preben S. *A Family in India*. Watts, 1984. *(P; I)*

Karan, P. P., ed. *India*. Gateway Press, 1988. *(I; A)*

Lye, Keith. *Take a Trip to India*. Watts, 1982. *(P)*

Ogle, Carol, and Ogle, John. *Through the Year in India*. David & Charles, 1983. *(I; A)*

Sandal, Veenu. *We Live in India*. Watts, 1984. *(I)*

Sarin, Amitra Vohra. *India: An Ancient Land, a New Nation*. Dillon, 1984. *(I)*

Tames, Richard. *India and Pakistan in the Twentieth Century*. David & Charles, 1981. *(I; A)*

Tigwell, Tony. *A Family in India*. Lerner, 1985. *(P)*

Traub, James. *India: The Challenge of Change*. Messner, 1985 (rev. ed.). *(I; A)*

INDIANA

Carpenter, Allan. *Indiana*. Children's, 1979. *(I)*

Fradin, Dennis. *Indiana: In Words and Pictures*. Children's, 1980. *(P; I)*

INDIANS, AMERICAN

Ashabranner, Brent. *To Live in Two Worlds: American Indian Youth Today*. Dodd, 1984. *(I; A)*

Beck, Barbara L. *The Ancient Mayas; The Incas*, both books rev. by Lorna Greenberg. Watts, 1983. *(I; A); The Aztecs*, rev. by Lorna Greenberg. Watts, 1983. *(I)*

Bierhorst, John, ed. *The Girl Who Married a Ghost and Other Tales from the North American Indians*. Scholastic, 1978. *(I; A)*

Blood, Charles. *American Indian Games and Crafts*. Watts, 1981. *(P)*

Cwiklik, Robert. *Sequoyah and the Cherokee Alphabet*. Silver Burdett, 1989. *(I)*

Freedman, Russell. *Indian Chiefs*. Holiday, 1987. *(I; A)*

Garbarino, Merwyn S. *The Seminole*. Chelsea House, 1988. *(A)*

Gorsline, Marie, and Gorsline, Douglas. *North American Indians*. Random, 1978. *(P)*

Graymont, Barbara. *The Iroquois*. Chelsea House, 1988. *(A)*

Hirschfelder, Arlene. *Happily May I Walk: American Indians and Alaska Natives Today*. Scribner, 1986. *(I; A)*

Hoyt-Goldsmith, Diane. *Totem Pole*. Holiday, 1990. *(P)*

Jacobson, Daniel. *Indians of North America*. Watts, 1983. *(I; A)*

Kelly, Lawrence C. *Federal Indian Policy*. Chelsea House, 1989. *(I; A)*

McClard, Megan, and Ypsilantis, George. *Hiawatha and the Iroquois League*. Silver Burdett, 1989. *(I)*

Osinski, Alice. *The Sioux*. Children's, 1984. *(P)*

Paterson, E. Palmer. *Indian Peoples of Canada*. Watts, 1982. *(I; A)*

Poatgieter, Hermina. *Indian Legacy: Native American Influences on World Life and Culture*. Messner, 1981. *(I; A)*

Purdy, Susan, and Sandak, Cass R. *North American Indians*. Watts, 1982. *(P; I)*

Robinson, Gail. *Raven the Trickster: Legends of North American Indians*. Atheneum, 1982. *(I)*

Shorto, Russell. *Tecumseh and the Dream of an American Indian Nation*. Silver Burdett, 1989. *(I)*

Sneve, Virginia Driving Hawk. *Dancing Teepees: Poems of American Indian Youth*. Holiday, 1989. *(P; I; A)*

Watson, Jane W. *The First Americans: Tribes of North America*. Pantheon, 1980. *(P)*

Weinstein-Farson, Laurie. *The Wampanoag*. Chelsea House, 1988. *(A)*

Weiss, Malcolm E. *Sky Watchers of Ages Past*. HM, 1982. *(I; A)*

Wheeler, M. J. *First Came the Indians*. Atheneum, 1983. *(P; I)*

Wilson, Terry P. *The Osage*. Chelsea House, 1988. *(A)*

Yue, Charlotte. *The Tipi: A Center of Native American Life*. Knopf, 1984. *(I)*

INDIAN WARS

Baldwin, Gordon C. *The Apache Indians: Raiders of the Southwest*. Scholastic, 1978. *(I; A)*

Black, Sheila. *Sitting Bull and the Battle of the Little Bighorn*. Silver Burdett, 1989. *(I)*

Brown, Dee. *Wounded Knee: An Indian History of the American West*. HR&W, 1974. *(I; A)*

Halliburton, Warren J. *The Tragedy of Little Bighorn*. Watts, 1989. *(P; I)*

Marrin, Albert. *War Clouds in the West: Indians & Cavalrymen 1860-1890*. Atheneum, 1984. *(A)*

McGaw, Jessie B. *Chief Red Horse Tells About Custer*. Lodestar, 1981. *(P; I)*

Mitchell, Barbara. *Tomahawks and Trombones*. Carolrhoda, 1982. *(P)*

Morris, Richard B. *The Indian Wars*. Lerner, 1986 (rev. ed.). *(I; A)*

INDONESIA. See SOUTHEAST ASIA.

INDUSTRY

Burne, Gordon. *Tools and Manufacturing*. Watts, 1984. *(I)*

Claypool, Jane. *Manufacturing*. Watts, 1984. *(I; A)*

Grigoli, Valorie. *Service Industries*. Watts, 1984. *(I)*

Sherwood, Martin. *Industry*. Watts, 1984. *(I)*

Vialls, Christine. *The Industrial Revolution Begins*. Lerner, 1982. *(I; A)*

INSECTS

The World In Your Backyard: And Other Stories of Insects and Spiders. Zaner-Bloser, 1989. *(P; I)*

Cole, Joanna. *An Insect's Body*. Morrow, 1984. *(P)*

dos Santos, Joyce A. *Giants of Smaller Worlds Drawn in Their Natural Sizes*. Dodd, 1983. *(P)*

Goor, Ron, and Goor, Nancy. *Insect Metamorphosis: From Egg to Adult*. Atheneum, 1990. *(P)*

Graham, Ada, and Graham, Frank. *Busy Bugs*. Dodd, 1983. *(I)*

Johnson, Sylvia. *Water Insects*. Lerner, 1989. *(P; I)*

Lavies, Bianca. *Backyard Hunter: The Praying Mantis*. Dutton, 1990. *(I)*

Milne, Lorus J., and Milne, Margery. *Nature's Clean-Up Crew: The Burying Beetles*. Dodd, 1982. *(I; A)*

Penn, Linda. *Young Scientists Explore Insects*. Good Apple, 1982. *(P)*

Podendorf, Illa. *Insects*. Children's, 1981. *(P)*

Selsam, Millicent E. *Where Do They Go? Insects in Winter*. Scholastic, 1982. *(P)*

Selsam, Millicent E., and Goor, Ronald, *Backyard Insects*. Scholastic, 1983. *(P)*

Shepherd, Elizabeth, *No Bones: A Key to Bugs & Slugs, Worms & Ticks, Spiders & Centipedes, & Other Creepy Crawlies*. Macmillan/Collier, 1988. *(P; I)*

INSURANCE

Van Gelder, Patricia. *Careers in the Insurance Industry*. Watts, 1978. *(A)*

INTERIOR DECORATING

Greer, Michael. *Your Future in Interior Design*. Rosen Group, 1980. *(I; A)*

James, Elizabeth, and Barkin, Carol. *A Place of Your Own*. Dutton, 1981. *(A)*

INTERNATIONAL RELATIONS

Goode, Stephen. *The Foreign Policy Debate: Human Rights in American Foreign Policy*. Watts, 1984. *(I; A)*

Hart, William B. *The United States and World Trade*. Watts, 1985. *(A)*

Wibberley, Leonard. *The Mouse That Roared*. Bantam, 1971. *(I; A)* (Fiction)

Woody, D. W. *The Kids of Mischief Island*. Carlton, 1981. *(I; A)* (Fiction)

INVENTIONS

Aaseng, Nathan. *The Unsung Heroes: Unheralded People Who Invented Famous Products*. Lerner, 1989. *(I)*

Benjamin, Alan. *One Thousand Inventions*. Scholastic, 1980. *(P)*

Klein, Aaron E., and Klein, Cynthia L. *The Better Mousetrap: A Miscellany of Gadgets, Labor-Saving Devices, and Inventions That Intrigue*. Beaufort NY, 1983. *(I; A)*

Richards, Norman. *Dreamers and Doers: Inventors Who Changed the World*. Atheneum, 1984. *(I; A)*

Weiss, Harvey. *How to Be an Inventor*. Har-Row, 1980. *(I; A)*

IOWA

Carpenter, Allan. *Iowa*. Childrens, 1979. *(I)*

Fradin, Dennis. *Iowa: In Words and Pictures*. Childrens, 1980. *(P; I)*

IRAN

Iran . . . in Pictures. Lerner, 1989. *(I; A)*

Mannetti, Lisa. *Iran and Iraq: Nations at War*. Watts, 1986. *(I; A)*

Sanders, Renfield. *Iran*. Chelsea House, 1990. *(I; A)*

IRAQ

Docherty, J. P. *Iraq*. Chelsea House, 1988. *(P)*

Mannetti, Lisa. *Iran and Iraq: Nations at War*. Watts, 1986. *(I; A)*

IRELAND

Cullen, L. M. *Life in Ireland*. David & Charles, 1979. *(I; A)*

James, Ian. *Take a Trip to Ireland*. Watts, 1984. *(P)*

Langford, Sondra G. *Red Bird of Ireland*. Atheneum, 1983. *(I; A)*

Meyer, Kathleen A. *Ireland: Land of Mist and Magic*. Dillon, 1983. *(I; A)*

Ryan, Joan, and Snell, Gordon, eds. *Land of Tales: Stories of Ireland for Children*. Dufour, 1983. *(P; I)*

IRON AND STEEL

Cherry, Mike. *Steel Beams and Iron Men*. Scholastic, 1980. *(I; A)*

Harter, Walter. *Steel: The Metal with Muscle*. Messner, 1981. *(P; I)*

Lambert, Mark. *Spotlight on Iron and Steel*. Rourke, 1988. *(P; I)*

Thompson, Brenda, and Giesen, Rosemary. *The Story of Steel*. Lerner, 1977. *(P)*

IRRIGATION. See DAMS.

IRVING, WASHINGTON

Irving, Washington. *Rip Van Winkle, the Legend of Sleepy Hollow, and Other Tales*. Putnam, n.d. *(I; A)*

ISLAM. See RELIGIONS OF THE WORLD.

ISLANDS

Rydell, Wendy. *All About Islands*. Troll, 1984. *(P; I)*

See also CARIBBEAN SEA AND ISLANDS; PACIFIC OCEAN AND ISLANDS.

ISRAEL

Ashabranner, Brent. *Gavriel and Jemal: Two Boys of Jerusalem*. Dodd, 1984. *(I)*

Burstein, Chaya M. *A Kid's Catalog of Israel*. Jewish Publication Society, 1988. *(I; A)*

Davidson, Margaret. *The Golda Meir Story*. Scribner, 1976. *(I)*

Feinstein, Steve. *Israel . . . in Pictures*. Lerner, 1988. *(P; I)*

Jones, Helen Hinckley. *Israel*. Children's, 1986. *(P)*

Kuskin, Karla. *Jerusalem, Shining Still*. Harper/Charlotte Zolotow, 1987. *(P)*

Lawton, Clive A. *Israel*. Watts, 1988. *(P; I)*

Levine, Gemma. *We Live in Israel*. Watts, 1984. *(I; A)*

Rachloff, Owen S. *Young Israel: A History of the Modern Nation the First 20 Years*. Lion, 1981. *(I; A)*

Rutland, Jonathan. *Take a Trip to Israel*. Watts, 1981. *(P)*

Taitz, Emily, and Henry, Sondra. *Israel: A Sacred Land*. Dillon, 1987. *(P; I)*

Taylor, Allegra. *A Kibbutz in Israel*. Lerner, 1987. *(P)*

Williams, Lorna, and Bergman, Denise. *Through the Year in Israel*. David & Charles, 1983. *(I; A)*

Worth, Richard. *Israel and the Arab States*. Watts, 1983. *(I; A)*

Zagoren, Ruby. *Chaim Weizmann: First President of Israel*. Garrard, 1972. *(I; A)*

ITALY

de Zulueta, Tana. *We Live in Italy*. Watts, 1984. *(I; A)*

DiFranco, Anthony. *Italy: Balanced on the Edge of Time*. Dillon, 1983. *(I; A)*

Fairclough, Chris. *Take a Trip to Italy*. Watts, 1981. *(P)*

Goldstein, Frances. *Children's Treasure Hunt Travel Guide to Italy*. Paper Tiger Pap, 1980. *(P; I)*

James, Ian. *Inside Italy*. Watts, 1988. *(P; I)*

Mariella, Cinzia. *Passport to Italy*. Watts, 1986. *(P)*

Powell. *Renaissance Italy*. Watts, 1980. *(I; A)*

Stein, R. Conrad. *Italy*. Children's, 1984. *(I; A)*

Ventura, Piero. *Venice: Birth of a City*. Putnam, 1988. *(I; A)*

IVES, CHARLES

Sive, Helen R. *Music's Connecticut Yankee: An Introduction to the Life and Music of Charles Ives*. Atheneum, 1977. *(I; A)*

IVORY COAST

Cote d'Ivoire . . . in Pictures. Lerner, 1988. *(I; A)*

JACKSON, ANDREW

Osinski, Alice. *Andrew Jackson: Seventh President of the United States*. Childrens, 1987. *(I)*

Remini, Robert V. *The Revolutionary Age of Andrew Jackson*. Har-Row, 1976. *(I)*

Stefoff, Rebecca. *Andrew Jackson, 7th President of the United States*. Garrett Educational Corp., 1988. *(A)*

See also PRESIDENCY OF THE UNITED STATES.

JACKSON, THOMAS JONATHAN (STONEWALL)

Fritz, Jean. *Stonewall*. Putnam, 1979. *(I; A)*

Harrison, and others. *Stonewall Jackson*. Dormac, 1981. *(P; I; A)*

JAMAICA. See CARIBBEAN SEA AND ISLANDS.

JAMESTOWN. See AMERICAN COLONIES.

JAPAN

Japan . . . in Pictures. Lerner, 1989. *(I)*

Ashby, Gwynneth. *Take a Trip to Japan*. Watts, 1981. *(P)*

Davidson, Judith. *Japan: Where East Meets West*. Dillon, 1983. *(I)*

Dolan, Edward F., Jr., and Finney, Shan. *The New Japan*. Har-Row, 1983. *(A)*

Jacobsen, Karen. *Japan*. Childrens, 1982. *(P)*

Kawamata, Kazuhide. *We Live in Japan*. Watts, 1984. *(I; A)*

Meyer, Carolyn. *A Voice From Japan: An Outsider Looks In*. HRJ/Gulliver, 1988, *(I; A)*

Pitts, Forrest R. *Japan*. Gateway Press, 1988. *(I; A)*

Robertson, John R. *From Shogun to Sony*. Atheneum, 1985. *(A)*

Spry-Leverton, Peter, and Kornicki, Peter. *Japan*. Facts On File, 1987. *(A)*

Stefoff, Rebecca. *Japan*. Chelsea House, 1988. *(P; I)*

Tames, Richard. *Japan in the Twentieth Century*. David & Charles, 1981. *(A); Passport to Japan*. Watts, 1988. *(I)*

JAZZ

Griffin, Clive D. *Jazz*. Batsford, dist. by David & Charles, 1989. *(I; A)*

Hughes, Langston. *The First Book of Jazz*. Watts, 1982 (rev. ed.). *(I)*

Iverson, Genie. *Louis Armstrong*. Har-Row, 1976. *(P)*

Jones, Max. *Talking Jazz*. Norton, 1988. *(A)*

Kliment, Bud. *Ella Fitzgerald*. Chelsea House, 1988. *(A)*

Montgomery, Elizabeth R. *Duke Ellington: King of Jazz*. Garrard, 1972. *(P; I)*

Terkel, Studs. *Giants of Jazz*. Har-Row, 1975 (rev. ed.). *(I; A)*

JEFFERSON, THOMAS

Adler, David A. *A Picture Book of Thomas Jefferson*. Holiday, 1990. *(P); Thomas Jefferson: Father of Our Democracy*. Holiday House, 1987. *(P)*

Bober, Natalie S. *Thomas Jefferson: Man on a Mountain*. Atheneum, 1988. *(A)*

Fisher, Leonard Everett. *Monticello*. Holiday, 1988. *(I)*

Hargrove, Jim. *Thomas Jefferson: Third President of the United States*. (Encyclopedia of presidents) Childrens, 1986. *(P; I)*

Milton, Joyce. *The Story of Thomas Jefferson: Prophet of Liberty*. Dell, 1990. *(I; A)*

Sabin, Francene. *Young Thomas Jefferson*. (Easy Biography Series) Troll, 1986. *(P; I)*

See also PRESIDENCY OF THE UNITED STATES; DECLARATION OF INDEPENDENCE; FOUNDERS OF THE UNITED STATES.

JELLYFISHES AND OTHER COELENTERATES

MacQuitty, Miranda. *Discovering Jellyfish*. Bookwright, dist. by Watts, 1989. *(P)*

JENNER, EDWARD. See DISEASES.

JERUSALEM. See ISRAEL.

JESUS CHRIST

Bennett, Marian. *Jesus, God's Son*. Standard, 1982. *(P)*

Collins, David R. *The Wonderful Story of Jesus*. Concordia, 1980. *(P; I)*

Nystrom, Carolyn. *Jesus Is No Secret*. Moody, 1983. *(P; I); Who Is Jesus?* 1980. *(P)*

Petersham, Maud, and Petersham, Miska. *Christ Child*. Doubleday, 1931. *(P; I)*

Sherlock, Connie. *Life of Jesus*. Standard, 1983. *(P; I)*

Storr, Catherine, and Lindvall, Ella K. *The Birth of Jesus*. Moody, 1983 (rev. ed.); *Jesus Begins His Work*, 1983 (rev. ed.). *(P; I)*

JET PROPULSION

Moxon, Julian. *How Jet Engines Are Made*. Facts on File, 1985. *(P; I)*

JEWS AND JUDAISM

Brownstone, David M. *The Jewish-American Heritage*. Facts on File, 1988. *(I; A)*

Chaikin, Miriam. *Sound the Shofar: The Story and Meaning of Rosh Hashanah and Yom Kippur*. Clarion, 1986. *(I; A)*

Costabel, Eva D. *The Jews of New Amsterdam*. Atheneum, 1988. *(P; I)*

Domnitz, Myer. *Judaism*. Watts/Bookwright Press, 1987. *(I; A)*

Finkelstein, Norman A. *The Other 1492: Jewish Settlement in the New World*. Scribner's, 1989. *(I; A)*

Freeman, Joan G., and Freeman, Grace R. *Inside the Synagogue*. UAHC, 1984. *(P)*

Geffner, Anne. *A Child Celebrates: The Jewish Holidays*. Double M Pr, 1980 (rev. 2nd ed.). *(P; I)*

Greenberg, Judith E., and Carey, Helen H. *Jewish Holidays*. Watts, 1985. *(P; I)*

Klaperman, Gilbert, and Klaperman, Libby. *The Story of the Jewish People*, 4 vols. Behrman, 1974. *(I; A)*

Meltzer, Milton. *Taking Root: Jewish Immigrants in America*. FS&G, 1976; *World of Our Fathers: The Jews of Eastern Europe*, 1974. *(I; A)*

Metter, Bert. *Bar Mitzvah, Bat Mitzvah: How Jewish Boys and Girls Come of Age*. HM, 1984. *(I)*

Muggamin, Howard. *The Jewish Americans*. Chelsea House, 1988. *(I; A)*

Rossel, Seymour. *Journey Through Jewish History*, Vol. 1. Behrman, 1981. *(P; I)*

Shamir, Ilana, and Shavit, Shlomo. *The Young Reader's Encyclopedia of Jewish History*. Viking, 1987. *(P; I)*

Swartz, Sarah Silberstein. *Bar Mitzvah*. Doubleday, 1985. *(I; A)*

Turner, Reuben. *Jewish Festivals*. Rourke, 1987. *(P; I)*

See also HANUKKAH; HOLOCAUST; PASSOVER; PURIM.

JOAN OF ARC, SAINT

Boutet de Monvel, Maurice. *Joan of Arc*. Viking, 1980. *(I)*

Brooks, Polly Schoyer. *Beyond the Myth: The Story of Joan of Arc*. Lippincott, 1990. *(A)*

Ready, Dolores. *Joan, the Brave Soldier: Joan of Arc*. Winston, 1977. *(P; I)*

JOGGING AND RUNNING. See TRACK AND FIELD.

JOHNSON, ANDREW

Kent, Zachary. *Andrew Johnson*. Childrens, 1989. *(P; I)*

Paley, Alan L. *Andrew Johnson: The President Impeached*. SamHar, 1972. *(I; A)*

Stevens, Rita. *Andrew Johnson: 17th President of the United States*. Garrett Educational Corp., 1989. *(I)*

See also PRESIDENCY OF THE UNITED STATES.

JOHNSON, JAMES WELDON

Egypt, Ophelia Settle. *James Weldon Johnson*. Har-Row, 1974. *(P)*

JOHNSON, LYNDON BAINES

Barton, Thomas F. *Lyndon B. Johnson: Young Texan*. Bobbs, 1973. *(P; I)*

Devaney, John. *Lyndon Baines Johnson, President*. Walker, Aug. 1986. *(I; A)*

Falkof, Lucille. *Lyndon B. Johnson: 36th President of the United States*. Garrett Educational Corp., 1989. *(I)*

Hargrove, Jim. *Lyndon B. Johnson*. Children's, 1988. *(P; I)*

Kaye, Tony. *Lyndon B. Johnson*. Chelsea House, 1988. *(I; A)*

See also PRESIDENCY OF THE UNITED STATES.

JOKES AND RIDDLES. See HUMOR.

JOLLIET, LOUIS, AND MARQUETTE, JACQUES

Stein, R. Conrad. *The Story of Marquette and Jolliet*. Childrens, 1981. *(P; I)*

JORDAN

Jordan . . . in Pictures. Lerner, 1988. *(I)*

Whitehead, Susan. *Jordan*. Chelsea House, 1988. *(P)*

JOURNALISM. See NEWSPAPERS.

JUDO AND KARATE

Atkinson, Linda. *Women in the Martial Arts: A New Spirit Rising*. Dodd, 1983. *(I; A)*

Brimner, Larry Dane. *Karate*. Watts, 1988. *(P; I)*

James, Stuart. *The Complete Beginner's Guide to Judo*. Doubleday, 1978. *(I; A)*

Parulski, George R., Jr. *Karate Power!: Learning the Art of the Empty Hand*. Contemporary Bks., 1985. *(P)*

Queen, J. Allen. *Karate to Win*. Sterling, 1988. *(I; A)*

Ribner, Susan, and Chin, Richard. *The Martial Arts*. Har-Row, 1978. *(A)*

JUNGLES

Forsyth, Andrian. *Journey Through a Tropical Jungle*. S. & S., 1989. *(P; I)*
Norden, Carroll R. *The Jungle*. Raintree, 1978. *(P)*
Pepe, Joyce. *A Closer Look at Jungles*. Watts, 1978. *(I)*
Rowland-Entwistle, Theodore. *Jungles and Rain Forests*. Silver Burdett, 1987. *(P)*

JURY. See LAW AND LAW ENFORCEMENT.

JUVENILE CRIME

Dolan, Edward F., Jr., and Finney, Shan. *Youth Gangs*. Messner, 1984. *(I; A)*
Hyde, Margaret O. *Juvenile Justice and Injustice*. Watts, 1983 (rev. ed.). *(I; A)*
LeShan, Eda. *The Roots of Crime: What You Need to Know About Crime and What You Can Do About It*. Scholastic, 1981. *(I; A)*
Riekes, Linda, and Ackerly, Sally M. *Juvenile Problems and Law*. West Pub, 1980 (2nd ed.). *(P; I)*
Shanks, Ann Z. *Busted Lives: Dialogues with Kids in Jail*. Delacorte, 1982. *(I; A)*

KAMPUCHEA (CAMBODIA). See SOUTHEAST ASIA.

KANGAROOS AND OTHER POUCHED MAMMALS

Arnold, Caroline. *Kangaroo*. Morrow, 1987. *(P)*
Eugene, Toni. *Koalas and Kangaroos: Strange Animals of Australia*. National Geog, 1981. *(P)*
Glendenning, Sally. *Little Blue and Rusty: Red Kangaroos*. Garrard, 1980. *(P)*
Hogan, Paula Z. *The Kangaroo*. Raintree, 1979. *(P)*
Lavine, Sigmund A. *Wonders of Marsupials*. Dodd, 1979. *(I)*
Rue, Leonard Lee, and Owen, William. *Meet the Opossum*. Dodd, 1983. *(P; I)*
Sherman, Geraldine. *Animals with Pouches: The Marsupials*. Holiday, 1978. *(P)*

KANSAS

Carpenter, Allan. *Kansas*. Childrens, 1979. *(I)*
Desmond, J. *Kansas Boy*. Roush Bks, 1979. *(I; A)*
Fradin, Dennis. *Kansas: In Words and Pictures*. Childrens, 1980. *(P; I)*
Wilder, Laura Ingalls. *Little House on the Prairie*. Har-Row, 1953. (Fiction) *(I)*

KARATE. See JUDO AND KARATE.

KARTING

Fichter, George S. *Karts and Karting*. Watts, 1982. *(P; I; A)*

Leonard, Jerry. *Kart Racing*. Messner, 1980. *(I; A)*
Radlauer, Ed. *Karting Winners*. Childrens, 1982. *(P; I)*

KASHMIR. See INDIA.

KELLER, HELEN

Keller, Helen. *The Story of My Life*. Scholastic, 1973. *(I; A)*
Peare, Catherine Owens. *The Helen Keller Story*. Har-Row, 1959. *(I; A)*
Sabin, Francene. *The Courage of Helen Keller*. Troll, 1982. *(P; I)*
Wepman, Dennis. *Helen Keller*. (American Women of Achievement) Chelsea House, 1987. *(I; A)*
Wilkie, Katherine E. *Helen Keller: From Tragedy to Triumph*. Bobbs, 1983. *(P; I)*

KENNEDY, JOHN F.

Denenberg, Barry. *John Fitzgerald Kennedy: America's 35th President*. Scholastic, 1988. *(I)*
Donnelly, Judy. *Who Shot the President? The Death of John F. Kennedy*. Random, 1988. *(P)*
Falkof, Lucille. *John F. Kennedy: 35th President of the United States*. Garrett, 1988. *(A)*
Frisbee, Lucy P. *John F. Kennedy: America's Youngest President*. Bobbs, 1983. *(P; I)*
Frolick, S. J. *Once There Was a President*. Black Star, 1980. *(P; I)*
Kent, Zachary. *John F. Kennedy: Thirty-fifth President of the United States*. Children's, 1987. *(P; I)*
Mills, Judie. *John F. Kennedy*. Watts, 1988. *(A)*
Waggoner, Jeffrey. *The Assassination of President Kennedy*. Greenhaven, 1990. *(I; A)*
See also PRESIDENCY OF THE UNITED STATES.

KENTUCKY

Fradin, Dennis. *Kentucky: In Words and Pictures*. Children's, 1981. *(P; I)*
McNair, Sylvia. *Kentucky*. Children's, 1988. *(P; I)*
Stuart, Jesse. *The Thread That Runs So True*. Scribner, 1958. *(I; A)*

KENYA

Kenya . . . in Pictures. Lerner, 1988. (I; A)
Khalfan, Zulf M., and Amin, Mohamed. *We Live in Kenya*. Watts, 1984. *(I; A)*
Maren, Michael. *The Land and People of Kenya*. Lippincott, 1989. *(I; A)*
Winslow, Zachary. *Kenya*. Chelsea House, 1987. *(A)*

KEYBOARD INSTRUMENTS. See MUSICAL INSTRUMENTS.

KIDD, CAPTAIN WILLIAM. See PIRATES AND PIRACY.

KING, MARTIN LUTHER, JR.

Adler, David A. *Martin Luther King, Jr.: Free at Last.* Holiday, 1987. *(P; I)*

Behrens, June. *Martin Luther King, Jr.* Children's, 1979. *(P)*

Faber, Doris, and Faber, Harold. *Martin Luther King, Jr.* Messner, 1986. *(P; I)*

Harris, Jacqueline. *Martin Luther King, Jr.* Watts, 1983. *(I; A)*

King, Martin Luther, Jr. *Why We Can't Wait.* Har-Row, 1964. *(A)*

Patterson, Lillie. *Martin Luther King, Jr. and the Freedom Movement.* Facts on File, 1989. *(I; A)*

Quayle, Louise. *Martin Luther King, Jr.: Dreams for a Nation.* Fawcett, 1990. *(I)*

Richardson, Nigel. *Martin Luther King, Jr.* David & Charles, 1983. *(P; I)*

Schloredt, Valerie. *Martin Luther King, Jr.: America's Great Nonviolent Leader in the Struggle for Human Rights.* Gareth Stevens, 1988. *(I)*

Thompson, Marguerite. *Martin Luther King, Jr.: A Story for Children.* Gaus, 1983. *(P; I)*

KIPLING, RUDYARD

Kamen, Gloria. *Kipling: Storyteller of East and West.* Atheneum, 1985. *(P; I)*

Kipling, Rudyard. *The Jungle Book.* Doubleday, 1981. *(I); Just So Stories.* Rand, 1982. *(P; I)* (Other publishers of both books and of other Kipling titles)

KIRIBATI. See Pacific Ocean and Islands.

KITES

Marks, Burton, and Marks, Rita. *Kites for Kids.* Lothrop, 1980. *(P; I)*

Moran, Tom. *Kite Flying Is for Me.* Lerner, 1983. *(P; I)*

Newnham, Jack. *Kites to Make and Fly.* Penguin, 1982. *(P; I)*

Nicklaus, Carol. *Flying, Gliding, and Whirling: Making Things That Fly.* Watts, 1981. *(P)*

KNIGHTS, KNIGHTHOOD, AND CHIVALRY

Gibson, Michael, and Pike, Tricia. *All About Knights.* EMC, 1982. *(P; I; A)*

Lasker, Joe. *A Tournament of Knights.* Crowell, Sept. 1986. *(I)*

Pyle, Howard. *Men of Iron.* Har-Row, 1930. *(A)*

See also Middle Ages.

KNITTING AND CROCHETING. See Sewing and Needlecraft.

KOREA

Ashby, Gwynneth. *A Family in South Korea.* Lerner, 1987. *(P)*

Farley, Carol. *Korea: A Land Divided.* Dillon, 1983. *(I; A)*

Shepheard, Patricia. *South Korea.* Chelsea House, 1988. *(P)*

So-un, Kim. *The Story Bag: A Collection of Korean Folk Tales.* Tuttle, 1955. *(I)*

KOREAN WAR

Fincher, E. B. *The War in Korea.* Watts, 1981. *(I; A)*

KUWAIT. See Middle East

KYOTO. See Japan.

LABOR

Claypool, Jane. *The Worker in America.* Watts, 1985. *(A)*

Lens, Sidney. *Strikemakers & Strikebreakers.* Lodestar, 1985. *(A)*

Meltzer, Milton. *Bread and Roses: The Struggle of American Labor, 1865–1915.* NAL, 1977. *(I; A)*

Morgen, Linda. *Heroes of American Labor.* Fleet, n.d. *(I; A)*

Morton, Desmond. *Labour in Canada.* Watts, 1982. *(I; A)*

Scott, Geoffrey, *Labor Day.* Carolrhoda, 1982. *(P)*

LAFAYETTE, MARQUIS DE. See Revolutionary War.

LAFITTE, JEAN. See Louisiana; Pirates and Piracy.

LAKES. See Rivers and Lakes.

LANGUAGES (Origin, History, and Usage)

Ashton, Christian. *Words Can Tell: A Book About Our Language.* Messner, 1989. *(P; I; A)*

Laird, Helen, and Laird, Charlton. *The Tree of Language.* World, 1977. *(I)*

Ludovici, L. J. *Origins of Language.* Putnam, 1965. *(I)*

LANGUAGES (Foreign Language Studies)

Colyer, Penrose. *I Can Read French.* Watts, 1981; *I Can Read Italian*, 1983; *I Can Read Spanish*, 1981. *(P; I)*

Cooper, Lee, and McIntosh, Clifton. *Fun with French.* Little, 1963; *Fun With German*, 1965; *Fun with Spanish*, 1960; *More Fun with Spanish*, 1967. *(I)*

Hautzig, Esther. *At Home: A Visit in Four Languages.* Macmillan, 1968. *(P)*

Woff, Diane. *Chinese Writing: An Introduction.* HR&W, 1975. *(I)*

LAOS. See Southeast Asia.

LAPLAND

Hagbrink, Bodil. *Children of Lapland.* Tundra, 1979. *(P; I)*

LA SALLE, ROBERT CAVELIER, SIEUR DE. See Jolliet, Louis, and Marquette, Jacques; Mississippi River.

LASERS

Bender, Lionel. *Lasers in Action.* Watts/Bookwright Pr., 1985. *(I; A)*

De Vere, Charles. *Lasers.* Watts, 1984. *(P; I)*

Filson, Brent. *Exploring with Lasers.* Messner, 1984. *(I; A)*

French, P. M. W., and Taylor, J. W. *How Lasers Are Made.* Facts on File, 1987. *(A)*

LATIN AMERICA

Pascoe, Elaine. *Neighbors at Odds: U.S. Policy in Latin America.* Watts, 1990. *(I; A)*

See also individual countries.

LAVOISIER, ANTOINE LAURENT

Grey, Vivian. *The Chemist Who Lost His Head: The Story of Antoine Laurent Lavoisier.* Putnam, 1982. *(I)*

LAW AND LAW ENFORCEMENT

Arnold, Caroline. *Why Do We Have Rules?* Watts, 1983. *(P)*

Atkinson, Linda. *Your Legal Rights.* Watts, 1982. *(I; A)*

Fincher, E. B. *The American Legal System.* Watts, 1980. *(I; A)*

Hyde, Margaret O. *The Rights of the Victim.* Watts, 1983. *(I; A)*

Smith, Elizabeth Simpson. *Breakthrough: Women in Law Enforcement.* Walker, 1982. *(I; A)*

Stern, Ron. *Law Enforcement Careers: A Complete Guide from Application to Employment.* Lawman Press; dist. by Quality Books, 1988. *(A)*

Weiss, Ann E. *The Supreme Court.* Enslow, 1986. *(A)*

Zerman, Melvyn B. *Beyond a Reasonable Doubt: Inside the American Jury System.* Har-Row, 1981. *(I; A)*

See also Police.

LAWYERS

Fry, William R., and Hoopes, Roy. *Legal Careers and the Legal System.* Enslow, 1988. *(A)*

Heath, Charles D. *Your Future as a Legal Assistant.* Rosen, 1982 (rev. ed.). *(I; A)*

LEAVES

Kirkpatrick, Rena K. *Look at Leaves.* Raintree, 1978. *(P)*

Selsam, Millicent E., and Hunt, Joyce, eds. *A First Look at Leaves.* Walker, 1972. *(P)*

Testa, Fulvio. *Leaves.* P. Bedrick, 1983. *(I)*

LEBANON

Lebanon . . . in Pictures. Lerner, 1988. *(I)*

Shapiro, William. *Lebanon.* Watts, 1984. *(I; A)*

LEE, ROBERT E.

Commager, Henry Steele, and Ward, Lynd. *America's Robert E. Lee.* HM, n.d. *(I)*

Monsell, Helen A. *Robert E. Lee: Young Confederate.* Bobbs, 1983. *(P; I)*

Weidhorn, Manfred. *Robert E. Lee.* Atheneum, 1988. *(I; A)*

See also Civil War.

LEGENDS. See Folklore and Fairy Tales.

LENIN

Rawcliffe, Michael. *Lenin.* Batsford, dist. by David & Charles, 1989. *(I; A)*

Resnick, Abraham. *Lenin: Founder of the Soviet Union.* Childrens, 1988. *(I)*

Topalian, Elyse. *V. I. Lenin.* Watts, 1983. *(I; A)*

See also Union of Soviet Socialist Republics.

LENSES

Brindze, Ruth. *Look How Many People Wear Glasses: The Magic of Lenses.* Atheneum, 1975. *(I)*

Goodsell, Jane. *Katie's Magic Glasses.* Houghton, 1978. *(P)*

LEONARDO DA VINCI

Cooper, Margaret. *The Inventions of Leonardo da Vinci.* Macmillan, 1968. *(I)*

Konigsburg, E. L. *The Second Mrs. Giaconda.* Atheneum, 1975. (Fiction) *(I)*

LESOTHO. See Africa.

LETTER WRITING

Dettmer, M. L. *Bag of Letters.* Western, 1977. *(I; A)*

Mischel, Florence D. *How to Write a Letter.* Watts, 1988. *(I)*

LEWIS AND CLARK EXPEDITION

Blumberg, Rhoda. *The Incredible Journey of Lewis & Clark.* Lothrop, 1987. *(P; I)*

McGrath, Patrick. *The Lewis and Clark Expedition.* Silver Burdett, 1985. *(I; A)*

LIBERIA

Hope, Constance Morris. *Liberia.* Chelsea House, 1987. *(A)*

Sullivan, Jo M. *Liberia . . . in Pictures.* Lerner, 1988. *(P; I)*

LIBERTY, STATUE OF

Burchard, Sue. *The Statue of Liberty: Birth to Rebirth.* HarBraceJ, 1985. *(I)*

Fisher, Leonard Everett. *The Statue of Liberty.* Holiday, 1985. *(P; I)*

Shapiro, Mary J. *How They Built the Statue of Liberty.* Random House, 1985. *(I)*

LIBERTY BELL

Boland, Charles M. *Ring in the Jubilee: The Story of America's Liberty Bell.* Chatham, 1973. *(I; A)*

LIBRARIES

Anders, Rebecca. *Careers in a Library.* Lerner, 1978. *(P; I)*

Cleary, Florence D. *Discovering Books and Libraries.* Wilson, 1977 (2nd ed.). *(I; A)*

Hardendorff, Jeanne B. *Libraries and How to Use Them.* Watts, 1979. *(P; I; A)*

Schurr, Sandra. *Library Lingo.* Incentive Pubns, 1981. *(P; I)*

Shapiro, Lillian L. *Teaching Yourself in Libraries.* Wilson, 1978. *(I; A)*

LIBYA

Brill, Marlene Targ. *Libya.* Children's, 1988. *(P; I)*

Sanders, Renfield. *Libya.* Chelsea House, 1987. *(A)*

LIES

Bawden, Nina. *Kept in the Dark.* Lothrop, 1982. *(I)*

Elliot, Dan. *Ernie's Little Lie.* Random, 1983. *(P)*

Moncure, Jane B. *Honesty.* Childs World, 1981 (rev. ed.); *John's Choice,* 1983. *(P; I)*

Ruby, Lois. *Two Truths in My Pocket.* Viking, 1982. *(I; A)*

Yep, Laurence. *Liar, Liar.* Morrow, 1983. *(I; A)*

LIGHT

Burkig, Valerie. *Photonics: The New Science of Light.* Enslow, 1986. *(A)*

Crews, Donald. *Light.* Greenwillow, 1981. *(P; I)*

Goor, Ron, and Goor, Nancy. *Shadows: Here, There, and Everywhere.* Har-Row, 1981. *(I)*

Hecht, Jeff. *Optics: Light for a New Age.* Scribner, 1988. *(A)*

Stuart, Gene S. *Hidden Worlds.* National Geog, 1981. *(P; I)*

Watson, Philip. *Light Fantastic.* Lothrop, 1983. *(P; I)*

White, Jack R. *The Invisible World of the Infrared.* Dodd, 1984. *(I)*

LIMA. See PERU.

LINCOLN, ABRAHAM

Adler, David A. *A Picture Book of Abraham Lincoln.* Holiday, 1989. *(P)*

Brandt, Keith. *Abe Lincoln: The Young Years.* Troll, 1982. *(P; I)*

Coolidge, Olivia. *The Apprenticeship of Abraham Lincoln.* Scribner, 1974. *(I; A)*

D'Aulaire, Ingri, and D'Aulaire, Edgar P. *Abraham Lincoln.* Doubleday, 1957 (rev. ed.). *(P)*

Freedman, Russell. *Lincoln, A Photobiography.* Clarion, 1987. *(P; I; A)*

Gross, Ruth Belov. *True Stories About Abraham Lincoln.* Lothrop, 1990. *(P)*

Hargrove, Jim. *Abraham Lincoln.* Childrens, 1988. *(I)*

Phelan, Mary Kay. *Mr. Lincoln's Inaugural Journey.* Har-Row, 1972. *(I)*

Sandburg, Carl. *Abe Lincoln Grows Up.* HarBraceJ, 1975. *(I)*

Stefoff, Rebecca. *Abraham Lincoln: 16th President of the United States.* Garrett Educational Corp., 1989. *(I)*

Stevenson, Augusta. *Abraham Lincoln: The Great Emancipator.* Bobbs, 1983. *(P; I)*

See also PRESIDENCY OF THE UNITED STATES.

LINCOLN-DOUGLAS DEBATES. See LINCOLN, ABRAHAM.

LINDBERGH, CHARLES

Collins, David R. *Charles Lindbergh: Hero Pilot.* Garrard, 1978. *(P; I)*

Lindbergh, Charles A. *The Spirit of St. Louis.* Scribner, 1956. *(A)*

Randolph, Blythe. *Charles Lindbergh.* Watts, 1990. *(I; A)*

LIONS AND TIGERS

Adamson, Joy. *Born Free.* Pantheon, 1960. *(A); Living Free.* HarBraceJ, 1961. *(A)*

Ashby, Ruth. *Tigers.* Atheneum, 1990. *(I)*

Lewin, Ted. *Tiger Trek.* Macmillan, 1990. *(P)*

McClung, Robert M. *Rajpur: Last of the Bengal Tigers.* Morrow, 1982. *(P; I)*

Overbeck, Cynthia. *Lions.* Lerner, 1981. *(P; I; A)*

Torgersen, Don. *Lion Prides and Tiger Marks.* Childrens, 1982. *(P; I)*

LIQUIDS. See MATTER.

LITTLE LEAGUE BASEBALL

Hale, Creighton H. *Official Little League Baseball Rules in Pictures.* Putnam, 1981. *(P; I)*

Remmers, Mary. *Ducks on the Pond: A Lexicon of Little League Lingo.* Shoal Creek Pub, 1981. *(P; I)*

Shirts, Morris. *Warm Up for Little League Baseball.* Sterling, 1976. *(P; I)*

Sullivan, George. *Baseball Kids.* Dutton, 1990. *(P; I)*

LIVESTOCK. See RANCH LIFE.

LIZARDS AND CHAMELEONS

Chace, G. Earl. *The World of Lizards*. Dodds, 1982. *(I; A)*

Schnieper, Claudia. *Chameleons*. Carolrhoda, 1989. *(P; I)*

LOBSTERS

Bailey, Jill. *Discovering Crabs and Lobsters*. Watts, 1987. *(P)*

LOCKS AND KEYS

Gibbons, Gail. *Locks and Keys*. Har-Row, 1980. *(P)*

LOCOMOTIVES. See RAILROADS.

LONDON. See ENGLAND.

LONGFELLOW, HENRY WADSWORTH

Holberg, Ruth L. *American Bard: The Story of Henry Wadsworth Longfellow*. Har-Row, 1963. *(I; A)*

Longfellow, Henry Wadsworth. *The Children's Own Longfellow*. HM, n.d. *(P; I)*; *Hiawatha*. Dial, 1983. *(P)*

LOS ANGELES. See CALIFORNIA.

LOUISIANA

Bridges, L. T. *Flags of Louisiana*. Claitors, 1971. *(I; A)*

Fradin, Dennis. *Louisiana: In Words and Pictures*. Children's, 1981. *(P; I)*

Kent, Deborah. *Louisiana*. Children's, 1988. *(P; I)*

LOUISIANA PURCHASE

Phelan, Mary K. *The Story of the Louisiana Purchase*. Har-Row, 1979. *(P; I)*

LUMBER AND LUMBERING

Abrams, Kathleen, and Abrams, Lawrence. *Logging and Lumbering*. Messner, 1980. *(P; I)*

Langley, Andres. *Timber*. (Spotlight on Resources) Rourke Enterprises, 1987. *(P; I)*

Newton, James R. *Forest Log*. Har-Row, 1980. *(P; I)*

See also FORESTS AND FORESTRY.

LUTHER, MARTIN

Fehlauer, Adolph. *The Life and Faith of Martin Luther*. Northwest Pub, 1981. *(I; A)*

O'Neill, Judith. *Martin Luther*. Lerner, 1978. *(I; A)*

MACHINES

Ackins, Ralph. *Energy Machines*. Raintree, 1980. *(P)*

Adkins, Jan. *Moving Heavy Things*. HM, 1980. *(I; A)*

Ardley, Neil. *Force and Strength*. Watts, 1985. *(P; I)*

Fenner, Sal. *Sea Machines*. Raintree, 1980. *(P)*

Gardner, Robert. *This Is The Way It Works: A Collection of Machines*. Doubleday, 1980. *(I; A)*

Horton, Casey. *The Amazing Fact Book of Machines*. A & P Bks, 1980. *(P; I)*

National Geographic editors. *How Things Work*. National Geog, 1983. *(P; I; A)*

Weiss, Harvey. *Machines and How They Work*. Har-Row, 1983. *(I)*

See also TECHNOLOGY.

MACKENZIE, SIR ALEXANDER. See EXPLORATION AND DISCOVERY.

MACRAMÉ

Bress, Helene. *The Craft of Macramé*. Scribner, 1977; *The Macramé Book*, 1972. *(I; A)*

Creative Educational Society Editors. *How to Have Fun with Macramé*. Creative Ed, 1973. *(P; I)*

La Croix, Grethe. *Beads Plus Macramé: Applying Knotting Techniques to Beadcraft*. Sterling, 1971. *(I; A)*

MADAGASCAR

Madagascar . . . in Pictures. Lerner, 1988. *(I)*

Stevens, Rita. *Madagascar*. Chelsea House, 1987. *(P; I)*

MADISON, JAMES

Leavell, J. Perry. *James Madison*. Chelsea House, 1988. *(A)*

See also PRESIDENCY OF THE UNITED STATES.

MAGELLAN, FERDINAND

Harley, Ruth. *Ferdinand Magellan*. Troll, 1979 (new ed.). *(P; I)*

Wilkie, Katherine. *Ferdinand Magellan: Noble Captain*. HM, 1963. *(P; I)*

MAGIC

Bernstein, Bob. *Monday Morning Magic*. Good Apple, 1982. *(P; I)*

Boyar, Jay. *Be a Magician! How to Put On a Magic Show and Mystify Your Friends*. Messner, 1981. *(I; A)*

Cohen, Daniel. *Real Magic*. Dodd, 1982. *(P; I)*

Dolan, Edward F. *Let's Make Magic*. Doubleday, 1981. *(P; I)*

Fortman, Jan. *Houdini and Other Masters of Magic*. Raintree, 1977. *(P; I)*

Lewis, Shari. *Abracadabra: Magic and Other Tricks*. Ballantine, 1984. *(P; I)*

Severin, Bill. *Magic with Rope, Ribbon, and String*. McKay, 1981. *(I; A)*

Shalit, Nathan. *Science Magic Tricks: Over 50 Fun Tricks That Mystify and Dazzle*. HR&W, 1981. *(P; I)*

Stoddard, Edward. *Magic*. Watts, 1983 (rev. ed.). *(I; A)*

White, Laurence B., Jr., and Broekel, Ray. *Math-a-Magic: Number Tricks for Magicians*. Albert Whitman, 1990. *(P; I)*

MAGNA CARTA. See ENGLAND, HISTORY OF.

MAGNETS AND MAGNETISM

Adler, David. *Amazing Magnets*. Troll, 1983. *(P; I)*

Branley, Franklyn M., and Vaughan, Eleanor K. *Mickey's Magnet*. Scholastic, n.d. *(P)*

Kirkpatrick, Rena K. *Look at Magnets*. Raintree, 1978. *(P)*

Schneider, Herman, and Schneider, Nina. *Secret Magnets*. Scholastic, 1979. *(P)*

MAINE

Cayford, John E. *Maine Firsts*. C & H Pub, 1980. *(I)*

Fradin, Dennis. *Maine: In Words and Pictures*. Children's, 1980. *(P; I)*

Harrington, Ty. *Maine*. Childrens, 1989. *(P; I)*

MALAWI

Malawi . . . in Pictures. Lerner, 1988. *(I)*

Sanders, Renfield. *Malawi*. Chelsea House, 1987. *(P; I)*

MALAYSIA. See SOUTHEAST ASIA.

MALI. See AFRICA.

MAMMALS

Anderson, Lucia. *Mammals and Their Milk*. Dodd, 1986. *(I)*

Board, Tessa. *Mammals*. Watts, 1983. *(P; I)*

Crump, Donald J., ed. *Giants from the Past*. National Geog, 1983. *(P; I)*

Parker, Steve. *Mammal*. Knopf, 1989. *(I)*

Selsam, Millicent E., and Hunt, Joyce. *A First Look at Mammals*. Scholastic, 1976. *(P)*

MANITOBA. See CANADA.

MAO TSE-TUNG. See CHINA.

MAPLE SYRUP AND MAPLE SUGAR

Gokay, Nancy H. *Sugarbush: Making Maple Syrup*. Hillsdale Educ, 1980. *(P)*

Lasky, Kathryn. *Sugaring Time*. Macmillan, 1983. *(I)*

Metcalf, Rosamund S. *The Sugar Maple*. Phoenix Pub, 1982. *(P; I)*

MAPS AND GLOBES

Arnold, Caroline. *Maps and Globes: Fun, Facts, and Activities*. Watts, 1984. *(P)*

Baynes, John. *How Maps Are Made*. Facts on File, 1987. *(I)*

Carey, Helen. *How to Use Maps and Globes*. Watts, 1983. *(I; A)*

Madden, James F. *The Wonderful World of Maps*. Hammond Inc., 1982. *(I; A)*

Rushdoony, Haig A. *The Language of Maps: A Map Skills Program for Grades 4–6*. Pitman Learning, 1983. *(P; I)*

MARIE ANTOINETTE. See FRENCH REVOLUTION.

MARS

Cattermole, Peter. *Mars*. Facts on File, 1990. *(P; I)*

See also PLANETS.

MARYLAND

Carpenter, Allan. *Maryland*. Childrens, 1979. *(I)*

Fradin, Dennis. *Maryland: In Words and Pictures*. Childrens, 1980. *(P; I)*

Rollo, Vera F. *A Geography of Maryland: Ask Me!* Maryland Hist Pr, 1981. *(P; I)*

Schaun, George, and Schaun, Virginia. *Everyday Life in Colonial Maryland*. Maryland Hist Pr, 1981. *(P; I; A)*

Seiden, Art. *Michael Shows Off Baltimore*. Outdoor Bks, 1982. *(P; I)*

MASSACHUSETTS

Fradin, Dennis. *Massachusetts: In Words and Pictures*. Children's, 1981. *(P; I)*

Kent, Deborah. *Massachusetts*. Children's, 1988. *(P; I)*

Smith, Robert. *The Massachusetts Colony*. Macmillan, 1969 *(I)*

MATHEMATICS

Bergamini, David. *Mathematics*. Silver, n.d. *(A)*

Burns, Marilyn. *Math for Smarty Pants: Or Who Says Mathematicians Have Little Pig Eyes*. Little, 1983. *(I; A)*

Dennis, J. Richard. *Fractions Are Parts of Things*. Har-Row, 1971. *(P; I)*

Overholt, James. *Dr. Jim's Elementary Math Prescriptions*. Scott F, 1978. *(P; I)*

MATTER. See PHYSICS.

MAURITANIA. See AFRICA.

MAYFLOWER

DeLage, Ida. *The Pilgrim Children on the Mayflower*. Garrard, 1980. *(P; I)*

Richards, Norman. *The Story of the Mayflower Compact*. Children's, 1967. *(I)*

See also AMERICAN COLONIES.

MCKINLEY, WILLIAM

Kent, Zachary. *William McKinley: Twenty-fifth President of the United States.* Childrens, 1988. *(P; I)*

MEAD, MARGARET

Castiglia, Julie. *Margaret Mead.* Silver Burdett, 1989. *(I; A)*

Epstein, Sam, and Epstein, Beryl. *She Never Looked Back: Margaret Mead in Samoa.* Putnam, 1980. *(I)*

Frevert, Patricia. *Margaret Mead Herself.* Creative Ed, 1981. *(I; A)*

Ludle, Jacqueline. *Margaret Mead.* Watts, 1983. *(I; A)*

Rice, Edward. *Margaret Mead: A Portrait.* Har-Row, 1979. *(I; A)*

Saunders, Susan. *Margaret Mead: The World Was Her Family.* Viking, 1987. *(P; I)*

MEDICINE

Ardley, Neil. *Health and Medicine.* Watts, 1982. *(P; I)*

Berger, Melvin. *Sports Medicine.* Har-Row, 1982. *(I; A)*

Drotar, David. L. *Microsurgery: Revolution in the Operating Room.* Beaufort NY, 1981. *(I; A)*

Englebardt, Stanley. *Jobs in Health Care.* Lothrop, 1983. *(I)*

Jackson, Gordon. *Medicine: The Body and Healing.* Watts, 1984. *(P; I)*

Oleksy, Walter G. *Paramedics.* Messner, 1983. *(I)*

MEDITERRANEAN SEA

Hargreaves, Pat. *The Mediterranean.* Silver, n.d. *(I; A)*

MENDEL, GREGOR JOHANN

Sootin, Harry. *Gregor Mendel: Father of the Science of Genetics.* Vanguard, 1959. *(I)*

MENSTRUATION

Berger, Gilda. *PMS: Premenstrual Syndrome.* Watts, 1984. *(I; A)*

Marzollo, Jean. *Getting Your Period: A Book About Menstruation.* Dial, 1989. *(I; A)*

Nourse, Alan E., M.D. *Menstruation: Just Plain Talk.* Watts, 1980. *(I; A)*

MENTAL HEALTH

Gilbert, Sara. *What Happens in Therapy.* Lothrop, 1982. *(I; A)*

Myers, Irma, and Myers, Arthur. *Why You Feel Down and What You Can Do About It.* Scribner, 1982. *(I; A)*

Olshan, Neal H. *Depression.* Watts, 1982. *(I; A)*

METALS AND METALLURGY

Coombs, Charles. *Gold and Other Precious Metals.* Morrow, 1981. *(P; I)*

Fodor, R. V. *Gold, Copper, Iron: How Metals Are Formed, Found, and Used.* Enslow, 1989. *(A)*

Kerrod, Robin, *Metals.* Silver, n.d. *(I; A)*

Lambert, Mark. *Spotlight on Copper.* Rourke, 1988. *(P; I)*

Lye, Keith. *Spotlight on Gold.* Rourke, 1988. *(P; I)*

Lyttle, Richard B. *The Golden Path: The Lure of Gold Through History.* Atheneum, 1983. *(I; A)*

Mitgutsch, Ali. *From Ore to Spoon.* Carolrhoda, 1981. *(P)*

Rickard, Graham. *Spotlight on Silver.* Rourke, 1988. *(P; I)*

Whyman, Kathryn. *Metals and Alloys.* Gloucester Press, dist. by Watts, 1988. *(P; I)*

METRIC SYSTEM. See WEIGHTS AND MEASURES.

MEXICAN WAR

Lawson, Don. *The United States in the Mexican War.* Har-Row, 1976. *(I; A)*

Murphy, Keith. *The Battle of the Alamo.* Raintree, 1979. *(P; I)*

See also TEXAS.

MEXICO

Casagrande, Louis B., and Johnson, Sylvia A. *Focus on Mexico: Modern Life in an Ancient Land.* Lerner, 1987. *(I)*

Epstein, Sam, and Epstein, Beryl. *Mexico.* Watts, 1983 (rev. ed.). *(I)*

Fincher, E. B. *Mexico and the United States: Their Linked Destinies.* Har-Row, 1983. *(I; A)*

Jacobsen, Peter O., and Kristensen, Preben S. *A Family in Mexico.* Watts, 1984. *(P; I)*

Jacobson, Karen. *Mexico.* Children's, 1982. *(P)*

Lye, Keith. *Take a Trip to Mexico.* Watts, 1982. *(P)*

Moran, Tom. *A Family in Mexico.* Lerner, 1987. *(P)*

Smith, Eileen L. *Mexico: Giant of the South.* Dillon, 1983. *(I; A)*

Visual Geography. *Mexico in Pictures.* Lerner, 1987. *(I)*

MICHIGAN

Fradin, Dennis. *Michigan: In Words and Pictures.* Children's, 1980. *(P; I)*

Hintz, Martin. *Michigan.* Watts, 1987. *(P; I)*

McConnell, David B. *Discover Michigan.* Hillsdale Educ, 1981. *(P)*

Parker, Lois, and McConnell, David. *A Little Peoples' Beginning on Michigan.* Hillsdale Educ, 1981. *(P)*

Stein, R. Conrad. *Michigan.* Children's, 1988. *(P; I)*

Zimmerman, Chanda K. *Detroit.* Dillon Press, 1989. *(P; I)*

MICROBIOLOGY

Anderson, Lucia. *The Smallest Life Around Us.* Crown, 1978. *(I)*

Patent, Dorothy Hinshaw. *Germs!* Holiday, 1983. *(P; I)*

MICROSCOPES AND OTHER OPTICAL INSTRUMENTS

Bleifeld, Maurice. *Experimenting with a Microscope*. Watts, 1988. *(I)*

Chaple, Glenn F., Jr. *Exploring with a Telescope*. Watts, 1988. *(I)*

Johnson, Gaylord, and Bleifeld, Maurice. *Hunting with the Microscope*. Arco, 1980 (rev. ed.). *(I; A)*

Klein, Aaron E. *The Complete Beginner's Guide to Microscopes and Telescopes*. Doubleday, 1980. *(I; A); Microscopes*. Wonder, n.d. *(P; I)*

Simon, Seymour. *Hidden Worlds*. Morrow, 1983. *(P; I)*

Stwertka, Eve and Stwertka, Albert. *Microscope: How to Use It and Enjoy It*. Messner, 1989. *(I)*

See also ASTRONOMY; LASERS; LENSES; LIGHT.

MICROWAVES

Asimov, Isaac. *How Did We Find Out About Microwaves?* Walker, 1989. *(P; I)*

MIDDLE AGES

Aliki. *A Medieval Feast*. Har-Row, 1983. *(P)*

Brooks, Polly S. *Queen Eleanor: Independent Spirit of the Medieval World*. Har-Row, 1983. *(I; A)*

Cosman, Madeleine P. *Medieval Holidays and Festivals: A Calendar of Celebrations*. Scribner, 1982. *(I; A)*

Lewis, Brenda R. *Growing Up in the Dark Ages*. David & Charles, 1980. *(I; A)*

Sancha, Sheila. *The Luttrell Village: Country Life in the Middle Ages*. Har-Row, 1983. *(I; A)*

Wright, Sylvia. *The Age of Chivalry: English Society, 1200–1400*. Warwick, dist. by Watts. *(P; I)*

MIDDLE EAST

Kuwait . . . in Pictures. Lerner, 1989. *(I)*

Abdallah, Maureen S. *The Middle East*. Silver, n.d. *(I; A)*

Beaton, Margaret. *Syria*. Childrens, 1988. *(I)*

Feinstein, Steve. *Turkey . . . in Pictures*. Lerner, 1988. *(P: I)*

Ferrara, Peter. *East vs. West in the Middle East*. Watts, 1983. *(I; A)*

Husain, Akbar. *The Revolution in Iran*. Rourke, 1988. *(A)*

Lawless, Richard, and Bleaney, Heather. *The Middle East Since 1945*. Batsford, dist. by David & Charles, 1990. *(A)*

Mulloy, Martin. *Kuwait*. Chelsea House, 1989. *(P; I)*

Mulloy, Martin. *Syria*. Chelsea House, 1988. *(P)*

Rice, Edward. *Babylon, Next to Nineveh: Where the World Began*. Scholastic, 1979. *(I; A)*

Spencer, William. *The Islamic States in Conflict*. Watts, 1983. *(I, A); The Land and People of Turkey*. Harper, 1990. *(I; A)*

Tarasar, Constance J. *New Friends—New Places*. Friend Pr., 1979. *(P)*

See also EGYPT; ISRAEL.

MILK. See DAIRYING AND DAIRY PRODUCTS.

MINES AND MINING

Mitgutsch, Ali. *From Ore to Spoon*. Carolrhoda, 1981. *(P)*

MINNESOTA

Densmore, Frances. *Dakota and Ojibwe People in Minnesota*. Minn Hist, 1977. *(I)*

Finsand, Mary J. *The Town That Moved*. Carolrhoda, 1983. *(P)*

Fradin, Dennis. *Minnesota: In Words and Pictures*. Children's, 1980. *(P; I)*

Stewart, Anne, and Roquitte, Ruth. *A Part of These United States: Riches from the Land*. Dillon, 1979. *(P; I)*

Wilder, Laura Ingalls. *On the Banks of Plum Creek*. Har-Row, 1953. (Fiction) *(I)*

MISSISSIPPI

Carson, Robert. *Mississippi*. Childrens, 1989. *(P; I)*

Fradin, Dennis. *Mississippi: In Words and Pictures*. Childrens, 1980. *(P; I)*

MISSISSIPPI RIVER

Cooper, Kay. *Journeys on the Mississippi*. Messner, 1981. *(P; I)*

Crisman, Ruth. *The Mississippi*. Watts, 1984. *(I; A)*

St. George, Judith. *The Amazing Voyage of the New Orleans*. Putnam, 1980. *(I; A)*

Zeck, Pam, and Zeck, Gerry. *Mississippi Sternwheelers*. Carolrhoda, 1982. *(P; I)*

MISSOURI

Fradin, Dennis. *Missouri: In Words and Pictures*. Children's, 1980. *(P; I)*

Wilder, Laura Ingalls, and Lane, Rose Wilder. *On the Way Home: The Diary of a Trip from South Dakota to Mansfield, Missouri, in 1894*. Har-Row, 1962. *(I)*

MODELING

Cantwell, Lois. *Modeling*. (First Book) Watts, 1986. *(I; A)*

Lasch, Judith. *The Teen Model Book*. Messner, 1986. *(A)*

MODERN ART. See ART AND ARTISTS.

MODERN MUSIC. See MUSIC AND MUSICIANS.

MONEY

Adler, David A. *All Kinds of Money*. Watts, 1984. *(P)*

Byers, Patricia, and Preston, Julia. *The Kids' Money Book*. Liberty, 1983. *(P; I)*

Cantwell, Lois. *Money and Banking*. Watts, 1984. *(I; A)*

Dolan, Edward F., Jr. *Money Talk*. Messner, 1986. *(I)*

Fodor, R. V. *Nickels, Dimes, and Dollars: How Currency Works*. Morrow, 1980. *(P; I)*

Oppenheim, Joanne. *Cents Sense: Small Change*. Milton Bradley, 1983. *(P)*

MONKEYS, APES, AND OTHER PRIMATES

Anderson, Norman D., and Brown, Walter R. *Lemurs*. Dodd, Mead, 1984. *(P)*

Barrett, N. S. *Monkeys and Apes*. Watts, 1988. *(P; I)*

Boorer, Michael. *The Life of Monkeys and Apes*, ad. by Tim Healey. Silver, 1978. *(I; A)*

Gelman, Rita Golden. *Monkeys and Apes of the World*. Watts, 1990. *(P)*

Goodall, Jane. *The Chimpanzee Family Book*. Picture Book Studio, 1989. *(P; I)*

Hunt, Patricia. *Gibbons*. Dodd, 1983. *(P; I)*

Lumley, Kathryn W. *Monkeys and Apes*. Children's, 1982. *(P)*

McDearmon, Kay. *Orangutans*. Dodd, 1983. *(P; I)*

Overbeck, Cynthia. *Monkeys*. Lerner, 1981. *(P; I; A)*

Schlein, Miriam. *Gorillas*. Atheneum, 1990. *(I)*

Whitehead, Patricia. *Monkeys*. Troll, 1982. *(P)*

MONROE, JAMES

Fitzgerald, Christine Maloney. *James Monroe: Fifth President of the United States*. Children's, 1987. *(I)*

Hanser, James. *The Glorious Hour of Lieutenant Monroe*. Atheneum, 1976. *(P; I)*

Wetzel, Charles. *James Monroe*. Chelsea House, 1989. *(I; A)*

See also PRESIDENCY OF THE UNITED STATES.

MONTANA

Carpenter, Allan. *Montana*. Children's, 1979. *(I)*

Fradin, Dennis. *Montana: In Words and Pictures*. Children's, 1981. *(P; I)*

Whitehead, Bruce, and Whitehead, Charlotte. *Montana Bound: An Activity Approach to Teaching Montana History*. Pruett, 1980. *(I)*

MONTREAL. SEE CANADA.

MOON

Adler, David. *All About the Moon*. Troll, 1983. *(P; I)*

Apfel, Necia H. *The Moon and Its Exploration*. Watts, 1982. *(I; A)*

Hughes, David. *The Moon*. Facts on File, 1990. *(P; I)*

Jay, Michael, and Henbest, Nigel. *The Moon*. Watts, 1982. *(P)*

Kerrod, Robin. *The Race for the Moon*. Lerner, 1980. *(P; I)*

Simon, Seymour. *The Moon*. Four Winds, 1984. *(P)*

Vaughan, Jenny. *On the Moon*. Watts, 1983. *(P)*

Zim, Herbert S. *The New Moon*. Morrow, 1980. *(P; I)*

MORMONS

Smith, Gary. *Day of Great Healing in Nauvoo*. Deseret, 1980. *(I; A)*

MOROCCO. See AFRICA.

MOSCOW. See UNION OF SOVIET SOCIALIST REPUBLICS.

MOSES. See BIBLE AND BIBLE STORIES.

MOSES, GRANDMA

Kallir, Jane Katherine. *Grandma Moses: The Artist Behind the Myth*. Clarkson N. Potter, 1982. *(I; A)*

Oneal, Zibby. *Grandma Moses: Painter of Rural America*. Viking Kestrel, 1986. *(I; A)*

MOSQUITOES

Bernard, George, and Cooke, John. *Mosquito*. Putnam, 1982. *(I; A)*

Patent, Dorothy Hinshaw. *Mosquitoes*. Holiday, 1987. *(I)*

MOTHER GOOSE. See Nursery Rhymes.

MOTION PICTURE INDUSTRY

Aylesworth, Thomas G. *Monsters from the Movies*. Bantam, 1981. *(P; I)*

Cherrell, Gwen. *How Movies Are Made*. Facts on File, 1989. *(I)*

Cohen, Daniel. *Horror in the Movies*. HM, 1982. *(P; I; A)*

Levine, Michael L. *Moviemaking: A Guide for Beginners*. Scribner, 1980. *(I; A)*

MOTORCYCLES

Baumann, Elwood D. *An Album of Motorcycles and Motorcycle Racing*. Watts, 1982. *(I; A)*

Cave, Joyce, and Cave, Ronald. *What About . . . Motorbikes*. Watts, 1982. *(P)*

Cleary, Beverly. *Lucky Chuck*. Morrow, 1984. *(P)* (Story)

Jefferis, David. *Trailbikes*. Watts, 1984. *(P; I)*

Jennings, Gordon. *Motorcycles*. P-H, 1981. *(I; A)*

Kerrod, Robin. *Motorcycles*. Gloucester, dist. by Watts, 1989. *(I)*

Naden, C. J. *Cycle Chase, the Championship Season*. Troll, 1980. *(P; I; A); High Gear*, 1980. *(P; I; A); I Can Read About Motorcycles*, 1979 (new ed.). *(P; I); Motorcycle Challenge, Trials and Races*, 1980. *(P; I; A)*

Radlauer, Ed, and Radlauer, Ruth. *Minibike Mania; Minibike Winners*. Children's, 1982. *(P; I)*

MOUNTAINS AND MOUNTAIN CLIMBING

Catchpole, Clive. *Mountains*. Dial, 1984. *(P)*

Dixon, Dougal. *Mountains*. Watts, 1984. *(P; I; A)* (Atlas format)

Douglas, William O. *Exploring the Himalaya*. Random, 1958. *(I; A)*

George, Jean Craighead. *One Day in the Alpine Tundra*. Har-Row, 1984. *(P; I)*

Hargrove, Jim, and Johnson, S. A. *Mountain Climbing*. Lerner, 1983. *(P; I; A)*

Lye, Keith. *Mountains*. Silver Burdett, 1987. *(P)*

Marcus, Elizabeth. *All About Mountains and Volcanoes*. Troll, 1984. *(P; I)*

Miller, Luree. *The Black Hat Dances: Two Buddhist Boys in the Himalayas*. Dodd, 1987. *(I)*

Radlauer, Ed. *Some Basics About Rock Climbing*. Children's, 1983. *(P; I; A)*

Updegraffe, Imelda, and Updegraffe, Robert. *Mountains and Valleys*. Penguin, 1983. *(I; A)*

MOZAMBIQUE

James, R. S. *Mozambique*. Chelsea House, 1987. *(P; I)*

MOZART, WOLFGANG AMADEUS. See MUSIC AND MUSICIANS.

MUNICIPAL GOVERNMENT

Eichner, James A., and Shields, Linda M. *The First Book of Local Government*. Watts, 1983 (rev. ed.). *(I)*

Hildebrandt, illus. *Who Runs the City?* Platt, 1978. *(P)*

MUSEUMS

Althea. *Visiting a Museum*. Cambridge U Pr, 1983. *(I; A)*

Cutchins, Judy, and Johnston, Ginny. *Are Those Animals Real? How Museums Prepare Wildlife Exhibits*. Morrow, 1984. *(I)*

Papajani, Janet. *Museums*. Childrens, 1983. *(P)*

Sandak, Cass R. *Museums: What They Are and How They Work*. Watts, 1981. *(P; I; A)*

Stan, Susan. *Careers in an Art Museum*. Lerner, 1983. *(P; I)*

Stein, R. Conrad. *The Story of the Smithsonian Institution*. Childrens, 1979. *(P; I)*

MUSHROOMS. See FUNGI.

MUSICAL COMEDY

Powers, Bill. *Behind the Scenes of a Broadway Musical*. Crown, 1982. *(P; I)*

MUSICAL INSTRUMENTS

Anderson, David. *The Piano Makers*. Pantheon, 1982. *(I)*

Blackwood, Alan. *Musical Instruments*. Watts, 1987. *(P)*

Boy Scouts of America. *Music and Bugling*. BSA, 1968. *(I; A)*

Darlow, Denys. *Musical Instruments*. Dufour, 1980. *(I; A)*

Fichter, George S. *American Indian Music and Musical Instruments*. McKay, 1978. *(I; A)*

Kettelkamp, Larry. *Electronic Musical Instruments: What They Do, How They Work*. Morrow, 1984. *(A)*

Walther, Tom. *Make Mine Music*. Little, 1981. *(P; I)*

MUSIC AND MUSICIANS

Ardley, Neil. *Music*. Knopf, 1989. *(P; I; A); Sound and Music*. Watts, 1984. *(P; I)*

Bailey, Eva. *Music and Musicians*. David & Charles, 1983. *(I; A)*

Davis, May, and Davis, Anita. *All About Music*. Oxford, 1977. *(I; A)*

Englander, Roger. *Opera! What's All the Screaming About?* Walker, 1983. *(I; A)*

Erickson, Helen. *Young Person's Guide to the Opera*. Silver, n.d. *(I; A)*

Glazer, Tom. *Music for Ones and Twos: Songs and Games for the Very Young Child*. Doubleday, 1983. *(P)*

Kendall, Catherine W. *Stories of Composers for Young Musicians*. Toadwood Pubs, 1982. *(P; I)*

Meyer, Carolyn. *Music Is for Everyone*. Good Apple, 1980. *(P; I)*

See also COUNTRY AND WESTERN MUSIC; JAZZ; ROCK MUSIC; UNITED STATES (ART, LITERATURE, AND MUSIC).

MUSSOLINI, BENITO

Hartenian, Larry. *Benito Mussolini*. Chelsea House, 1988. *(A)*

Lyttle, Richard B. *Il Duce: The Rise and Fall of Benito Mussolini*. Atheneum, 1987. *(I)*

MYTHOLOGY

Asimov, Isaac. *Words from the Myths*. HM, 1961. *(I)*

Benson, Sally. *Stories of the Gods and Heroes*. Dial Bks Young, 1940 *(P; I)*

D'Aulaire, Ingri, and D'Aulaire, Edgar P. *D'Aulaire's Book of Greek Myths*. Doubleday, 1962. *(P; I)*

Evslin, Bernard. *Hercules*. Morrow, 1984. *(I)*

Kingsley, Charles. *The Heroes*. Smith Pubs, 1980. *(P; I)*

Richardson, I. M. *Demeter and Persephone: The Seasons of Time; Prometheus and the Story of Fire*. Troll, 1983. *(P; I)*

Ross, Harriet, comp. by. *Myths and Legends of Many Lands*. Lion, 1982. *(I; A)*

Switzer, Ellen and Costas. *Greek Myths: Gods, Heroes and Monsters: Their Sources, Their Stories and Their Meanings*. Atheneum, 1988. *(A)*

Zimmerman. *Dictionary of Classical Mythology*. Bantam, n.d. *(I; A)*

NAMES AND NICKNAMES

Asimov, Isaac. *Words on the Map*. HM, 1962. *(I; A)*

Hazen, Barbara S. *Last, First, Middle, and Nick: All About Names*. P-H, 1979. *(P)*

Hook, J. N. *The Book of Names*. Watts, 1984. *(A)*

Lee, Mary P. *Your Name: All About It*. Westminster, 1980. *(P; I; A)*

Lee, Mary Price, and Lee, Richard S. *Last Names First . . . And Some First Names, Too*. Westminster, 1985. *(I; A)*

NAMIBIA. See AFRICA

NAPOLEON I

Masters, Anthony. *Napoleon*. McGraw, 1981. *(I; A)*

Robbins, Ruth. *The Emperor and the Drummer Boy*. Parnassus, 1962. *(P; I)*

NARCOTICS. See DRUGS.

NASSER, GAMAL ABDEL

DeChancie, John. *Gamal Abdel Nasser*. Chelsea House, 1987. *(I: A)*

NATIONAL ANTHEMS AND PATRIOTIC SONGS

Bangs, Edward. *Yankee Doodle*. Scholastic, 1980. *(P)*

Browne, C. A. *The Story of Our National Ballads*. Har-Row, 1960. *(I)*

Lyons, John Henry. *Stories of Our American Patriotic Songs*. Vanguard, n.d. *(I; A)*

Spier, Peter. *The Star-Spangled Banner*. Doubleday, 1973. *(P; I)*

NATIONAL PARK SYSTEM

Annerino, John. *Hiking and Grand Canyon*. Sierra Club/Random, 1986. *(A)*

National Park Service, Department of the Interior, Washington. D.C. 20240—a source of printed materials about the National Park System and the individual units.

Radlauer, Ruth. Books describing individual U.S. national parks: *Acadia; Bryce Canyon; Denali; Glacier; Grand Canyon; Grand Teton; Haleakala, Mammoth Cave; Mesa Verde; Olympic; Shenandoah; Zion*. Childrens, 1977–1982. *(P; I; A)*

NATURAL GAS. See ENERGY.

NEBRASKA

Fradin, Dennis. *Nebraska: In Words and Pictures*. Childrens, 1980. *(P; I)*

Hargrove, Jim. *Nebraska*. Childrens, 1989. *(P; I)*

Manley, Robert N. *Nebraska: Our Pioneer Heritage*. Media Prods & Mktg, 1981. *(I)*

Thompson, Kathleen. *Nebraska*. Raintree, 1988. *(P; I)*

NEBULAS. See ASTRONOMY.

NEEDLEPOINT. See SEWING AND NEEDLECRAFT.

NEHRU, JAWAHARLAL. See INDIA.

NEPAL, SIKKIM, AND BHUTAN

Nepal . . . in Pictures. Lerner, 1989. *(I; A)*

Foster, Leila Merrell. *Bhutan*. Childrens, 1989. *(I)*

Knowlton, MaryLee, and Sachner, Mark J. *Nepal*. Gareth Stevens, 1987. *(P)*

Redford, Lora B. *Getting to Know the Central Himalayas: Nepal, Sikkim, Bhutan*. Coward, 1964. *(I)*

Watanabe, Hitomi. *Nepal*. Gareth Stevens, 1987. *(P)*

NERO. See ROME (ANCIENT).

NETHERLANDS

Dodge, Mary M. *Hans Brinker*. Putnam, n.d. (Fiction) *(I)*

Fairclough, Chris. *Take a Trip to Holland*. Watts, 1984. *(P; I)*

Fradin, Dennis B. *The Netherlands*. Childrens, 1983. *(I; A)*

Jacobsen, Peter O., and Kristensen, Preben S. *A Family in Holland*. Watts, 1984. *(P; I)*

NEVADA

Carpenter, Allan. *Nevada*. Children's, 1979. *(I)*

Fradin, Dennis. *Nevada: In Words and Pictures*. Children's, 1981. *The New Hampshire Colony*, 1988. *(P; I)*

NEW BRUNSWICK. See CANADA.

NEWFOUNDLAND. See CANADA.

NEW GUINEA. See SOUTHEAST ASIA.

NEW HAMPSHIRE

Fradin, Dennis. *New Hampshire: In Words and Pictures*. Children's, 1981; *The New Hampshire Colony*, 1988. *(P; I)*

Giffen, Daniel H. *The New Hampshire Colony*. Macmillan, 1970. *(I)*

NEW JERSEY

Cook, Fred J. *The New Jersey Colony*. Macmillan, 1969. *(I)*

Fradin, Dennis. *New Jersey: In Words and Pictures*. Children's, 1980. *(P; I)*

Homer, Larona. *The Shore Ghosts and Other Stories of New Jersey*. Mid Atlantic, 1981. *(P; I)*

Kent, Deborah. *New Jersey*. Children's, 1988. *(P; I)*

Murray, Thomas C., and Barnes, Valerie. *The Seven Wonders of New Jersey—And Then Some*. Enslow, 1981. *(P; I)*

Rabold, Ted, and Fair, Phillip. *New Jersey: Yesterday and Today*. Penns Valley, 1982. *(P; I)*

NEW MEXICO

Fradin, Dennis. *New Mexico: In Words and Pictures*. Children's, 1981. *(P; I)*
Stein, R. Conrad. *New Mexico*. Children's, 1988. *(P)*

NEWSPAPERS

Carey, Helen, and Greenberg, Judith H. *How to Read a Newspaper*. Watts, 1983. *(I; A)*
English, Betty Lou. *Behind the Headlines at a Big City Paper*. Lothrop, 1985. *(A)*
Fisher, Leonard Everett. *The Newspapers*. Holiday, 1981. *(I; A)*
Koral, April. *Headlines and Deadlines*. Messner, 1981. *(P; I)*
Leedy, Loreen. *The Furry News: How to Make a Newspaper*. Holiday, 1990. *(P)*
Lipson, Greta, and Greenberg, Bernice. *Extra! Extra! Read All About It*. Good Apple, 1981. *(P; I)*
Miller, Margaret. *Hot off the Press! A Day at the Daily News*. Crown, 1985. *(I)*
Waters, Sarah. *How Newspapers Are Made*. Facts on File, 1989. *(I)*

NEWTON, ISAAC

Ipsen, D. C. *Isaac Newton: Reluctant Genius*. Enslow, 1986. *(I; A)*
Tiner, John H. *Isaac Newton: The True Story of His Life*. Mott, 1976. *(P; I)*

NEW YEAR CELEBRATIONS AROUND THE WORLD. See HOLIDAYS.

NEW YORK

Stein, R. Conrad. *New York*. Childrens, 1989. *(P; I)*
Thompson, Kathleen. *New York*. Raintree, 1988. *(P; I)*

NEW YORK CITY

Adams, Barbara Johnston. *New York City*. Dillon, 1988. *(P)*
Krustrup, Erik V. *Gateway to America: New York City*. Creative Ed, 1982. *(I; A)*
Lovett, Sarah. *Kidding Around New York City: A Young Person's Guide to the City*. John Muir, 1989. *(I; A)*
Munro, Roxie. *The Inside-Outside Book of New York City*. Dodd, 1985. *(P)*

NEW ZEALAND

Anderson, Margaret J. *Light in the Mountain*. Knopf, 1982. *(I)*
Armitage, Ronda. *New Zealand*. Bookwright, dist. by Watts, 1988. *(P)*
Ball, John. *We Live in New Zealand*. Watts, 1984. *(I; A)*

Knowlton, MaryLee, and Sachner, Mark J. *New Zealand*. Gareth Stevens, 1987. *(P)*
Sterling Publishing Company Editors. *New Zealand in Pictures*. Sterling, n.d. *(I)*
Yanagi, Akinobu. *New Zealand*. Gareth Stevens, 1987. *(P; I)*

NICARAGUA. See CENTRAL AMERICA.

NIGER. See AFRICA.

NIGERIA

Nigeria . . . in Pictures. Lerner, 1988. *(P; I)*

NIGHTINGALE, FLORENCE

Koch, Charlotte. *Florence Nightingale*. Dandelion, 1979. *(P; I)*
Peach, L. Dugarde. *Florence Nightingale*. Merry Thoughts, n.d. *(I; A)*

NILE RIVER

Percefull. Aaron W. *The Nile*. Watts, 1984. *(I; A)*
Worthington, Barton. *The Nile*. Silver, 1978. *(I; A)*

NIXON, RICHARD M.

Cook, Fred J. *The Crimes of Watergate*. Watts, 1981. *(A)*
Hargrove, Jim. *Richard M. Nixon*. Children's, 1985. *(I; A)*
Lillegard, Dee. *Richard Nixon: Thirty-seventh President of the United States*. Children's, 1988. *(P; I)*
Ripley, C. Peter. *Richard Nixon*. Chelsea House, 1987. *(A)*
See also PRESIDENCY OF THE UNITED STATES.

NOBEL PRIZES

Abrams, Irwin. *The Nobel Peace Prize and the Laureates: An Illustrated Biographical History 1901–1987*. Hall, 1988. *(A)*
Asseng, Nathan. *The Disease Fighters: The Nobel Prize in Medicine*. Lerner, 1987. *(P; I)*; *The Inventors: Nobel Prizes in Chemistry, Physics, and Medicine*, 1988. *(I)*; *The Peace Seekers: The Nobel Peace Prize*, 1987. *(I)*
Meyer, Edith P. *In Search of Peace: The Winners of the Nobel Peace Prize, 1901–1975*. Abingdon, 1978. *(A)*

NOISE

Finney, Shan. *Noise Pollution*. Watts, 1984. *(I; A)*

NORSE MYTHOLOGY

Colum, Padraic. *The Children of Odin*. Haverton Bks. 1920. *(I; A)*
Coolidge, Olivia. *Legends of the North*. HM, 1951. *(I; A)*

D'Aulaire, Ingri, and D'Aulaire, Edgar P. *Norse Gods and Giants*. Doubleday, 1967. *(P; I)*

Green, Roger L. *Myths of the Norsemen*. Penguin, 1970. *(I; A)*

Hodges, Margaret. *Baldur and the Mistletoe: A Myth of the Vikings*. Little, 1974. *(P)*

NORTH AMERICA

Asimov, Isaac. *The Shaping of North America*. HM, 1973. *(I; A)*

See also individual countries, states, and provinces.

NORTH CAROLINA

Carpenter, Allan. *North Carolina*. Children's, 1979. *(I)*

Fradin, Dennis. *North Carolina: In Words and Pictures*. Children's, 1980. *(P; I)*

NORTH DAKOTA

Carpenter, Allan. *North Dakota*. Children's, 1979. *(I)*

Fradin, Dennis. *North Dakota: In Words and Pictures*. Children's, 1981. *(P; I)*

Tweton, D. Jerome, and Jelliff, Theodore B. *North Dakota: The Heritage of a People*. N Dak Inst, 1976. *(I; A)*

NORTH POLE. See ARCTIC.

NORTHWEST PASSAGE. See EXPLORATION AND DISCOVERY.

NORWAY

Hintz, Martin. *Norway*. Children's, 1982. *(I; A)*

Sterling Publishing Company Editors. *Norway in Pictures*. Sterling, n.d. *(I; A)*

St. John, Jetty. *A Family in Norway*. Lerner, 1988. *(P)*

NOVA SCOTIA. See CANADA.

NUCLEAR ENERGY

Ardley, Neil. *Atoms and Energy*. Watts, 1982. *(I; A)*

Bentley, Judith. *The Nuclear Freeze Movement*. Watts, 1984. *(I; A)*

Coble, Charles. *Nuclear Energy*. Raintree, 1983. *(I; A)*

Feldbaum, Carl B., and Bee, Ronald J. *Looking the Tiger in the Eye: Confronting the Nuclear Threat*. Harper, 1988. *(A)*

Fradin, Dennis B. *Nuclear Energy*. Children's, 1987. *(P)*

Haines, Gail Kay. *The Great Nuclear Power Debate*. Dodd, 1985. *(A)*

Halacy, Daniel. *Nuclear Energy*. Watts, 1984 (rev. ed.). *(I; A)*

Lens, Sidney. *The Bomb*. Dutton, 1982. *(I; A)*

Pringle, Laurence. *Nuclear Energy: Troubled Past, Uncertain Future*. Macmillan Children's Books, 1989.

(I; A); Radiation: Waves and Particles/Benefits and Risks. Enslow, 1983. *(I; A)*

Smoke, Richard. *Nuclear Arms Control: Understanding the Arms Race*. Walker, 1988. *(A)*

Williams, Gene B. *Nuclear War, Nuclear Winter*. Watts, 1987. *(I; A)*

NUMBERS AND NUMBER SYSTEMS

Sitomer, Harry, and Sitomer, Mindel. *How Did Numbers Begin?* Har-Row, 1976; *Zero Is Not Nothing*, 1978. *(P)*

Srivastava, Jane. *Number Families*. Har-Row, 1979. *(P)*

Tallarico, Tony. *Numbers*. Tuffy Bks, 1982. *(P; I)*

Watson, Clyde. *Binary Numbers*. Har-Row, 1977. *(I)*

NURSERY RHYMES

Blegvad, Lenore, ed. *Hark! Hark! the Dogs Do Bark: And Other Rhymes About Dogs*. Atheneum, 1976. *(P)*

Bodecker, N. M. *It's Raining Said John Twaining: Danish Nursery Rhymes*. Atheneum, 1973. *(P)*

De Angeli, Marguerite. *Book of Nursery and Mother Goose Rhymes*. Doubleday, 1954. *(P; I)*

DePaola, Tomie. *Tomie dePaola's Mother Goose*. Putnam, 1985. *(P)*

Greenaway, Kate, illus. *Mother Goose: Or, the Old Nursery Rhymes*. Warne, 1882. *(P)*

Lewis, Bobby, illus. *Mother Goose: Home Before Midnight*. Lothrop, 1984. *(P)*

Lobel, Arnold. *The Random House Book of Mother Goose*. Random House, 1986. *(P; I)*

Opie, Iona, and Opie, Peter. *A Nursery Companion*. Oxford, 1980; *Oxford Nursery Rhyme Book*, 1955. *(P)*

Potter, Beatrix. *Appley Dapply's Nursery Rhymes*. Warne, 1917; *Cecily Parsley's Nursery Rhymes*, 1922. *(P)*

Provensen, Alice, and Provensen, Martin, illus. *Old Mother Hubbard*. Random, 1982. *(P)*

Rackham, Arthur, illus. *Mother Goose, the Old Nursery Rhymes*. S J Durst, 1978. *(P)*

Rockwell, Anne. *Gray Goose and Gander and Other Mother Goose Rhymes*. Har-Row, 1980. *(P)*

Rojankovsky, Feodor. *Tall Book of Mother Goose*. Har-Row, 1942. *(P)*

Rossetti, Christina G. *Sing Song: A Nursery Rhyme Book*. Dover, 1969. *(P; I)*

Wyndham, Robert. *Chinese Mother Goose Rhymes*. Putnam, 1982. *(P)*

NURSES AND NURSING

Donahue, M. Patricia. *Nursing, the Finest Art: An Illustrated History*. Abrams, 1986. *(A)*

Seide, Diane. *Nurse Power: New Vistas in Nursing*. Lodestar, 1985. *(A)*

Wandro, Mark, and Blank, Joani. *My Daddy Is a Nurse*. A-W, 1981. *(P; I)*

Witty, Margot. *A Day in the Life of an Emergency Room Nurse*. Troll, 1981. *(P; I)*

NUTRITION

Baldwin, Dorothy, and Lister, Claire. *Your Body Fuel*. Watts, 1984. *(I; A)*

Franz, William, and Franz, Barbara. *Nutritional Survival Manual for the 80's: A Young People's Guide to Dietary Goals for the United States*. Messner, 1981. *(I; A)*

Fretz, Sada. *Going Vegetarian: A Guide for Teenagers*. Morrow, 1983. *(I; A)*

Peavy, Linda, and Smith, Ursula. *Food, Nutrition, and You*. Scribner, 1982. *(I; A)*

Perl, Lila. *Junk Food, Fast Food, Health Food—What America Eats and Why*. HM, 1980. *(I; A)*

Sanchez, Gail Jones, and Gerbino, Mary. *Overeating: Let's Talk About It*. Dillon Press, 1986. *(I; A)*

Thompson, Paul, *Nutrition*. Watts, 1981. *(I; A)*

NYLON AND OTHER SYNTHETIC FIBERS. See TEXTILES.

OAKLEY, ANNIE

Alderman, Clifford L. *Annie Oakley and the World of Her Time*. Macmillan, 1979. *(I; A)*

Harrison, and others. *Annie Oakley*. Dormac, 1981. *(P; I; A)*

OASES. See DESERTS.

OATS. See GRAIN AND GRAIN PRODUCTS.

OCEANS AND OCEANOGRAPHY

Adler, David. *Our Amazing Oceans*. Troll, 1983. *(P; I)*

Althea. *Signposts of the Sea*. Cambridge U Press, 1983. *(A)*

Asimov, Isaac. *How Did We Find Out About Life in the Deep Sea?* Walker, 1981. *(I)*

Ballard, Robert D. *Exploring the Titanic*. Scholastic, 1988. *(P; I)*

Blair, Carvel Hall. *Exploring the Sea: Oceanography Today*. Random, 1986. *(I)*

Blumberg, Rhoda. *The First Travel Guide to the Bottom of the Sea*. Lothrop, 1983. *(I)*

Bramwell, Martyn. *Oceanography*. Watts, 1989. *(P; I)*; *Oceans*. Watts, 1984. *(P; I)* (Atlas format)

Carson, Rachel L. *The Sea Around Us*. Oxford, 1961. *(A)*

Carter, Katherine J. *Oceans*. Childrens, 1982. *(P)*

Cook, Jan L. *The Mysterious Undersea World*. Natl Geog, 1980. *(P; I)*

Elting, Mary. *Mysterious Seas*. Putnam, 1983. *(P; I)*

Fine, John Christopher. *Oceans in Peril*. Atheneum, 1987. *(A)*

Lambert, David. *The Oceans*. Watts, 1984. *(I; A)*

Lampton, Christopher. *Undersea Archaeology*. Watts, 1988. *(I)*

Meyerson, A. Lee. *Seawater: A Delicate Balance*. Enslow, 1988. *(I; A)*

Morris, R. *Mysteries and Marvels of Ocean Life*. EDC, 1983. *(P; I)*

Polking, Kirk. *Oceans of the World: Our Essential Resource*. Putnam, 1983. *(I; A)*

Poynter, Margaret, and Collins, Donald. *Under the High Seas: New Frontiers in Oceanography*. Atheneum, 1983. *(I)*

Russell, Solveig P. *What's Under the Sea?* Abingdon, 1982. *(P)*

Sedge, Michael H. *Commercialization of the Oceans*. Watts, 1987. *(I; A)*

Simon, Anne W. *Neptune's Revenge: The Ocean of Tomorrow*. Watts, 1984. *(A)*

Updegraff, Imelda, and Updegraff, Robert. *Seas and Oceans*. Penguin, 1983. *(I; A)*

OHIO

Carpenter, Allan. *Ohio*. Childrens, 1979. *(I)*

Cockley, David H. *Over the Falls: A Child's Guide to Chagrin Falls*. Aschley Pr., 1981. *(P; I)*

Fox, Mary Virginia. *Ohio*. Watts, 1987. *(P; I)*

Fradin, Dennis. *Ohio: In Words and Pictures*. Children's, 1977. *(P; I)*

Kent, Deborah. *Ohio*. Childrens, 1989. *(P; I)*

O'KEEFFE, GEORGIA

Berry, Michael. *Georgia O'Keeffe*. Chelsea House, 1988. *(A)*

Gherman, Beverly. *Georgia O'Keeffe: The Wideness and Wonder of Her World*. Atheneum, 1986. *(I; A)*

OKLAHOMA

Carpenter, Allan. *Oklahoma*. Childrens, 1979. *(I)*

Fradin, Dennis. *Oklahoma: In Words and Pictures*. Childrens, 1981. *(P; I)*

Heinrichs, Ann. *Oklahoma*. Childrens, 1989. *(P; I)*

Newsom, D. Earl. *The Birth of Oklahoma*. Evans Pubns, 1983. *(I; A)*

OLD AGE. See AGING.

OLYMPIC GAMES

Glubok, Shirley, and Tamarin, Alfred. *Olympic Games in Ancient Greece*. Har-Row, 1976. *(A)*

Wallechinsky, David. *The Complete Book of the Olympics*. Viking, 1987. *(A)*

ONTARIO. See CANADA.

OPERA. See MUSIC AND MUSICIANS.

OPERETTA. See MUSIC AND MUSICIANS.

OPTICAL ILLUSIONS

O'Neill, Catherine. *You Won't Believe Your Eyes!* National Geog, 1987. *(P; I)*

Simon, Seymour. *The Optical Illusion Book*. Scholastic, 1976. *(I)*

White, Laurence B., and Broekel, Ray. *Optical Illusions*. Watts, 1986. *(P; I)*

OPTICAL INSTRUMENTS. See MICROSCOPES.

ORCHESTRA

English, Betty Lou. *You Can't Be Timid with a Trumpet: Notes from the Orchestra*. Lothrop, 1980. *(I)*

Kuskin, Karla. *The Philharmonic Gets Dressed*. Har-Row, 1982. *(P)*

Rubin, Mark. *The Orchestra*. Douglas & McIntyre, 1984. *(P)*

Storms, Laura. *Careers with an Orchestra*. Lerner, 1983. *(P; I)*

OREGON

Carpenter, Allan. *Oregon*. Childrens, 1979. *(I)*

Cloutier, James. *This Day in Oregon*. Image West, 1981. *(I; A)*

Fradin, Dennis. *Oregon: In Words and Pictures*. Childrens, 1980. *(P; I)*

Stein, R. Conrad. *Oregon*. Childrens, 1989. *(P; I)*

ORGAN. See MUSICAL INSTRUMENTS.

ORIGAMI

Araki, Chiyo. *Origami in the Classroom*. Tuttle, 1968. *(I)*

Murray, William D., and Rigney, Francis J. *Paperfolding for Beginners*. Dover, n.d. *(P; I)*

Nakano, Dokuohtei. *Easy Origami*. Viking Kestrel, 1986. *(P)*

Sarasas. Claude. *The ABC's of Origami*. Tuttle, 1964. *(I)*

Takahama, Toshie. *Origami for Fun: Thirty-one Basic Models*. Tuttle, 1980. *(P; I)*

ORTHODONTICS. See DENTISTS AND DENTISTRY.

OSMOSIS. See PLANTS.

OSTRICHES AND OTHER FLIGHTLESS BIRDS

Arnold, Carolyn. *Ostriches and Other Flightless Birds*. Carolrhoda, 1990. *(I)*

Lavine, Sigmund A. *Wonders of Flightless Birds*. Dodd, 1981. *(I; A)*

OTTAWA. See CANADA.

OTTERS AND OTHER MUSTELIDS

Ashby, Ruth. *Sea Otters*. Atheneum, 1990. *(I)*

Hurd, Edith T. *Song of the Sea Otter*. Pantheon, 1983. *(P; I)*

Lavine, Sigmund A. *Wonders of Badgers*. Dodd, 1985. *(I)*

Scheffer, Victor B. *The Amazing Sea Otter*. Scribner, 1981. *(I)* (Story)

OUTDOOR COOKING AND PICNICS

Haines, Gail K. *Baking in a Box, Cooking on a Can*. Morrow, 1981. *(I)*

OVERLAND TRAILS. See WESTWARD MOVEMENT.

OWLS

Burton, Jane. *Buffy the Barn Owl*. Gareth Stevens, 1989. *(P)*

Hunt, Patricia. *Snowy Owls,* Dodd, 1982. *(P; I)*

Sadoway, Margaret W. *Owls: Hunters of the Night*. Lerner, 1981. *(P; I)*

Storms, Laura. *The Owl Book*. Lerner, 1983. *(P; I)*

Zim, Herbert S. *Owls*. Morrow, 1977 (rev. ed.). *(P; I)*

OYSTERS, OCTOPUSES, AND OTHER MOLLUSKS

Carrick, Carol. *Octopus*. HM, 1978. *(P)*

PACIFIC OCEAN AND ISLANDS

Deverell, Gweneth. *Follow the Sun . . . to Tahiti, to Western Samoa, to Fiji, to Melanesia, to Micronesia*. Friends Pr, 1982. *(P)*

Gittins, Anne. *Tales from the South Pacific Islands*. Stemmer, 1977. *(I)*

Hargreaves, Pat. *The Pacific*. Silver, n.d. *(I; A)*

Kamikamica, Esiteri, comp. by. *Come to My Place: Meet My Island Family*. Friend Pr, 1982. *(P; I)*

PADDLE TENNIS. See TENNIS.

PAINTING

Couch, Tony. *Watercolor: You Can Do It!* North Light (Dist. by Writer's Digest), 1987. *(A)*

Cumming, Robert. *Just Look: A Book About Paintings*. Scribner, 1980. *(P; I)*

Foste. *A Guide to Painting*. EDC, 1981. *(P; I)*

Holme, Bryan. *Creatures of Paradise: Pictures to Grow Up With*. Oxford, 1980; *Enchanted World: The Magic of Pictures,* 1979. *(I; A)*

Peppin. *The Story of Painting*. EDC, 1980. *(I; A)*

See also ART AND ARTISTS.

PAKISTAN AND BANGLADESH

Laure, Jason, and Laure, Ettagale. *Joi Bangla! The Children of Bangladesh*. FS&G, 1974. *(I)*

Wright, R. E. *Bangladesh*. Chelsea House, 1988. *(P)*

Yusufali, Jabeen. *Pakistan: An Islamic Treasure*. Dillon, 1990. *(I)*

PALESTINE. See ISRAEL; MIDDLE EAST.

PANAMA. See CENTRAL AMERICA.

PANAMA CANAL AND ZONE. See CANALS.

PANDAS

Barrett, N. S. *Pandas*. Watts, 1988. *(P; I)*
McClung, Robert M. *Lili: A Giant Panda of Sichuan*. Morrow, 1988. *(P: I)*
Wexo, John Bonnett. *Giant Pandas*. Creative Education, 1988. *(P)*

PAPER

Perrins, Lesley. *How Paper is Made*. Facts on File, 1985. *(P; I)*

PAPUA NEW GUINEA. See SOUTHEAST ASIA.

PARAGUAY AND URUGUAY

Naverstock, Nathan A. *Paraguay in Pictures*. Lerner, 1988. *(P: I)*

PARIS. See FRANCE.

PARKS AND PLAYGROUNDS

Anderson, Norman D., and Brown, Walter R. *Ferris Wheels*. Pantheon, 1983. *(I)*
Hahn, Christine. *Amusement Park Machines*. Raintree, 1979. *(P)*
Van Steenwyk, Elizabeth. *Behind the Scenes at the Amusement Park*. Whitman, 1983. *(P; I)*

PARLIAMENTARY PROCEDURE

Jones, O. Garfield. *Parliamentary Procedure at a Glance*. Dutton, 1971. *(A)*

PARROTS AND OTHER "TALKING" BIRDS. See BIRDS.

PARTIES

Brinn, Ruth E., and Saypol, Judyth R. *101 Mix and Match Party Ideas for the Jewish Holidays*. Kar Ben, 1981. *(P)*
Highlights editors. *Party Ideas with Crafts Kids Can Make*. Highlights, 1981. *(P; I)*
Pitcher, Caroline. *Party Time*. Watts, 1984. *(P)*

PASSOVER

Adler, David A. *Passover Fun Book: Puzzles, Riddles, and More*. Hebrew Pub, 1978. *(P; I); A Picture Book of Passover*. Holiday, 1982. *(P)*

Drucker, Malka. *Passover: A Season of Freedom*. Holiday, 1981. *(I; A)*
Kustanowitz, Shulamit, and Foont, Ronnie. *A First Haggadah*. Hebrew Pub, 1980. *(P; I)*
Rosen, Anne, and others. *Family Passover*. Jewish Pubn, 1980. *(P; I; A)*

PASTEUR, LOUIS

Birch, Beverley. *Louis Pasteur*. Gareth Stevens, 1989. *(I)*
Johnson, Spencer, and Johnson, Ann D. *The Value of Believing in Yourself: The Story of Louis Pasteur*. Western, 1979. *(P; I)*
Sabin, Francene. *Louis Pasteur: Young Scientist*. Troll, 1983. *(P; I)*

PATRICK, SAINT

Corfe, Tom. *St. Patrick and Irish Christianity*. Lerner, 1978. *(I; A)*

PEACE MOVEMENTS

Fitzgerald, Merni Ingrassia. *The Peace Corps Today*. Dodd, 1986. *(P; I)*
Meltzer, Milton. *Ain't Gonna Study War No More: The Story of America's Peace Seekers*. Harper, 1985. *(A)*

PEKING. See CHINA.

PELICANS

Cooper, Lester. *Pelicans*. Handel & Sons, 1979. *(P; I)*
Wildsmith, Brian. *Pelican*. Pantheon, 1983. *(P)*

PENGUINS

Arnold, Caroline. *Penguin*. Morrow, 1988. *(P; I)*
Bonners, Susan. *A Penguin Year*. Delacorte, 1981. *(P)*
Coldrey, Jennifer. *Penguins*. Andre Deutsch, 1983. *(P)*
Lepthien, Emilie U. *Penguins*. Children's, 1983. *(P)*
Sømme, Lauritz and Kalas, Sybille. *The Penguin Family Book*. Picture Book Studio, 1988. *(P)*
Strange, Ian J. *Penguin World*. Dodd, 1981. *(I; A)*
Tenaza, Richard. *Penguins*. Watts, 1982. *(I; A)*
Todd, Frank S. *The Sea World Book of Penguins*. Sea World, 1981. *(I)*

PENN, WILLIAM

Foster, Genevieve. *The World of William Penn*. Scribner, 1973. *(I)*

PENNSYLVANIA

Cornell, William A., and Altland, Millard. *Our Pennsylvania Heritage*. Penns Valley, 1978. *(I; A)*
Costabel, Eva D. *The Pennsylvania Dutch*. Atheneum, 1986. *(P; I)*
De Angeli, Marguerite. *Henner's Lydia*. Doubleday, 1936; *Whistle for the Crossing*, 1977. *(P; I)*

Fradin, Dennis. *Pennsylvania: In Words and Pictures.* Children's, 1980. *(P; I)*

Fritz, Jean. *Brady.* Putnam, 1960; *The Cabin Faced West,* 1958. *(P; I)*

Kent, Deborah. *Pennsylvania.* Children's, 1988. *(P)*

Knight, James E. *The Farm, Life in Colonial Pennsylvania.* Troll, 1982 *(I; A)*

Meyer, Carolyn. *Amish People: Plain Living in a Complex World.* Atheneum, 1976. *(I; A)*

PERCUSSION INSTRUMENTS. See MUSICAL INSTRUMENTS.

PERRY, COMMODORE

Blumberg, Rhoda. *Commodore Perry in the Land of the Shogun.* Lothrop, 1985. *(I; A)*

PERU

Bleeker, Sonia. *The Inca: Indians of the Andes.* Morrow, 1960. *(P; I)*

Clark, Ann Nolan. *Secret of the Andes.* Viking, 1952. *(A)*

Gemming, Elizabeth. *Lost City in the Clouds: The Discovery of Machu Picchu.* Putnam, 1980. *(P; I)*

Mangurian, David. *Children of the Incas.* Scholastic, 1979. *(P; I)*

Visual Geography. *PERU . . . In Pictures.* Lerner, 1987. *(I; A)*

PETER THE GREAT

Stanley, Diane. *Peter the Great.* Macmillan/Four Winds, 1986. *(P; I)*

PETROLEUM

Alvarez, A. *Offshore: a North Sea Journey.* Houghton, 1986. *(A)*

Asimov, Isaac. *How Did We Find Out About Oil?* Walker, 1980. *(I)*

Mitgutsch, Ali. *From Oil to Gasoline.* Carolrhoda, 1981. *(P)*

Olney, Ross R. *Offshore!* Dutton, 1981. *(I; A)*

Pampe, William R. *Petroleum: How it is Found and Used.* Enslow, 1984. *(A)*

Piper, Allan. *Oil.* Watts, 1980. *(I)*

Rutland, Jonathan. *See Inside an Oil Rig and Tanker.* Watts, 1979. *(I; A)*

Scott, Elaine. *Doodlebugging: The Treasure Hunt for Oil.* Warne, 1982. *(I)*

Stephen, R. J. *Oil Rigs.* Watts, 1987. *(P)*

Swanson, Glen. *Oil and Water.* P-H, 1981. *(P; I)*

PETS

Arnold, Caroline. *Pets Without Homes.* HM, 1983. *(P)*

Blumberg, Leda. *Pets.* Watts, 1983. *(P; I)*

Case, Marshal T. *Look What I Found! The Young Conservationist's Guide to the Care and Feeding of Small Wildlife.* Devin, 1983. *(P; I)*

Fields, Alice. *Pets.* Watts, 1981. *(P)*

Hess, Lilo. *Bird Companions.* Scribner, 1981. *(I)*

Marrs, Texe, and Marrs, Wanda. *The Perfect Name for Your Pet.* Heian Intl. 1983. *(P; I; A)*

Weber, William J. *Care of Uncommon Pets.* HR&W, 1979; *Wild Orphan Babies—Mammals and Birds: Caring for Them/Setting Them Free,* 1978. *(I; A)*

PHILADELPHIA

Balcer, Bernadette and O'Byrne-Pelham, Fran. *Philadelphia.* Dillon, 1989. *(P; I)*

Gantshar, Barbara R. *Philadelphia: The City and the Bell.* Artistic Endeavors, 1976. *(P; I)*

Knight, James E. *Seventh and Walnut, Life in Colonial Philadelphia.* Troll, 1982. *(I; A)*

Loeper, John J. *The House on Spruce Street.* Atheneum, 1982. *(I)*

PHILIPPINES. See SOUTHEAST ASIA.

PHILOSOPHY

Allington, Richard L., and Krull, Kathleen. *Thinking.* Raintree, 1980. *(P)*

Post, Beverly, and Eads, Sandra. *Logic, Anyone? One Hundred Sixty-five Brain-Stretching Problems.* Pitman, 1982. *(I; A)*

PHOTOGRAPHY

Boy Scouts of America. *Photography.* BSA, 1983. *(I; A)*

Cooper, Miriam. *Snap! Photography.* Messner, 1981. *(I)*

Craven, John, and Wasley, John. *Young Photographer.* Sterling, 1982. *(I)*

Cumming, David. *Photography.* Steck-Vaughn, 1989. *(I)*

Knudsen-Owens, Vic. *Photography Basics: An Introduction for Young People.* P-H, 1983. *(P; I)*

Noren, Catherine. *The Way We Looked: The Meaning and Magic of Family Photographs.* Lodestar, 1983. *(I; A)*

Sandler, Martin W. *The Story of American Photography.* Little, 1979. *(A)*

PHOTOSYNTHESIS. See PLANTS.

PHYSICAL FITNESS. See HEALTH AND PHYSICAL FITNESS.

PHYSICS

Ardley, Neil. *Exploring Magnetism.* Watts, 1984. *(I); Hot and Cold,* 1983. *(P; I; A); Making Things Move.* 1984. *(P; I; A)*

Berger, Melvin. *Our Atomic World.* Watts, 1989. *(P; I); Solids, Liquids, and Gases.* Putnam, 1989. *(I; A)*

Chester, Michael. *Particles: An Introduction to Particle Physics.* Macmillan, 1978. *(I; A)*

Cobb, Vicki. *Why Can't You Unscramble An Egg?: and Other Not Such Dumb Questions About Matter.* Lodestar, 1990. *(P; I)*

Henbest, Nigel, and Couper, Heather. *Physics.* Watts, 1983. *(I; A)*

Watson, Philip. *Liquid Magic.* Lothrop, 1983. *(P; I)*

PIANO. See MUSICAL INSTRUMENTS.

PICASSO, PABLO

Frevert, Patricia D. *Pablo Picasso: Twentieth Century Genius.* Creative Ed, 1981. *(I; A)*

Raboff, Ernest. *Pablo Picasso.* Doubleday, 1982. *(P; I)*

Venezia, Mike. *Picasso.* Children's, 1988. *(P)*

PIERCE, FRANKLIN

Brown, Fern G. *Franklin Pierce.* Garrett Educational Corp., 1989. *(I)*

Hoyt, Edwin P. *Franklin Pierce: The Fourteenth President of the United States.* Har-Row, 1972. *(I)*

Simon, Charnan. *Franklin Pierce.* Childrens, 1988. *(I)*

See also PRESIDENCY OF THE UNITED STATES.

PIGS. See AGRICULTURE.

PIONEER LIFE. See WESTWARD MOVEMENT.

PIRATES AND PIRACY

McCall, Edith. *Pirates and Privateers.* Children's, 1980. *(P; I; A)*

Stein, R. Conrad. *The Story of the Barbary Pirates.* Children's, 1982. *(P; I)*

PIZARRO, FRANCISCO. See EXPLORATION AND DISCOVERY.

PLANETARIUM. See ASTRONOMY.

PLANETS

Asimov, Isaac. *Colonizing the Planets and Stars.* Gareth Stevens, 1990. *(P; I); Pluto: A Double Planet?* Gareth Stevens, 1990. *(P; I); Saturn: The Ringed Beauty.* Gareth Stevens, 1989. *(P; I); Uranus: The Sideways Planet.* Gareth Stevens, 1988. *(P; I)*

Berger, Melvin. *If You Lived on Mars.* Dutton/Lodestar, 1988. *(P; I)*

Branley, Franklyn M. *The Planets in Our Solar System.* Crowell, 1987. *(P); Uranus: The Seventh Planet.* Crowell, 1988. *(I; A)*

Dunbar, Robert E. *Into Jupiter's World.* Watts, 1981. *(I; A)*

Halliday, Ian. *Saturn.* Facts on File, 1990. *(P; I)*

Lampton, Christopher. *Stars and Planets.* Doubleday, 1988. *(P)*

Lauber, Patricia. *Journey to the Planets,* Crown, 1987. *(I; A)*

Levasseur-Regourd, Anny Chantal. *Our Sun and the Inner Planets.* Facts on File, 1990. *(P; I)*

Nourse, Alan E. *The Giant Planets.* Watts, 1982. *(I; A)*

Petersen, Carolyn Collins. *Jupiter.* Facts on File, 1990. *(P; I)*

Petty, Kate. *The Planets.* Watts, 1984. *(P)*

Simon, Seymour. *Jupiter.* Morrow, 1985. *(I; A); Mars,* 1987. *(P); Mars,* 1987; *Saturn,* 1985; *Uranus,* 1987. *(I; A)*

Vogt, Gregory. *Mars and the Inner Planets.* Watts, 1982. *(I; A)*

Yeomans, Don K. *The Distant Planets.* Facts on File, 1990. *(P; I)*

PLANTS

Burnie, David. *Plant.* Knopf, 1989. *(I)*

Cross, Diana H. *Some Plants Have Funny Names.* Crown, 1983. *(P)*

Dowden, Anne O. *From Flower to Fruit.* Har-Row, 1984. *(I; A)*

Janulewicz, Mike. *Plants.* Watts, 1984. *(I; A)*

Johnson, Sylvia A. *Mosses.* Lerner, 1983. *(I)*

Lambert, Mark. *Plant Life.* Watts, 1983. *(I; A)*

Lauber, Patricia. *Seeds: Pop, Stick, Glide.* Crown, 1981. *(P)*

Lerner, Carol. *Pitcher Plants: The Elegant Insect Traps.* Morrow, 1983. *(P; I); Plant Families.* Morrow, 1989. *(P; I)*

Marcus, Elizabeth. *Amazing World of Plants.* Troll, 1984. *(P; I)*

Podendorf, Illa. *Weeds and Wildflowers.* Childrens, 1981. *(P)*

Pringle, Laurence P. *Being a Plant.* Har-Row, 1983. *(I; A)*

Rahn, Joan E. *Plants Close Up.* HM, 1981; *Seven Ways to Collect Plants.* Atheneum, 1978. *(P; I)*

Selsam, Millicent E. *Catnip.* Morrow, 1983; *Eat the Fruit, Plant the Seed,* 1980; *The Plants We Eat,* 1981 (rev. ed.). *(P; I)*

Shuttleworth, Floyd S., and Zim, Herbert. *Non-Flowering Plants.* Western, 1967. *(I; A)*

Welch, Martha M. *Close Looks in a Spring Woods.* Dodd, 1982. *(P; I)*

Wexler, Jerome. *Secrets of the Venus Fly Trap.* Dodd, 1981. *(P; I)*

PLASTICS

Dineen, Jacqueline. *Plastics.* Enslow, 1988. *(I)*

Lambert, Mark. *Spotlight on Plastics.* Rourke, 1988. *(P; I)*

Whyman, Kathryn. *Plastics.* Gloucester Press; dist. by Watts, 1988. *(P; I)*

PLATYPUS AND SPINY ANTEATERS. See MAMMALS.

PLUMBING

Zim, Herbert S., and Skelly, James R. *Pipes and Plumbing Systems*. Morrow, 1974. *(I)*

PLYMOUTH COLONY. See AMERICAN COLONIES.

POCAHONTAS. See SMITH, JOHN.

POETRY

Adoff, Arnold, ed. *I Am the Darker Brother: An Anthology of Modern Poems by Black Americans*. Macmillan, 1970; *The Poetry of Black America: Anthology of the Twentieth Century*. Har-Row, 1973. *(I; A)*

Adshead, Gladys L., and Duff, Annis, eds. *An Inheritance of Poetry*. HM, 1948. *(I)*

Bierhorst, John, ed. *The Sacred Path: Spells, Prayers, and Power Songs of the American Indians*. Morrow, 1983. *(I)*

Bogan, Louise, and Smith, William J., eds. *The Golden Journey: Poems for Young People*. Contemp Bks, 1976. *(P; I; A)*

Cole, Joanna, comp. *A New Treasury of Children's Poetry: Old Favorites and New Discoveries*. Doubleday, 1984. *(P; I)*

Cummings, E. E. *Hist Whist and Other Poems for Children,* ed. by George J. Firmage. Liveright, 1983. *(P; I)*

Hodges, Margaret, ad. *Saint George and the Dragon,* ad. from Edmund Spenser's *Faerie Queene*. Little, 1984. *(P; I)*

Janeczko, Paul B., ed. *Strings: A Gathering of Family Poems*. Bradbury, 1984. *(I; A)*

Jones, Hettie, ed. *The Trees Stand Shining: The Poetry of the North American Indians*. Dial Bks Young, 1976. *(P; I; A)*

Knudson, R. R., and Swenson, May, selector and ed. *American Sports Poems*. Watts/Orchard, 1988. *(I; A)*

Larrick, Nancy, ed. *Piping Down the Valleys Wild*. Dell, 1982. *(I; A)*

Lindsay, Vachel. *Johnny Appleseed and Other Poems*. Buccaneer, 1981. *(I)*

Livingston, Myra Cohn, ed. *Listen, Children, Listen: An Anthology of Poems for the Very Young*. HarBraceJ, 1972. *(P); Sky Songs*. Holiday, 1984. *(P; I; A)*

Merriam, Eve. *If Only I Could Tell You*. Knopf, 1983. *(I; A)*

Millay, Edna St. Vincent. *Poems Selected for Young people*. Har-Row, 1979. *(I; A)*

Prelutsky, Jack. *It's Snowing! It's Snowing!* Greenwillow, 1984. *(P); The Random House Book of Poetry for Children*. Random, 1983. *(P; I)*

Stevenson, Robert Louis. *A Child's Garden of Verses*. Scribner, n.d. (Other eds. and pubs.) *(P; I)*

Wildsmith, Brian, illus. *Oxford Book of Poetry for Children*. Merrimack, n.d. *(P; I)*

POISONS AND ANTIDOTES

Haines, Gail Kay. *Natural and Synthetic Poisons*. Morrow, 1978. *(P; I)*

POLAND

Greene, Carol. *Poland,* Childrens, 1983. *(I; A)*
Sandak, Cass R. *Poland*. Watts, 1986. *(I)*
Zyskind, Sara. *Stolen Years*. Lerner, 1981. *(I; A)*

POLICE

Broekel, Ray. *Police*. Childrens, 1981. *(P)*
Hewett, Joan. *Motorcycle on Patrol: The Story of a Highway Officer*. Clarion/T. & F., 1986. *(P)*
Scott, Paul. *Police Divers*. Messner, 1982. *(I)*

POLITICAL PARTIES AND POLITICS

Hoopes, Ray. *Political Campaigning*. Watts, 1979. *(I; A)*
Kronenwetter, Michael. *Are You a Liberal? Are You a Conservative?* Watts, 1984. *(I; A)*
Levenson, Dorothy. *Politics: How to Get Involved*. Watts, 1980. *(I; A)*
Raynor, Thomas. *Politics, Power, and People: Four Governments in Action*. Watts, 1983. *(I; A)*
Weiss, Ann E. *Party Politics, Party Problems*. Har-Row, 1980. *(I; A)*

POLK, JAMES K.

Lillegard, Dee. *James K. Polk: Eleventh President of the United States*. Children's, 1988. *(P; I)*
See also PRESIDENCY OF THE UNITED STATES.

POLLUTION

Bright, Michael. *The Dying Sea*. Gloucester Press, dist. by Watts, 1988. *(I)*
Gay, Kathlyn. *Acid Rain*. Watts, 1983. *(I; A); Ozone*. Watts, 1989. *(I; A); Silent Killers: Radon and Other Hazards*. Watts, 1988. *(I; A)*
Kronenwetter, Michael. *Managing Toxic Wastes*. Messner, 1989. *(I; A)*
O'Connor, Karen. *Garbage*. Lucent Books, 1989. *(P; I)*
Pringle, Lawrence. *Rain of Troubles: The Science and Politics of Acid Rain*. Macmillan, 1988. *(A)*
Weiss, Malcolm E. *Toxic Waste: Clean up or Cover Up?* Watts, 1984. *(I; A)*
Zipko, Stephen J. *Toxic Threat: How Hazardous Substances Poison Our Lives*. Messner, 1990 (rev. ed.). *(A)*
See also NOISE.

POLO, MARCO. See EXPLORATION AND DISCOVERY.

POMPEII. See ROME (ANCIENT).

PONCE DE LEÓN, JUAN. See EXPLORATION AND DISCOVERY.

PONY EXPRESS

McCall, Edith. *Mail Riders*. Childrens, 1980. *(P; I; A)*

Stein, R. Conrad. *The Story of the Pony Express*. Childrens, 1981. *(P; I)*

POPULATION

Becklake, John and Becklake, Sue. *The Population Explosion*. Gloucester Press, dist. by Watts, 1990. *(I)*

McGraw, Eric. *Population Growth*. Rourke, 1987. *(I; A)*

Nam, Charles B. *Our Population: The Changing Face of America*. Walker, 1988. *(A)*

Stwertka, Eve, and Stwertka, Albert. *Population: Growth, Change, and Impact*. Watts, 1981. *(I; A)*

PORTUGAL

Laure, Jason, and Laure, Ettagale. *Jovem Portugal: After The Revolution*. FS&G, 1977. *(I; A)*

Skalon, Ana de, and Stadtler, Christa. *We Live in Portugal*. Watts/Bookwright Press, 1987. *(P)*

POSTAL SERVICE

Gibbons, Gail. *The Post Office Book: Mail and How It Moves*. Har-Row, 1982. *(P)*

McAfee, Cheryl Weant. *The United States Postal Service*. Chelsea House, 1987. *(I; A)*

Roth, Harold. *First Class! The Postal System in Action*. Pantheon, 1983. *(I)*

POTATOES

Hughes, Meredith Sayles. *The Great Potato Book*. Macmillan, 1986. *(P)*

Johnson, Sylvia A. *Potatoes*. Lerner, 1986. *(I)*

POTTERY. See CERAMICS.

POULTRY

Hopf, Alice L. *Chickens and Their Wild Relatives*. Dodd, 1982. *(I)*

POVERTY

Dudley, William, ed. *Poverty*. Greenhaven Press, 1988. *(A)*

Meltzer, Milton. *Poverty in America*. Morrow, 1986. *(A)*

O'Connor, Karen. *Homeless Children*. Lucent, 1989. *(I; A)*

POWER PLANTS. See ENERGY; NUCLEAR ENERGY

PRAYER

Bogot, Howard, and Syme, Daniel. *Prayer Is Reaching*. UAHC, 1981. *(P)*

Cook, Walter L. *Table Prayers for Children*. Bethany, 1977. *(P)*

Field, Rachel. *Prayer for a Child*. Macmillan, 1973. *(P)*

Hallinan, P. K. *I'm Thankful Each Day*. Childrens, 1981. *(P)*

Nystrom, Carolyn. *What Is Prayer?* Moody, 1980. *(P; I)*

Tudor, Tasha. *First Graces*. McKay, 1955. *(P)*

PREHISTORIC ANIMALS

Cohen, Daniel. *Prehistoric Animals*. Doubleday, 1988. *(P; I)*

Cole, Joanna. *Saber-Toothed Tiger and Other Ice Age Mammals*. Morrow, 1977. *(P; I)*

Dixon, Dougal. *A Closer Look at Prehistoric Reptiles*. Watts, 1984. *(I; A)*

Eldridge, David. *Flying Dragons: Ancient Reptiles That Ruled the Air; Sea Monsters: Ancient Reptiles That Ruled the Sea*. Troll, 1980. *(P; I)*.

Hall, Derek. *Prehistoric Mammals*. Watts, 1984. *(P; I)*

Lampton, Christopher. *Prehistoric Animals*. Watts, 1983. *(I)*

Moody, Richard. *100 Prehistoric Animals*. Putnam/Grosset, 1988. *(P; I)*

National Geographic editors. *Giants from the Past*. National Geog, 1983. *(P; I; A)*

Zallinger, Peter. *Prehistoric Animals*. Random, 1981. *(P)*

See also DINOSAURS.

PREHISTORIC PEOPLE. See ANTHROPOLOGY.

PRESIDENCY OF THE UNITED STATES

Beard, Charles A. *The Presidents in American History*. Messner, 1985 (rev. ed.). *(A)*

Blassingame, Wyatt. *The Look-It-Up Book of Presidents*. Random, 1990. *(I; A)*

Cooke, Donald E. *Atlas of the Presidents*. Hammond, 1981. *(I; A)*

Coy, Harold. *Presidents*. Watts, 1981 (updated). *(I)*

Frank, Sid, and Melick, Arden. *Presidents: Tidbits and Trivia*. Hammond, 1980. *(P; I; A)*

Miers, Earl S. *America and Its Presidents*. Putnam, 1982. *(P; I; A)*

Parker, Nancy Windlow, *The President's Car*. Har-Row, 1981. *(P; I)*

Seuling, Barbara. *The Last Cow on the White House Lawn, and Other Little-Known Facts About the Presidency*. Doubleday, 1978. *(P; I; A)*

PRINCE EDWARD ISLAND. See CANADA.

PRINTING. See BOOKS.

PRISONS

Rickard, Graham. *Prisons and Punishments*. Watts, 1987. *(P)*

Weiss, Anne E. *Prisons: A System in Trouble*. Enslow, 1988. *(A)*

PROBABILITY. See STATISTICS.

PSYCHOLOGY

Kalb, Jonah, and Viscott, David. *What Every Kid Should Know.* HM, 1976. *(I)*

Stwertka, Eve. *Psychoanalysis: From Freud to the Age of Therapy.* Watts, 1988 *(I; A)*

Weinstein, Grace W. *People Study People: The Story of Psychology.* Dutton, 1979. *(I; A)*

PUBLIC SPEAKING

Detz, Joan. *You Mean I Have To Stand Up and Say Something?* Atheneum, 1986. *(I; A)*

Gilford, Henry. *How to Give a Speech.* Watts, 1980. *(I; A)*

PUBLISHING. See BOOKS.

PUERTO RICO

Griffiths, John. *Take a Trip to Puerto Rico.* Watts, 1989. *(P; I)*

Perl, Lisa. *Puerto Rico: Island Between Two Worlds.* Morrow, 1979. *(A)*

Visual Geography. *Puerto Rico in Pictures.* Lerner, 1987. *(I)*

PUMPS

Zubrowski, Bernie. *Messing Around with Water Pumps and Siphons: A Children's Museum Activity Book.* Little, 1981. *(P; I)*

PUNCTUATION

Forte, Imogene. *Punctuation Power.* Incentive Pubns, 1981. *(P; I)*

Gregorich, Barbara. *Apostrophe, Colon, Hyphen.* EDC, 1980; *Comma,* 1980; *Period, Question Mark, Exclamation Mark,* 1980; *Quotation Marks and Underlining,* 1980. *(P; I)*

Rigsby, Annelle. *Punctuation.* Enrich, 1980. *(P)*

PUNIC WARS. See HANNIBAL; ROME (ANCIENT)

PUPPETS AND MARIONETTES

Griffith, Bonnie. *The Tree House Gang: Puppet Plays for Children.* Standard, 1983. *(P; I)*

Krisvoy, Juel. *The Good Apple Puppet Book.* Good Apple, 1981. *(P; I)*

Lasky, Kathryn. *Puppeteer.* Macmillan, 1985. *(I)*

Marks, Burton, and Marks, Rita. *Puppets and Puppet-Making.* Plays, 1982. *(P; I)*

Oldfield, Margaret J. *Finger Puppets and Finger Plays.* Creative Storytime, 1981; *Tell and Draw Paper Bag Puppet Book,* 1981 (2nd ed.). *(P)*

Supraner, Robyn, and Supraner, Lauren. *Plenty of Puppets to Make.* Troll, 1981. *(P; I)*

Venning, Sue, illus. *Jim Henson's Muppet Show Bill.* Random, 1983. *(P; I)*

Wright, Lyndie. *Puppets.* Watts, 1989. *(P)*

PURIM

Chaikin, Miriam. *Make Noise, Make Merry: The Story and Meaning of Purim.* HM, 1983. *(I)*

Cohen, Barbara. *Here Comes the Purim Players.* Lothrop, 1984. *(P)*

Greenfeld, Howard. *Purim.* HR&W, 1983. *(P; I)*

QUAKERS. See RELIGIONS OF THE WORLD.

QUASARS AND PULSARS. See ASTRONOMY.

QUEBEC. See CANADA.

QUEBEC CITY. See CANADA.

RABBITS AND HARES

Bare, Colleen S. *Rabbits and Hares.* Dodd, 1983. *(P; I)*

Burton, Jane. *Freckles the Rabbit.* Gareth Stevens, 1989. *(P)*

Henrie, Fiona. *Rabbits.* Watts, 1980. *(P; I)*

Hess, Lilo. *Diary of a Rabbit.* Scribner, 1982. *(I)*

Oxford Scientific Films. *The Wild Rabbit.* Putnam, 1980. *(I; A)*

RACCOONS

Freschet, Berniece. *Raccoon Baby.* Putnam, 1984. *(P)*

MacClintock, Dorcas. *A Natural History of Raccoons.* Scribner, 1981. *(I); A Raccoon's First Year.* 1982. *(P)*

Patent, Dorothy H. *Raccoons, Coatimundis, and Their Family.* Holiday, 1979. *(I; A)*

RACES, HUMAN. See ANTHROPOLOGY; GENETICS AND GENETIC ENGINEERING.

RACQUETBALL

Hogan, Marty, and Wong, Ken. *High-performance Racquetball.* HP Books, 1985. *(A)*

RADIATION. See NUCLEAR ENERGY.

RADIO, AMATEUR

Ferrell, Nancy Warren. *The New World of Amateur Radio.* Watts, 1986. *(I; A)*

Kuslan, Louis I., and Kuslan, Richard D. *Ham Radio.* P-H, n.d. *(I: A)*

RADIO

Carter, Alden R. *Radio: From Marconi To the Space Age.* Watts, 1987. *(P; I)*

Edmonds, I. G., and Gebhardt, William H. *Broadcasting for Beginners.* HR&W, 1980. *(I; A)*

Gilmore, Susan. *What Goes On at a Radio Station?* Carolrhoda, 1983. *(P; I)*

Hawkins. *Audio and Radio*. EDC, 1982. *(I; A)*

Lerner, Mark. *Careers with a Radio Station*. Lerner, 1983. *(P; I)*

RAILROADS

Marshall, Ray. *The Train: Watch it Work by Operating the Moving Diagrams!* Viking, 1986. *(P)*

Sheffer, H. R. *Trains*. Crestwood, 1982. *(P; I)*

Wilson, Keith. *Railways in Canada: The Iron Link*. Watts, 1982. *(I; A)*

Yepsen, Roger. *Train Talk*. Pantheon, 1983. *(I; A)*

RAIN, SNOW, SLEET, AND HAIL

Bennett, David. *Rain*. Bantam, 1988. *(P)*

Brandt, Keith. *What Makes It Rain?* Troll, 1981. *(P)*

Branley, Franklyn M. *Rain and Hail*. Har-Row, 1983. *(P)*

Williams, Terry T., and Major, Ted. *The Secret Language of Snow*. Pantheon, 1984. *(I; A)*

RALEIGH, SIR WALTER. See ENGLAND, HISTORY OF.

RANCH LIFE. See COWBOYS.

REAGAN, RONALD WILSON

Fox, Mary Virginia. *Mister President: The Story of Ronald Reagan*. Enslow, 1986 (rev. ed.). *(I; A)*

Sullivan, George. *Ronald Reagan*. Messner, 1985. *(A)*

Tax, Mary V. *Mister President: The Story of Ronald Reagan*. Enslow, 1982. *(I; A)*

See also PRESIDENCY OF THE UNITED STATES.

RECIPES. See COOKING.

RECONSTRUCTION PERIOD

Sterling, Dorothy, ed. *The Trouble They Seen: Black People Tell the Story of Reconstruction*. Doubleday, 1976. *(I; A)*

RED CROSS

Barton, Clara. *The Story of the Red Cross*. Airmont, 1968. *(P; I)*

Gilbo, Patrick. *The American Red Cross*. Chelsea House, 1987. *(I; A)*

See also BARTON, CLARA.

REFRIGERATION

Ford, Barbara. *Keeping Things Cool: The Story of Refrigeration and Air Conditioning*. Walker, 1986. *(I; A)*

REFUGEES

Ashabranner, Brent, and Ashabranner, Melissa. *Into A Strange Land*. Dodd, 1987. *(I; A)*

Bentley, Judith. *Refugees: Search for a Haven*. Messner, 1986. *(P; I)*

Loescher, Gil, and Loescher, Ann D. *The World's Refugees: A Test of Humanity*. HarBraceJ, 1982. *(I; A)*

RELATIVITY

Apfel, Necia H. *It's All Relative: Einstein's Theory of Relativity*. Lothrop, 1981. *(I)*

Fisher, David E. *The Ideas of Einstein*. HR&W, 1980. *(P; I)*

Tauber, Gerald E. *Relativity: From Einstein to Black Holes*. Watts, 1988. *(I; A)*

RELIGIONS OF THE WORLD

Ahsan, M. M. *Muslim Festivals*. Rourke, 1987. *(P; I)*

Bates, Sylvia. *Religions of the World*. Silver, n.d. *(I; A)*

Berger, Gilda. *Religions*. Watts, 1983. *(I; A)*

Daves, Michael. *Young Reader's Book of Christian Symbolism*. Abingdon, 1967. *(I)*

Edmonds, I. G. *Hinduism*. Watts, 1978. *(I; A)*

Faber, Doris. *The Perfect Life: The Shakers in America*. FS&G, 1974. *(A)*

Haskins, James. *Religions*. Har-Row, 1973. *(A)*

Kanitkar, V. P. (Hemant). *Hinduism*. Watts/Bookwright Press, 1987. *(I; A)*

Kettelkamp, Larry. *Religions East and West*. Morrow, 1972. *(I; A)*

Martin, Nancy. *Christianity*. Watts/Bookwright Press, 1987. *(I; A)*

McNeer, May, and Ward, Lynd. *John Wesley*. Abingdon, n.d. *(I)*

Moktefi, Mokhtar. *The Rise of Islam*. Silver Burdett, 1987. *(P; I)*

Moskin, Marietta D. *In the Name of God*. Atheneum, 1980. *(I; A)*

Naylor, Phyllis. *An Amish Family*. Lamplight, 1977. *(I)*

Peare, Catherine O. *John Woolman: Child of Light*. Vanguard, n.d. *(I; A)*

Rice, Edward. *American Saints and Seers: American-born Religions and the Genius Behind Them*. Scholastic, 1982. *(I; A)*

Seeger, Elizabeth. *Eastern Religions*. Har-Row, 1973. *(I; A)*

Serage, Nancy. *The Prince Who Gave Up a Throne: A Story of the Buddha*. Har-Row, 1966. *(P; I)*

Snelling, John. *Buddhism*. Watts/Bookwright Press, 1987. *(I; A)*

Tames, Richard. *Islam*. (Dictionaries of World Religions Series). David & Charles, 1985. *(A)*

REMBRANDT. See ART AND ARTISTS.

RENAISSANCE

Caselli, Giovanni. *The Renaissance and the New World*. Harper, 1986. *(I; A)*

Setton, Kenneth M., and others. *Renaissance: Maker of Modern Man*. Natl Geog, 1970. *(A)*

REPRODUCTION, HUMAN

Cole, Joanna. *How You Were Born*. Morrow, 1984. *(P)*
Girard, Linda W. *You Were Born on Your Very First Birthday*. Whitman, 1983. *(P)*
Jessel, Camilla. *The Joy of Birth*. Hillside, 1982. *(P; I)*
Johnson, Eric W. *Love and Sex in Plain Language*. Har-Row, 1977. *(I; A)*
Nilsson, Lennart. *How Was I Born? A Photographic Story of Reproduction and Birth for Children*. Delacorte, 1975. *(P; I)*
Nourse, Alan E. *Birth Control*. Watts, 1988. *(A); Menstruation*, 1987. *(I; A)*
Showers, Paul. *Baby Starts to Grow*. Har-Row, 1969. *(P)*
Stein, Sarah B. *Making Babies*. Walker, 1974. *(P; I)*

REPTILES

Ballard, Lois. *Reptiles*. Childrens, 1982. *(P; I)*
Cook, David. *Small World of Reptiles*. Watts, 1981. *(P)*
Daly, Kathleen N. *A Child's Book of Snakes, Lizards, and Other Reptiles*. Doubleday, 1980. *(P)*
DeTreville, Susan, and DeTreville, Stan. *Reptiles and Amphibians*. Troubador Pr, 1981. *(P; I)*
Fichter, George S. *Reptiles and Amphibians of North America*. Random, 1982. *(P; I)*
George, Lindsay Barrett, and George, William T. *Box Turtle at Long Pond*. Greenwillow Books, 1989. *(P)*
Kuchalla, Susan. *What Is a Reptile?* Troll Assocs, 1982. *(P)*
Mattison, Chris. *The Care of Reptiles and Amphibians in Captivity*. Blandford, 1987. *(A)*
McNaughton, Lenor. *Turtles, Tadpoles, and Take-Me-Homes*. Good Apple, 1981. *(P; I)*

RETAIL STORES

Gibbons, Gail. *Department Stores*. Har-Row, 1984. *(P)*
Stanhope, Lavinia. *Careers in a Department Store*. Raintree, 1976. *(P; I)*

RETARDATION, MENTAL

Byars, Betsy. *The Summer of the Swans*. Viking Pr, 1970. (Fiction) *(I)*
Cleaver, Vera, and Cleaver, Bill. *Me Too*. Har-Row, 1973. *(I)*
Dunbar, Robert E. *Mental Retardation*. Watts, 1978. *(I)*
Sobol, Harriet Langsam. *My Brother Steven Is Retarded*. Macmillan, 1977. *(I)*

REVERE, PAUL

Brandt, Keith. *Paul Revere: Son of Liberty*. Troll, 1982. *(P; I)*
Forbes, Esther. *America's Paul Revere*. HM, 1976. *(P; I)*
Lee, Martin. *Paul Revere*. Watts, 1987. *(P)*

REVOLUTIONARY WAR

Benchley, Nathaniel. *George the Drummer Boy*. Har-Row, 1977. *(P)*
Bliven, Bruce, Jr. *The American Revolution*. Random, 1981. *(I; A)*
Carter, Alden R. *At the Forge of Liberty; Birth of the Republic; Colonies in Revolt; Darkest Hours*. Watts, 1988. *(P; I)*
Clapp, Patricia. *I'm Deborah Sampson: A Soldier in the War of the Revolution*. Lothrop, 1977. *(I)*
Davis, Burke. *George Washington and the American Revolution*. Random, 1975. *(I; A)*
Evans, R. E. *The American War of Independence*. Lerner, 1977. *(I; A)*
Forbes, Esther. *Johnny Tremain*. HM, 1943. *(I)*
Fritz, Jean. *Can't You Make Them Behave, King George?* Putnam, 1982. *(P; I)*
Meltzer, Milton. *The American Revolutionaries*. Harper/Crowell, 1987. *(A)*
Phelan, Mary K. *The Story of the Boston Massacre*. Har-Row, 1976. *(I; A)*
Stein, R. Conrad. *The Story of Lexington and Concord*. Children's, 1983. *(P; I)*

RHINOCEROSES

Lavine, Sigmund A. *Wonders of Rhinos*. Dodd, 1982. *(I)*

RHODE ISLAND

Carpenter, Allan. *Rhode Island*. Childrens, 1979. *(P; I)*
Eaton, Jeannette. *Lone Journey: The Life of Roger Williams*. HarBraceJ, 1966. *(A)*
Fradin, Dennis. *Rhode Island: In Words and Pictures*. Childrens, 1981. *(P; I); The Rhode Island Colony*. Childrens, 1989. *(P; I)*

RICE. See GRAIN AND GRAIN PRODUCTS.

RICHELIEU, CARDINAL. See FRANCE.

RIO DE JANEIRO. See BRAZIL.

RIVERS AND LAKES

Bains, Rae. *Wonders of Rivers*. Troll, 1981. *(P)*
Bellamy, David. *The River*. Clarkson N. Potter; dist. by Crown, 1988. *(P)*
Carlisle, Norman, and Carlisle, Madelyn. *Rivers*. Children's, 1982. *(P)*
Dabcovich, Lydia. *Follow the River*. Dutton, 1980. *(P)*
Emil, Jane, and Veno, Joseph. *All About Rivers*. Troll, 1984. *(P; I)*
Mulherin, Jenny. *Rivers and Lakes*. Watts, 1984. *(P; I)* (Atlas format)
Rowland-Entwistle, Theodore. *Rivers and Lakes*. Silver Burdett, 1987. *(P; I)*
Updegraffe, Imelda, and Updegraffe, Robert. *Rivers and Lakes*. Penguin, 1983. *(I; A)*

ROADS AND HIGHWAYS

Crockett, Mary. *Roads and Traveling*. Sportshelf, n.d. *(P; I)*

Gibbons, Gail. *New Road!* Har-Row, 1983. *(P)*

Williams, Owen. *How Roads Are Made*. Facts on File, 1989. *(I)*

ROBINSON, JACK ROOSEVELT (JACKIE)

Farr, Naunerle C. *Babe Ruth—Jackie Robinson*. Pendulum, 1979. *(P; I; A)*

Frommer, Harvey. *Jackie Robinson*. Watts, 1984. *(I; A)*

Scott, Richard. *Jackie Robinson*. Chelsea House, 1987. *(I; A)*

ROBOTS

Billard, Mary. *All About Robots*. Putnam, 1982. *(P; I)*

Chester, Michael. *Robots: Facts Behind Fiction*. Macmillan, 1983. *(P; I)*

Hawkes, Nigel. *Robots and Computers*. Watts, 1984. *(I; A)*

Knight, David C. *Robotics: Past, Present and Future*. Morrow, 1983. *(I; A)*

Liptak, Karen. *Robotics Basics: An Introduction for Young People*. Prentice-Hall, 1984. *(I)*

Litterick, Ian. *Robots and Intelligent Machines*. Watts, 1984. *(I)*

Silverstein, Alvin, and Silverstein, Virginia. *The Robots Are Here*. P-H, 1983. *(P; I)*

ROCKETS. See SATELLITES: SPACE EXPLORATION AND TRAVEL.

ROCK MUSIC

Fornatale, Pete. *The Story of Rock 'n' Roll*. Morrow, 1987. *(A)*

Hanmer, Trudy J. *An Album of Rock and Roll*. Watts, 1988. *(P; I)*

Tobler, John. *Thirty Years of Rock*. Exeter Books, 1985. *(A)*

ROCKS, MINERALS, AND ORES

Harris, Susan. *Gems and Minerals*. Watts, 1982. *(P)*

Kehoe, Michael. *The Rock Quarry Book*. Carolrhoda, 1981. *(P)*

Marcus, Elizabeth. *Rocks and Minerals*. Troll, 1983. *(P; I)*

McGowen, Tom. *Album of Rocks and Minerals*. Rand, 1981. *(P; I)*

Podendorf, Illa. *Rocks and Minerals*. Childrens, 1982. *(P)*

Symes, R. F. and the staff of the Natural History Museum. *Rocks and Minerals*. Knopf, 1988. *(I)*

Whyman, Kathryn. *Rocks and Minerals*. Gloucester, dist. by Watts, 1989. *(P; I)*

RODENTS

Bare, Colleen S. *Tree Squirrels*. Dodd, 1983. *(P; I)*

Lane, Margaret. *The Squirrel*. Dial, 1981. *(P)*

Lavine, Sigmund. *Wonders of Mice*. Dodd, 1980; *Wonders of Woodchucks*, 1984. *(I)*

McConoughey, Jana. *The Squirrels*. Crestwood, 1983. *(P; I)*

Newton, James R. *The March of the Lemmings*. Har-Row, 1976. *(P)*

See also GUINEA PIGS, HAMSTERS, AND GERBILS.

RODEOS

Fain, James W. *Rodeos*. Children's, 1983. *(P)*

Munn, Vella. *Rodeo Riders*. Harvey, 1981. *(P; I; A)*

Tinkelman, Murray. *Rodeo: The Great American Sport*. Greenwillow, 1982. *(I; A)*

ROLLER SKATING

Herda, D. J. *Roller Skating*. Watts, 1979. *(I; A)*

Olney, Ross R., and Bush, Chan. *Roller Skating!* Lothrop, 1979. *(I)*

ROMAN ART AND ARCHITECTURE. See ROME (ANCIENT).

ROMAN NUMERALS. See NUMBERS AND NUMBER SYSTEMS.

ROME (ANCIENT)

Asimov, Isaac. *Roman Empire*. HM, 1967; *Roman Republic*, 1966. *(I; A)*

Chisholm, Jan. *Roman Times*. EDC, 1982. *(I; A)*

Corbishley, Mike. *The Romans*. Watts, 1984. *(I; A)*

Glubok, Shirley. *The Art of Ancient Rome*. Har-Row, 1965; *The Art of the Etruscans*, 1967. *(P; I)*

James, Simon. *Rome: 750 B.C.–500 A.D.* Watts, 1987. *(I)*

Lapper, Ivan. *Small World of Romans*. Watts, 1982. *(P)*

Lewis, Brenda R. *Growing Up in Ancient Rome*. David & Charles, 1980. *(I; A)*

Mulvihill, Margaret. *Roman Forts*. Watts, 1990. *(I)*

Purdy, Susan, and Sandak, Cass R. *Ancient Rome*. (Civilization Project Book) Watts, 1982. *(I)*

Robinson, Charles A., Jr. *Ancient Rome*, rev. by Lorna Greenberg. Watts, 1984. *(I; A)*

Rutland, Jonathan. *See Inside a Roman Town*. Warwick/Watts, 1986. *(I)*

ROOSEVELT, ELEANOR

Jacobs, William J. *Eleanor Roosevelt: A Life of Happiness and Tears*. Putnam, 1983. *(I)*

Roosevelt, Eleanor. *The Autobiography of Eleanor Roosevelt*. Har-Row, 1961. *(A)*

Roosevelt, Elliott. *Eleanor Roosevelt, With Love: A Centenary Remembrance*. Lodestar, 1984. *(A)*

Toor, Rachel. *Eleanor Roosevelt*. Chelsea House, 1989. *(I; A)*

ROOSEVELT, FRANKLIN D.

Devaney, John. *Franklin Delano Roosevelt, President*. Walker, 1987. *(I; A)*

Feinberg, Barbara S. *Franklin D. Roosevelt: Gallant President*. Lothrop, 1981. *(P; I)*

Greenblatt, Miriam. *Franklin D. Roosevelt: 32nd President of the United States*. Garrett Educational Corp., 1989. *(I)*

Hacker, Jeffrey H. *Franklin D. Roosevelt*. Watts, 1983. *(I; A)*

Lawson, Don. *FDR's New Deal*. Har-Row, 1979. *(A)*

See also PRESIDENCY OF THE UNITED STATES.

ROOSEVELT, THEODORE

Kent, Zachary. *Theodore Roosevelt: Twenty-sixth President of the United States*. Children's, 1988. *(P; I)*

Osinski, Alice. *Franklin D. Roosevelt*. Children's, 1988. *(P; I)*

Sabin, Louis. *Teddy Roosevelt: Rough Rider*. (Easy Biography Series) Troll, 1986. *(P; I)*

Stefoff, Rebecca. *Theodore Roosevelt: 26th President of the United States*. Garrett Educational Corp., 1988. *(A)*

See also PRESIDENCY OF THE UNITED STATES.

RUMANIA

Carran, Betty B. *Romania*. Children's, 1988. *(P; I)*

Diamond, Arthur. *The Romanian Americans*. Chelsea House, 1988. *(I; A)*

RWANDA. See AFRICA.

SAFETY

Brown, Marc, and Krensky, Stephen. *Dinosaurs, Beware! A Safety Guide*. Little, 1982. *(P)*

Chlad, Dorothy. *Matches and Fireworks Are Not Toys; Strangers; When I Cross the Street—By Myself*. Children's, 1982. *(P)*

Keller, Irene. *Thingumajig Book of Health and Safety*. Children's, 1982. *(P)*

Vogel, Carol G., and Goldner, Kathryn A. *The Danger of Strangers*. Dillon, 1983. *(I)*

SAILING

Adkins, Jan. *The Craft of Sail: A Primer of Sailing*. Walker, 1983. *(I)*

Burchard, Peter. *Venturing: An Introduction to Sailing*. Little, Brown, 1986. *(I; A)*

Paulsen, Gary. *Sailing: From Jibs to Jibbing*. Messner, 1981. *(I; A)*

Slocombe, Lorna. *Sailing Basics*. P-H, 1982. *(P; I)*

Vandervoort, Tom. *Sailing Is for Me*. Lerner, 1981. *(P; I)*

SAINT KITTS—NEVIS. See CARIBBEAN SEA AND ISLANDS.

SAINT LAWRENCE RIVER AND SEAWAY

Hanmer, Trudy J. *The St. Lawrence*. Watts, 1984. *(I; A)*

SAINT LUCIA. See CARIBBEAN SEA AND ISLANDS.

SAINT VINCENT AND THE GRENADINES. See CARIBBEAN SEA AND ISLANDS.

SALES AND MARKETING

Boy Scouts of America. *Salesmanship*. BSA, 1971. *(I; A)*

Orent, Norman B. *Your Future in Marketing*. Rosen, 1978. *(I; A)*

SAMOA. See PACIFIC OCEAN AND ISLANDS.

SANDBURG, CARL

Hacker, Jeffrey H. *Carl Sandburg*. Watts, 1984. *(I; A)*

Melin, Grace. *Carl Sandburg: Young Singing Poet*. Bobbs, n.d. *(P; I)*

Sandburg, Carl. *Prairie-Town Boy*. HarBraceJ, 1977. *(A)*; *Rootabaga Stories*, n.d. *(P; I)*

SAN FRANCISCO. See CALIFORNIA.

SAO TOME AND PRINCIPE. See AFRICA.

SASKATCHEWAN. See CANADA.

SATELLITES

Berger, Melvin. *Space Shots, Shuttles, and Satellites*. Putnam, 1983. *(I; A)*

Furniss, Tim. *Space Rocket*. Gloucester, dist. by Watts, 1988. *(P; I)*

Irvine, Mat. *Satellites and Computers*. Watts, 1984. *(I; A)*

Petty, Kate. *Satellites*. Watts, 1984. *(P)*

Saunders, Mike, illus. *Satellites*. Watts, 1984. *(P)*

White, Jack R. *Satellites of Today and Tomorrow*. Dodd, 1985. *(I; A)*

SAUDI ARABIA

Saudi Arabia . . . in Pictures. Lerner, 1989. *(I)*

Lye, Keith. *Take a Trip to Saudi Arabia*. Watts, 1984. *(P; I)*

SCANDINAVIA

Booss, Claire, ed. *Scandinavian Folk & Fairy Tales*. Crown, 1985. *(A)*

Franck, Irene M. *The Scandinavian-American Heritage*. Facts on File, 1988. *(I; A)*

See also DENMARK; FINLAND; LAPLAND; NORSE MYTHOLOGY; NORWAY; SWEDEN.

SCHLIEMANN, HEINRICH. See ARCHAEOLOGY.

SCHOOLS. See EDUCATION.

SCHWEITZER, ALBERT

Daniel, Anita. *The Story of Albert Schweitzer,* Random, 1957. *(I)*

SCIENCE, HISTORY OF

Asimov, Isaac. *Great Ideas of Science.* HM, 1969. *(A); How Did We Find Out About the Speed of Light?* Walker, 1986. *(I)*

Ross, Frank, Jr. *Oracle Bones, Stars, and Wheelbarrows: Ancient Chinese Science and Technology.* HM, 1982. *(I; A)*

Tannenbaum, Beulah and Tannenbaum, Harold E. *Science of the Early American Indians.* Watts, 1988. *(I)*

SCIENCE FICTION

Cohen, Daniel. *The Monsters of Star Trek.* Archway, 1980. *(P; I)*

Elwood, Roger, ed. *Science Fiction Tales: Invaders, Creatures, and Alien Worlds.* Rand, 1973. *(I; A)*

Heinlein, Robert A., ed. *Tomorrow, the Stars.* Berkley, 1983. *(I; A)*

LeGuin, Ursula. *The Last Book of Earthsea.* Atheneum, 1990. *(I)*

Liebman, Arthur, ed. *Science Fiction: Creators and Pioneers.* Rosen, 1979. *(I; A)*

Science Fiction Hall of Fame, 2 vols. Avon, 1983. *(I; A)*

SCIENCE PROJECTS. See EXPERIMENTS AND OTHER SCIENCE ACTIVITIES.

SCOTLAND

Lye, Kenneth. *Take a Trip to Scotland.* Watts, 1984. *(P; I)*

Meek, James. *The Land and People of Scotland.* Lippincott, 1990. *(I; A)*

Mitcheson, Rosalind. *Life in Scotland.* David & Charles, 1978. *(I; A)*

Sutcliff, Rosemary. *Bonnie Dundee.* Dutton, 1984. *(I; A)*

SCULPTURE

Fine, Joan. *I Carve Stone.* Har-Row, 1979. *(I)*

Haldane, Suzanne. *Faces on Places: About Gargoyles and Other Stone Creatures.* Viking, 1980. *(P; I)*

Hunt, L. C., ed. *American Sculpture.* HR&W, 1973. *(A)*

SEASONS

Bennett, David. *Seasons.* Bantam, 1988. *(P)*

Brandt, Keith. *Wonders of the Seasons.* Troll, 1981. *(P)*

Lambert, David. *The Seasons.* Watts, 1983. *(P)*

McNaughton, Colin. *Autumn.* Dial Bks Young, 1983; *Spring,* 1983; *Summer,* 1983; *Winter,* 1983. *(P)*

Nestor, William. *Into Winter: Discovering a Season.* HM, 1982. *(I)*

Penn, Linda. *Young Scientists Explore the Seasons.* Good Apple, 1983. *(P)*

Provensen, Alice, and Provensen, Martin. *A Book of Seasons.* Random, 1978. *(P)*

Vaughan, Jenny. *The Four Seasons.* Watts, 1983. *(P)*

Zolotow, Charlotte. *Summer Is. . . .* Har-Row, 1983. *(P)*

SEGREGATION

Bentley, Judith. *Busing: The Continuing Controversy.* Watts, 1982. *(I; A)*

Bullard, Pamela, and Stoia, Judith. *The Hardest Lesson: Personal Stories of a School Desegregation Crisis.* Little, 1980. *(I; A)*

SENEGAL

Lutz, William. *Senegal.* Chelsea House, 1987. *(P; I)*

Senegal . . . in Pictures. Lerner, 1988. *(I; A)*

SETS. See NUMBERS AND NUMBER SYSTEMS.

SEWING AND NEEDLECRAFT

Cone, Ferne G. *Classy Knitting: A Guide to Creative Sweatering for Beginners.* Atheneum, 1984; *Crazy Crocheting.* Atheneum, 1981. *(I; A)*

Eaton, Jan. *The Encyclopedia of Sewing Techniques.* Barron's, 1987. *(A)*

Harayda, Marel. *Needlework Magic with Two Basic Stitches.* McKay, 1978. *(A)*

Hodgson, Mary Anne, and Paine, Josephine Ruth. *Fast and Easy Needlepoint.* Doubleday, 1978. *(I)*

Mahler, Celine. *Once Upon a Quilt: Patchwork Design and Technique.* Van Nostrand, 1973. *(I; A)*

Rubenstone, Jessie. *Knitting for Beginners.* Har-Row, 1973. *(P; I)*

Sommer, Elyse, and Sommer, Joeellen. *A Patchwork, Applique, and Quilting Primer.* Lothrop, 1975. *(P; I)*

Wilson, Erica. *Erica Wilson's Children's World: Needlework Ideas from Childhood Classics.* Scribner, 1983; *Erica Wilson's Christmas World,* 1982; *Erica Wilson's Embroidery Book,* 1979; *Fun with Crewel Embroidery,* 1965; *More Needleplay,* 1979; *Needleplay,* 1975; *Erica Wilson's Quilts of America,* Oxmoor, 1979. *(I; A)*

SEXUAL ABUSE

Hyde, Margaret O. *Sexual Abuse: Let's Talk About It.* Westminster, 1987. *(A)*

SHAKESPEARE, WILLIAM

Brown, John Russell. *Shakespeare and His Theatre.* Lothrop, 1982. *(I)*

Chute, Marchette. *An Introduction to Shakespeare*. Dutton, 1957; *Stories from Shakespeare*. NAL, 1971. *(I; A)*

Hodges, C. Walter. *Shakespeare's Theatre*. Putnam, 1980. *(I)*

Lamb, Charles, and Lamb, Mary. *Tales from Shakespeare*. Biblio Dist, 1981. *(I)*

Miles, Bernard. *Favorite Tales from Shakespeare*. Rand, 1977. *(I)*

SHARKS, SKATES, AND RAYS

Sharks. Facts on File, 1990. *(I)*

Albert, Burton. *Sharks and Whales*. Grosset, 1989. *(P)*

Blassingame, Wyatt. *Wonders of Sharks*. Dodd, 1984. *(P; I)*

Bunting, Eve. *The Great White Shark*. Messner, 1982; *The Sea World Book of Sharks*. HarBraceJ, 1980. *(P; I)*

Langley, Andrew. *The World of Sharks*. Bookwright, dist. by Watts, 1988. *(P)*

Selsam, Millicent, and others. *A First Look at Sharks*. Walker, 1979. *(P)*

SHEEP AND GOATS

Chiefari, Janet. *Kids Are Baby Goats*. Dodd, 1984. *(P; I)*

Levine, Sigmund A., and Scuro, Vincent. *Wonders of Goats*. Dodd, 1980; *Wonders of Sheep*, 1983. *(P; I)*

McDearmon, Kay. *Rocky Mountain Bighorns*. Dodd, 1983. *(P; I)*

Moon, Cliff. *Sheep on the Farm*. Watts, 1983. *(P; I)*

SHELLS

Abbott, R. Tucker. *Seashells of North America*. Western, 1969; *Seashells of the World*, 1962. *(A)*

Arthur, Alex. *Shell*. Knopf, 1989. *(I)*

Goudey, Alice E. *Houses from the Sea*. Scribner, 1959. *(P)*

Morris, Dean. *Animals That Live in Shells*. Raintree, 1977. *(P)*

Selsam, Millicent E., and Hunt, Joyce A. *A First Look at Seashells*. Walker, 1983. *(P)*

SHIPS AND SHIPPING

Bushey, Jerry. *The Barge Book*. Carolrhoda, 1984. *(P; I)*

Carter, Katherine. *Ships and Seaports*. Childrens, 1982. *(P)*

Gibbons, Gail. *Boat Book*. Holiday, 1983. *(P)*

Rutland, Jonathan. *Ships*. Watts, 1982 (updated ed.). *(I; A)*

Stephen, R. J. *The Picture World of Warships*. Watts, 1990. *(P)*

Thomas, David A. *How Ships Are Made*. Facts on File, 1989. *(I)*

Tunis, Edwin. *Oars, Sails, and Steam: A Picture Book of Ships*. Har-Row, 1977. *(I)*

Williams, Brian. *Ships and Other Seacraft*. Watts, 1984. *(P; I; A)*

SIBERIA

Hautzig, Esther. *The Endless Steppe: A Girl in Exile*. Scholastic, n.d.; *Endless Steppe: Growing Up in Siberia*. Har-Row, 1968. *(I; A)*

SIERRA LEONE. See AFRICA.

SILK

Johnson, Sylvia A. *Silkworms*. Lerner, 1982. *(P; I)*

SILVER. See METALS AND METALLURGY.

SINGAPORE. See SOUTHEAST ASIA.

SKATEBOARDING

Cassorla, Albert. *The Ultimate Skateboard Book*. Running Press, 1989. *(I; A)*

SKATING

Ryan, Margaret. *Figure Skating*. Watts, 1987. *(P)*

SKIING

Berry, I. William. *The Great North American Ski Book*. Scribner, 1982 (rev. ed.). *(I)*

Boy Scouts of America. *Skiing*. BSA, 1980. *(I; A)*

Campbell, Stu, and others. *The Way to Ski!* HP Books/Body Press, 1987. *(A)*

Marozzi, Alfred. *Skiing Basics*. Prentice-Hall, 1984. *(P; I)*

Sullivan, George. *Cross-country Skiing; A Complete Beginner's Book*. Messner, 1980. *(P; I)*

Washington, Rosemary G. *Cross-Country Skiing Is for Me*. Lerner, 1982. *(I)*

SKIN DIVING. See SWIMMING AND DIVING.

SKY-DIVING

Benson, Rolf. *Skydiving*. Lerner, 1979. *(P; I; A)*

Nentl, Jerolyn. *Skydiving*. Crestwood, 1978. *(P)*

SLAVERY

Buckmaster, Henrietta. *Flight to Freedom: The Story of the Underground Railroad*. Har-Row, 1958. *(A)*

Lester, Julius. *To Be a Slave*. Dial, 1968. *(I; A)*

Meltzer, Milton. *All Times, All Peoples: A World History of Slavery*. Har-Row, 1980. *(A)*

Monjo, F. N. *The Drinking Gourd*. Har-Row, 1969; 1983 (paper). (Fiction) *(P)*

Smucker, Barbara. *Runaway to Freedom*. Har-Row, 1979. (Fiction) *(P; I)*

See also CIVIL WAR, UNITED STATES; DOUGLASS, FREDERICK; TUBMAN, HARRIET.

SLEEP

Eldred, Patricia M. *What Do We Do When We're Asleep?* Creative Ed, 1981. *(P)*

Selsam, Millicent. *How Animals Sleep*. Scholastic, 1969. *(P)*

Silverstein, Alvin and Virginia. *The Mystery of Sleep*. Little, Brown, 1987. *(P; I)*

SMITH, JOHN

Foster, Genevieve. *The World of Captain John Smith*. Scribner, 1959. *(I; A)*

Fritz, Jean. *The Double Life of Pocahontas*. Putnam, 1983. *(P; I)*

SMOKING

Berger, Gilda. *Smoking Not Allowed: The Debate*. Watts, 1987. *(A)*

Gano, Lila. *Smoking*. Lucent Books, 1989. *(I; A)*

Sonnett, Sherry. *Smoking*. Watts, 1988. *(I: A)*

Ward, Brian R. *Smoking and Health*. Watts, 1986. *(I; A)*

SNAKES

Anderson, Robert. *A Step-By-Step Book About Snakes*. TFH Publications, 1988. *(I; A)*

Broekel, Ray. *Snakes*. Children's, 1982. *(P)*

Cole, Joanna. *A Snake's Body*. Morrow, 1981. *(P)*

Fichter, George S. *Poisonous Snakes*. Watts, 1982. *(P; I)*; *Snakes Around the World*, 1980. *(P)*

Freedman, Russell. *Rattlesnakes*. Holiday, 1984. *(P)*

Lauber, Patricia. *Snakes Are Hunters*. Crowell, 1988. *(P)*

Leen, Nina. *Snakes*. HR&W, 1979. *(I; A)*

McClung, Robert M. *Snakes: Their Place in the Sun*. Garrard, 1979. *(P; I)*

SOAP BOX DERBY

Radlauer, Ed, and Radlauer, Ruth. *Soap Box Winners*. Childrens, 1983. *(P; I)*

SOCCER

Butterfield, S. M. *The Wonderful World of Soccer*. Putnam, 1982. *(P; I; A)*

Cohen, Mervyn D. *Soccer for Children and Their Parents*. Brunswick, 1983. *(P; I)*

Delson, Paul. *Soccer Sense: Terms, Tips, and Techniques*. Bradson, 1983. *(I; A)*

Gutman, Bill. *Modern Soccer Superstars*. Dodd, 1980. *(P; I; A)*

Jackson, Paul. *How to Play Better Soccer*. Har-Row, 1978. *(P; I)*

Rosenthal, Bert. *Soccer*. Childrens, 1983. *(P)*

Yannis, Alex. *Soccer Basics*. P-H, 1982. *(P; I)*

SOFTBALL

Madison, Arnold. *How to Play Girls' Softball*. Messner, 1981. *(P; I)*

Sandak, Cass R. *Baseball and Softball*. Watts, 1982. *(P)*

Washington, Rosemary G. *Softball Is for Me*. Lerner, 1982. *(P; I)*

SOILS

Boy Scouts of America. *Soil and Water Conservation*. BSA, 1968. *(I; A)*

Leutscher, Alfred. *Earth*. Dial Bks Young, 1983. *(P; I)* (A book about soils)

SOLAR ENERGY

Asimov, Isaac. *How Did We Find Out About Solar Power?* Walker, 1981. *(P; I)*

Kaplan, Sheila. *Solar Energy*. Raintree, 1983. *(P; I)*

Spetgang, Tilly, and Wells, Malcolm. *The Children's Solar Energy Book*. Sterling, 1982. *(P; I)*

SOLAR SYSTEM

Adams, Richard. *Our Wonderful Solar System*. Troll, 1983. *(P; I)*

Lambert, David. *The Solar System*. Watts, 1984. *(I; A)*

Roop, Peter, and Roop, Connie. *The Solar System*. Greenhaven Press, 1988. *(A)*

See also PLANETS; SUN.

SOLIDS. See MATTER.

SOLOMON ISLANDS. See PACIFIC OCEAN AND ISLANDS.

SOMALIA. See AFRICA.

SOUND AND ULTRASONICS

Branley, Franklyn M. *High Sounds, Low Sounds*. Har-Row, 1975. *(P)*

Kettelkamp, Larry. *The Magic of Sound*. Morrow, 1982. *(I)*

Knight, David. *All About Sound*. Troll, 1983. *(P; I)*

Wicks, Keith. *Sound and Recording*. Watts, 1982. *(I; A)*

SOUTH AFRICA

Harris, Sarah. *Timeline: South Africa*. Dryad, 1988. *(I; A)*

Jacobsen, Karen. *South Africa*. Childrens, 1989. *(P)*

Meyer, Carolyn. *Voices of South Africa: Growing up in a Troubled Land*. Gulliver/Harcourt, 1986. *(I; A)*

Naidoo, Beverly. *Journey to Jo'burg: A South African Story*. Lippincott, 1986. *(I; A)*

Pascoe, Elaine. *South Africa: Troubled Land*. Watts, 1987. *(A)*

Paton, Jonathan. *The Land and People of South Africa*. Lippincott, 1990. *(A)*

Stein, R. Conrad. *South Africa*. Children's, 1986. *(P)*

Watson, R. L. *South Africa . . . in Pictures*. Lerner, 1988. *(P; I)*

SOUTH AMERICA

Beatty, Noelle B., *Suriname*. Chelsea House, 1987. *(P; I)*
Carter, William E. *South America*. Watts, 1983 (rev. ed.). *(I; A)*
See also individual countries.

SOUTH CAROLINA

Burney, Eugenia. *Fort Sumter*. Childrens, 1975. *(P; I)*
Carpenter, Allan. *South Carolina*. Childrens, 1979. *(I)*
Fradin, Dennis. *South Carolina: In Words and Pictures*. Childrens, 1980. *(P; I)*
Osborne, Anne R. *A History of South Carolina*. Sandlapper Pub, 1983. *(P; I)*

SOUTH DAKOTA

Carpenter, Allan. *South Dakota*. Childrens, 1978. *(P; I)*
Fradin, Dennis. *South Dakota: In Words and Pictures*. Childrens, 1981. *(P; I)*
Wilder, Laura Ingalls. *Little Town on the Prairie*. Har-Row, 1953. *(I)*; *The Long Winter*, 1953. *(I)*

SOUTHEAST ASIA

Malaysia . . . in Pictures. Lerner, 1989. *(I)*
Thailand . . . in Pictures. Lerner, 1989. *(I)*
Bjener, Tamiko. *Philippines*. Gareth Stevens, 1987. *(P)*
Cordero Fernando, Gilda. *We Live in the Philippines*. Watts/Bookwright Pr., 1986. *(P; I)*
Elder, Bruce. *Malaysia. Singapore*. Watts, 1985. *(P)*
Fairclough, Chris. *We Live in Indonesia*. Watts/Bookwright Pr., 1986. *(P; I)*
Goldfarb, Mace. *Fighters, Refugees, Immigrants: A Story of the Hmong*. Carolrhoda, 1982. *(P; I)*
Huynh Quang Nhuong. *The Land I Lost: Adventures of a Boy in Vietnam*. Har-Row, 1982. *(I)*
Knowlton, MaryLee, and Sachner, Mark J. *Burma*. Gareth Stevens, 1987. *(P)*; *Indonesia*, 1987. *(P)*; *Malaysia*, 1987. *(P)*
Lye, Keith. *Indonesia*. Watts, 1985. *(P)*
Nickelson, Harry. *Vietnam*. Lucent Books, 1989. *(I; A)*
Smith, Datus C., Jr. *The Land and People of Indonesia*. Har-Row, 1983 (rev. ed.). *(I)*
Stein, R. Conrad. *The Fall of Singapore*. Children's, 1982. *(P; I)*
Thomson, Ruth and Neil. *A Family in Thailand*. Lerner, 1988. *(P)*
Warren, James A. *Portrait of a Tragedy: America and the Vietnam War*. Lothrop, 1990. *(A)*
Withington, William A. *Southeast Asia*. Gateway Press, 1988. *(I; A)*
Wright, David K. *Malaysia*. Children's, 1988. *(P; I)*

SOUTH POLE. See ANTARCTICA.

SPACE EXPLORATION AND TRAVEL

Asimov, Isaac. *Piloted Space Flights*. Gareth Stevens, 1990. *(P; I)*
Bendick, Jean. *Space Travel*. Watts, 1982. *(I; A)*
Berger, Melvin. *Space Shots, Shuttles, and Satellites*. Putnam, 1983. *(I; A)*
Branley, Franklyn M. *From Sputnik to Space Shuttles: Into the new Space Age*. Harper/Crowell, 1986. *(P; I)*
Dwiggins, Don. *Flying the Space Shuttles*. Dodd, 1985. *(I)*; *Hello? Who's Out There?: The Search for Extraterrestrial Life*, 1987. *(P; I)*
Lampton, Christopher. *Rocketry: From Goddard to Space Travel*. Watts; 1988. *(P,I)*
Long, Kim. *The Astronaut Training Book for Kids*. Dutton/Lodestar, 1990. *(I)*
Muarer, Richard. *The Nova Space Explorer's Guide: Where to Go and What to See*. Crown, 1985. *(I; A)*
Sandak, Cass R. *The World of Space*. Watts, 1989. *(P; I)*
Schefter, James L. *Aerospace Careers*. Watts, 1987. *(A)*
Schick, Ron, and Van Haaften, Julia. *The View from Space*. Clarkson N. Potter, 1988. *(A)*
Spangenburg, Ray, and Moser, Diane. *Opening the Space Frontier*. Facts on File, 1989. *(I; A)*
Vogt, Gregory. *Space Laboratories*. Watts, 1990. *(P; I)*; *Spaceships*. Watts, 1990. *(P; I)*

SPAIN

Lye, Keith. *Passport to Spain*. Watts, 1987. *(P)*
Miller, Arthur. *Spain*. Chelsea House, 1989. *(P; I)*
Rutland, Jonathan. *Take a Trip to Spain*. Watts, 1981. *(P)*
Woods, Geraldine. *Spain: A Shining New Democracy*. Dillon Press, 1987. *(P; I)*
Yokoyama, Masami. *Spain*. Gareth Stevens, 1987. *(P; I)*

SPANISH-AMERICAN WAR

Lawson, Don. *The United States in the Spanish-American War*. Har-Row, 1976. *(I; A)*

SPEECH AND SPEECH DISORDERS

Adams, Edith. *The Noisy Book Starring Yakety Yak*. Random, 1983. *(P)*
Berger, Gilda. *Speech and Language Disorders*. Watts, 1981. *(I; A)*
Carlisle, Jock A. *Tangled Tongue*. Univ. of Toronto, 1985. *(A)*
Minn, Loretta. *Teach Speech*. Good Apple, 1982. *(P; I)*
Showers, Paul. *How You Talk*. Har-Row, 1967; 1975 (paper). *(P)*
Silverstein, Alvin and Virginia. *Wonders of Speech*. Morrow, 1988. *(A)*
See also PUBLIC SPEAKING.

SPELLING

Daniel, Charlie, and Daniel, Becky. *Super Spelling Fun*. Good Apple, 1978. *(P; I)*

Gordon, Sharon. *The Spelling Bee*. Troll, 1981. *(P)*

Preksto, Peter W., Jr., and Schaefer, Patricia S. *Spelling Skills*. Creative Ed, 1979. *(P; I; A)*

Wittels, Harriet, and Greisman, Joan. *How to Spell It: A Dictionary of Commonly Misspelled Words*. Putnam, 1982. *(P; I; A)*

SPELUNKING. See CAVES AND CAVERNS.

SPIDERS AND THEIR RELATIVES

Billings, Charlene W. *Scorpions*. Dodd, 1983. *(I; A)*

Dallinger, Jane. *Spiders*. Lerner, 1981. *(P; I; A)*

Lane, Margaret. *The Spider*. Dial Bks Young, 1982. *(P)*

Schnieper, Claudia. *Amazing Spiders*. Carolrhoda, 1989. *(P; I)*

Selsam, Millicent E., and Hunt, Joyce A. *A First Look at Spiders*. Walker, 1983. *(P)*

Webster, David. *Spider Watching*. Messner, 1984. *(I)*

SPIES

Cohen, Daniel. *The Science of Spying*. McGraw, 1977. *(I; A)*

Surge, Frank. *Famous Spies*. Lerner, 1969. *(I; A)*

SPIRITUALS. See HYMNS AND SPIRITUALS.

SQUIRRELS

Gurnell, John. *The Natural History of Squirrels*. Facts on File, 1987. *(A)*

SRI LANKA

Sri Lanka . . . in Pictures. Lerner, 1989. *(I; A)*

Wilber, Donald N. *The Land and People of Ceylon*. Har-Row, 1972. *(I; A)*

STAINED-GLASS WINDOWS. See CATHEDRALS.

STALIN, JOSEPH

Blassingame, Wyatt. *Joseph Stalin and Communist Russia*. Garrard, 1971. *(P; I)*

Marrin, Albert. *Stalin: Russia's Man of Steel*. Viking, 1988. *(A)*

STAMPS AND STAMP COLLECTING

Allen, Judy. *Guide to Stamps and Stamp Collecting*. EDC, 1981. *(P; I)*

Boy Scouts of America. *Stamp Collecting*. BSA, 1974. *(I; A)*

Hobson, Burton. *Getting Started in Stamp Collecting*. Sterling. 1982 (rev. ed.) *(I; A)*

STARFISHES AND THEIR RELATIVES

Zim, Herbert S., and Krantz, Lucretia. *Sea Stars and Their Kin*. Morrow, 1976. *(P; I)*

STARS

Apfel, Necia H. *Nebulae: The Birth and Death of Stars*. Lothrop, 1988. *(P)*; *Stars and Galaxies*. Watts, 1982. *(I; A)*

Berger, Melvin. *Bright Stars, Red Giants, and White Dwarfs*. Putnam, 1983. *(I; A)*

Branley, Franklyn M. *The Sky Is Full of Stars*, 1981. *(P)*; *Star Guide*, 1987. *(P; I)*

Gallant, Roy A. *The Constellations: How They Came to Be*. Scholastic, 1979. *(I; A)*

Rymon, Chet. *365 Starry Nights*. P-H, 1982. *(I; A)*

STATE GOVERNMENTS

Bentley, Judith. *State Government*. Watts, 1978. *(I; A)*

Goode, Stephen. *The New Federalism: States' Rights in American History*. Watts, 1983. *(I; A)*

STATISTICS

Arthur, Lee, and others. *Sportsmath: How It Works*. Lothrop, 1975. *(I; A)*

Riedel, Manfred G. *Winning with Numbers: A Kid's Guide to Statistics*. P-H, 1978. *(I; A)*

Srivastava, Jane J. *Statistics*. Har-Row, 1973. *(P; I)*

STEAM ENGINES. See TECHNOLOGY.

STOWE, HARRIET BEECHER

Jakoubek, Robert E. *Harriet Beecher Stowe: Author and Abolitionist*. Chelsea House, 1989. *(I; A)*

Scott, John A. *Woman Against Slavery: The Story of Harriet Beecher Stowe*. Har-Row, 1978. *(I; A)*

STRINGED INSTRUMENTS. See MUSICAL INSTRUMENTS.

STUDY, HOW TO

Farnette, Cherrie. *The Study Skills Shop*. Incentive Pubns, 1980. *(P; I)*

James, Elizabeth, and Barkin, Carol. *How to Be School Smart: Secrets of Successful Schoolwork*. Lothrop, Lee & Shepard, 1988. *(I; A)*

Kesselman-Turkel, Judi, and Peterson, Franklynn. *Study Smarts: How to Learn More in Less Time*. Contemp Bks 1981. *(I; A)*

SUBMARINES

Graham, Ian. *Submarines*. Gloucester, dist. by Watts, 1989. *(I)*

Rossiter, Mike. *Nuclear Submarine*. Watts, 1983. *(I; A)*

Stephen, R. J. *The Picture World of Submarines*. Watts, 1990. *(P)*

Sullivan, George. *Inside Nuclear Submarines*. Dodd, 1982. *(I; A)*

Weiss, Harvey. *Submarines and Other Underwater Craft*. Crowell, 1990. *(P; I)*

White, David. *Submarines*. Rourke, 1988. *(P)*

SUDAN

Sudan . . . in Pictures. Lerner, 1988. *(I)*

Stewart, Judy. *A Family in Sudan*. Lerner, 1988. *(P)*

SUEZ CANAL. See CANALS.

SUGAR

Cobb, Vicki. *Gobs of Goo*. Har-Row, 1983. *(P)*

Mitgutsch, Ali. *From Beet to Sugar*. Carolrhoda, 1981. *(P)*

SUN

Adams, Richard. *Our Amazing Sun*. Troll, 1983. *(P; I)*

Ardley, Neil. *Sun and Light*. Watts, 1983. *(P; I)*

Asimov, Isaac. *How Did We Find Out About Sunshine?* Walker, 1987. *(P; I)*

Fields, Alice. *The Sun*. Watts, 1980. *(P)*

Gibbons, Gail. *Sun Up, Sun Down*. HarBraceJ, 1983. *(P; I)*

Jaber, William. *Exploring the Sun*. Messner, 1980. *(P; I)*

Lampton, Christopher. *The Sun*. Watts, 1982. *(I; A)*

Palazzo, Janet. *Our Friend the Sun*. Troll, 1982. *(P)*

SUPERMARKETS. See RETAIL STORES.

SUPERSTITIONS

Nevins, Ann. *Super Stitches: A Book of Superstitions*. Holiday, 1983. *(P)*

Perl, Lila. *Don't Sing Before Breakfast, Don't Sleep in the Moonlight: Everyday Superstitions and How They Began*. Clarion Books, 1988. *(I)*

SUPREME COURT OF THE UNITED STATES

Coy, Harold. *The Supreme Court,* rev. by Lorna Greenberg. Watts, 1981. *(I; A)*

Fox, Mary V. *Justice Sandra Day O'Connor*. Enslow, 1983. *(I; A)*

Goode, Stephen. *The Controversial Court: Supreme Court Influences on American Life*. Messner, 1982. *(I; A)*

Greene, Carol. *Sandra Day O'Connor: First Woman of the Supreme Court*. Children's, 1982. *(P)*

Rierden, Anne B. *Reshaping the Supreme Court: New Justices, New Directions*. Watts, 1988. *(A)*

Stein, R. Conrad. *The Story of the Powers of the Supreme Court*. Childrens, 1989. *(I)*

SURFING

Coombs, Charles. *Be a Winner in Windsurfing*. Morrow, 1982. *(P; I)*

Evans, Jeremy. *The Complete Guide To Short Board Sailing*. International Marine, 1987. *(A)*

Freeman, Tony. *Beginning Surfing*. Children's, 1980. *(P; I)*

SURINAME. See SOUTH AMERICA.

SWANS

Scott, Jack Denton. *Swans*. Putnam, 1988. *(P; I)*

SWAZILAND. See AFRICA.

SWEDEN

Bjener, Tamiko. *Sweden*. Gareth Stevens, 1987. *(P; I)*

Knowlton, MaryLee, and Sachner, Mark J. *Sweden*. Gareth Stevens, 1987. *(P)*

Lye, Keith. *Take a Trip to Sweden*. Watts, 1983. *(P)*

McGill, Allyson. *The Swedish Americans*. Chelsea House, 1988. *(I; A)*

Olsson, Kari. *Sweden: A Good Life for All*. Dillon, 1983. *(I; A)*

SWIMMING AND DIVING

Boy Scouts of America. *Swimming*. BSA, 1980. *(I; A)*

Briggs, Carole S. *Diving Is for Me*. Lerner, 1983. *(P; I)*

Chiefari, Jane, and Wightman, Nancy. *Better Synchronized Swimming for Girls*. Dodd, 1981. *(I)*

Gleasner, Diana C. *Illustrated Swimming, Diving, and Surfing Dictionary for Young People*. Harvey, 1980. *(P; I; A)*

Libby, Bill. *The Young Swimmer*. Lothrop, 1983. *(P; I)*

Orr, C. Rob, and Tyler, Jane B. *Swimming Basics*. P-H, 1980. *(P; I; A)*

Sullivan, George. *Better Swimming for Boys and Girls*. Dodd, 1982. *(A)*

SWITZERLAND

Cameron, Fiona, and Kristensen, Preben. *We Live in Switzerland*. Watts/Bookwright Press, 1987. *(P)*

Hintz, Martin. *Switzerland*. Childrens, 1986. *(P)*

Lye, Keith. *Take a Trip to Switzerland*. Watts, 1984. *(P; I)*

Schrepfer, Margaret. *Switzerland: The Summit of Europe*. Dillon Press, 1989. *(P; I)*

SYRIA. See MIDDLE EAST.

TABLE TENNIS

Sullivan, George. *Better Table Tennis for Boys and Girls*. Godd, 1972. *(I)*

TAFT, WILLIAM HOWARD

Casey, Jane Clark. *William Howard Taft*. Childrens, 1989. *(P; I)*

TAIWAN

Cooke, David C. *Taiwan, Island China*. Dodd, 1975. *(I)*
Yu, Ling. *Taiwan . . . in Pictures*. Lerner, 1989. *(I)*

TAJ MAHAL. See INDIA.

TANZANIA. See AFRICA.

TAXATION

Taylor, Jack. *The Internal Revenue Service*. Chelsea House, 1987. *(A)*

TAXIDERMY

Cutchins, Judy, and Johnston, Ginny. *Are Those Animals Real? How Museums Prepare Wildlife Exhibits*. Morrow, 1984. *(P; I)*

TAXONOMY

Gutnik, Martin J. *The Science of Classification: Finding Order Among Living and Non-Living Objects*. Watts, 1980. *(I; A)*
Selsam, Millicent E. *Benny's Animals and How He Put Them in Order*. Har-Row, 1966. *(P)*

TAYLOR, ZACHARY

Collins, David R. *Zachary Taylor: 12th President of the United States*. Garrett Educational Corp., 1989. *(I)*
Kent, Zachary. *Zachary Taylor: Twelfth President of the United States*. Children's, 1988. *(P; I)*
See also PRESIDENCY OF THE UNITED STATES.

TCHAIKOVSKY, PETER ILYICH. See MUSIC AND MUSICIANS.

TEACHERS

Shockley, Robert J., and Cutlip, Glen W. *Careers in Teaching*. Rosen, 1988. *(A)*

TECHNOLOGY

Ardley, Neil. *Fact or Fantasy*. Watts, 1982. *(I; A)*
Macaulay, David. *The Way Things Work*. Houghton, 1988. *(I; A)*
McKie, Robin. *Technology: Science at Work*. Watts, 1984. *(I; A)*
Pollard, Michael. *How Things Work*. Larousse, 1979. *(I)*
Smith, Norman F., and Douglas W. *Simulators*. Watts, 1989. *(I; A)*

TEETH

Nourse, Alan. *The Tooth Book*. McKay, 1977. *(I; A)*
Pluckrose, Henry. *Teeth*. Watts, 1988. *(P)*
See also DENTISTS AND DENTISTRY.

TELEPHONE AND TELEGRAPH

Cavanagh, Mary. *Telephone Power*. Enrich, 1980. *(P; I)*
Math, Irwin. *Morse, Marconi, and You: Understanding and Building Telegraph, Telephone, and Radio Sets*. Scribner, 1979. *(I; A)*
See also BELL, ALEXANDER GRAHAM.

TELESCOPES. See ASTRONOMY.

TELEVISION.

Beale, Griffin. *TV and Video*. EDC, 1983. *(P; I)*
Drucker, Malka, and James, Elizabeth. *Series TV: How a Television Show Is Made*. H-M, 1983. *(I; A)*
Fields, Alice. *Television*. Watts, 1981. *(P)*
Jaspersohn, William. *A Day in the Life of a Television News Reporter*. Little, 1981. *(I)*
Scott, Elaine. *Ramona: Behind the Scenes of a Television Show*. Morrow, 1988. *(P; I)*
Smith, Betsy. *Breakthrough: Women in Television*. Walker, 1981. *(A)*

TENNESSEE

Carpenter, Allan. *Tennessee*. Children's, 1979. *(I)*
Fradin, Dennis. *Tennessee: In Words and Pictures*. Children's, 1980. *(P; I)*
Steele, William O. *The Perilous Road*. HarBraceJ, 1965. *(P; I)*

TENNIS

Ashe, Arthur, and Robinson, Louie. *Getting Started in Tennis*. Atheneum, 1977. *(I; A)*
Braden, Vic, and Bruns, Bill. *Vic Braden's Quick Fixes*. Little, Brown, 1988. *(I; A)*
Knudson, R. R. *Martina Navratilova: Tennis Power*. Viking Kestrel, 1986. *(P; I)*
LaMarche, Bob. *Tennis Basics*. P-H, 1983. *(P; I)*
Sullivan, George. *Better Tennis for Boys and Girls*. Dodd, 1987. *(I)*

TERRARIUMS

Broekel, Ray. *Aquariums and Terrariums*. Childrens, 1982. *(P)*
Mattison, Christopher. *The Care of Reptiles and Amphibians in Captivity*. Blandford Press, 1987. *(I; A)*
Steinberg, Phil. *You and Your Pet: Terrarium Pets*. Lerner, 1978. *(P; I)*

TERRORISM

Arnold, Terrell E., and Kennedy, Moorhead. *Think About Terrorism: The New Warfare*. Walker, 1988. *(A)*
Coker, Chris. *Terrorism and Civil Strife*. Watts, 1987. *(I)*
Edwards, Richard. *International Terrorism*. Rourke, 1988. *(I)*

TEXAS

Adams, Carolyn. *Stars over Texas*. Eakin Pubns, 1983. *(P; I)*

Carpenter, Allan. *Texas*. Childrens, 1979. *(I)*

Fradin, Dennis. *Texas: In Words and Pictures*. Childrens, 1981. *(P; I)*

Peacock, Howard. *The Big Thicket of Texas: America's Ecological Wonder*. Little, 1984. *(I; A)*

Phillips, Betty Lou and Bryce. *Texas*. Watts, 1987. *(P; I)*

Stein, R. Conrad. *Texas*. Childrens, 1989. *(P; I)*

Warren, Betsy. *Let's Remember When Texas Belonged to Spain*. Hendrick-Long, 1982; *Let's Remember When Texas Was a Republic*, 1983; *Texas in Historic Sites and Symbols*, 1982. *(I; A)*

Younger, Jassamine. *If These Walls Could Speak: A Story of Early Settlement in Texas*. Henrick-Long, 1981. *(I)*

See also MEXICAN WAR.

TEXTILES

Cobb, Vicki. *Fuzz Does It!* Har-Row, 1982. *(P)*

Macaulay, David. *Mill*. HM, 1983. *(I; A)*

Whyman, Kathryn. *Textiles*. Gloucester Press, dist. by Watts, 1988. *(P; I)*

See also CLOTHING; COTTON; SILK; WEAVING; WOOL.

THAILAND. See SOUTHEAST ASIA.

THANKSGIVING DAY

Anderson, Joan. *The First Thanksgiving Feast*. Clarion/Houghton, 1984. *(I)*

Baldwin, Margaret. *Thanksgiving*. Watts, 1983. *(I; A)*

Barkin, Carol, and James, Elizabeth. *Happy Thanksgiving!* Lothrop, 1987. *(P; I)*

Barth, Edna. *Turkey, Pilgrims, and Indian Corn: The Story of the Thanksgiving Symbols*. HM, 1981. *(P; I)*

Gibbons, Gale. *Thanksgiving Day*. Holiday, 1983. (I)

Kessel, Joyce K. *Squanto and the First Thanksgiving*. Carolrhoda, 1983. *(P)*

Penner, Ruth. *The Thanksgiving Book*. Hastings, 1983. *(I; A)*

THATCHER, MARGARET

Faber, Doris. *Margaret Thatcher: Britain's "Iron Lady."* Viking Kestrel, 1985. *(I)*

Levin, Angela. *Margaret Thatcher*. David & Charles, 1981. *(P; I)*

THEATER

Gillette, J. Michael. *Theatrical Design and Production*. Mayfield, 1987. *(A)*

Greenberg, Jan. *Theater Careers*. HR&W, 1983. *(I; A)*

Haskins, James S. *Black Theater in America*. Har-Row, 1982. *(I; A)*

Hewett, Joan. *On Camera: The Story of a Child Actor*. Clarion Books, 1987. *(P)*

Huberman, Caryn, and Wetzel, JoAnne. *Onstage/Backstage*. Carolrhoda, 1987. *(P)*

Judy, Susan, and Judy, Stephen. *Putting On a Play*. Scribner, 1982. *(I)*

Lowndes, Rosemary. *Make Your Own World of the Theater*. Little, 1982. *(I; A)*

Loxton, Howard, *Theater*. Steck-Vaughn, 1989. *(I)*

Williamson, Walter. *Behind the Scenes: The Unseen People Who Make Theater Work*. Walker, 1987. *(I; A)*

THOREAU, HENRY DAVID

Burleigh, Robert. *A Man Named Thoreau*. Atheneum, 1985. *(P)*

THUNDER AND LIGHTNING

Branley, Franklyn M. *Flash, Crash, Rumble, and Roll*. Har-Row, 1964. *(P)*

Cutts, David. *I Can Read About Thunder and Lightning*. Troll, 1979 (new ed.). *(P; I)*

TIDES

Stephens, William. *Life in the Tidepool*. McGraw, 1975. *(P; I)*

TIGERS. See LIONS AND TIGERS.

TIME

Baumann, Hans. *What Time Is It Around the World?* Scroll, 1979. *(P; I)*

Burns, Marilyn. *This Book Is About Time*. Little, 1978. *(I; A)*

Grey, Judith. *What Time Is It?* Troll, 1981. *(P)*

Humphrey, Henry, and Humphrey, Deirdre. *When Is Now: Experiments with Time and Timekeeping Devices*. Doubleday, 1981. *(I)*

Livoni, Cathy. *Elements of Time*. HarBraceJ, 1983. *(I; A)*

Simon, Seymour. *The Secret Clocks: Time Senses of Living Things*. Penguin, 1981. *(I; A)*

Ziner, Feenie, and Thompson, Elizabeth. *Time*. Children's, 1982. *(P)*

TOGO

Winslow, Zachery. *Togo*. Chelsea House, 1987. *(P; I)*

TOLKIEN, J. R. R.

Helms, Randel. *Tolkien's World*. HM, 1975. *(I; A)*

TONGA. See PACIFIC OCEAN AND ISLANDS.

TOOLS

Gibbons, Gail. *The Tool Book*. Holiday, 1982. *(P)*

Robbins, Ken. *Tools*. Scholastic, 1983. *(P)*

Rockwell, Anne. *The Toolbox*. Macmillan, 1971. *(P)*

TOPOLOGY

Froman, Robert. *Rubber Bands, Baseballs, and Dough-nuts: A Book About Topology*. Har-Row, 1972. *(P)*

TORONTO. See CANADA.

TOYS

Churchill, E. Richard. *Fast & Funny Paper Toys You Can Make*. Sterling, 1990. *(P; I; A)*

Gogniat, Maurice. *Indian and Wild West Toys You Can Make*. Sterling, 1980. *(P; I; A)*

Lerner, Mark. *Careers in Toy Making*. Lerner, 1980. *(P; I)*

Loeper, John J. *The Shop on High Street: Toys and Games of Early America*. Atheneum, 1978. *(P; I)*

Olney, Ross. *The Amazing Yo-Yo*. Lothrop, 1980; *Tricky Discs: Frisbee Saucer Flying*, 1979. *(P; I; A)*

Sibbett, Ed, Jr. *Easy-to-Make Articulated Wooden Toys: Patterns and Instructions for 18 Playthings That Move*. Dover, 1983. *(P; I; A)*

TRACK AND FIELD

Aaseng, Nathan. *Track's Magnificent Milers*. Lerner, 1981. *(P; I; A)*

Lyttle, Richard B. *Jogging and Running*. Watts, 1979. *(I; A)*

McMane, Fred. *Track and Field Basics*. P-H, 1983. *(P; I)*

Owens, Jesse, and O'Connor, Dick. *Track and Field*. Atheneum, 1976. *(I; A)*

Ryan, Frank. *Jumping for Joy: The High Jump, the Pole Vault, the Long Jump, and the Triple Jump*. Scribner, 1980. *(P; I)*

Sullivan, George. *Better Cross-country Running for Boys and Girls*, 1983; *Better Field Events for Girls*, 1982; *Better Track for Boys*, 1985; *Better Track for Girls*, 1981; *Marathon: The Longest Race*, 1980; *Run, Run Fast*, 1980; *Track and Field: Secrets of the Champions*, 1980. Dodd. *(I; A)*

TRADEMARKS

Arnold, Oren. *What's In a Name: Famous Brand Names*. Messner, 1979. *(I; A)*

Campbell, Hannah. *Why Did They Name It*. Fleet, 1964. *(I; A)*

TRANSPORTATION

Arnold, Caroline. *How Do We Travel?* Watts, 1983. *(P)*

Graham, Ian. *Transportation*. Watts, 1989. *(P; I)*

Hamer, Mick. *Transport*. Watts, 1982. *(I)*

Scarry, Huck. *On Wheels*. Philomel, 1980. *(P)*

Taylor, Ron. *50 Facts About Speed and Power*. Watts, 1983. *(I)*

See also AUTOMOBILES; AVIATION; RAILROADS; ROADS AND HIGHWAYS; SHIPS AND SHIPPING; TRUCKS AND TRUCKING.

TREES

Arnold, Caroline. *The Biggest Living Thing*. Carolrhoda, 1983. *(P; I)*

Boulton, Carolyn. *Trees*. Watts, 1984. *(P; I)*

Brandt, Keith. *Discovering Trees*. Troll, 1981. *(P)*

Burnie, David. *Tree*. Knopf, 1988. *(P; I)*

Dickinson, Jane. *All About Trees*. Troll, 1983. *(P; I)*

Hamer, Martyn. *Trees*. Watts, 1983. *(P)*

Podendorf, Illa. *Trees*. Children's, 1982. *(P)*

Selsam, Millicent E. *Tree Flowers*. Morrow, 1984. *(P; I)*

Zim, Herbert S., and Martin, Alexander C. *Trees*. Western, 1952. *(I; A)*

See also FORESTS AND FORESTRY.

TRICKS AND PUZZLES

Anderson, Doug. *Picture Puzzles for Armchair Detectives*. Sterling, 1983. *(I; A)*

Barry, Sheila Anne. *Super-Colossal Book of Puzzles, Tricks, and Games*. Sterling, 1978. *(I)*

Churchill, Richard. *I Bet I Can—I Bet You Can't*. Sterling, 1982. *(P; I)*

TRINIDAD AND TOBAGO. See CARIBBEAN SEA AND ISLANDS.

TROPICS. See JUNGLES.

TRUCKS AND TRUCKING

Abrams, Kathleen S., and Abrams, Lawrence F. *The Big Rigs: Trucks, Truckers, and Trucking*. Messner, 1981. *(P; I)*

Gibbons, Gail. *Trucks*. Har-Row, 1981. *(P)*

Haddad, Helen R. *Truck and Loader*. Greenwillow, 1982. *(P)*

Lerner, Mark. *Careers in Trucking*. Lerner, 1979. *(P; I)*

Lines, Cliff. *Looking at Trucks*. Watts, 1984. *(P; I)*

Radlauer, Ed. *Some Basics About Minitrucks*. Children's, 1982; *Some Basics About Vans*, 1978; *Trucks*, 1980. *(P; I)*

Rockwell, Anne F. *Trucks*. Dutton, 1984. *(P)*

Wolverton, Ruth, and Wolverton, Mike. *Trucks and Trucking*. Watts, 1983. *(I; A)*

TRUMAN, HARRY S.

Greenberg, Morrie. *The Buck Stops Here: A Biography of Harry Truman*. Dillon Press, 1989. *(I)*

Hargrove, Jim. *Harry S. Truman: Thirty-third President of the United States*. Children's, 1987. *(P; I)*

Leavell, J. Perry, Jr. *Harry S. Truman*. Chelsea House, 1987. *(A)*

Melton, David. *Harry S Truman: The Man Who Walked with Giants*. Ind Pr MO, 1980. *(I; A)*

See also PRESIDENCY OF THE UNITED STATES.

TRUSTS AND MONOPOLIES. See ECONOMICS.

TUBMAN, HARRIET

Epstein, Sam, and Epstein, Beryl. *Harriet Tubman: Guide to Freedom.* Garrard, 1968. *(P; I)*

Petry, Ann. *Harriet Tubman: Conductor on the Underground Railroad.* Archway, 1971. *(I; A)*

TUNISIA. See AFRICA.

TUNNELS

Epstein, Sam, and Epstein, Beryl. *Tunnels.* Little, 1985. *(I)*

Gibbons, Gail. *Tunnels.* Holiday, 1984. *(P)*

Rickard, Graham. *Tunnels.* Bookwright, dist. by Watts, 1988. *(P)*

TURKEY. See MIDDLE EAST.

TURKS AND CAICOS ISLANDS. See CARIBBEAN SEA AND ISLANDS.

TURTLES AND TORTOISES

Jahn, Johannes. *A Step-by-Step Book About Turtles.* TFH Publications, 1988. *(I; A)*

Riedman, Sarah R., and Witham, Ross. *Turtles: Extinction or Survival?* Har-Row, 1974. *(I; A)*

Waters, John. *The Hatchlings: A Book About Baby Turtles.* Walker, n.d. *(P)*

TUVALU. See PACIFIC OCEAN AND ISLANDS.

TWAIN, MARK

Frevert, Patricia D. *Mark Twain, an American Voice.* Creative Ed, 1981. *(I; A)*

Meltzer, Milton. *Mark Twain: A Writer's Life.* Watts, 1985. *(I; A)*

Twain, Mark. *Mark Twain's Best.* Scholastic, 1969. *(I; A)*

TYLER, JOHN

Lillegard, Dee. *John Tyler.* Children's, 1988. *(P; I)*

See also PRESIDENCY OF THE UNITED STATES.

TYPE. See BOOKS.

UGANDA

Creed, Alexander. *Uganda.* Chelsea House, 1987. *(P; I)*

UKRAINE. See UNION OF SOVIET SOCIALIST REPUBLICS.

UNDERWATER EXPLORATION. See OCEANS AND OCEANOGRAPHY.

UNIDENTIFIED FLYING OBJECTS

Asimov, Isaac. *Unidentified Flying Objects.* Gareth Stevens, 1989. *(P; I)*

Berger, Melvin. *UFOs, ETs and Visitors From Space.* Putnam, 1988. *(I)*

UNION OF SOVIET SOCIALIST REPUBLICS

Barlow, Pamela. *Through the Year in the U.S.S.R.* David & Charles, 1981. *(I; A)*

Bernards, Neal, ed. *The Soviet Union.* Greenhaven Press, 1987. *(A)*

Campling, Elizabeth. *The Russian Revolution.* David & Charles, 1985. *(I; A); How and Why: The Russian Revolution.* Batsford, 1987. *(A)*

Gillies, John. *The Soviet Union: The World's Largest Country.* Dillon, 1985. *(P; I)*

Jackson, W. A. Douglas. *Soviet Union.* Gateway Press, 1988. *(I; A)*

Keeler, Stephen. *Soviet Union.* (Passport to) Watts, 1988. *(P; I)*

Lye, Keith. *Take a Trip to Russia.* Watts, 1982. *(P)*

Oparenko, Christina. *The Ukraine.* Chelsea House, 1988. *(P; I)*

Riordan, James. *Soviet Union: The Land and Its People.* Silver Burdett, 1987. *(P; I)*

Ross, Stewart. *The Russian Revolution.* Bookwright Press, dist. by Watts, 1989. *(I; A)*

Williams, Brian. *Come to Russia.* Watts, 1979. *(I)*

UNITED KINGDOM

Sutherland, Dorothy B. *Wales.* (Enchantment of the World) Children's, 1987. *(P; I)*

Warner, Marina. *The Crack in the Teacup: Britain in the Twentieth Century.* HM, 1979. *(I; A)*

See also ENGLAND; ENGLAND, HISTORY OF; SCOTLAND; IRELAND.

UNITED NATIONS

Carroll, Raymond. *The Future of the United Nations.* Watt, 1985. *(I; A)*

Parker, Nancy Winslow. *The United Nations from A to Z.* Dodd, 1985. *(I)*

Ross, Stewart. *The United Nations.* Watts, 1990. *(I; A)*

Woods, Harold, and Woods, Geraldine. *The United Nations.* Watts, 1985. *(I)*

UNITED STATES

Arnold, Pauline, and White, Percival. *How We Named Our States.* Har-Row, 1966. *(I)*

Berger, Gilda. *The Southeast States.* Watts, 1984. *(I)*

Brandt, Sue R. *Facts About the Fifty States.* Watts, 1979 (rev. ed.). *(I)*

Gilfond, Henry. *The Northeast States.* Watts, 1984. *(I)*

Jacobson, Daniel. *The North Central States.* Watts, 1984. *(I)*

Lawson, Don. *The Pacific States.* Watts, 1984. *(I)*

Ronan, Margaret. *All About Our Fifty States.* Random, 1978 (rev. ed.). *(I; A)*

Ross, Frank. *Stories of the States: A Reference Guide to*

the Fifty States and the U.S. Territories. Har-Row, 1969. *(I)*

Taylor, L. B., and Taylor, C. *The Rocky Mountain States.* Watts, 1984. *(I)*

Woods, Harold, and Woods, Geraldine. *The South Central States.* Watts, 1984. *(I)*

See also MISSISSIPPI RIVER; NATIONAL PARK SYSTEM; NEW ENGLAND; NORTH AMERICA; and names of individual states.

UNITED STATES (Art, Literature, and Music)

Famous American Artists. Denison, n.d. *(I; A)*

Famous American Fiction Writers. Denison, n. d. *(I; A)*

Famous American Musicians. Denison, n.d. *(I; A)*

Foley, Mary M. *The American House.* Har-Row, 1981. *(I; A)*

Glubock, Shirley. *The Art of America in the Early Twentieth Century.* Macmillan, 1974; *The Art of Colonial America,* 1970; *The Art of the New American Nation,* 1972. *(P; I; A)*

Hancock, Carla. *Seven Founders of American Literature.* Blair, 1976. *(I; A)*

Kraske, Robert. *America the Beautiful: Stories of Patriotic Songs.* Garrard, 1972. *(P; I)*

Plotz, Helen, ed. *The Gift Outright: America to Her Poets.* Greenwillow, 1977. *(I; A)*

Thum, Marcella. *Exploring Literary America.* Atheneum, 1979. *(I; A)*

UNITED STATES (History and Government)

Bartz, Carl F. *The Department of State.* Chelsea House, 1988. *(A)*

Bender, David L. *The Arms Race: Opposing Viewpoints.* Greenhaven, 1982. *(I; A)*

Bender, David L., ed. *American Government.* Greenhaven Press, 1987. *(A)*

Commager, Henry S. *The Great Constitution.* Bobbs, 1961. *(I; A)*

Coy, Harold. *Congress,* rev. by Barbara L. Dammann. Watts, 1981. *(I; A)*

Ellis, Rafaela. *The Central Intelligence Agency.* Chelsea House, 1987. *(A)*

Faber, Doris, and Faber, Harold. *The Birth of a Nation: The Early Years of the United States.* Scribner, 1989. *(I; A)*

Fritz, Jean. *Shh! We're Writing the Constitution.* Putnam, 1987. *(I)*

Goode, Stephen. *The New Federalism: States' Rights in American History.* Watts, 1983; *The New Congress.* Messner, 1980. *(I; A)*

Hilton, Suzanne. *The Way It Was—1876.* Westminster, 1975. *(I; A)*

Hoopes, Roy. *What a United States Senator Does.* Har-Row, 1975. *(P; I; A)*

Lomask, Milton. *The Spirit of 1787: The Making of Our Constitution.* FS&G, 1980. *(P; I; A)*

Maestro, Betsy. *A More Perfect Union: The Story of Our Constitution.* Lothrop, 1987. *(P; I)*

McGrath, Edward, and Krauss, Bob, eds. *A Child's History of America.* Little, 1976. *(P; I)*

Ragsdale, Bruce A. *The House of Representatives.* Chelsea House, 1988. *(A)*

Ritchie, Donald A. *The U.S. Constitution.* Chelsea House, 1988. *(A)*

Short, Max H., and Felton, Elizabeth N. *The United States Book: Facts and Legends About the Fifty States.* Lerner, 1975. *(P; I; A)*

Spier, Peter. *We The People: The Constitution of the United States of America.* Doubleday, 1987. *(P)*

See also AMERICAN COLONIES; CIVIL WAR, UNITED STATES; REVOLUTIONARY WAR; WESTWARD MOVEMENT AND PIONEER LIFE; WORLD WAR I; WORLD WAR II.

UNITED STATES ARMED FORCES

Bradley, Jeff. *A Young Person's Guide to Military Service.* Kampmann, 1987. *(A)*

Cohen, Andrew and Heinsohn, Beth. *The Department of Defense.* Chelsea House, 1990. *(I; A)*

Colby, C. B. *Two Centuries of Sea Power.* Putnam, 1976. *(P; I)*

Ferrell, Nancy Warren. *The U.S. Coast Guard.* Lerner, 1989. *(I; A)*

Fisch, Arnold G., Jr. *The Department of the Army.* Chelsea House, 1987. *(A)*

Halliburton, Warren. *The Fighting Redtails: America's First Black Airmen.* Silver, 1978. *(I; A)*

Holmes, Burnham. *Basic Training: A Portrait of Today's Army.* Scholastic, 1979. *(I; A)*

Palladin, Arthur. *Careers in the Army.* Lerner, 1978. *(P; I)*

Rummel, Jack. *The U.S. Marine Corps.* Chelsea House, 1990. *(I; A)*

Stefoff, Rebecca. *The U.S. Coast Guard.* Chelsea House, 1989. *(I; A)*

UNITED STATES COAST GUARD AND MERCHANT MARINE

Martin, Nancy. *Search and Rescue: The Story of the Coast Guard Service.* David & Charles, 1975. *(P; I)*

Petersen, Gwenn B. *Careers in the United States Merchant Marine.* Lodestar, 1983. *(I; A)*

UNIVERSE. See ASTRONOMY.

UNIVERSITIES AND COLLEGES

The *Yale Daily News* Staff, Eds. *The Insider's Guide to the Colleges, 1986–1987.* St. Martin's Pr., 12th ed., 1986. *(A)*

UPPER VOLTA. See AFRICA.

URBAN PLANNING. See CITIES.

URUGUAY

Uruguay in Pictures. Lerner, 1987. *(I; A)*

UTAH

Carpenter, Allan. *Utah.* Children's, 1979. *(I)*
Fradin, Dennis. *Utah: In Words and Pictures.* Children's, 1980. *(P; I)*

VACCINATION AND INOCULATION. See DISEASES.

VALENTINES

Barth, Edna. *Hearts, Cupids, and Red Roses: The Story of the Valentine Symbols.* HM, 1982. *(P; I)*
Brown, Fern G. *Valentine's Day.* Watts, 1983. *(I; A)*
Prelutsky, Jack. *It's Valentine's Day.* Greenwillow, 1983. *(P)*
Sandak, Cass R. *Valentine's Day.* Watts, 1980. *(P)*
Supraner, Robyn. *Valentine's Day: Things to Make and Do.* Troll, 1981. *(P; I)*

VAN BUREN, MARTIN

Ellis, Rafaela. *Martin Van Buren.* Garrett Educational Corp., 1989. *(I)*
Hargrove, Jim. *Martin Van Buren.* Children's, 1988. *(P; I)*
See also PRESIDENCY OF THE UNITED STATES.

VANCOUVER. See CANADA.

VANUATU. See PACIFIC OCEAN AND ISLANDS.

VEGETABLES

Blanchet, Francoise, and Doornekamp, Rinke. *What to Do with . . . Vegetables.* Barron, 1981. *(P; I)*
Brown, Elizabeth B. *Vegetables: An Illustrated History with Recipes.* P-H, 1981. *(I; A)*
Johnson, Sylvia. *Potatoes.* Lerner, 1984. *(I)*
Sobol, Harriet L. *A Book of Vegetables.* Dodd, 1984. *(P)*

VENEZUELA

Sterling Publishing Company Editors. *Venezuela in Pictures.* Sterling, 1965. *(I; A)*
Venezuela in Pictures. Lerner, 1987. *(I; A)*
Morrison, Marion. *Venezuela.* Childrens, 1989. *(I)*

VENICE. See ITALY.

VENTRILOQUISM

Bergen, Edgar. *How to Become a Ventriloquist.* Presto Bks, 1983. *(P; I; A)*

Hutton, Darryl. *Ventriloquism: How to Put on an Act, Use the Power of Suggestion, Write a Clever Accompanying Patter, and Make Your Own Dummy.* Sterling, 1982. *(I; A)*
Ritchard, Dan, and Moloney, Kathleen. *Ventriloquism for the Total Dummy.* Random/Villard, 1988. *(A)*

VERMONT

Carpenter, Allan. *Vermont.* Children's, 1979. *(I)*
Cheney, Cora. *Vermont: The State with the Storybook Past.* Greene, 1981. *(P; I)*
Fradin, Dennis. *Vermont: In Words and Pictures.* Children's, 1980. *(P; I)*

VERNE, JULES. See SCIENCE FICTION.

VETERINARIANS

Bellville, Rod, and Bellville, Cheryl W. *Large Animal Veterinarians.* Carolrhoda, 1983. *(P)*
Carris, Joan Davenport. *Pets, Vets, and Marty Howard.* Lippincott, 1984. *(I)*
Riser, Wayne H. *Your Future in Veterinary Medicine.* Rosen, 1982. *(I; A)*
Sobol, Harriet Langsam. *Pet Doctor.* Putnam, 1988. *(I)*

VICE PRESIDENCY OF THE UNITED STATES

Alotta, Robert I. *Number Two: A Look at the Vice Presidency.* Messner, 1981. *(I; A)*
Feerick, John D., and Feerick, Emalie P. *Vice-Presidents.* Watts, 1981 (updated ed.). *(I)*
Hoopes, Roy. *The Changing Vice-Presidency.* Har-Row, 1981. *(I; A)*

VICTORIA, QUEEN. See ENGLAND, HISTORY OF.

VIDEO RECORDING

Cooper, Carolyn E. *VCRs.* Watts, 1987. *(P)*
Irvine, Mat. *TV & Video.* Watts, 1984. *(I)*
Meigs, James B., and Stern, Jennifer. *Make Your Own Music Video.* Watts, Oct. 1986. *(I; A)*
Shachtman, Tom and Harriet. *Video Power: A Complete Guide to Writing, Planning, and Shooting Videos.* Holt, 1988. *(I; A)*
Yurko, John. *Video Basics.* P-H, 1983. *(P; I)*

VIENNA. See AUSTRIA.

VIETNAM. See SOUTHEAST ASIA.

VIETNAM WAR

Bender, David L., ed. *The Vietnam War.* Greenhaven Pr., 1984. *(A)*
Dolan, Edward F. *America After Vietnam: Legacies of a Hated War.* Watts, 1989. *(I; A)*
Fincher, E. B. *The Vietnam War.* Watts, 1980. *(I; A)*

Hauptly, Denis J. *In Vietnam*. Atheneum, 1985. *(A)*

Lawson, Don. *The War in Vietnam*. Watts, 1981. *(I); An Album of the Vietnam War,* 1986. *(A)*

VIKINGS

Atkinson, Ian. *The Viking Ships*. Lerner, 1980. *(I; A)*

Benchley, Nathaniel. *Snorri and the Strangers*. Har-Row, 1976. *(P)*

Ferguson, Sheila. *Growing Up in Viking Times*. David & Charles, 1981. *(I)*

Glubok, Shirley. *The Art of the Vikings*. Macmillan, 1978. *(P; I; A)*

Hughes, Jill. *Vikings*. Watts, 1984 (rev. ed.). *(P; I; A)*

Janeway, Elizabeth. *The Vikings*. Random, 1981. *(I; A)*

Jones, Terry. *The Saga of Erik the Viking*. Schocken, 1983. *(P; I)*

Martell, Hazel. *The Vikings*. Warwick Press/Watts, 1986. *(I)*

Pluckrose, Henry, ed. *Small World of Vikings*. Watts, 1982. *(P)*

VIOLIN. See Musical Instruments.

VIRGINIA

Campbell, Elizabeth A. *The Carving on the Tree*. Little, 1968. *(P)*

McNair, Sylvia. *Virginia*. Childrens, 1989. *(P; I)*

Thane, Elswyth. *The Virginia Colony*. Macmillan, 1969. *(I)*

VIRUSES

Knight, David C. *Viruses: Life's Smallest Enemies*. Morrow, 1981. *(I)*

Nourse, Alan E. *Viruses*. Watts, 1983 (rev. ed.). *(I; A)*

VITAMINS

Nourse, Alan. *Vitamins*. Watts, 1977. *(I)*

VOCATIONS AND CAREERS

Berman, Steve, and Weiss, Vivian. *What to Be*. P-H, 1981. *(I)*

Claypool, Jane. *How to Get a Good Job*. Watts, 1982. *(I; A)*

Collins, Robert F. *America at Its Best: Opportunities in the National Guard*. Rosen, 1989. *(A)*

Epstein, Rachel. *Careers in Health Care*. Chelsea House, 1989. *(A)*

Girl Scouts of the U.S.A. *Careers to Explore for Brownie and Junior Girl Scouts*. GS, 1979. *(I; A)*

Lobb, Charlotte. *Exploring Apprenticeship Careers*. Rosen, 1982; *Exploring Vocational School Careers,* 1982 (2nd rev. ed.). *(I; A)*

Sipiera, Paul. *I Can Be an Oceanographer*. Childrens, 1989. *(P)*

See also names of specific fields.

VOLCANOES

Asimov, Isaac. *How Did We Find Out About Volcanoes?* Walker, 1981. *(P; I)*

Aylesworth, Thomas G., and Aylesworth, Virginia L. *The Mount St. Helens Disaster: What We've Learned*. Watts, 1983. *(I; A)*

Branley, Franklyn M. *Volcanoes*. Crowell, 1985. *(P)*

Carson, James. *Volcanoes*. Watts, 1984. *(I)*

Fradin, Dennis. *Disaster! Volcanoes*. Children's, 1982. *(I)*

Lauber, Patricia. *Volcano: The Eruption and Healing of Mount St. Helens*. Bradbury, 1986. *(I)*

Marcus, Elizabeth. *All About Mountains and Volcanoes*. Troll, 1984. *(P; I)*

Place, Marian T. *Mount St. Helens: A Sleeping Volcano Awakes*. Dodd, 1981. *(I)*

Simon, Seymour. *Volcanoes*. Morrow, 1988. *(P; I)*

Taylor, G. Jeffrey. *Volcanoes in Our Solar System*. Dodd, 1983. *(I; A)*

VOLLEYBALL

Sullivan, George. *Better Volleyball for Girls*. Lerner, 1980. *(P; I)*

Thomas, Art. *Volleyball Is for Me*. Lerner, 1980. *(P; I)*

WALES. See United Kingdom.

WALRUSES, SEA LIONS, AND SEALS

Brady, Irene. *Elephants on the Beach*. Scribner, 1979. *(P; I)*

Brown, Joseph E. *Wonders of Seals and Sea Lions*. Dodd, 1976. *(I)*

Fields, Alice. *Seals*. Watts, 1980. *(P)*

Myers, Susan. *Pearson: A Harbor Seal Pup*. Dutton, 1981. *(P; I)*

Rabinowich, Ellen. *Seals, Sea Lions, and Walruses*. Watts, 1980. *(I)*

Scott, Jack Denton. *The Fur Seals of Pribilof*. Putnam, 1983. *(I; A)*

WAR OF 1812

Richards, Norman. *The Story of Old Ironsides*. Childrens, 1967. *(P; I)*

WASHINGTON

Carpenter, Allan. *Washington*. Childrens, 1979. *(I)*

Field, Nancy, and Machlis, Sally. *Discovering Mount Rainier*. Dog Eared Pubns, 1980. *(P; I)*

Fradin, Dennis. *Washington: In Words and Pictures*. Childrens, 1980. *(P; I)*

Olson, Joan, and Olson, Gene. *Washington Times and Trails*. Windyridge, 1983. *(I; A)*

WASHINGTON, BOOKER T.

Poole, Susan. *Booker T. Washington*. Dandelion, n.d. *(P)*
Washington, Booker T. *Up from Slavery*. Airmont, n.d. *(I; A)*

WASHINGTON, D.C.

Aikman, Lonnelle. *We, the People: The Story of the United States Capital, Its Past and Its Promise*. U.S. Capital Historical Society, 1978. *(I)*
Munro, Roxie. *The Inside-Outside Book of Washington, D.C.* Dutton, 1987. *(P)*
Sandak, Cass R. *The White House*. Watts, 1981. *(I)*

WASHINGTON, GEORGE

Adler, David A. *A Picture Book of George Washington*. Holiday, 1989. *(P); George Washington, Father of Our Country: A First Biography*. Holiday, 1988. *(P)*
D'Aulaire, Ingri, and D'Aulaire, Edgar P. *George Washington*. Doubleday, n.d. *(P)*
Falkof, Lucille. *George Washington: 1st President of the United States*. Garrett Educational Corp., 1989. *(I)*
Foster, Genevieve. *George Washington's World*. Scribner, 1977. *(A)*
Fritz, Jean. *George Washington's Breakfast*. Putnam, 1969. *(I)* (Fiction)
Heilbroner, Joan. *Meet George Washington*. Random, 1965. *(P; I)*
Kent, Zachary. *George Washington: First President of the United States*. (Encyclopedia of Presidents) Childrens, 1986. *(P; I)*
Meltzer, Milton. *George Washington and the Birth of Our Nation*. Watts, 1986. *(I; A)*
Santrey, Laurence. *George Washington: Young Leader*. Troll, 1982. *(P; I)*
See also PRESIDENCY OF THE UNITED STATES.

WATCHES AND CLOCKS

Breiter, Herta S. *Time and Clocks*. Raintree, 1978. *(P)*
Jespersen, James, and Fitz-Randolph, Jane. *Time and Clocks for the Space Age*. Atheneum, 1979. *(I; A)*
Perry, Susan. *How Did We Get Clocks and Calendars?* Creative Ed, 1981. *(P)*
Trivett, Daphne, and Trivett, John. *Time for Clocks*. Har-Row, 1979. *(P; I)*

WATER

Ardley, Neil. *Working with Water*. Watts, 1983. *(P)*
Bain, Iain. *Water on the Land*. Watts, 1984. *(I)*
Branley, Franklyn M. *Water for the World*. Har-Row, 1982. *(I)*
Dickinson, Jane. *Wonders of Water*. Troll, 1983. *(P; I)*
Gardner, Robert. *Water, the Life Sustaining Resource*. Messner, 1982. *(A)*
Ginsburg, Mirra. *Across the Stream*. Morrow, 1982. *(P)*
Goldin, Augusta. *The Shape of Water*. Doubleday, 1979.

(P); Water—Too Much, Too Little, Too Polluted? HarBraceJ, 1983. *(I; A)*
Leutscher, Alfred. *Water*. Dutton, 1983. *(P)*
Smeltzer, Patricia, and Smeltzer, Victor. *Thank You for a Drink of Water*. Winston, 1983. *(P; I)*

WATER POLLUTION. See POLLUTION.

WATERSKIING

Radlauer, Ed. *Some Basics About Water Skiing*. Childrens, 1980. *(I)*

WEATHER

Adler, David. *The World of Weather*. Troll, 1983. *(P; I)*
Bramwell, Martyn. *Weather*. Watts, 1988. *(I)*
DeBruin, Jerry. *Young Scientists Explore the Weather*. Good Apple, 1983. *(P; I)*
Dickinson, Terence. *Exploring the Sky by Day: The Equinox Guide to Weather and the Atmosphere*. Camden House, dist. by Firefly Books, 1988. *(P; I)*
Gibbons, Gail. *Weather Words and What They Mean*. Holiday, 1990. *(P)*
Lambert, David. *Weather*. Watts, 1983. *(P)*
Purvis, George, and Purvis, Anne. *Weather and Climate*. Watts, 1984. *(I; A)*
Webster, Vera. *Weather Experiments*. Childrens, 1982. *(P)*
Wolff, Barbara. *Evening Gray, Morning Red: A Handbook of American Weather Wisdom*. Macmillan, 1976. *(P; I)*
Yvart, Jacques, and Forgeot, Claire. *The Rising of the Wind: Adventures Along the Beaufort Scale*. Green Tiger, 1986. *(I)*
See also CLIMATE.

WEATHER FORECASTING

Cosner, Shaaron. *Be Your Own Weather Forecaster*. Messner, 1982. *(P; I)*
Hill, Malcolm. *Forecast*. Dell, 1980. *(I)*
Palazzo, Janet. *What Makes the Weather*. Troll, 1982. *(P)*

WEAVING

Alexander, Marthann. *Simple Weaving*. Taplinger, n.d. *(P; I)*
Hobden, Eileen. *Fun with Weaving*. Sportshelf, n.d. *(I)*
Rubenstone, Jessie. *Weaving for Beginners*. Lippincott, 1975. *(I)*

WEEDS

Collins, Pat L. *Tumble, Tumble, Tumbleweed*. Whitman, 1981. *(P)*
Kirkpatrick, Rena K. *Look at Seeds and Weeds*. Raintree, 1978. *(P)*
Podendorf, Illa. *Weeds and Wild Flowers*. Childrens, 1981. *(P)*

Selsam, Millicent E., and Wexler, Jerome. *The Amazing Dandelion*. Morrow, 1977. *(P; I)*

WEIGHT LIFTING

Smith, Tim. *Junior Weight Training and Strength Training*. Sterling, 1985. *(I; A)*

WEIGHTS AND MEASURES

Ardley, Neil. *Making Metric Measurements*. Watts, 1984. *(I)*

Arnold, Caroline. *Measurements: Fun, Facts, and Figures*. Watts, 1984. *(P)*

Baird, Eva-Lee, and Wyler, Rose. *Going Metric the Fun Way*. Doubleday, 1980. *(I; A)*

Bendick, Jeanne. *How Much & How Many? The Story of Weights and Measures*. Watts, 1989. *(P; I)*

Branley, Franklyn M. *Measure with Metric*. Har-Row, 1975. *(P); Think Metric!* 1973. *(P; I)*

WESLEY, JOHN. See Religions of the World.

WEST INDIES. See Caribbean Sea and Islands.

WEST VIRGINIA

Carpenter, Allan. *West Virginia*. Childrens, 1979. *(I)*

Fradin, Dennis. *West Virginia: In Word and Pictures*. Childrens, 1980. *(P; I)*

WESTWARD MOVEMENT AND PIONEER LIFE

Bercuson, David, and Palmer, Howard. *Pioneer Life in the West*. Watts, 1984. *(I; A)* (Canadian West)

Carr, Mary Jane. *Children of the Covered Wagon*. Har-Row, 1957. *(I)*

Collins, James L. *Exploring the American West*. Watts, 1989. *(P; I)*

Flatley, Dennis R. *The Railroads: Opening the West*. Watts, 1989. *(P; I)*

Fradin, Dennis B. *Pioneers*. Childrens, 1984. *(P)*

Freedman, Russell. *Children of the Wild West*. HM, 1983. *(I)*

Gorsline, Marie, and Gorsline, Douglas. *The Pioneers*. Random, 1983. *(P)*

Guthrie, Alfred B., Jr. *The Big Sky: The Way West*. Bantam, 1972. *(I; A)*

Hilton, Suzanne. *Getting There: Frontier Travel Without Power*. Westminster, 1980. *(I; A)*

Holbrook, Stewart. *Wyatt Earp: U.S. Marshall*. Random, 1956. *(P; I)*

Jassem, Kate. *Sacajawea, Wilderness Guide*. Troll, 1979. *(P; I)*

Laycock, George. *How the Settlers Lived*. McKay, 1980. *(I; A)*

Lyons, Grant. *Mustangs, Six-Shooters, and Barbed Wire: How the West Was Really Won*. Messner, 1981. *(P; I)*

McCall, Edith. *Cumberland Gap and Trails West; Hunters Blaze the Trails; Pioneering on the Plains; Wagons over the Mountains*. Childrens, 1980. *(P; I; A)*

Poole, Frederick King. *Early Exploration of North America*. Watts, 1989. *(P; I)*

Stein, R. Conrad. *The Story of the Homestead Act*. Childrens, 1978. *(P; I)*

Strait, Treva. *The Price of Free Land*. Har-Row, 1979. *(I)*

Ulyatt, Kenneth. *Outlaws*. Har-Row, 1978. *(A)*

WHALES AND WHALING

Whales. Facts on File, 1990. *(I)*

Bunting, Eve. *The Sea World Book of Whales*. HarBraceJ, 1980. *(I)*

Gardner, Robert. *The Whale Watchers' Guide*. Messner, 1984. *(P; I)*

Hoke, Helen, and Pitt, Valerie. *Whales*. Watts, 1981 (rev. ed.). *(I)*

Mallory, Kenneth, and Conley, Andrea. *Rescue of the Stranded Whales*. S & S, 1989. *(I)*

Patent, Dorothy Hinshaw. *Whales: Giants of the Deep*. Holiday, 1984. *(P; I)*

Sattler, Roney Helen. *Whales, the Nomads of the Sea*. Lothrop, 1987. *(P; I)*

Selsam, Millicent E., and Hunt, Joyce. *A First Look at Whales*. Walker, 1980. *(P)*

Simon, Seymour. *Whales*. Crowell, 1989. *(P; I)*

Stein, R. C. *The Story of the New England Whalers*. Childrens, 1982. *(P; I)*

Torgersen, Don. *Killer Whales and Dolphin Play*. Childrens, 1982. *(P; I)*

WHEAT. See Grain and Grain Products.

WHEELS

Barton, Byron. *Wheels*. Har-Row, 1979. *(P)*

Scarry, Huck. *On Wheels*. Putnam, 1980. *(P)*

Tunis, Edwin. *Wheels: A Pictorial History*. Har-Row, 1977. *(I)*

WILLIAMS, ROGER

Eaton, Jeanette. *Lone Journey: The Life of Roger Williams*. HarBraceJ, 1966. *(A)*

WILLIAM THE CONQUEROR. See England, History of.

WILSON, WOODROW

Collins, David R. *Woodrow Wilson: 28th President of the United States*. Garrett Educational Corp., 1989. *(I)*

Jacobs, David. *An American Conscience: Woodrow Wilson's Search for World Peace*. Har-Row, n.d. *(I; A)*

Osinski, Alice. *Woodrow Wilson*. Childrens, 1989. *(P; I)*

See also Presidency of the United States.

WIND INSTRUMENTS. See Musical Instruments.

WINNIPEG. See Canada.

WISCONSIN

Fradin, Dennis B. *Wisconsin in Words and Pictures.* Children's, 1977. *(P; I)*

Stein, R. Conrad. *Wisconsin.* Children's, 1988. *(P; I)*

Wilder, Laura Ingalls. *Little House in the Big Woods.* Har-Row, 1953. (Fiction) *(I)*

WITCHCRAFT

Jack, Adrienne. *Witches and Witchcraft.* Watts, 1981. *(P; I)*

Jackson, Shirley. *The Witchcraft of Salem Village.* Random, 1956. *(I)*

Petry, Ann. *Tituba of Salem Village.* Har-Row, 1964. *(I)*

Zeinert, Karen. *The Salem Witchcraft Trials.* Watts, 1989. *(I; A)*

WOLVES

Hansen, Rosanna. *Wolves and Coyotes.* Putnam, 1981. *(P; I)*

Johnson, Sylvia A., and Aamodt, Alice. *Wolf Pack: Tracking Wolves in the Wild.* Lerner, 1985. *(I)*

McConoughey, Jana. *The Wolves.* Crestwood, 1983. *(I)*

Murphy, Jim. *The Call of the Wolves.* Scholastic, 1989. *(P; I)*

Pringle, Laurence. *Wolfman: Exploring the World of Wolves.* Scribner, 1983. *(I; A)*

WOMEN, ROLE OF

Berger, Gilda. *Women, Work and Wages.* Watts, 1986. *(A)*

Fisher, Maxine P. *Women in the Third World.* Watts, 1989. *(I; A)*

Gutman, Bill. *Women Who Work with Animals.* Dodd, 1982. *(I)*

Haber, Louis. *Women Pioneers of Science.* HarBraceJ, 1979 (rev. ed.). *(I; A)*

Hodgman, Ann, and Djabbaroff, Ruby. *Skystars: The History of Women in Aviation.* Atheneum, 1981. *(I)*

Ingraham, Gloria D. and Leonard W. *An Album of American Women: Their Changing Role.* Watts, 1987. *(P; I)*

Levinson, Nancy S. *The First Women Who Spoke Out.* Dillon, 1983. *(I; A)*

Peavy, Linda, and Smith, Ursula. *Women Who Changed Things.* Scribner, 1983. *(I; A)*

Scheader, Catherine. *Contributions of Women: Music.* Dillon Pr., 1985. *(I; A)*

Stein, R. Conrad. *The Story of the Nineteenth Amendment.* Childrens, 1982. *(P; I)*

Whitney, Sharon. *The Equal Rights Amendment: The History of the Movement.* Watts, 1984. ·*(I; A)*; *Women in Politics,* 1986. *(A)*

WOOD, GRANT

Goldstein, Ernest. *Grant Wood: American Gothic.* NAL, 1984. *(I; A)*

WOOD AND WOOD PRODUCTS. See Lumber and Lumbering.

WOOD CRAFTS

Boy Scouts of America. *Wood Carving.* BSA, 1966; 1970. *(I; A)*

Brown, William F. *Wood Works: Experiments with Common Wood and Tools.* Atheneum, 1984. *(I)*

WOOL

Mitgutsch, Ali. *From Sheep to Scarf.* Carolrhoda, 1981. *(P)*

WORLD WAR I

Gurney, Gene. *Flying Aces of World War I.* Random, 1965. *(I; A)*

Hoobler, Dorothy, and Hoobler, Thomas. *An Album of World War I.* Watts, 1976. *(I; A)*

Ross, Stewart. *The Origins of World War I.* Bookwright Press, dist. by Watts, 1989. *(I; A)*

Snyder, Louis L. *World War I.* Watts, 1981 (rev.). *(I; A)*

Wright, Nicolas. *The Red Baron.* McGraw, 1977. *(I)*

WORLD WAR II

Bliven, Bruce. *From Casablanca to Berlin: The War in North Africa and Europe, 1942–1945.* Random, 1965; *From Pearl Harbor to Okinawa: The War in the Pacific, 1941–45,* 1960; *The Story of D-Day,* 1956. *(I; A)*

Carter, Hodding. *The Commandos of World War II.* Random, 1981. *(I; A)*

Dank, Milton. *D-Day.* Watts, 1984. *(I; A)*

Davis, Daniel S. *Behind Barbed Wire: The Imprisonment of Japanese Americans During World War II.* Dutton, 1982. *(I; A)*

Foreman, Michael. *War Boy: A Country Childhood.* Arcade, dist. by Little, Brown, 1990. *(I)*

Frank, Anne. *Anne Frank: The Diary of a Young Girl.* Doubleday, 1967 (rev. ed.). *(I)*

Gordon, Sheila. *3rd September 1939.* Batsford, dist. by David & Charles, 1988. *(I; A)*

Graff, Stewart. *The Story of World War II.* Dutton, 1978. *(P; I)*

Hoobler, Dorothy, and Hoobler, Thomas. *An Album of World War II.* Watts, 1977. *(I; A)*

Jones, Madeline. *Find Out About Life in the Second World War.* David & Charles, 1983. *(I; A)*

Lawson, Ted. *Thirty Seconds over Tokyo.* Random, 1981. *(I)*

Loomis, Robert D. *Great American Fighter Pilots of World War II.* Random, 1961. *(I; A)*

Markl, Julia. *The Battle of Britain.* Watts, 1984. *(I; A)*

Marrin, Albert. *The Airman's War: World War II in the Sky*. Atheneum, 1982; *Victory in the Pacific*, 1983. *(I; A)*

Maruki, Toshi. *Hiroshima No Pika*. Lothrop, 1982. *(I; A)*

McGowen, Tom. *Midway and Guadalcanal*. Watts, 1984. *(I; A)*

Messenger, Charles. *The Second World War*. (Conflict in the Twentieth Century) Watts, 1987. *(A)*

Miner, Jane C. *Hiroshima and Nagasaki*. Watts, 1984. *(I; A)*

Richardson, Nigel. *How and Why: The Third Reich*. Batsford, dist. by David & Charles, 1988. *(I; A)*

Saunders, Alan. *The Invasion of Poland*. Watts, 1984. *(I; A)*

Shapiro, William E. *Pearl Harbor*. Watts, 1984. *(I; A)*

Snyder, Louis L. *World War II*. Watts, 1981 (rev. ed.). *(I; A)*

Sullivan, George. *Strange But True Stories of World War II*. Walker, 1983. *(I; A)*

WORMS

Hess, Lilo. *The Amazing Earthworm*. Scribner, 1979. *(I)*

O'Hagan, Caroline, ed. *It's Easy to Have a Worm Visit You*. Lothrop, 1980. *(P)*

WRESTLING

Hellickson, Russ, and Baggott, Andrew. *An Instructional Guide to Amateur Wrestling*. Putnam, Perigee, 1987. *(A)*

Thomas, Art. *Wrestling Is for Me*. Lerner, 1979. *(P; I)*

WRIGHT, WILBUR AND ORVILLE

Reynolds, Quentin. *The Wright Brothers: Pioneers of American Aviation*. Random, 1981. *(I; A)*

Sabin, Louis. *Wilbur and Orville Wright: The Flight to Adventure*. Troll, 1983. *(I)*

Stein, R. Conrad. *The Story of the Flight at Kitty Hawk*. Childrens, 1981. *(I)*

WRITING (AUTHORSHIP)

Dubrovin, Vivian. *Write Your Own Story*. Watts, 1984. *(I; A)*

Duncan, Lois. *Chapters: My Growth as a Writer*. Little, 1982. *(I)*

Hackwell, W. John. *Signs, Letters, Words: Archaeology Discovers Writing*. Scribner, 1987. *(I; A)*

Henderson, Kathy. *Market Guide for Young Writers*. Shoe Tree Press, dist. by Talman, 1988. *(I; A)*

James, Elizabeth, and Barkin, Carol. *How to Write Your Best Book Report; How to Write A Great School Report; How to Write a Term Paper*. Lothrop, Lee & Shepard, 1988. *(I; A)*

Judy, Susan, and Judy, Stephen. *Gifts of Writing: Decorative Projects with Words and Art*. Scribner, 1980. *(I)*

Tchudi, Susan. *The Young Writer's Handbook*. Scribner, 1984. *(I; A)*

WYOMING

Carpenter, Allan. *Wyoming*. Childrens, 1979. *(I)*

Fradin, Dennis. *Wyoming: In Words and Pictures*. Childrens, 1980. *(P; I)*

O'Hara, Mary. *Green Grass of Wyoming*. Har-Row, 1946; *My Friend Flicka*, 1973 (new ed.) *(I; A)*

Willems, Arnold, and Hendrickson, Gordon. *Living Wyoming's Past*. Pruett, 1983. *(P; I)*

YANGTZE RIVER. See CHINA.

YEMEN (ADEN). See MIDDLE EAST.

YEMEN (SANA). See MIDDLE EAST.

YUGOSLAVIA. See BALKANS.

YUKON AND NORTHWEST TERRITORIES. See CANADA.

ZAÏRE

Stefoff, Rebecca. *Republic of Zaire*. Chelsea House, 1987. *(A)*

ZAMBIA. See AFRICA.

ZEBRAS

Arnold, Caroline. *Zebra*. Morrow, 1987. *(P; I)*

ZIMBABWE (RHODESIA)

Barnes-Svarney, Patricia. *Zimbabwe*. Chelsea House, 1989. *(I)*

Lauré, Jason. *Zimbabwe*. Children's, 1988. *(P; I)*

Stark, Al. *Zimbabwe: A Treasure of Africa*. Dillon Pr., 1986. *(I)*

Zimbabwe . . . in Pictures. Lerner, 1988. *(A)*

ZOOS

Anderson, Madelyn Klein. *New Zoos*. Watts, 1987. *(P; I)*

Barton, Miles. *Zoos and Game Reserves*. Gloucester Press; dist. by Watts, 1988. *(P; I)*

Hoffmeister, Donald F. *Zoo Animals*. Western, 1967. *(P)*

Jacobson, Karen. *Zoos*. Children's, 1982. *(P)*

Moss, Miriam. *Zoos*. Watts, 1987. *(P)*

Rinard, Judith E. *Zoos Without Cages*. National Geog, 1981. *(P; I)*

Thomson, Peggy. *Keepers and Creatures at the National Zoo*. Crowell, 1988. *(P; I)*

HOME AND SCHOOL
STUDY GUIDE

THE NEW BOOK OF KNOWLEDGE

HOME AND SCHOOL
STUDY GUIDE

THE NEW BOOK
OF KNOWLEDGE

GROLIER
INCORPORATED
DANBURY, CONN

THE HOME AND SCHOOL READING GUIDE

HOME AND SCHOOL STUDY GUIDE

Dear Parents:

Each of your children is a unique individual in your unique family. This is why there can be no sure set of rules for child-rearing. How a child will develop depends partly on characteristics inherited from both sides of the family and partly on experiences inside and outside the home.

You want your children to have the best that life can offer. You want them to enjoy life, to succeed in life, and to fulfill your dreams as well as their own. These are the desires of all parents.

When your children are very young, you are their comforters. You heal their bruises. You praise each fumbling effort and offer encouragement after each childish defeat. You satisfy their curiosity. However, the day comes when their horizons widen. They discover much that is new and strange and come to you for information. Out of your learning and experience you try to answer all questions. Suddenly you realize how much more children have to learn today than when you went to school.

The fact is that recent years have seen an explosion of knowledge—amazing advances in science, prodigious progress in technology, and a rapid succession of world events. At the same time, a host of new words has been added to our vocabulary. *Laser, quasar, bioluminescence, genetic engineering, videodisc, microcomputer,* and *computer-assisted instruction* are only a few of the words or terms that have become part of our language in recent years. What can parents do to help children understand and master this bewildering array of new knowledge? What can parents do to help children keep up with the ever-widening horizons of our world? The wise parent turns to books for help. THE NEW BOOK OF KNOWLEDGE, a comprehensive encyclopedia especially designed for children and for family use, is the logical choice.

An encyclopedia suitable for children contains the information children are likely to seek. It presents this information in language that children can read and understand. It is organized so that children can find information easily. The style of writing captures the interest and imagination of children and encourages further reading. And it includes a wealth of illustrations in full color—photographs, artwork, maps, and diagrams to supplement and clarify the text. Your NEW BOOK OF KNOWLEDGE meets all these criteria. It answers the questions that arise from your children's school studies because it is keyed to every area of the school curriculum—science, mathematics, language arts, history, geography, social studies, economics, anthropology, sociology, art, music, and health education.

The habit of turning to reference books for information is invaluable. But the close association of parents and children searching together for knowledge is even more valuable. Thus parents share with their children the experiences of each child's growing up.

Sometimes parents try to help children with their homework. In conference with your children's teachers, you can discover the teachers' objectives for their classes and what the children are studying. Then if you take this HOME AND SCHOOL STUDY GUIDE and turn to the grade your child is in, you will find keys to the wealth of material in THE NEW BOOK OF KNOWLEDGE. The STUDY GUIDE will suggest many ways in which you can help your children both in school work and in the learning opportunities at home.

You can help your children, secure in the knowledge that school and home are working harmoniously together. With a gesture as easy as turning the pages of a book, you can increase opportunities for learning and multiply your children's powers.

THE EDITORS
THE NEW BOOK OF KNOWLEDGE

To the Teacher:

We who have to do with children know that many facts we teach are soon forgotten. Not so the skills and concepts that we build, for children retain these throughout life if they are taught well.

One of the most useful of these skills is that of reference and research. You can teach children where and how to look for information and help them form the habit of seeking it out and using it correctly. Once they have learned to use resources, they can help themselves toward any goal.

THE NEW BOOK OF KNOWLEDGE was planned and made by educators—classroom teachers as well as school administrators. The founding editor in chief was a teacher for ten years and a curriculum co-ordinator for six years. The senior editor in charge of social studies had similar experience; the indexer is a librarian, and many staff members are former teachers.

Beyond that, material was tested with children in the classroom before being published. Research in schools established the arrangement easiest for young searchers to use and the pronunciation system that they could understand. Twenty-five school systems—in cities and towns and rural areas—co-operated in testing articles with children to determine reading level and understandability.

Reader motivation is built into THE NEW BOOK OF KNOWLEDGE. We don't say that THE NEW BOOK OF KNOWLEDGE makes teaching easy; we do say that it will make your teaching more effective.

THE EDITORS
THE NEW BOOK OF KNOWLEDGE

CONTENTS

Although grade levels are suggested in the HOME AND SCHOOL STUDY GUIDE, parents and teachers should also refer to related topics described for other grades. All references to THE NEW BOOK OF KNOWLEDGE are given by letter volume and page, thus: A100 (Volume A, page 100).

HOME AND SCHOOL WORK TOGETHER

Parents are a child's first teachers. At no other time in life are growth and development as rapid as in the preschool years. It is sometimes hard to keep up with the changes that take place in youngsters from day to day. There are new words, new ideas, new interests, sudden changes in likes and dislikes. Learning is going on every waking moment.

Parents and the environment they provide influence children's learning both in and out of school. More important than what children learn is their attitude toward learning. Frequent successful experiences at home give them confidence to go on to new and more difficult tasks. Learning becomes an adventure—an enjoyable, challenging part of life.

▶ SCHOOL IS A FRIENDLY PLACE

Children should look forward to school as an important and interesting part of life. The attitudes that they have already formed before entering school can help or hinder that vital first adjustment to school life. You, as parents, can shape those attitudes. You can help your children to make the emotional adjustment between home and school.

References to school should be frequent, casual, happy ones. Children need opportunities to ask questions and generally feel right about this approaching adventure. They should look forward to meeting their teachers as new adults in their lives who will help and guide them. The teachers will be friendly persons who like and understand children. At school, children will be in contact with other adults, too—the principal, other teachers, the school secretary, health officer, custodian, traffic officer, and the school bus driver. Your youngsters should understand that all these people will be helping them in one way or another.

Ideally, children should have an opportunity to visit the school building before the first day. Perhaps you can arrange to visit the school grounds before that time. Walk around the building, look at the playground, and talk about what's inside. Give assurance that teachers and the other children will help newcomers find their way—to their room, the bathroom, the place to get a drink of water, the lunchroom. These details are often the things that are most worrisome to a child.

Find out what the opening-day procedure is. Some schools ask parents to leave immediately. Others feel it is better for them to stay part or all of the first morning. In any case, children can be prepared for the fact that parents may not be able to stay. This sometimes comes as a surprise to the child who has never really thought about it.

▶ **SCHOOL IS AN INTERESTING PLACE**

Children will be working with all kinds of materials—paper, paint, crayons, clay, blocks, wood, tools. Some of these are already familiar. Some are new and strange but are fun to try. They will find old favorites among the books in the classroom as well as many new and interesting books. They will hear music and learn new songs and games. There will be many things to talk about. There may be trips in the neighborhood and plants and pets to care for. There will be times to work quietly, times to listen, and times to be active and even noisy. Wise teachers will take advantage of the child's natural desire to try many things. They will give every child the chance to achieve at the child's own level by providing jobs that can be completed satisfactorily.

▶ **SCHOOL IS A PLACE FOR LEARNING**

Children want to learn. They are eager to gain new skills and abilities, new knowledge and ideas. Schools recognize that children's natural interest and curiosity form a valuable basis for teaching. The model of the neighborhood they are building with blocks and toy cars in their classroom may lead to a visit to the shopping center. What children learn there is reinforced by reading, mathematics, writing, science, and social studies.

Besides the basic subjects that are uppermost in parents' minds when they think about school, there are other learnings, too. All through elementary and even secondary school, children will be taught to communicate effectively through the use of pictures, speech, and written words. Early in kindergarten and first grade they will learn to plan their work and to carry out these plans. They will learn to work well with others and to be contributing members of a group. Every day they will gain in self-reliance, in the realization of their own capacities, and in their understanding of other people.

▶ **HOME-SCHOOL RELATIONSHIPS**

Just as children bring home the happenings of the school day, so they carry to school the things that are influencing them at home. No child can simply shut a door on one part of daily life and then take up another. For this reason, schools recognize the need for good home-school communication and mutual objectives. Many schools use parent-teacher conferences as a means of reporting progress. Others use conferences in combination with written reports. If your school does not provide time for regularly scheduled conferences, you should arrange to speak informally with your child's teacher. There are many things you can tell each other that will help both of you in working with your child.

▶ YOUR CHILD'S TEACHER

A teacher's greatest satisfaction comes from knowing that he or she has a part in a child's achievement. Teachers know that each child must progress at an individual rate. Here is another place where parent-teacher conferences can play an important part. Find out exactly what the school is trying to do, how the teacher is working with your child, the aims for the school year. Clear up misunderstandings before they have a chance to color your attitude, and your child's attitude, toward school. Criticism of school can hardly help a child feel that school is important.

▶ WHAT ABOUT HOMEWORK?

Teachers recognize that some of the best learning often comes from direct experiences outside of school. There are many opportunities for learning at home. The five-year-old setting the table sees the necessity for simple counting. Fractions and measurements come alive for youngsters who help bake a cake. Helping children write thank-you notes for birthday and Christmas gifts gives practice in writing and spelling. A visit to the supermarket or the place where a parent works is an exercise in social studies. These are examples of homework in the best sense of the word.

Sometimes the best homework bears little relation to the work being done at school but serves to enrich the child's total living. Music or dancing lessons, a trip to the zoo or the museum, travel to another city, membership in a club—all these are contributions to the child's education in the broadest sense.

Your child's own library of reference books, stories, and factual books is important, too. Books keep alive a child's interest in reading for pleasure and information and help to build a foundation for developing the reading habit. The HOME AND SCHOOL READING GUIDE, which accompanies your NEW BOOK OF KNOWLEDGE, contains many valuable suggestions.

▶ HOME ENVIRONMENT AND THE TOOLS FOR LEARNING

We hear a great deal about providing children with an enriched environment—the kind that has nothing to do with money. This simply means purposely creating an environment in which children have the opportunity to develop and to learn. It isn't difficult to build this environment for your children when you remember what children need.

Children need security—security that comes from knowing that they are real members of the family and have the loving support of their parents.

Children need freedom—both physical and mental.

Children need limits—thoughtfully and firmly established and consistently maintained.

Children need help, not hovering overprotection; guidance, not interference; and just enough supervision for their protection.

Children need honest praise and encouragement.

Children need an example of good living.

Children need a well-organized home.

Children need a quiet corner where they can read a book or use the encyclopedia or other reference materials.

Tools for Learning

Given this kind of atmosphere to grow in, children also need the tools for learning.

Children need music—opportunities to hear good music on radio, television, and the wonderful records produced for children today; experiences in creating music with simple instruments, and later with real instruments, and by singing.

Children need arts and crafts materials—clay, paint, paper, crayons, cloth, paste, wood, scissors, and other tools. All these things become wonderful play materials for children.

Children need all kinds of books to meet their different needs—realistic and fanciful stories, reference books for factual information, books to be shared by the whole family and books to be enjoyed by a child alone, picture books to look at and talk about.

Learning begins and continues at home. You can help your child to be eager to learn, to be enthusiastic about trying new things. You can encourage your child to think independently, to be creative and ready to explore. That is learning.

KINDERGARTEN AND GRADES 1–3

▶ MEET THE EARLY SCHOOL CHILD

Even though each child grows and learns at an individual pace, nearly all children go through similar stages of development. Teachers in kindergarten and the early childhood grades recognize these growth characteristics. At the same time, they take into account the individual physical, emotional, and mental differences of young children when they plan the program for the level known as early childhood education.

Teachers know that large muscles develop more rapidly than small muscles. Consequently, early graders need outdoor play—jumping, running, and climbing. While they jump, run, and climb, children learn a great deal about the world and the people around them, for they learn in many ways—with their eyes, ears, and bodies, as well as with their minds.

Children need quiet times and rest periods, too, for they tire easily. Their hearts are growing rapidly, while their lungs are still relatively small. And so there are times for rest, for listening to songs and stories, and poring over picture books, and for caring for plants and animals.

This is a time of transition. It has not been easy for your child to leave the warm comfort of home and familiar surroundings, even though school offers excitement and the glamour of growing up. Tears sometimes well up quickly. Tempers sometimes flare. Feelings can be hurt and possessions disputed. Young children have much to learn about themselves and about getting along with others. They need understanding and a chance to develop self-confidence.

Each early grader develops according to an individual growth rate. Some children may be full of action and speed, fidgety and restless, and eager to run or to throw a ball. Others, whose control of smaller muscles is more advanced, may enjoy sewing, cutting, pasting, drawing, coloring, and writing. But all youngsters at this developmental level are quite concerned with large ideas—with the immensity of space and the universe, with the wonders of nature and of God.

This is a wonderful age, but it is a trying one for both children and parents because children are reaching out in their own way to a wide and exciting new world. Early graders are still very young, and much is expected of them. They need support, understanding, and friendship. And they need to feel that you accept them and appreciate what they can do.

LANGUAGE ARTS

The language arts started in the crib, for that is where children began to learn the many sounds they now use in talking and listening. With their first lusty cries they began to realize that sound carries both meaning and feeling. Your response taught them that. As they grew, they gradually understood that spoken words are messengers that carry meaning from speaker to listener.

As you read to your children, they saw the printed words in the book. They couldn't read the words, of course, but they did understand that written and printed words have meaning. In the primary grades they learn the magic of unlocking meaning from those printed symbols on a page.

Many things influence children's language, but those nearest to them—you, their parents—have the greatest effect on their language growth. As they catch your attitudes, feelings, and thoughts, they realize that what you say and how you say it tell others what you mean and how you mean it.

Where you live, your choice of words, your work, your personality, and many other factors influence family talk and your children's speech. As they use words to express feelings and facts, questions and answers, they learn that we use language as we seek information. When you ask, "What do you think?" they learn that children do not have a monopoly on questions and that you care about their opinions. When they see you look it up in THE NEW BOOK OF KNOWLEDGE, they learn that although adults do not know all the answers, we do know where and how to find many of them.

In dozens of ways parents teach preschoolers the meaning and use of language. Once children go out into the neighborhood and to schools, other influences shape their language. Television, radio, and motion pictures introduce new words, new accents, and new uses of words to their sharp young ears and tongues. Books bring freshly minted phrases from a writer's rich imagination. The neighbor's children share more than toys, for they share their language inheritance, too. But of all the many influences that affect your children's language, yours is still the strongest. Consciously or not, you are still their most important teachers. You can help your children to select and edit their speech, to spark it, and stretch for new ways of expressing ideas, facts, and feelings. You can help them develop discrimination in television viewing. And you can expose them early to the joys of reading.

▶ THE LANGUAGE ARTS IN EARLY CHILDHOOD EDUCATION

Ours is a verbal society. How much children learn both in and out of school depends largely on their ability to use and understand language. As they learn by watching and doing, they use words to clarify ideas. As they listen, talk with others, read, and write, schoolchildren use words as they think.

The language arts are used and taught throughout the school day. Of course, special periods are set aside for skill development in listening, speaking, reading, writing, and spelling, but language is used in social studies, science, mathematics, and in all other studies and activities in the classroom and on the playground.

The description of the language-arts curriculum that follows presents ways parents can tie home and school experiences together as they help their children learn to use our language well.

▶ LISTENING

This is truly an age of listening. Television, motion pictures, lectures, the theater, radio, and recordings have attuned our ears to the talk of others. All through school and life we must listen courteously and attentively when others speak.

The art of listening must be taught to children, and kindergarten and primary grade teachers do this with plan and purpose. They know that children who sit at rigid attention with folded hands may be far away from the words that are floating in their direction. Teachers know, too, that if they wish to catch the child's ear, they must capture interest through purposeful teaching.

During kindergarten and the primary years, youngsters learn to listen to (a) simple rules and directions, (b) answers to their many questions, (c) stories and poems, (d) recordings, the school public-address system, radio, television, motion pictures, and filmstrips with sound.

Of course, you do these things at home, too. Home is the place for varied and informal oral language. In dozens of ways parents encourage children to speak well and listen carefully. THE NEW BOOK OF KNOWLEDGE provides material for many and varied language-arts experiences. These include stories, poems, plays, games, selections for reading aloud, suggestions for listening experiences, games, riddles, and puzzles.

▶ SPEAKING

We express feelings and meaning through the tone, inflection, rhythm, and mood of our speech as well as through our words.

Poetry. Listening to poetry can help children hear the rhythm, the lilt, and the richness of our language. Rhyme not only delights children but alerts them to the similarity of sounds. If the ideas and the imagery are simple, poems can introduce youngsters to new words and help them expand their imagination and their vocabularies.

Courtesy. If children are to communicate effectively, they must learn to use appropriate language and observe language courtesy. When you say "Please" and "Thank you," your child learns that consideration for others dictates good manners and that good manners can be expressed verbally.

Observation. Children learn to speak best when they have something they want to say. Help your children enjoy the world around them. Teach them to observe and to talk about what they see. Help them to engage in activities that they can discuss and describe. The youngster who is encouraged this way has something to share with others. Dozens of activities described in THE NEW BOOK OF KNOWLEDGE help children observe the natural wonders around them and engage in experimentation and construction. These experiences provide opportunities for developing new interests, understandings, and enthusiasms. Such interests are necessary for future reading and speaking success.

SPEAKING AND LISTENING

Your child's teacher will try to create a comfortable, receptive, and lively classroom atmosphere so that children will talk easily and well. The teacher will guide the children by helping them to organize and edit their thoughts, by helping them develop a sense of idea sequence, and by showing them how to stick to a point in conversation. Using various tools and techniques, the teacher will teach spoken language skills as these are used in conversation, discussion, planning, reporting, interviewing, telephoning, delivering messages, extending invitations and thank-you's, making announcements, storytelling, oral reading, reciting poetry, group, or choral, reading, and dramatic play.

Your child's teacher sets aside special times each day when the children are encouraged to share special experiences. They learn to stand on their feet and communicate with ease and charm. The modern classroom is a place of continuously shared experiences and ideas, for as children learn, they engage in the easy exchange of ideas carried on through talk.

▶ READING AND LITERATURE

The reading program that begins in the primary grades has as its objectives mastery of the mechanics of reading, increase in comprehension, and the development of lifetime reading habits.

In the primary grades children will learn to read and understand simple signs, charts, and books. They will learn that certain groups of letters have particular sounds. They will learn that words often take their meanings from other words in the sentence, and they learn how to judge what they read. They will read for fun as well as for information, ideas, and facts.

Parents can help children at home, too. When you look at pictures together, you can help them grasp meanings, discern likenesses and differences, and group similar ideas. They may describe what they see as they grasp the meaning of a picture. This is important preparation for learning to read, because they will have to recognize printed symbols that stand for words. They will have to learn to organize and interpret what they read. Pictures help children link their visual experiences with the printed page. Photographs capture reality; drawings create mood. Both can provide additional information to supplement the printed page, and both are important. THE NEW BOOK OF KNOWLEDGE is a rich source of carefully selected photographs, drawings, art-work, and diagrams—many in exciting, accurate full color.

As children picture-read, they handle books. They learn that we turn pages from right to left as we start to read from the front of a book. They learn to read from left to right and from the top of the page to the bottom.

Your Children's Knowledge Grows as You Read to Them

Human beings differ from all other living creatures in their ability to learn through indirect experiences. Through reading, we conquer time and space, and we reach out beyond our physical limits. We help our youngsters understand this when we read aloud to them.

You can read aloud without being an actor. Fortunately, children make a warmly appreciative audience. A little practice and a few hints should make you a good reader.

Read a selected story or poem to yourself first so you will understand it, feel its mood, and tailor your reading tone to the mood of the selection. Remember, too, that there is no one kind of story or poem or subject of an article that everyone must like. Tastes differ. Children's present interests determine the kind of story or poem they like now. With time, growth, and guidance, their interests will widen, and their taste will improve.

Children like to be read to for many reasons. They delight in your individual attention. They enjoy humor. They like to identify themselves with a brave hero or heroine. They want to extend their understanding of the world around them. They want to distinguish between fact and fancy. They are interested in hearing about the people who do the world's work and how we all help one another. They want to know about other ways of living in other places and other times. They particularly want to know how children live across the border of space and time. They want to find out how to do things and why things are as they are.

Home Activities in Reading and Literature

Reading to your youngsters is your early invitation to them to share the mysteries of the printed page with you. How proud they will be when, after completing their first preprimer or primer, they bring it home to share with you. They want and need your attentive audience. They may need some help with troublesome words. Encourage them by accepting their achievement, however simple it may seem to you. The teacher will encourage and help each child to move along as fast as possible. Success in small details develops self-confidence.

▶ HOW YOUR CHILD LEARNS TO READ

Teachers know that there are many ways to teach reading. No one way is best for all children or for any child at all times. That is why teachers use many methods and many materials.

Sight vocabulary. Many children begin to read by learning a sight vocabulary. These are simple words that your child learns to recognize on sight.

Phonics. Another method is the use of phonics. This is the association of speech sounds with a letter or a group of letters. Later, children will learn to identify words by dividing them into their structural parts. This technique is useful in identifying longer and more difficult words encountered for the first time.

Context. Children learn new words by their context in a sentence. The surrounding words and pictures tell them the meaning of the new word. Completing a sentence is one of the word-attack skills.

Experience charts. Children may be asked to dictate sentences describing an experience, an activity, or a story that the teacher prints on the chalkboard or on a chart. When children read these sentences, they learn to recognize words common to their own experiences. They may themselves print these words, their own names, and the names of classmates. Spelling is introduced in this way.

Basal readers. Many schools build the beginning reading program around a series of basal readers. These are graded books that have the special function of teaching reading.

Workbooks and programmed materials. The basal readers are often supplemented by workbooks and programmed materials. This type of material uses small sections or "frames" of reading content followed by a question, directions, or a blank space to fill in. Thus, children work at their own speed.

Individualized reading. A program of personal, or individualized, reading is also carried on by the school in connection with the how-to-read program. Children select books related to their own interests.

Reading Problems

Teachers watch for signs of reading difficulty and take steps to help a child before the problem becomes a block to progress. They recognize that some children have ear or eye defects that are not detected before they enter school. Sometimes reading instruction is begun before a child is "ready." Some young children cannot distinguish between sounds and words that are similar.

Many schools now provide reading teachers trained to make diagnoses and provide corrective help for children who have reading problems. If you feel that your child requires special help, go to the teacher or principal, who can recommend appropriate action.

How You Can Help Your Preschool Child

When parents read aloud to their preschool children, they are providing the best preparation for learning to read in school.

Answer children's questions and tell them what a word is if they are curious about it.

Research shows that young children who have been taught the letters of the alphabet at home may learn to read more quickly in school.

▶ SPELLING

Children learn to spell as they learn to read and write. The words they learn are those they need to express their ideas in writing. Spelling learned for a real purpose is not easily forgotten.

Readiness for spelling begins in the earliest grades. Children examine alphabet books. They learn to identify letters. They learn alphabetical sequence by singing alphabet songs and playing alphabet games. Children learn to make and use a picture dictionary. They learn to duplicate letters of the alphabet and to play spelling games like Word Lotto.

Systematic instruction in spelling is begun when children have a large enough reading vocabulary, when they can write in manuscript, and when they can copy words correctly.

POEMS, NURSERY RHYMES, AND SONGS

▶ WRITING

As oral expression takes permanent form on paper and becomes writing, children learn to express their ideas and feelings in written language that others can read easily.

Teachers realize that children write best when they have something to say and a reason for saying it on paper. Children's "Dear Santa" letters are readable because there is a reason for writing clearly. In school, children will write simple labels, signs, charts, and letters as needed in the school day. They will probably use manuscript writing at first because it is easier to read and write, and it resembles the printed words in books. Toward the end of second grade, children will usually change over to the connected writing we call "cursive," in which the pencil is not lifted from the paper until the end of the word.

The teacher will encourage pride in legibility. As soon as children are ready, they will be taught proper page placement and letter formation. They will be helped to see that good writing requires proper physical balance. This means that the arm must rest comfortably on the desk and that writing implements are comfortable to children's small fingers and limited physical ability. If a child is left-handed, the teacher will show how to position the paper and use the left hand correctly.

Children develop clear, legible handwriting when standards are set and maintained. Writing includes correct usage, spelling, punctuation, capitalization, and the ability to compose clear sentences and paragraphs. These skills take a long time to develop and require much practice.

Writing is used in copying individual and co-operative stories, preparing a report, writing a letter of invitation or an original story, composing titles for pictures and illustrations, and making a notebook.

During the primary years children will learn simple facts about these skills. Capitalization and punctuation will be taught as they are needed and used. Acceptable usage is taught as it is heard, for in these early grades "grammar" is taught largely by sound, rather than as a formal skill.

Creative Written Expression

Most children love to express their feelings, ideas, and experiences through talk. If properly encouraged, they will enjoy expressing themselves in writing, too. By creating a warm and friendly atmosphere, by encouraging youngsters who want to share creative poems, stories, and reports, teachers develop creative writing in school. They respect children's creative efforts and present those efforts with dignity and respect.

The poems composed lovingly for Mother's or Father's day or a birthday are also examples of creative writing. Encourage such efforts, and show your appreciation. Your child may never be a professional writer, but creative writing, like music and art, offers another path to self-expression and enjoyment.

WRITING

THE SOCIAL STUDIES, OR SOCIAL SCIENCES

The social studies (also called the social sciences) are the study of people and how they live. These studies include geography, history, government, economics, citizenship education, anthropology, and sociology. Naturally, in the earliest grades none of these individual disciplines will be identified by name. In fact, young children seldom realize that they are learning any of the social sciences. Yet they are actually building the foundation for these studies in later grades.

Learning that they belong to a family group is children's first social studies lesson. Your youngster learns that "belonging" also brings with it responsibility for others and that it means people depending upon one another.

Gradually youngsters learn that each family is part of a larger group—the community. During their school years they will learn about their own community and about the larger communities—state and region, the nation and the world. As they do this, they see that just as membership in a family entails responsibility and caring for others, so does membership in the city, state, nation, or world.

Children have a deep sense of morality, nourished by their experiences with the adults around them. Although they may not always understand your words, they do understand the feelings behind your interest in the daily news and in the problems of other people.

Children Learn Social Studies in Many Ways

As youngsters gather information from many sources—people, trips, radio, television, displays, pictures, and printed materials—they acquire understandings and facts that must be put together. In school, the teacher will present the larger meanings behind facts and will help your child develop important concepts. Your child will also be taught how and where to find the facts and how best to make use of them.

The teacher will excite your child's imagination in many ways, using different materials and methods. An antique spinning wheel may be brought to school when the children are studying pioneer life. Pictures and letters from children in faraway lands add both fun and fact as they show similarities and differences of peoples around the world. A doll can tell much about how people dress or work. Stamp collections, photographs, slides, films, books, and realia supplement the information found in textbooks and reference books. Used wisely, both at home and in school, such resources extend a youngster's understanding of other people and other times.

Your child's teacher may take the class on educational trips—to the post office or a farm or the zoo. Through such actual contact, children learn how social institutions and organizations work—how people work together. A local police officer may come into the classroom to talk about traffic rules and the reasons for them. A mail carrier may tell how letters are delivered, and a member of the fire department may discuss fire prevention.

Films, filmstrips, opaque projectors, transparencies, pictures, and picture postcards all illuminate the study of times, places, and people. Perhaps the most important visual aids are the illustrations in children's books. The illustrations—photographs, artwork, diagrams, and maps—in THE NEW BOOK OF KNOWLEDGE have been selected carefully so that children will understand both the idea and the feeling behind them.

Often the right story or poem explains an idea in social studies with crystal clarity. THE NEW BOOK OF KNOWLEDGE has a rich supply of stories, legends, and poems for the kindergartner and primary grader.

▶ **SOCIAL STUDIES IN EARLY CHILDHOOD EDUCATION**

Social studies include the study of people and their relation to their environment. Through social studies, teachers help children prepare to live as democratic citizens in an ever-changing world. They help children acquire basic knowledge and understanding of the world in which they live and guide them in the development of worthwhile attitudes toward other people. Children also are helped to attain skill in study and work habits, in social living, in problem solving, and in critical thinking. And they are taught to appreciate their heritage, its values, and its ideals.

These are objectives of all education, not merely of the social studies. Teachers know that school is only one avenue by which children will attain these worthwhile attitudes, skills, and habits. They rely on the home to supplement the school.

Teachers and parents working together can help young children achieve these objectives by such teachings as these:

Teaching children to live, work, and play together at home, in school, and in the community.

Teaching young children that people everywhere help one another and that many people help us by supplying the services and goods that we need.

Teaching children that just as we have our ways of living, working, and playing, so people in other lands have theirs.

The following social studies topics are part of the early childhood curriculum in most elementary schools. They lend themselves ideally to additional learning at home under guidance.

Homes and Families

"Home" is a special word that brings up an image of family living. Children know its meaning. As soon as they are able, they visit their neighbors' homes. It isn't long before they know that people live in many different kinds of homes. With their parents they may watch a house being built in the neighborhood. At home they may build a playhouse with blocks. Perhaps they help a member of the family repair a household appliance, paint a room, or build bookshelves.

During the early school years children will learn about other people who live in quite different dwellings. They may learn how people live in hot desert regions, in the cold Arctic, or in a tropical rain forest. And they will learn about animal homes and families, too, as they watch a mother cat care for her kittens or a robin carry worms to its young in a nearby nest.

Children know that home is a place of comfort and love. They know, too, that families live and work together in their homes. They see parents create the feeling of a home. They share the family work when they are able to help set the table or dry the dishes, when they tidy their rooms and put their toys away, when they help in the garden or take care of tools, and when they walk the dog or feed the cat.

Families have fun together, and children learn from these experiences, too. Radio, television, picnics, visits to the zoo, story reading time, ice-skating, swimming, listening to records, playing games together, sharing a hobby like stamp or coin collecting—all these are educational as well as recreational experiences.

HOME AND FAMILY LIFE

Our School and Neighborhood

One of the most difficult tasks that young school children face is getting along with other children and adults. They soon learn that everyone must follow rules if people are to live and work together happily. The way they feel about themselves and other people and the attitudes they have learned from you will shape their adjustment.

As children ride the school bus or walk to school or a place of worship or the neighborhood store, they learn where their friends live, what happens in different community buildings, what streets and roads are dangerous to cross, and where the traffic lights and friendly police officers are. They carry a mental map of their home-school neighborhood.

During the primary years children gather in groups as they play in the school yard or playground. They sing songs and play games that you knew when you were young. A bit later many join Cub Scouts, Brownies, Y's, and Boys' and Girls' clubs as they seek well-rounded and guided group play.

SCHOOLS

THE COMMUNITY AND NEIGHBORHOOD

Days We Celebrate

Seasons and holidays are very important in the lives of young children. By sharing in festivities with other children at school, with others of their family, and with the community, your children link themselves with their cultural and national heritage.

Birthdays, Mother's Day, Father's Day, Valentine's Day, Halloween, Thanksgiving, Hanukkah, Christmas, and Easter are among the days for special observance. Celebrations are a time for sharing.

There is a tendency to decry the commercialism that characterizes holidays today. Parents should not allow this to interfere with their own family observance and celebration. Family holidays that commemorate happy events—even trivial events—are valuable learning experiences for children. Parents can help young children acquire a sense of obligation to remember others with thoughtfulness and kindness on birthdays and anniversaries.

Patriotic holidays introduce children to their country's history and heritage. The flag displayed at home as well as at school can mark an event or the birthday of a national figure and be the inspiration for family storytelling, reading, or singing.

Many articles in THE NEW BOOK OF KNOWLEDGE describe interesting activities that can help parents as well as teachers observe holidays. Some of the articles listed below provide background information. Others are "how to make" and "how to do" articles.

HOLIDAYS AND DAYS WE CELEBRATE

Parties	P89–93; H10–11; M23–25, 91
Passover	P97–98; E43
Purim	P549
Religious holidays	R153–55
Saint Patrick's Day	H152; P102
Seasons	S108–12; F324–26
Thanksgiving Day	T154–55, 172; F339; P346
Valentine's Day	V266–68; G373
Veterans' Day	H156–57
Washington's Birthday	H151–52; C13; W36–43

▶ **INDIANS**

Once upon a time other people lived in this part of the world, and they did not live as we do. Since young children have little notion of past time, their interest in history will be quite simple. But an introduction to the life of American Indians who once lived where they now live may start them on the path to a better understanding of the people of the world, today and yesterday. The articles listed below suggest a wealth of pictures and text.

INDIANS

INDIANS, AMERICAN	I 162–201
Algonkian	I 177–78; Q10a
Apache	I 184–85, 205; A407; N185
Assiniboin	I 180
Athapascans	A153
Aztecs	A571–74; I 172–73; C551; M247–48
Blackfoot	I 180
Cherokee	I 178; A144; G147
Cheyenne	I 180
Chinook	I 188
Chippewa (Ojibway)	I 190
Choctaw	I 178; A144
Creek	I 178; A144; F273
Crow	I 180
Five civilized tribes	O80, 84, 94–95
Gatherers	I 172–80
Haida	I 188; A154
Hopi	I 183; A407
Huron	I 175; C71
Incas	I 107–110
Iroquois	I 175–76, 190; C71, 187; N224; Q10a
Lenni-Lenape	D94; N178
Maya	M184–87; I 167; C461; L68; N401–02
Micmac	I 177
Mound Builders	I 156; O74
Navajo	I 184–85; A407; N185
Nez Percé	I 188, 205
Paiute	I 183
Plains Indians	I 205
Pomo	I 186
Pueblo	I 172; H173–74
Seminole	I 178, 205; F259, 273; T31
Shoshoni	I 180
Sioux	I 179–80, 178, 205; S324, 326; W337
Tlingit	A154
Toltec	I 172; M569–70
Tsimshian	A154
Ute	C437, 445
Zuni	I 183
FAMOUS INDIANS	
Atahualpa	I 173; P163, 266
Black Hawk	I 74–75
Joseph Brant	B370–71; R205
Cochise	C608
Crazy Horse	C629
Geronimo	G189
Joseph	I 59, 205
Massasoit	P346
Metacomet (Philip)	P562
Montezuma I	M622
Montezuma II	I 172–73; M247, 622
Osceola	O240
Philip (Metacomet)	P561–62
Pocahontas	J22, 23; S201
Pontiac	O74; P382
Powhatan	P584
Red Cloud	R377
John Ross	R400
Sacajawea	I 59; L163
Seattle	W25
Sequoya	S124; G145; O93
Sitting Bull	I 182; B429; N337; S325
Tecumseh	T42; H42; I 157, 204

MATHEMATICS

By the time children enter school, they have had many experiences with numbers. They may enjoy counting. They know that numbers are used for telephoning and for television channels, and they know how old they are. Children recognize the differences between coins, even though they may not be sure of the actual value, and they have already learned something about fractions when they ask for half a glass of milk. Though their ideas of number may still be inaccurate, those ideas furnish a starting point for the teacher.

The Mathematics Program

The mathematics program in elementary schools has undergone changes in recent times. In mathematics, the classroom is a laboratory containing materials that children can handle and use for experimentation. Mathematics emphasizes the development of concepts and logical thinking. Instead of stressing only the memorization of numbers, tables, and rules, mathematics teaches children to discover mathematical relationships. Basic facts and techniques of computation—and the reasons why they work—are mastered for the purpose of solving problems.

Your Child's Classroom

Walk into your child's classroom and look around. You will probably see an abacus, dominoes, and play money. These are called experience materials. You will also probably see place-value cards, disks, tens frames, and squared materials. These are called representative materials because they are concrete representations of abstract numbers. Instruments of measure will include a real clock, a tape measure, a meter stick, a real thermometer, and transparent containers to measure dry and liquid substances.

Your Child's Teacher

Using many materials and many methods, your child's teacher introduces youngsters to mathematical concepts from the earliest grades. Experiences are an excellent means of developing mathematical concepts. A tape measure helps children measure how tall they and their classmates are. Play money is changed into smaller denominations. A clock with movable hands stands ready to teach time. Children are taught to compute mentally, to find solutions by using a variety of methods, and to explain their reasoning to the class. They are encouraged to "estimate" the answer before solving a mathematical problem and then to compare the answer with the original estimate. They are introduced to the idea of "sets" and "set theory."

How You Can Help Your Child with Mathematics

Even first graders will occasionally bring home mathematics "homework." Their teachers may ask them to cut out from the newspaper or supermarket advertisement pictures of articles with their prices. Another time they may be asked to complete an unfinished page from their workbook. As they prepare their assignments, discuss the assignment with them and provide whatever guidance is needed.

Concepts, understandings, and skills in mathematics are cumulative. If children do not understand one mathematical concept, they may find difficulty in mastering a new one. Ask the teacher how you can help them at home.

Out-of-school experiences are an excellent means of developing mathematical understanding. Children practice mathematics when they help you plan a birthday party. How many children will they invite? How many invitations will they need, and what will the stamps cost? How many favors, cakes, cups, plates, and balloons shall they buy? How much change should they expect?

Help your children understand words like little and big, short and tall, centimeter and meter. Provide them with a ruler to measure their growth against a mark on the wall. Help them to estimate the cost of single items when they go to the supermarket with you.

The teacher uses similar experiences as the starting point for teaching mathematics. You can help your child in the same way. Learned this way, mathematics has more meaning for children and so is easier to understand and to learn.

SCIENCE

Although you may hold no teaching certificate, you have probably been teaching your youngsters science since they first toddled after a butterfly or watched you bake a cake. When you showed them how to feed the goldfish or pick up a kitten or plant seeds in a window box, you were teaching them about the world of living things and about the rhythmic changes of life. As you shared your enthusiasm and encouraged their interest, you introduced them to scientific methods of learning and using knowledge.

There are many ways by which you teach your children science.

Observation. You teach your children to learn by observation when you stand at the window to see how the stars twinkle or watch the snow fall.

Doing. You teach them to learn by doing when you collect leaves and help them see the differences in size and shape or when you let them hold a seashell to their ears so they can hear its curious sound.

Experimentation. You teach them to learn by experiment when you pop corn or change a fuse or use a lever to move a heavy object.

Scientific knowledge. You teach your children to use scientific knowledge when you read the thermometer to see whether they should wear heavy sweaters or when you help them build a picnic fire and teach them the proper precautions.

will be helped to recognize that science affects our ways of living, thinking, feeling, and doing and that scientific knowledge carries with it certain responsibilities. Children are also helped to realize that all people depend on one another and upon plants and animals.

Children learn something about weather and how it affects our lives. They begin to learn about the living things that move in the air. They learn about sound and electricity and magnets; about the sun, the stars, and the moon; and about machines that help us travel and communicate with one another.

The following references in THE NEW BOOK OF KNOWLEDGE will help you meet or whet your child's curiosity about science. They will help you answer the questions children often ask. The pictures help youngsters understand many things, even though they may not be ready to read the printed explanations. Because children usually learn best by doing, many activities are included—things for parents and children to do together for fun as well as for information.

You will know best how much information to share with your child and the right time for sharing. The references in THE NEW BOOK OF KNOWLEDGE can help you help your child to discover the wonders and the joys of science.

Science in the Primary Grades

During their early school years children begin to understand about themselves, about the world of living and nonliving things, and about the forces of nature surrounding them. Their teachers help them to use simple scientific methods of thinking and acting. They

SCIENCE

Air	A481–82
Airplanes	A108–21
Animals	A262–74
Aquariums	A340–43
Birds	B199–244; P178–79
Fishes	F181–204; A343; P181
Flowers and seeds	F279–86
Heat	H84–93
Insects	I 230–50; B471–79

Articles in THE NEW BOOK OF KNOWLEDGE that describe specific animals and plants are too numerous to be listed here. Information can be found in the Index under the name of the particular animal or plant.

ART AND MUSIC

Your children began to enjoy art and music long before they reached school age. You introduced them to aesthetic experiences when you sang nursery songs and lullabies, when you played singing and dancing games. You stimulated them when you shared pictures with them and when you encouraged their early efforts by giving them the materials they needed and the appreciation they wanted.

Art

When your children start school, they already have a background of creative experiences. Their teachers encourage them so that they feel free to express their ideas through many art media. In school children have access to a variety of materials. They use bright-colored poster and finger paints, chalks and crayons, clay, paper, and fabrics of different textures. Because teachers know that large muscles must be developed during early school years, they encourage children to work with large sheets of paper, large brushes, and thick crayons.

There are developmental stages in the use of art materials, as in all learning. Children need time to explore and to manipulate art media before attempting representation. Teachers do not impose adult standards or techniques. They know that young children get satisfaction from merely experimenting with materials and may not always make a finished product.

Teachers encourage children to experiment with a variety of brushstrokes. They know that copying and filling in outlines are not creative art experiences. Dependence on prescribed outlines thwarts children's creative instincts and prevents them from expressing themselves with freedom and satisfaction.

You can help your children develop their creative ability at home. Help them to see that they have experiences and ideas worth expressing. Don't ridicule their efforts. Along with paper, blunt scissors, crayons, clay, chalk, pencils, and paint, give them scraps of colored cloth, string, yarn, bottle corks, empty spools, feathers, ribbons, and paste. Provide a table to work on, a large square of plastic or oilcloth to catch the spills, an old shirt to use as a smock, and an easel or piece of wallboard to help them use new media and methods.

Display the results of your children's work but do not expect their art products to be easily recognizable, and do not ask, "What is it?" Instead, encourage children to talk about their art efforts when they wish to. Don't set too high a standard of accomplishment or tell them how to express their ideas.

ARTS AND CRAFTS

Clay modeling	C354–55
Collage	C400–01
Découpage	D80
Finger painting	F126–28
Making greeting cards	G374
Making puppets and marionettes	P544–48
Needlecraft	N95–103
Planning a party	P89–93
Origami	O232–35
Paper chromatography	E397
Papier-mâché	P58b–58c
Sand art	S25
Weaving	W96–98b
Wire sculpture	W190b–191
Woodworking	W230–34

Music

Young children sing spontaneously. They imitate the sounds of cars, trains, boats, and planes. They enjoy singing nursery rhymes, nonsense songs, and songs about holidays, seasons, and home.

Teachers use music throughout the day. They will use records and tapes. They may play the piano and even a guitar, an accordion, or a recorder. Children sing, listen to music, engage in rhythmic exercises and dramatic play, and even play simple rhythm instruments, such as drums and tambourines.

You can encourage your child to love music. The recorded music you buy and the radio and television programs you select provide opportunities for the whole family to enjoy and appreciate music. Children's concerts and operettas are often featured in larger metropolitan areas. Family "sings" on holidays introduce children to traditional and seasonal music, and religious music in houses of worship provides an opportunity for children to sing with others.

HEALTH AND SAFETY

School helps to keep children safe and healthy. Each morning, teachers check each child's appearance for signs of illness. Ears, eyes, teeth, height, and weight are checked at regular intervals.

Children learn the importance of taking care of their own health and of being considerate of the health of others. School activities are planned so that physical activity is alternated with periods of relaxation.

Children's safety is an important concern of the school. The safe way to use materials and equipment, to behave in an emergency, to cross the street, and to play after school are constantly emphasized.

You can help your children by setting an example of good health and safety practices at home and by explaining the reasons for these. Teach them to avoid accidents by obeying traffic, water safety, and fire prevention rules. Encourage them to practice good personal habits of nutrition and cleanliness.

Schools are including study of the environment in many parts of the curriculum. Air and water pollution, noise pollution, and solid-waste disposal are concerns vital to your children's health and safety, and it is increasingly important that they learn the causes and solutions of these problems. This area can be studied from both its social and scientific aspects. Field trips can be arranged to recycling points where the responsibility of the public in such matters is demonstrated.

MEET THE MIDDLE SCHOOL CHILD

The middle school child can be delightful to teach. This is an age of balance and calm compared with the earlier period of transition from home to school that marks the primary years or compared with the later period of stress that marks the teens.

Children in the middle school are interested in the world around them. Their teachers not only try to answer this interest but also try to broaden and deepen understanding sparked by children's needs and enthusiasm.

Because of their interest in the adult world, children of middle school age fit in well with family schedules and plans. They cherish their sense of growing independence. Yet they want and accept limits. They hate to be bossed, but they respond to courteous treatment. They are eager to find their place in their own age group. They love to conform and to belong to a team, a group, or a club. They may pursue such an interest for weeks or forget all about it in a day. Youngsters work out their needs in their own way if we allow them opportunity for choice and selection.

Youngsters love to help plan family projects, trips, hobbies, and jobs that can be done together. They enjoy the wonderful feeling of companionship and the prestige their appreciated efforts bring.

Middle school children are eager to know what things are, how they work, how they were discovered, and how they are used. Children of this age have great need to understand the meaning behind the facts and to see their connections. They collect things with enthusiasm. They may collect bottle tops, coins, stamps, marbles, minerals—or any of a hundred other things. Through these collections, youngsters reach out to learn about the world around them.

While many children pass from interest to interest as they go through the grades, any worthwhile enthusiasm can open new doors of understanding at different times. Rocks or seashells are pretty to pick up and play with when a child is four or five. They may be fun for second graders to carry home and display in their rooms, but fifth graders may enjoy collecting and identifying them.

Essays or reports demanding the ability to generalize may pose problems, and your children may need your help. But if they are asked to write about the dog they trained or the tropical fish they raise, they will surprise you with lively descriptions filled with carefully observed details. They may even wish to draw pictures to illustrate their reports, for they are eager to share exact meanings.

You can use your youngsters' interest in the specific as you help them develop reading skills and a respect for accuracy. You can help them use the tools and techniques of learning if you remember that children differ and that they therefore learn differently. One youngster may require a great deal of help. Another may merely need a clue or suggested reference. A third may prefer to proceed independently without your help. Censure or comparisons may foster feelings of inadequacy in a child, for confidence stems from gradual achievement. Being a middle school child isn't always easy. There are standards to be met at home, at school, in the neighborhood, and in the special world of one's own feelings. Confidence comes slowly, and children need help in developing it.

Middle school children may become lost in a maze of details. Help them organize and review what they have learned. Teachers do this. They help select the important facts and ideas in any study. When called upon, you can help your children arrange and organize information, materials, and assignments. Of course, you won't always be successful. Some youngsters welcome an occasional suggestion. Some prefer to have their teachers, not their parents, suggest methods. And some youngsters just can't or won't organize the way parents wish they would. Gentle suggestions at the right time without "pushing" may in time bear satisfying fruit. There is always time.

There are many ways you can help your children indirectly, too. You can help them at home. A carefully planned party can be a lesson in learning to "follow through." Your youngsters will let you know how much responsibility they can or will assume and what limits they need.

LANGUAGE ARTS

Children read with many purposes. Some seek knowledge of people, places, and things. Some find comfort as they read about children like themselves. Sometimes children read for fun and pleasure or just to while away the time.

No one type of reading matter or story appeals to all youngsters. There are stories that strike the spark of enthusiasm in children and start them on their reading way. Some youngsters prefer fairy tales. Others like science fiction, adventure stories, or animal stories. Whatever kinds of stories your children read, they are living vicariously—traveling in a time machine to other places and times and into the minds and hearts of other people.

Librarians and Teachers Encourage Reading

Both librarians and teachers are dedicated to the task of helping children find the right reading material at the right time. Your children's teachers may try to capture their interests in these ways:

By having library times when children may read for fun.

By displaying books attractively, making them hard to resist.

By encouraging book reviews and reports, not just to see whether the child has read the stories but rather to share reactions to good stories.

By appointing a library committee so children can check their own books in and out as they use the class card catalog.

By allowing time for "book talk." Shared enthusiasm sparks reading faster than anything else.

By taking the class to the school library or media center or the public library regularly.

By sponsoring plans such as Children's Book Week or a summer reading program in which children receive bookmarks or award certificates for participation.

By finding a special story for a certain child.

Most of all, by sharing their own delight in reading.

While both librarians and teachers try to capture children's enthusiasm for reading, encouraging lifetime reading habits is largely the business of the home. Here is where parents can really help their children.

Parents Encourage Reading at Home

Parents who enjoy reading can share their pleasure by reading to very young children. But middle school children also need to hear stories read to them. Perhaps they need this experience in the middle school more than they did before because Scouts, sports, clubs, hobbies, music lessons, and myriad other activities take up their time and energy.

Help your children find the kinds of stories that interest them. Their interests will expand and change from time to time. Explore the lists of stories in THE NEW BOOK OF KNOWLEDGE, found on pages 86–87 of this Guide. The HOME AND SCHOOL READING GUIDE that accompanies your set of THE NEW BOOK OF KNOWLEDGE lists recommended books according to subjects in the encyclopedia. Your school or community library will suggest books and book lists to meet each child's interests. Encourage the habit of reading aloud to other members of the family.

▶ **THE NEW BOOK OF KNOWLEDGE—A BRIDGE TO WIDER READING**

Not all youngsters read equally well, nor do they all read the same kind of story. One outstanding value of THE NEW BOOK OF KNOWLEDGE is the inclusion of excellent stories for different reading levels and tastes.

Teachers know that the more youngsters read with enjoyment, the more they will want to read. Getting started is sometimes difficult for middle school children who have not read very much before. Some reading authorities suggest that such children be encouraged to read simple stories that interest them until they gain the confidence they need. With each successful reading experience, children become more competent as well as more confident readers. If they read stories with enjoyment, the experience has meaning for them.

THE NEW BOOK OF KNOWLEDGE can help parents provide a bridge to wider reading. Often children just don't know what they want to read. Browsing through THE NEW BOOK OF KNOWLEDGE will help them discover many possibilities. As children handle the volumes, spotting stories that they like, you can help them expand their reading by finding other stories in THE NEW BOOK OF KNOWLEDGE and in other books at home.

Help them become acquainted with the inexhaustible storehouse of good reading in the local public library. And finally, help them to build up their personal libraries by gifts of books from time to time.

Reading Is Thinking

In the middle school, children are taught to think as they read. Training in thoughtful reading does begin in the primary grades. But in the middle school, both general reading skills and special reading skills are emphasized.

Children learn to find information in libraries, in books, in chapters, on pages, and in paragraphs. And they learn how to use the appropriate sources of information.

Reading growth is a complex process. Teachers remember that each child is an individual with differences that become evident in reading. Therefore, they tailor reading instruction to each child's needs and purposes. Strong supplementary support at home can be most effective when parents and teachers work together.

How You Can Help Your Children Improve Their Reading

Understand that reading skills improve slowly but surely as they are used and as children grow and develop. Encourage your children by providing opportunities to use their reading skills. Help them develop the habit of seeking information in reference books. Encourage their enthusiasm and interests.

See that your child wears glasses if they are needed. Provide the child with a quiet place for working, reading, and doing home assignments. Provide a good reading light and a comfortable chair and desk.

It is important to encourage and appreciate efforts and accomplishments and to share children's interests and enthusiasms in what they have read or are working on.

Provide a basic collection of suitable reference books so that your children's needs for information can be satisfied as they arise. THE NEW BOOK OF KNOWLEDGE can be the foundation of such a collection. A suitable dictionary, an annual almanac, an atlas, a yearbook, and a globe are a few of the useful reference tools that can help children improve their reading skills and develop the habit of reading for information.

▶ **READING SKILLS**

In the middle school, children learn and improve many reading skills, including the following:

Using the dictionary for word meaning and to expand their vocabularies.

Recognizing word structure.

Tackling new words by breaking them into syllables and by guessing the meaning of the word through its familiar parts.

Thinking critically as they read.

Distinguishing between fact and opinion.

Using different speeds for different reading purposes.

Outlining and taking notes as they read.

Using the parts of a book—table of contents, index, glossary, footnotes, chapter and paragraph headings, guide words.

Selecting a book for a particular purpose.

Teachers help children with the particular reading skills they need to improve. Foundations of reading were laid in earlier grades. But reading skills must be used and expanded as children grow in ability.

Reading is taught all day long, as children use different kinds of printed materials.

LITERATURE

▶WRITTEN EXPRESSION

Writing means handwriting, correct usage, spelling, and composing clear sentences and paragraphs. Children must express themselves in writing when they make a report, write a letter or invitation, do homework, take notes, create stories, or review books. Parents and teachers can encourage children by creating an atmosphere conducive to good writing.

Formal Writing

In writing invitations, thank-you notes, homework assignments, reports, minutes, and letters asking for information, children learn that there are certain acceptable forms and usages for each type of written expression.

Formal grammar may not be taught di-

rectly in the middle school, but correct usage is taught as part of the planned program and informally throughout the school day when the need arises.

Parents can help children use acceptable language by using correct forms themselves. When you write a letter, a list, or a note to the teacher, you can observe the correct and acceptable form and usage that youngsters are urged to adopt. Provide children with opportunities for using correct written forms at home. Help your youngster write the invitations to a party, a thank-you note for a gift, or a letter to a friend or relative. There are many opportunities for intelligent practice at home. But the child must know that there is a reason for writing.

Creative Writing

Just as children learn at school to express themselves in acceptable formal written language, so they learn to write creatively. Creative writing (stories, poems, plays, and reports of experiences, feelings, and observations) gives children a channel of expression and a chance to sharpen and share their perceptions. Many children love to write creatively if they receive encouragement.

Perhaps you have never encouraged creative writing knowingly at home. But you can. The important ingredient is your response. When your youngster describes an experience with excitement, you might say, "That would make an exciting story. I'd love to see you write it."

Provide your youngster with the encouragement of a truly accepting audience. And share your own creative efforts, too. Some families play storytelling games. Others collect special stories, riddles, and jokes to tell at dinner. There are many ways. But an attentive audience and an accepting atmosphere are two important elements needed if children are to write creatively.

▶ SPELLING

By the end of grade six, children probably have a writing vocabulary of about 3,000 words. These words have been learned functionally, as well as from graded spelling lists that are based on national research.

In the middle school, children learn to use a dictionary for word definitions, pronunciation, and syllabication, as well as for spelling. They are taught to proofread their own writing for errors and to keep their own lists of words they frequently misspell.

You can help by providing your children with a suitable dictionary. Encourage them to use the dictionary and to proofread their writing at home for spelling errors. Many educators believe there is a close correlation between legible handwriting and the ability to spell. Learning to type is also considered a good way to improve a child's spelling ability.

The first article in each volume of THE NEW BOOK OF KNOWLEDGE describes a letter of the alphabet. Illustrating each of these letter articles is a model of the accepted form of that letter in both manuscript and cursive writing.

▶ ORAL EXPRESSION

Children acquire their basic speech patterns, accents, and habits of enunciation from their parents and families, from their neighborhood friends, and from the speech of the region in which they live. Their speech patterns are largely formed by the time they start school.

The school can do much, however, to improve speech habits by providing instruction in oral expression. Teachers and parents recognize that children speak and listen more frequently than they read and write. Teachers provide many opportunities for children to practice oral expression. These range from making simple announcements to taking part in group discussions. In the middle school, children report on individual and group projects, tell about personal experiences, impart and explain information, give directions, answer questions, tell stories, recite poetry, engage in conversation, take part in dramatics and choral speaking, make introductions, conduct interviews, read aloud to the class, and dramatize telephone conversations.

How Parents Can Help

If your child needs remedial speech help, the school may either provide such trained attention or refer you to someone who is qualified to give it. The oral expression of children who do not need special speech therapy can be encouraged and guided if you provide the opportunities.

Answering the telephone, ordering food, family conversation, and informal conversation with neighbors are all different kinds of talk. Children should learn that we often talk differently for different occasions. Certain kinds of talk are appropriate in one situation and not in others. Children want to talk. Parents, by creating acceptance at home, can encourage good speech. There are many ways, but they all center on the habit of listening to what children say and accepting their verbal offerings with enthusiasm. At home, parents can encourage good speech by speaking well themselves, by avoiding interrupting children to correct their speech but by using the correct form soon after, and by respecting the child's right to an attentive audience.

▶ LISTENING

There is a direct relationship between the kind of speaking and reading that children do and the way in which they listen. Encouraging them to speak so that others can understand them will improve children's listening habits. Whatever teachers and parents can do to improve children's ability to listen with understanding also contributes to their ability to understand reading materials.

One of the best ways in which parents can encourage good listening is to listen courteously and attentively when children speak. Reading aloud to children encourages good listening habits. Listening to recordings, radio, television, and motion pictures offers wonderful opportunities to improve listening skills. Discussing what one has heard is an excellent way to make listening more purposeful.

If you want your children to learn to listen well, you might ask yourself the following questions: Do I talk in a way I'd like to hear if I were a child? Do I speak simply and to the point, or do I confuse my children with words and ideas they can't understand? Do I repeat the same message over and over, so that my children no longer want to hear it? Do I address my children mostly when I want to scold, advise, or order? Do I address my children as courteously as I do my guests, or do I reserve polite language for strangers? The simple, natural courtesy you show your child and other members of the family is the most important factor in encouraging good listening habits.

SPEAKING AND LISTENING

SOCIAL STUDIES

Social studies in the middle school broaden children's understanding of the world around them and strengthen their appreciation of their heritage. The social studies curriculum in the middle school varies from school to school. In general, however, pupils learn how people use the earth to satisfy basic needs for food, clothing, and shelter. They learn how people live together in neighborhoods, communities, states and nations, and in the world of nations. They learn about their city and state; about the history and geography of the United States and other nations in the Western Hemisphere; about continents and nations of the world; about America's historical and cultural roots in other countries; and about the role of the United States in world affairs. They learn about these broad topics through the study of history, biography, current affairs, political science, economics, and even anthropology.

Methods of teaching social studies vary from school to school. Children may study the social studies disciplines as separate subjects—chiefly history and geography. In general, social studies will be taught through the study of major topics or units with such titles as Transportation, Life in the Polar Regions, How the United States Became an Industrial Nation, and so forth. Units based on topics of this kind may involve many subjects in the curriculum—science, language arts, mathematics, and music, for example, as well as all the aspects of the social studies. A unit may touch on many parts of the world and on many periods of history. Biography and literature, group projects and activities, trips and discussions are all used by teachers to develop social studies concepts and to impart factual information.

Teachers Develop Children's Understandings, Concepts, and Skills

Whatever organization or method is used, teachers try to help children develop certain understandings, concepts, and skills. These include understanding our way of life; appreciating the events and people that influenced the history of our country; understanding the geographic influences that affect the ways people live; and understanding the techniques of research and problem-solving in the pursuit of information.

Social Studies Skills Begin in the Elementary Grades

Children cannot understand the past or the present without certain important study skills. We know that skills develop slowly as the child matures and becomes physically, emotionally, and mentally ready to use them. We know, too, that skills are developed gradually as they are needed and used.

In the middle school, children perfect their reading skills because reading is the basic skill on which much of their learning will depend.

They learn how to use maps, globes, and atlases. They interpret map symbols, the map index, and the legend. They construct maps, locate places, estimate distances, understand the relationship of places through direction, and interpret information on maps. They learn that there are many kinds of maps and that maps can be used for special purposes.

Study skills are not limited to the social studies; they extend into other curriculum areas. Children learn to use the encyclopedia. This means learning to locate information by using the index and guide words.

They learn to locate references to a topic by using bibliographies and the library card catalog. They use the dictionary to find the meaning of a word and so come to understand the special vocabulary of the social studies. They learn to read graphs, charts, and diagrams. When they need special information, they learn how to write letters and to interview people. They work on committees; use parliamentary procedure; participate in discussions; organize, prepare, and deliver oral and written reports; and write for their class or school newspaper.

Because the future of our nation and of the world depends upon intelligent and informed citizens, children will study current affairs. Some classes subscribe to professionally prepared school newspapers designed for a particular grade level. Such newspapers present the news simply and graphically. Many schools use educational television and radio programs to stimulate current-affairs discussion. In many schools, people with special qualifications are invited to address children.

How Parents Can Help

You can help your children in social studies by understanding that not all children develop all skills at the same time, at the same rate, or with equal facility. Help your children find the information they need, if they want help. Help them find the special maps they need. You use road maps and depend on them. Show your children how the scale and the legends on an automobile map help you determine your route. Let them take charge of the road map and direct the driver of the car on your next automobile trip.

Show them how to use reference books.

Provide them with a good dictionary, an up-to-date atlas, and a globe; and help them to use these valuable tools. Teach them to use the daily newspaper and the weekly news magazine. Discuss important news events at the family table. Help your children distinguish between sensational gossip, unfounded rumor, and important current events. Personalize social studies. Try to tie in current events and ideas with their lives by asking such questions as "Why are people interested in this question?" Show them that you care about your local and national government. Explore ways of extending your children's interest in history, government, social processes, and geography. Plan family trips to museums and historic places that illuminate their study. Make birthdays and holidays a time for giving books that will build the child's personal library.

PREHISTORIC TIMES

ANCIENT CIVILIZATIONS

See outline on page 68

MIDDLE AGES

Agriculture	F99–103; A98
Armor and coats of arms	A433–35; H110–12; K272–73
Art and architecture	A375–77, 438, 438e; B438, 483–90; C133–35; D75; E202–03; G165–66; H178–79; I 391–94; P17–18; S393–94; U54–56
Black Death	M297; E240; R293
Byzantine Empire	B491–92; C522, 586–88
Castles	C131–32; F375; A377; E257
Charlemagne	C188–89, 290; A375–76; E77–78; G158–59; H160; J155; L129–33; M292; R291
Chivalry	K274–75, 277; F435
Clothing	C375–76
Crafts and guilds	G174, 401–03; L110; J94; M295
Crusades	C586–88; B492; E403; I 349
Duels and tournaments	D345; A444–45; K274
Education	E77–79; L188; M296–97; U217
Fairs and expositions	F10
Feudalism	F99–103; C327; L87; M292; R112d
Fiefs	F100
Flags and banners	H110–12
Food	F333–34; B386
Growth of cities and towns	C318–19; M294–95; U232
Heraldry	H110–12
Holy Roman Empire	H160–63; C188–89
Homes	H178–79; F102
Hundred Years War	H281–82; F415; M294, 297
Illuminated manuscripts	I 77–78; B320; C461; G165; K202–03; P17–18
King Arthur	A442–45; E269; L129; M568
Knighthood	K272–77; A433–35
Libraries	L188
Magna Carta	M24, 293; B180; E239; F101; T26
Medical knowledge	M204–05
Middle Ages	M291–97
Miracle plays	M339–40; D297; E271
Monks and monasteries	M295–96, 348–49; B319–21; A377; C289, 461; L188; R290
Mummers	D297
Music	M298–99; B137
Norman Conquest	E238
Printing and bookmaking	B319–22; C461, 462; E79; G173, 427; P472
Religion	M295–97; C290–91, 586–88; D297; J107–08, 112; R291
Round Table	A442, 444; E269
Serfs and serfdom	F102; M294; R112d; S197
Tapestries	T20
Trades	M294–95; S174; H113
Vassals	F100–01; R112d
William the Conqueror	M293; E238; W173

AGE OF EXPLORATION AND DISCOVERY

Allouez, Claude Jean	W206
Almagro, Diego de	C253–54; P266
Alvarado, Pedro de	A597
Argall, Sir Samuel	D102
Ayllón, Lucas de	S309
Balboa, Vasco Núñez de	B20; E412; P48
Barents, Willem	E416
Bering, Vitus	B142; A160
Bienville, Jean Baptiste Lemoyne, Sieur de	L361, 362
Block, Adriaen	B522; C516
Brébeuf, Jean de, Saint	B534
Cabeza de Vaca, Álvar Núñez	C565
Cabot, John and Sebastian	C3, 70; E409
Cabral, Pedro Alvares	E407; P395
Cabrillo, Juan Rodríguez	C565
Cadillac, Sieur Antoine de la Mothe	C566
Cartier, Jacques	C126, 70–71; E409; Q14; S16
Cavendish, Thomas	C583
Champlain, Samuel de	C185, 71; E410; Q14; S16; V320
Charcot, Jean Baptiste	C588
Charlevoix, Pierre	C589
Chouart, Médart	M336
Columbus, Bartolomé	D282
Columbus, Christopher	C447–48; E406; D284; F88; H153
Cook, James	C531; A161
Coronado, Francisco	E409
Cortes, Hernando	C551; E409; M247–48
Crusades	C586–88; E403
De Soto, Hernando	D138; A144, 431; E409; F272; G147; M362
Dias, Bartholomeu	E406
Drake, Sir Francis	D293; C18; E408
Ericson, Leif	E307–08, 402; V339
Eric the Red	E308; G370–71; V339
Exploration and Discovery	E400–20
Ferdinand and Isabella	F88
Frobisher, Sir Martin	E416
Frontenac, Comte Louis de	F558
Fuca, Juan de	F559
Gama, Vasco da	G7; A67; E407–08
Gilbert, Sir Humphrey	G453; T165
Gosnold, Bartholomew	G461; M149
Grenville, Sir Richard	G471
Greysolon, Daniel	M336
Hennepin, Louis	M336, 364
Henry the Navigator	P395; E405–06
Hudson, Henry	H272–73; E409
Iberville, Pierre Lemoyne, Sieur d'	I 493; L362
Jolliet, Louis	J127; E410; G328
Kublai Khan	M416; C269; E403–04
La Salle, Robert Cavelier, Sieur de	L46; C71; E410
La Vérendrye, Sieur de	L389; N336
Magellan, Ferdinand	M21; E408
Marco Polo	P380; C269; E403–04
Marquette, Father Jacques	J127; E410
Mendoza, Pedro de	S294
Narváez, Pánfilo de	N431
Nicolet, Jean	N250; G328; W192, 206, 207
Norsemen	V338–40; E307–08, 402; S58e
Ojeda, Alonso de	O283
Orellana, Francisco de	A194f

COLONIAL LIFE IN AMERICA

THE REVOLUTIONARY WAR

FAMOUS SAYINGS

FAMOUS PEOPLE IN THE AMERICAN REVOLUTION

PIONEER LIFE AND WESTWARD EXPANSION

THE FIFTY STATES OF THE UNITED STATES

THE NEW BOOK OF KNOWLEDGE describes the fifty states in a series of comprehensive articles prepared by experts in the states. Some schools study their state in the middle grades; some in the upper grades. The state articles in THE NEW BOOK OF KNOWLEDGE are written and organized so that children can locate and select the exact information they need for a particular grade.

Each state article is introduced with an exciting anecdote about the state. Each article is handsomely illustrated with many full-color photographs. These include the state flag, tree, bird, and flower, as well as photographs of important aspects of the state's geography, economy, and places of interest. Fact boxes help children find the exact information they need. The many and varied maps that accompany each state article appear adjacent to the text information that relates to each map. Each state article follows this outline:

The land—landforms; rivers and lakes; climate; natural resources.

The people and their work—where they live; industries and products; transportation and communication.

Education—schools and colleges; libraries and museums.

Places of interest—parks, memorials, and other places of interest.

Cities—the capital city and other important cities.

Government.

Famous people—biographies of people associated with the state.

History.

The state's future.

STORIES ABOUT THE STATES

Many of the state articles in THE NEW BOOK OF KNOWLEDGE are introduced by a story. The subjects are listed below.

CANADA

PHYSICAL GEOGRAPHY

MATHEMATICS

Mathematics in the middle school contains new subject matter and ideas and new ways of looking at old subject matter. Children continue to perfect their skills in the basic computational operations of mathematics— addition, subtraction, multiplication, and division of numbers. But they are taught to apply new ideas and methods. These ideas and methods run throughout all mathematics from kindergarten to college. Thus, in the middle school, children continue to apply set theory. They learn about the associative and distributive properties of numbers. They work with experience materials and representative materials as they did in earlier grades. And they are taught to reason, to recognize mathematical relationships, and to solve problems.

THE NEW BOOK OF KNOWLEDGE articles listed below describe the most modern practices in mathematics. As parents, you will find the articles invaluable in understanding your children's mathematics program and in helping them with their homework.

SCIENCE

During the primary grades, children learned to see, to do, to try, to wonder, to question, to experiment, and to judge science phenomena. Their enthusiasm helped to shape the science program. The teachers guided the children's efforts and encouraged them to use scientific methods of thinking.

During the middle school years, teachers continue to encourage scientific curiosity and attitudes while leading children to a systematic understanding of the importance of science information.

Science All Day

Science plays an important part in children's school day. In school they learn that civilization continues to unfold as people progress in understanding their physical environment. They learn the importance of body health and muscular development. They learn that the sounds of music are composed of loudness, pitch, and quality. If they plant a school garden, they learn that plants need sun and water. They learn about volcanoes, earthquakes, glaciers, rivers, seas, the wind, people, and the other forces that continually change the surface of the earth.

Science helps children understand the importance of community health and safety. They learn about the relationship of the earth to the other heavenly bodies. They discover that people adjust to the changing climate and surface of the earth. They learn that people depend on plants and animals and that people are responsible for wise use and conservation of natural resources. Children are helped to appreciate the many forms of energy that are used to improve our way of living. And they learn about some of the great men and women of science.

Science learning would be of little value to children if they did not apply it to daily living. That is why teachers help develop the following attitudes:

"I don't know, but let's find out." By using scientific methods of observation, research, and investigation and by weighing evidence and forming judgments, children see that educated people want to learn. This attitude lies behind all scientific progress. An open mind is imperative in scientific thinking.

"Let's get the facts and use them." This attitude has saved and lengthened lives and eliminated disease. Basic facts about health and safety, cleanliness and diet, rest and proper clothing, and people's needs and their obligations for the well-being of others are stressed in the middle school.

"What does this really mean?" Critical thinking helps youngsters weigh evidence, judge pertinent data, and determine the truth. What is fact? What is opinion? During the middle school years, science can teach children to recognize faulty thinking. Critical thinking can help children see cause-and-effect relationships. Through science and education, children learn to question, to think critically, to apply scientific methods, and to use science knowledge as they learn to adjust to their environment.

"How does science help us?" Children are taught to judge scientific discoveries in terms of their contributions to humankind. They learn that science helps us to live more comfortably, makes us healthier, and teaches us to think more clearly. It also helps us extend our ability to enjoy, to sympathize, and to feel secure. Learning about the unknown may help children conquer their fear of it.

When they learn to understand, protect, and love living things, they find increased comfort in the order of the universe.

"There's much to enjoy in life." One of the finest contributions that science can make to your youngsters' lives is that of increasing their pleasure in the living world around them. As enthusiasm expands, it brings children greater pleasure in living and learning.

How Parents Can Help

Parents can help their middle school children develop the scientific attitudes, the openmindedness, and the purposes their teachers are encouraging. Specifically, parents can do the following:

Stimulate their interests. Help them get the supplies and tools they need.

Share your enthusiasm with them, for it is contagious. And share their enthusiasm, too.

Help them find and use appropriate sources of information (museums, government agencies, reference books, local nature experts).

Understand the important concepts, facts, and ideas that the teacher is stressing. Find examples and experiments that illustrate these concepts.

Show children the science all around us—in the refrigerator, the television set, the air conditioner, the daily newspaper, the backyard.

SCIENCE

HEALTH AND SAFETY

Your children's health and safety continue to be important concerns of teachers in the middle school. Children's cumulative health records follow them from grade to grade and help their teachers adjust their instruction to individual needs.

Health education is taught in connection with science, social studies, and language arts. But planned units in health, safety, and physical education are also part of the program.

Children continue to practice health and safety rules. They learn about first aid; good food and eating practices; body structure; care of teeth, eyes, and ears; the importance of sleep and rest; and the dangers of stimulants, narcotics, and tobacco.

In physical education, children learn group games and folk dancing. They are taught to derive satisfaction from self-achievement rather than from competition.

How You Can Help

All parents want their children to be healthy. But good health is more than not being sick.

Food, exercise, and rest are only part of the health story. Teach your children the importance of safety rules, of hand-washing, of caring for their teeth, of sleep, and of exercise. Planning exercise for middle school children may seem foolish. To many parents, the problem appears to be the opposite. Yet it is sometimes necessary to see that children exercise actively. They are more likely to enjoy this if it comes under the heading of sports and play rather than exercise. Children will benefit if they are not pressured to engage in a particular sport or to become a star performer.

Physical activities that children can use all their lives are preferable. These include swimming, ice-skating, dancing, tennis, and golf.

HEALTH AND SAFETY

AIDS	A100b
Air pollution	A122–25; D212; E299–300; F289
Alcoholism	A175
Antiseptics and disinfectants	D214; M202
Baseball	B76–93; L314–17
Bicycle safety	B174
Body building	B289–90
Camping	C41–47
Consumerism	C527–28
Detergents	D139–41; E297
Drug abuse	D329–32, 334; N13–15
Environment	E295–302
Exercise	P224–29; H75
Eye	E429–32
Eyes, care of	B283–85; L286–87; M208g; O181–82
Fertilizers	F96–98; E297
Fire prevention	F154–55
First aid	F157–63
Folk and square dancing	F297–301; L68–69
Food, care of	F341–45, 351–53
Food regulations and laws	F346–47
Guidance	G397–400
Health	H82–85; M223–25; N423–26; P222–29; V370–71
Health Foods	H78–79
Hearing	B285; M208h
Heart	H80–83
Hiking and backpacking	H124–125
Ice-skating	I 38–45
Insect control	E299
Jogging and running	J113–14
Little League Baseball	L314–17; B85
Medical supplies in the home	F162
Medicine, tools and techniques of	M208d–211
Noise	N270
Nutrition	N423–26; F331–40; H74–75; V370a–71
Physical fitness	P224–29
Poisonous plants	P321–23; F499; L115
Pollution	E295–302
Population explosion	P387–88; E296–97
Racket sports	R34, 34a–34c
Roller-skating	R284
Safety	S3–7; B174, 261–63; E148–49; F154–55; H76; M152; P323, 355–56; T187
Sanitation	S32–33; D211–12; E297–98; W64–69
Skateboard safety	S182–83
Skiing	S184d
Skin, care of	C552; D187
Sleep	S200–01; H75
Soccer	S216–19; P120
Sunburn	S235; R44
Swimming	S494–99, 6
Teeth, care of	T44; D114–16; F286–87; H76

MUSIC

In the middle school, children begin to learn two-part songs and even how to read simple music. As they listen to live or recorded musical performances, middle schoolers learn to recognize and appreciate the various forms that music takes. Many children of this age experiment with musical instruments at home and also at school, where they often have an opportunity to play in a band or orchestra.

MUSIC

ART

Art is an important school experience for middle school children, just as it was in earlier grades. They paint, draw, model in clay, design posters, construct with wood, make puppets, and work with paper, cloth, and yarn. Much of their creative artwork will be related to personal experiences in and out of school and to other subjects.

You can add to your children's art experiences by referring to the beautiful color reproductions that illustrate the history of art articles listed below. In addition, THE NEW BOOK OF KNOWLEDGE contains many "how to" articles that will help develop children's artistic abilities and supplement their school craft work.

ART AROUND THE WORLD

Art	A437–438g
African art	A70–76
Art in the United States	U133–42
Canadian Art	C81–83
Chinese Art	C274–77
Dutch and Flemish Art	D351–64
Egyptian art and architecture	E110–17; A438b
English art and architecture	E256–64
French art and architecture	F421–32; A438g
German art and architecture	G165–71
India, art and architecture of	I 135–39
Islamic art and architecture	I 354–59
Italian art and architecture	I 391–403; A438f
Japanese art and architecture	J48–51
Korean art	K297–98
Latin-American art and architecture	L62–67
Oriental art and architecture	O222–29
Russian art and architecture	U54–59
Spanish art and architecture	S360–65; A438g

ARTS AND CRAFTS

Clay modeling	C354–55
Collage	C400–01
Crocheting	C577–79
Découpage	D80
Finger painting	F126–28
Leaf prints	L118
Macramé	M6–7, 7a, 7b
Making greeting cards	G374
Making puppets and marionettes	P544–48
Needlecraft	N95–103
Origami	O232–35
Papier-mâché	P58b–59
Photography	P198–218
Planning a party	P89–93
Rubbings	R348–348a
Sand art	S25
Weaving	W96–98, 98a, 98b
Wire sculpture	W190b–191
Woodworking	W230–34
Wrapping gifts	G206–07

RELATED ART ARTICLES

Animation	A296–99
Architecture	A368–386a
Art	A437–438g
Cartoons	C127–29
Color	C424–29
Design	D132–37
Drawing	D306–12
Drawing, history of	D313–16
Fountains	F394–95
Graphic arts	G302–08
Mosaic	M463
Museums	M514–28
Hermitage Museum	H116
Louvre	L266–68
Metropolitan Museum of Art	M239–239a
National Gallery (London)	N34–35
National Gallery of Art (Washington, D.C.)	N36–38
National Gallery of Canada	N39–40
Prado	P424–25
Uffizi Gallery	U2–3
Obelisks	O5
Painting	P14–32
Perspective	D311–12
Posters	P402
Pottery	P407–13
Sculpture	S90–105
Watercolor	W58–61

GRADES 7, 8, AND 9

There are moments when the parents of teenagers say—or at least think—"Why don't you act your age?" But what age are young adolescents to act? One minute they are twelve years old; the very next they seem sixteen; and a moment later they revert to childish behavior. The betwixt-and-between junior high school pupil offers parents and teachers an exciting challenge, for adults cannot guide seventh, eighth, and ninth graders without growing themselves.

These are years of rapid change. Your teenagers' perplexities start with bodily changes. Almost as soon as young teenagers begin to understand and accept these physical changes, they have a different body to accept. Their legs and arms seem to grow like weeds. Girls often become heavier and taller than boys of the same age, though this difference seems to level out at the end of the junior high school period. Along with rapid growth comes an increased appetite or finickiness about foods. Young teenagers' skin may pose new problems, for the glands are working in new ways.

Most junior high school pupils have reached the age of puberty. Many accept these startling changes gracefully. Others worry excessively about their health and their bodies. They may translate their worries into aggressive or withdrawn behavior. Some youngsters may seem sluggish; others may exude energy. New croaking voices may seem unpredictable and shocking, and the adolescent boy may find it hard to believe that *this* voice came from his mouth. Girls may find their newly obvious breasts a source of embarrassment and make ineffectual efforts to hide them. Others are quite proud of these signs of maturity. Adults can help young adolescents accept their new growth by helping them understand that what is happening to them is a perfectly natural part of growing up.

REACHING FOR INDEPENDENCE

Physical changes color the emotions of young adolescents. They have been striving for independence since childhood. This effort gains greater force during grades seven, eight, and nine. Strong, surging needs dominate their entire personalities. These needs are the following:

The need to establish independence from adult authority.

The need to conform to the code of their peers, for their friends and their friends' values are all-important to the adolescent.

The need to adjust to friends of their own sex and to know how to behave with members of the opposite sex.

The need to accept themselves as worthwhile.

Home, school, and community can help youngsters temper these urges and route them into healthy, acceptable channels.

The young adolescent's need for independence shows itself in many ways. Some youngsters want part-time jobs. As they earn spending money or live within their allowances, growing children develop healthy attitudes toward work and money management, especially if they are wisely guided by adults who have come to terms with similar problems. If they are occasionally allowed to make mistakes, they will learn from their own mismanagement. Through their need for independence and their interest in working, they begin to wonder, "What shall I do when I grow up?"

WHY YOUNG ADOLESCENTS ACT AS THEY DO

Just as their new physical growth affects the way youngsters feel, so it affects the way they act. Boys and girls alike wonder, "What kind of person will I be?" "What's ahead for me?" They look to parents and teachers for guidance and for acceptance in the strange world of grown-ups. They may challenge parents or other older people to a swimming race or a game of tennis. Parents, understanding their children's need to gain acceptance, hide their fatigue and resolve not to be beaten.

Teenagers, hitherto tractable and helpful, may become suddenly rebellious. They may flatly refuse to tidy their rooms. They may ask, "Why don't you act like other parents do?" Or they may withdraw into their own world and become almost strangers.

While imitating adult behavior at one moment, young adolescents may at the next feel compelled to devise their own codes of behavior—codes that may be in direct conflict with adult standards. Teenagers experiment with many roles before they find the personality that is their own. Because they feel a strong need to conform to their friend's standards, teenagers may say, "Tom is allowed to go hunting; why can't I?" or "Peggy is allowed to go to the movies during the week; why can't I?"

This is the golden age for organized clubs and groups. At the same time, young adolescents are principally concerned with themselves. Wrapped up in their own hobbies, they often find it difficult to appreciate their friends' different interests. They are intensely afraid of ridicule, though they have a splendid sense of humor. They are oversensitive and highly self-critical. Of course, children differ. But studies indicate that an overwhelming number of seventh, eighth, and ninth graders show these characteristics.

THINKING AND LEARNING

Along with their changing bodies, feelings, and actions, young adolescents have new abilities and new ways of learning. Their ability to think abstractly and to express their ideas has increased. They are fascinated by large concepts like justice, democracy, friendship, citizenship, and the obligations of freedom. And they love to explore "big ideas."

Their time sense is developing. They can begin to understand the sequence of past events, and they like to relate historical events one to the other. Because they are eager to see causes and effects, they will find THE NEW BOOK OF KNOWLEDGE a source of great help.

Just as they once collected string, shells, and other objects, junior high school pupils collect facts and information. They have intense interests. They may have several at a time, or one may follow another. Persistent interests may even fashion life careers or avocations. Do not be afraid when these multiple interests have short lives. Behind the hobbies and the changing interests, learning and maturing are going on.

In their eagerness and enthusiasm to learn many skills and extend their interests, young adolescents may make more plans than they will ever carry out. Many plans for parties, games, and hobbies never reach completion. The planning alone satisfies the urge to be up and doing. Don't insist on a carry-through.

▶ THE ADOLESCENT'S STANDARDS

Just as adolescents try to measure their independence, just as they compete with their friends in athletics and measure their ability to get along with others, so they explore a new kind of measurement—the ethical and moral measurement of human beings. Young adolescents love to read about the heroism of great people. They thrill to the concepts of friendship and loyalty. They are interested in religious and ethical values and in the differences they find in such values. They love to discuss the "right and wrong" kinds of behavior, to evaluate the ethics of a situation.

Their own free reading and their junior high school curriculum reflect this interest in values. The many biographies, classics, and stories found throughout THE NEW BOOK OF KNOWLEDGE were selected by curriculum experts and librarians for this purpose.

▶ HOMEWORK

Young adolescents will probably experience a more departmentalized school program and meet many more teachers than they did in their earlier school years. Larger amounts of homework are usually assigned in grades seven, eight, and nine than in earlier grades. How, parents ask, can we help our children with home assignments? Here are some basic suggestions:

Provide proper physical conditions for studying—good light, a desk, and a comfortable chair in a quiet place.

Help your youngsters establish regular study habits and times.

Provide a good dictionary and an atlas. THE NEW BOOK OF KNOWLEDGE will provide excellent reference information. Help them find other materials, too.

Create a calm home environment. Few of us can study if we are emotionally upset.

Some children need a great deal of help with homework. Some want suggestions. Others want only occasional aid in tracking down references and sources. Your interest is needed now. If homework becomes a battlefield, little is accomplished.

Homework can afford an opportunity for friendly contact between parents and children. Actually, children learn more if parents do not know the answers to every question. The phrase "Let's look it up" has magic. THE NEW BOOK OF KNOWLEDGE can furnish many answers.

LANGUAGE ARTS

The language arts in grades seven, eight, and nine include literature, grammar, spelling, and oral and written communication. Extensive reading from a variety of materials meets changing interests.

The language arts continue to bear an important relationship to other subjects, even though your child may attend a departmentalized school. The need for expressional skills in speaking and writing and the dependence of other subjects on reading, speaking, and listening emphasize this relationship. Your child's language arts teacher teaches skills that are used in every other curriculum area.

REFERENCE AND RESEARCH

Bibliography	B170; R129
Book reports and reviews	B314–17
Card catalog	L199–200
Dictionaries	D154–55; R129, 183
Encyclopedias	E204–08; R129, 175, 183
Indexes and indexing	I 114–15; E205; L197; R129, 183
Library skills	L195–200; R129, 182–83
Opinion surveys	O169–70; R182
Reference books	R129, 183; M92–99
Research	R129, 175–76, 182–83; E204–08; I 114–15; T141–42
Reader's Guide	R129
Textbooks	T141–42; S441
Word origins	W238–41; V372
Yearbooks	R129, 183

LITERATURE

African literature	A76a–76d
American literature	A195–215
Ballads	B23–24; F310–11, 303; S58f
Bible	B152–62
Biography, autobiography	B185–86; A196, 214a–214b; P536–37
Book awards for children's literature	C228–31
Book reports and reviews	B314–17; L310–12
Books	B314–34
Canadian literature	C84–85
Classics in literature	C233–37
Children's literature	C232–48
Chinese literature	C278–79
Diaries	D147–48; A196; E276

Drama	D294–305; P335–40; T157–62
Elegies and epitaphs	P354
English literature	E268–90
Epigrams	E323; P354
Essays	E274–75, 279, 322–23
Fiction	F109–12; C244–46; L310–12; W318
Folklore	F302–17; A76a; C243–44
French literature	F435–43; D299; L128; N360
German literature	G174–81, 376–86; D300; N361
Giants	G201–03
Greek literature	G350–55; A229; D296–97; H166
Greek mythology	G356–65; I 61; O51–52; T316
Haiku	J52
Hebrew literature	H99–101; B152–59; T13
Humor	H277–81; A195, 203, 205–06; C234–35; N272–76; P354
India, literature of	I 140–42
Ireland, literature of	I 325–28; D302
Italian literature	I 404–09; R159–60
Japanese literature	J52–53
Latin-American literature	L70–73
Latin literature	L76–80
Legends	L128–34; F109–10
Literary criticism	L309; A211, 215
Literature	L310–12
Magazines	M16–20
Miracle plays	M339–40; D297
Mystery and detective stories	M561–64
Norse mythology	N277–81
Novels	N358–63; A76b–76c; E280–82, 283; F110–11; L311–12
Odes	O50; P354
Plays	P335–40; T157–62
Poetry	P349–54; A76a–76d; B23–24; C248; L311
Prayer	P430–31
Quotations	Q19–20; S133–37
Russian literature	U60–64; F22; N363
Scandinavian literature	S58f–58g; N277–81
Science fiction	S83–85
Short stories	S161–65; F112; L312
Sonnets	E272; P353
Spanish literature	S366–72; N358–59; D298–99
Theater	T157–62; D33; M550–51; P335–40
Yiddish literature	Y350–51

MASS MEDIA

Advertising	A27–34
Animation	A296–99; C453; M477
Audiovisual aids	E91–92; L173
Billboards and posters	P402; A29–30
Books	B329–34; P523–25; W321
Cartoons	C127–29; A215
Comic books	C453–54
Communications satellites	C468; S55; T67
Magazines	M16–20
Mass communication	C469; A27–34
Motion pictures	M474–93; P212
Newspapers	N197–205; A28; J135–38
Paperback books	P58–58a, 524

SPEAKING AND LISTENING

WRITING

BIOGRAPHIES OF FAMOUS AUTHORS

SOCIAL STUDIES

In grades seven, eight, and nine, the social studies teach young people about our cultural heritage and about the foundations of our democracy. Young adolescents continue to learn history, geography, economics, government, anthropology, and even some sociology, just as they did in earlier grades.

However, junior high school youngsters now learn to "study in depth." They learn to use a variety of instructional materials and to seek out original sources. They are encouraged to pursue a social studies interest deeply; to look for causes, effects, and relationships: to interpret and evaluate information and sources.

THE NEW BOOK OF KNOWLEDGE provides accurate, objective, and thorough information about people, places, and events associated with every part of the globe and with every period in history. It provides youngsters with the best first source of background information to supplement their schoolbooks and to pursue an intensive study of social studies topics.

CIVIL WAR

TOWARD INTERNATIONAL UNDERSTANDING

ECONOMICS

AUSTRALIA, NEW ZEALAND, OCEANIA

ANTARCTICA

ANCIENT CIVILIZATIONS

SCIENCE

Science is an exciting subject for seventh-, eighth-, and ninth-grade pupils. Junior high school science provides stimulating exploratory experiences in biology, chemistry, physics, earth science, and other specialized courses taught in senior high school. General science is frequently a ninth-grade subject, but in many junior high schools it is taught over a period of two or three years.

The science content of THE NEW BOOK OF KNOWLEDGE reflects the latest information and the newest theories in this ever-expanding field. Your junior high school youngster will find articles on such current science topics as electronics and computers, exploration of the planets, underwater exploration, lasers, quasars, and black holes, as well as more familiar though no less exciting science topics.

BIOGRAPHIES OF FAMOUS SCIENTISTS

Agassiz, Jean Louis Rodolphe	A80; I 8–9
Archimedes	A367; F250–51
Audubon, John James	A490–91
Bacon, Roger	B9
Bell, Alexander Graham	B134–35; A560; C466; O57
Banting, Sir Frederick Grant	B59
Beaumont, William	B109; M207
Bohr, Niels	B304; C211; P232
Boyle, Robert	B354; C207–08; G56
Brahe, Tycho	B361; A472
Burbank, Luther	B450
Carver, George Washington	C130; A143; M377; P110
Copernicus	C544–45; A472; R160–61
Curie, Marie and Pierre	C599, 210–11
Darwin, Charles Robert	D40–41; B192–93; C548; E376–78; H296; S73–74
Davy, Sir Humphry	D44; A194c; C209; M27
De Forest, Lee	D383; I 285; R55
Descartes, René	D123; P190, 501; U206
Edison, Thomas Alva	E70–73; C462; L282; P194–95
Einstein, Albert	E118–20; G325; M174; P238; R139–44; S76
Faraday, Michael	F47; E133; P236, 237

Fermi, Enrico	F92; P237
Fleming, Sir Alexander	F247; A311, 315; M208a
Galileo	G5–7; A472; C207; E380–81; F34; H86–87; I 285; L142; M205, 449; P230; R182; S68; T61
Galvani, Luigi	M206; E138
Gilbert, William	G119; P235; M30; S67
Goddard, Robert Hutchings	G244–46
Halley, Edmund	H318; C449, 450; S246
Harvey, William	H44; B188, 189; M205; S69
Herschel family	H337
Jenner, Edward	J76; M207; V260
Kepler, Johannes	K234; A472; B361; M107; S68, 241–42
Koch, Robert	K291; M208, 274–75
Langmuir, Irving	L35, 284
La Place, Pierre Simon	S247
Lavoisier, Antoine	L86; C208–09; M206; S72
Leeuwenhoek, Anton van	L127, 141; B190; M206, 274
Linnaeus, Carolus	L301; B191; T26
Lister, Joseph	L308; M208
Marconi, Guglielmo	M102; C467; R55
Mendel, Gregor	M220; B194; G79–80
Morse, Samuel F. B.	M462; C466; T53–54
Osler, Sir William	O241; M208a
Newton, Sir Isaac	N206–07; A472–73; G320–21; L267–68; M471–73; P230; R140; S69, 241–42; T59
Pasteur, Louis	P99–100; B194; F90–91; M208; S73
Pavlov, Ivan	B195; L99; P103, 504
Piccard, Auguste	P244; B36
Priestley, Joseph	P457
Ptolemy	G99; A471; M98; S79
Rutherford, Lord Ernest	R361; C211; P232, 237
Sabin, Albert B.	S509; D199
Salk, Jonas E.	D199; V260
Schick, Béla	S521
Schliemann, Heinrich	S58h; T316
Szilard, Leo	S585
Thompson, Benjamin	T180
Volta, Alessandro	E138; I 277

SCIENCE

Acid rain	A7–9
Aerodynamics	A36–41, 558–59; B204–05; G239; H301; S469–73
Amphibians	F470–78; M76
Animals	See page references for Grades 4–6.
Anthropology	A304–09, 349, 362; P438–42; R29–32
Archaeology	A348–63, 304, 307–08; P432–42; S58h; U20–21
Astronomy	A470–76; B361; C544–45; G6–7; K234; R69–76; S239–49

MATHEMATICS

Mathematics in grades seven, eight, and nine contains many new ideas and new ways of looking at old subject matter. When your girls and boys talk about their junior high school mathematics, they may use terms that are unfamiliar to you. They may talk about sets and set theory, properties and structure of numbers, probability, and topology.

You can help your youngsters by familiarizing yourself with the meanings of these and other terms. Articles in THE NEW BOOK OF KNOWLEDGE explain the latest ideas in mathematics with clarity and simplicity. They not only will help your child to understand mathematics but will help you, too.

FOREIGN LANGUAGE

Foreign language study in junior high school is both a skill and a cultural subject.

The ability to understand a foreign language has practical value in view of our country's worldwide responsibilities and the increasing numbers of people who travel abroad. Foreign language study will help your child learn more about other countries and how the people of those countries have contributed to our own culture.

Your child will probably begin a foreign language in grade eight or nine. However, some schools begin the study of a foreign language in the elementary grades. The study of a foreign language in the elementary and junior high schools is largely conversational. Listening and speaking skills learned in the elementary grades are valuable in helping children learn a new language.

FOREIGN LANGUAGE

Languages	L37–40
African languages	A55
Asian languages	A459–60
Chinese language and literature	C258–59
French language	F433–35; D47
French literature	F435–43, 3, 22; L128
German language	G174–81; D46
German literature	G174–81
Greek language	G349–50; A193
Greek literature	G350–55, 356–65; D296–97; H166; A229
Hebrew language	H98–100; C461; I 369–70
Hebrew literature	H99–101; B152–59; T13
India, languages of	I 118
Italian language	I 404–05
Italian literature	I 404–09
Japanese language	J30
Latin language	L76–77; K249; W238–39
Latin literature	L76–80
Latin-American languages	L49–50
Russian language	U60
Russian literature	U60–64; F22; D301
Scandinavian literature	S58f–58g; N277–81
Spanish language	S365–66; L50; D46
Spanish literature	S366–72; L70–73

HEALTH AND PHYSICAL EDUCATION

Health education is taught sometimes as part of the junior high school general science course and sometimes as a course in hygiene. Physical education is usually conducted separately, but its contribution to the health and adjustment of young adolescents is not overlooked. Sportsmanship, teamwork, and leadership are as important as the skills.

Articles on health topics and problems that concern young people are a feature of THE NEW BOOK OF KNOWLEDGE. Your young adolescent will find reassuring articles on care of the skin, hair, eyes, and teeth; on disease, physical fitness, and exercise; on adolescence, guidance, and mental health.

Sports and games are discussed by well-known athletes; and accurate rules, directions, and diagrams accompany the sports articles. In addition to "how to" articles on such familiar team sports as baseball, basketball, soccer, and football, experts have prepared articles on popular individual sports such as skiing, jogging and running, racket sports, ice-skating, golf, and many more.

HEALTH AND PHYSICAL EDUCATION

MUSIC

In grades seven, eight, and nine, music is usually taught by a music specialist. Your child will have many opportunities to participate in a variety of musical experiences both alone and with others. These may include part-singing in school assemblies and glee clubs, playing a musical instrument in a school orchestra or band, and taking part in musical productions.

Learning about the history of music, forms of music, and the biographies of great composers and performers is often co-ordinated with experiences in listening to recordings. The musical contributions of nations and cultures are sometimes studied as part of the social studies.

Your NEW BOOK OF KNOWLEDGE contains major articles on musical instruments, on the history and forms of music, and on the biographies of famous composers and performers. Many country articles feature special sections devoted to music.

Because teenagers like to perform with musical groups outside of school, THE NEW BOOK OF KNOWLEDGE features articles on folk music and folk music instruments, country and western music, and rock music.

MUSIC

BIOGRAPHIES OF FAMOUS MUSICIANS

Beatles, The	**B108**	Mendelssohn, Felix	**M221**
Beethoven, Ludwig van	**B124—25**	Mozart, Wolfgang Amadeus	**M508**
Berlioz, Hector	**B145**	Offenbach, Jacques	**O52**
Brahms, Johannes	**B362**	Palestrina	**P41**
Chopin, Frédéric	**C282**	Prokofiev, Sergei	**P485**
Copland, Aaron	**C545**	Puccini, Giacomo	**P525**
Dvořák, Antonin	**D368**	Schoenberg, Arnold	**S58h**
Foster, Stephen	**F388**	Schubert, Franz	**S58j**
Franck, César	**F450**	Schumann, Robert	**S59**
Gershwin, George	**G190**	Sibelius, Jean	**S169**
Gluck, Christoph Willibald	**G241**	Strauss, Johann, Jr.	**S437**
Grieg, Edvard	**G376**	Stravinsky, Igor	**S437**
Handel, George Frederick	**H21**	Tchaikovsky, Peter Ilyich	**T33**
Haydn, Joseph	**H67**	Toscanini, Arturo	**T247**
Ives, Charles	**I 415**	Verdi, Giuseppe	**V304**
Liszt, Franz	**L309**	Wagner, Richard	**W2**
Macdowell, Edward	**M4**		
Mahler, Gustav	**M34**		

ART

Art instruction in grades seven to nine provides boys and girls with a variety of art experiences. They experiment with different art media, tools, and processes. They learn to apply art principles in their daily lives at home and in the community.

Art in the seventh, eighth, and ninth grades is exploratory and experimental. Color and design are stressed because these are fundamental to all art learning. Children will experiment with poster making, lettering, puppetry, painting, illustration, clay modeling, costume design, advertising design, and interior and stage decoration. Many schools organize after-school art clubs for boys and girls with special abilities and interests in art.

Art education provides a means of personal satisfaction for your child. Your set of THE NEW BOOK OF KNOWLEDGE offers a treasure-house of art information. There are articles presenting the history of art from prehistoric to modern times. Articles dealing with major countries of the world contain special sections devoted to art. THE NEW BOOK OF KNOWLEDGE describes art processes and art media, provides biographies of famous artists, and gives practical "how to" directions. THE NEW BOOK OF KNOWLEDGE is unique in its lavish use of the finest full-color art reproductions.

PRACTICAL ARTS

The practical arts in grades seven, eight, and nine include industrial arts, home economics, and typewriting.

Through industrial arts, boys and girls learn about the tools, materials, and processes of modern industry. Most schools teach woodworking. Many also teach metalwork, electrical work, mechanical drawing, printing, general crafts, and ceramics.

Home economics courses pertain to many different aspects of the home and family life —foods and food preparation, household care, decorating, child care, sewing, budgeting, and much more. Boys as well as girls study the many aspects of home economics.

Typewriting instruction develops a functional skill that boys and girls will find useful in the preparation of schoolwork as well as throughout their lives.

Articles in THE NEW BOOK OF KNOWLEDGE describing the practical arts were prepared by experts. These articles provide background information and in many cases include instructions and diagrams for young people to follow.

TO PARENTS

THE NEW BOOK OF KNOWLEDGE is a valuable source of information for you, as well as for your children.

For Preschool Days

Even before your children are old enough to attend school, you will want to read to them from the many nursery rhymes, poems, and stories contained in THE NEW BOOK OF KNOWLEDGE. You will share with your preschooler the delights of looking at pictures. You will want to refer to the articles on storytelling, children's games, toys, early childhood education, and indoor activities for rainy days. You will find much to interest you in articles on health, child growth and development, psychology, and family life.

For School Days

Once your child begins school, you will turn to articles on learning, education, kindergarten, and schools. As your child progresses from the early and middle grades to grades seven, eight, and nine, your NEW BOOK OF KNOWLEDGE will help you to understand your child's school curriculum. Each curriculum area is explained in articles prepared by experts. The most recent trends in education and curriculum are reflected in these articles.

When your child needs help in perfecting study skills, you can turn to articles that explain how to write a book report, how to study, or how to use reference materials. If bad weather or illness confines your child to the house, you will discover games, puzzles, and things to do or make in THE NEW BOOK OF KNOWLEDGE.

For High School Days

For the older student in your family there are many articles related to the high school curriculum. These articles are both scholarly and interesting. For science there are articles on taxonomy, genetics, vectors, and quasars; for mathematics, topology, probability, and computers; for English, the novel, the short story, and drama; for the humanities, the history of civilization, religion, art, architecture, and music.

The high school student will find practical use for the articles on colleges and universities, tests and test taking, college entrance examinations, adolescence, and vocations. The Index entry "Vocations" leads to information about careers in many different fields. The topics listed on the pages that follow are only a sampling of other references useful to older students.

For Parents

Are you called upon to participate in a P.T.A. program? There are articles in THE NEW BOOK OF KNOWLEDGE on such topics as parent-teacher associations, mental health, juvenile delinquency, drug and alcohol abuse, driver education, programmed instruction, guidance, computers, and vocations. Other articles of particular interest to parents are listed on page 92 of this STUDY GUIDE.

For the Family

When the entire family sits down to dinner, there is often talk about world events, sports, entertainment, fashions, foods, or any of the hundreds of topics that families discuss. This is when THE NEW BOOK OF

KNOWLEDGE rounds out its usefulness for everyone. In the Dictionary Index that concludes each volume are concise, accurate entries on thousands of additional subjects not usually included in a children's encyclopedia. How satisfying it is to be able to turn to the Dictionary Index in THE NEW BOOK OF KNOWLEDGE and find the answer to a question quickly, easily, and at the exact moment of high interest.

HOBBIES AND LEISURE ACTIVITIES

A hobby is a favorite way of spending leisure time. Your children may share their hobbies with you or with their friends, or they may follow an enthusiasm by themselves.

THE NEW BOOK OF KNOWLEDGE is an especially valuable resource for pursuing a variety of hobbies. The articles listed below not only describe hobbies but offer simple directions for each activity.

HOBBIES AND LEISURE ACTIVITIES

LITERATURE IN THE NEW BOOK OF KNOWLEDGE

Many literary selections are contained in THE NEW BOOK OF KNOWLEDGE. All the selections were chosen with the advice of librarians and curriculum specialists and are studied in schools from grades four through nine. At the same time, the selections are all suitable for the pure pleasure of reading at home.

The literary selections include fiction, nonfiction, and poetry—classics, short stories, legends, fairy tales, fables, myths, and rhymes. Some selections accompany the biography of a famous writer. Others appear in articles that discuss a particular type of literature. Selections suitable for younger children are listed in the K-3 section of this guide.

PROJECTS AND EXPERIMENTS

WONDER QUESTIONS

ARTICLES OF PARTICULAR INTEREST TO PARENTS